The
Bipolar
Child

The Bipolar Child

The Definitive and
Reassuring Guide to
Childhood's Most
Misunderstood Disorder

DEMITRI F. PAPOLOS, M.D.,
AND JANICE PAPOLOS

REVISED AND EXPANDED EDITION

 BROADWAY BOOKS   NEW YORK

BROADWAY

PRINTED IN THE UNITED STATES OF AMERICA

BROADWAY BOOKS and its logo, a letter B bisected on the diagonal, are trademarks of Broadway Books, a division of Random House, Inc.

Visit our website at www.broadwaybooks.com

First edition published 2002.

Designed by Jessica Shatan

Illustrated by Jackie Aher

Charts and graphs by Kris Tobiassen

Grateful acknowledgment is made for permission to reprint:
    Excerpts from the *Diagnostic and Statistical Manual of Mental Disorders, Fourth Edition*. Reprinted with permission from the American Psychiatric Association. Copyright © 1994.
    Excerpts from "I Couldn't Help My Daughter," by Swanee Hunt and Lillian Hunt-Meeks. Copyright © 1996 by Swanee Hunt and Lillian Hunt-Meeks. Originally published in *Good Housekeeping*. Reprinted with permission from the authors.
    Excerpts from "Diagnosing Bipolar vs. ADHD: A Pharmacological Point of View," by Charles Popper, M.D. Reprinted from *The Link* 13 (1996). Reprinted with permission of the author.
    Excerpt from "On Diagnostic Gore in a Child's Nightmares," by Charles Popper, M.D. From *The American Academy of Child and Adolescent Psychiatry Newsletter*, Fall 1990. Reprinted with permission of the author.
    Venn diagram on page 41 from "Obsessive-Compulsive Disorder in Children and Adolescents: A Review," by Daniel Geller, Joseph Biederman, et al. From *The Harvard Review of Psychiatry*, page 265 of Volume 5, Issue 5. Reprinted with permission from Oxford University Press.
    Lithium Dosing chart on page 80. Adapted from "Lithium Dosage Guide for Prepubertal Children: A Preliminary Report," by Elizabeth B. Weller, Ronald A. Weller, and Mary A. Fristad, from the *Journal of the American Academy of Child Psychiatry*. Reprinted with permission.
    "Keepers of the Storm." Song and lyrics by Diane MacKenzie. Copyright © 1998. Reprinted with permission of the composer.

Cataloging-in-Publication Data is on file with the Library of Congress.

ISBN 0-7679-1285-3

10 9 8 7 6 5 4 3 2 1

For
Alex and Jordy,
and for
all the children

Contents

Part IV. Life Goes On

Preface to the Revised Edition

Just prior to *The Bipolar Child*'s release in January of 2000, we launched an informational site on the World Wide Web; and thanks to a feedback and comments section, we have always enjoyed very close communication with readers of the book. In the past two and a half years, we have heard from thousands of parents and educators, and their stories, comments, and questions have given us much to think about. These readers let us know what concerns they have, and what specific information they need and want. So often we've commented to each other: "If only that were in the book"; "If only we'd gotten a chance to explore that aspect more." While our email newsletter keeps parents current about new medications or new debates and developments in the field, we were always wistful that all the new information wasn't handy right in the book itself.

So when our editor Gerald Howard called to discuss the possibility of a revised edition, we were more than delighted to have a second opportunity to detail some of the newest developments in the fields of research and pharmacology, to address some subjects in greater depth, and to answer many of those questions that repeatedly come to us through cyberspace. Let us outline some of the changes we've made in this new edition of *The Bipolar Child*.

Stability is the start of all things good, and readers of the original version of the book will notice quite a lot of new information in the Prescriptions for Treatment chapter. We've added a detailed section on the new mood stabilizer, Trileptal (oxcarbazepine), as well as an in-depth discussion of the omega-3 essential fatty acids, which reportedly enhance mood stability for many children. In the first edition of *The Bipolar Child,* we were hopeful but cautious about the mood stabilizer Lamictal (lamotrigine), the only mood stabilizer shown to have robust antidepressant effects. New studies show that an extremely gradual dosing pattern has lessened the risks of serious side effects, and we've discussed these research findings as this medication may turn out to be uniquely helpful for adolescents with the illness.

It is now becoming apparent that many children may require one of the new atypical antipsychotic drugs in their medication regimens—either in the initial stabilization period, or as a maintenance drug. These medications are extremely effective against rage, agitation, and psychosis, with a reduced risk of the movement disorders caused by the older generation of antipsychotic drugs. However, emerging evidence is showing that the risks of type II diabetes and changes in the children's lipid profiles could become a substantial problem, and we discuss this as well as give guidelines for a monitoring schedule that will alert doctors and parents to these untoward side effects.

Three years ago, we sounded the alarm of the potential adverse reactions bipolar children have to stimulants and, most especially, to antidepressants. The stories that continue to reach us through email about the increased cycling, increased aggression, switches into mania and mixed states, psychosis, suicidal feelings and actions, as well as the hundreds of hospitalizations that have been caused as a result of this prescribing practice, have led us to strengthen and underscore our original warnings throughout the book.

Second only to the difficulties of diagnosis and treatment is the piece of the puzzle called school. Therefore, we've expanded Chapter 10 to include information about ways to head off school detentions, suspensions, and expulsions. We've also included a more realistic picture of due process proceedings, along with more information on that ever thorny subject: attorney's fees and who pays what and when. We want those parents who need to pursue due process to walk into the situation understanding all the risks and up-front costs as they make the decisions they will surely be forced to make as a due process hearing moves forward.

Also in Chapter 10, we've profiled the first school to develop a model program for children with bipolar disorder, one that can be reproduced anywhere throughout the country. What goes on every day in a small school called the Austin Harvard School in Austin, Texas, is working for these children, and we want parents and educators to know why. We fully describe the school's philosophy, as well as the exciting CD-ROM curriculum that makes such a school economically feasible.

Readers of the first edition will notice a totally new chapter following the school discussion. It is becoming increasingly apparent that many children with bipolar disorder have co-occurring learning disabilities, and that most of these children are turning out to have deficits in the areas of the brain that govern "executive functions." If the bipolar disorder is treated, but the child, parents, and teachers don't understand the impact these (possibly subtle) deficits have on the child's performance in school, and elsewhere, then the stage is being set for frustration, anger, and low self-esteem that may have little to do with the mood disorder. These learning problems can begin to dog that child and cause him or her to simply "quit the playing field," especially as the years go on and the schoolwork becomes more complex.

This new Chapter 11, called "The Neuropsychological Testing of a Bipolar Child," explains the need for a complete neuropsychological evaluation for each child diagnosed with a bipolar disorder. The chapter explains the battery of tests that examine all the different cognitive and motor domains so that more of the child's vulnerabilities (as well as strengths) come into focus. Ideas and strategies for helping the child deal with executive function deficits are detailed in this chapter also.

In many ways, "The Impact on the Family" chapter is the heart of this book. Here, we have included a new section dealing with the complexities that occur when several family members have bipolar disorder (not surprising, given that the vulnerability to develop the illness is transmitted genetically). You will hear the voice of a mother who refers to her illness and her son's as rendering their family "bp-squared"; as well as a mother who dubs her household "bp-saturated" as she speaks about her husband and two of three children who have the illness. Their sharing of their stories, their philosophies, and the coping strategies they've been forced to develop will be helpful to other families, and hopefully reduce some of the guilt and isolation such families feel.

Finally, we have added a new section in the chapter about adolescence. Because teenagers with bipolar disorder are at particular risk for addiction to alcohol and drugs, we explore programs that can help turn those addicted youngsters around and bring them back, not only to recovery but also to family. Resources that prepare parents to act if the need arises are also detailed in this section.

Again we want to give our sincere thanks to the professionals who answered our questions and shared their time and expertise: Sherri Burch, Carolyn J. Cheesum, Nancy Halle, Diana H. King, Jennifer D. Laviano, Esq., Kristen H. Laviano, Anngela Ritter, and Joseph Ruggiero, Ph.D.

We want to give special mention to Edwin H. Cook, M.D., Thomas J. Croke, R. George DeLong, M.D., Gianni L. Faedda, M.D., Steven Mattis, Ph.D., Dana Z. Luck, Ph.D., and Rosalie Greenberg, M.D., who granted us long interviews and followed up their points with thoughtful phone calls and email messages.

Pam Bernstein has guided this book to its perfect home at Broadway and was instrumental in seeing it through the revision process. Patricia Medved, our editor, was also invaluable.

A number of people helped in ways that were extremely meaningful to us. Our heartfelt thanks go to: Ann Baumbach, Thomas Casey, Cheryl Hart, Mary Jane Hatton, Tana McGrady, Sandi Norelli, Laura Spector, and Louise Woo—truly women and men of valor.

And, finally, two men have taken this journey with us on two previous books, but we were indeed blessed to have their combined wisdom and expertise focused on this one: Gerald Howard of Doubleday Broadway; and Ross J. Baldessarini, M.D., of Harvard Medical School. To both of you, our deepest gratitude.

Demitri F. Papolos, M.D.
Janice Papolos
Westport, Connecticut, 2002

Preface

When we first moved to our town, we met a couple who had a seven-year-old child who was extraordinarily bright but was prone to strange and agitated awakenings in the night. During the day his need to not be separated from his mother was so great that he insisted she carry a walkie-talkie so that he could always be in touch with her. He preferred his mother in his sight lines at all times.

As a baby he could go for days without sleeping, and the "terrible-two" temper tantrums persisted through toddlerhood and seemed to grow proportionately with each birthday. He was extremely oppositional and his mother and father couldn't find a way to discipline him, although they tried every parenting technique and spent a great deal of time in parenting classes and family therapies. Friends began pulling away, and their home—and any semblance of a family life—was being destroyed by his explosive behavior and erratic moods.

One evening the couple told us their story over dinner. It seems that they had a family history of manic-depression (now called bipolar disorder) on both sides going back generations; their son was showing all the signs of early-onset bipolar disorder—bipolar disorder that seems to present with temperamental features even in infancy. After listening carefully to Demitri's discussion of the illness, they said that their son fit the clinical description "to a T."

A few weeks later the boy threw his television set through the window in a fit of rage, and they took him to see a colleague of Demitri's, who did in fact diagnose him with the condition.

After a time on a mood stabilizer the tantrums and erratic behaviors ceased and the parents began to pick up the shards of their family life. Their son was able to use his great perceptive abilities in therapy and he began to monitor his own behavior at home and in school. While it hasn't been a perfect path, the before-and-after differences are significant and have made all the difference for the boy and his family.

It has long been thought in the psychiatric community that children could not be given a diagnosis of bipolar disorder until the mid- to late teens and that mania in children was extremely rare. But scientists in the research vanguard are beginning to prove that the disorder can begin very early in life and that it is far more common than was previously supposed. Because the illness looks so different in childhood, however, these children cannot be shoehorned into the adult criteria of the *Diagnostic and Statistical Manual (DSM-IV)*—the guidebook for psychiatrists. As a result, either they go undiagnosed or they are misdiagnosed.

When our book *Overcoming Depression* was first published in 1987, we included a small section on mood disorders in children. At that time little was known about bipolar disorder in the very young, and there was a handful of medication studies in this age group. But in 1996, as we began work on the tenth-anniversary edition of the book, the professional literature had mushroomed, and Demitri was involved in research focusing on bipolar disorder in children. There was so much to say, and although we did expand the discussion of childhood mood disorders in that edition, we felt that the subject of bipolar disorder in children deserved a volume of its own. Yet no book was published for either the layperson or the professional.

We decided to team up again and write a book that would be as comprehensive and reassuring about the childhood form of bipolar disorder as *Overcoming Depression* is about mood disorders in adults. We wanted to let parents know what is and is not known about the condition and how to get proper help for their children.

In the very early stages of this book, we were extremely fortunate to be invited to subscribe to BPParents, a listserv of several hundred mothers and fathers of bipolar children who email one another. This group gave us permission to "listen" to their postings in order to let us see what living with the illness was really like. The extensive questionnaire that we had constructed (reprinted on pages 416–419) was displayed on the website Parents of Bipolar Children.

The response was overwhelming. The voices and written statements from parents all over the United States—from Maine to Alaska—and from Canada, England, the Netherlands, and New Zealand began pouring into our computer and mailbox. Each day over 175 messages were delivered to our email address, and for over a year we sat in front of the computer screen and read and downloaded the postings, carefully noting the questions the parents asked.

Being members of this listserv offered us a unique vantage point from which to write about this disorder. In contrast to seeing a child once a month in a clinical situation, this was akin to watching two hundred children with bipolar disorder and their families in something like real time—hour by hour, day by day, season by season.

Because of the parents' frank and revealing postings, we got to "see" how these children woke up in the morning, whether the mothers could comb their hair that day, what outfit they insisted on wearing, and in what mood they boarded the school bus. We read about their activities and moods in the afternoon, what they would and would not eat for dinner, and their difficulties as the day came to a close. We learned how these children reacted on Christmas morning and at their birthday parties and how they handled unstructured time when school was not in session. Remarkably, several times mothers were online while their sons or daughters were raging in the background. Their graphic descriptions of the children's lengthy explosions seemed a way to preserve the parents' sanity—a sort of SOS to the only other people on earth who could possibly fathom what they were withstanding.

We got to see how lonely and isolated these parents had become before they discovered this cybercommunity, how they had blamed themselves for the difficult behaviors of their children, and how they worried about the effects of the illness on their well children. Yet they never stopped reaching out to one another to offer advice, share solutions they had found, and make other heartbroken parents only an email address away feel less lonely and more supported and embraced.

These incredible women and men offered us the same support they offered to one another. Not only did they fill out our questionnaires carefully and thoughtfully, but from thirty-four states they sent hospital and school records, diaries and journals, charts of their children's mood disorders, and notes inviting us to call them and use "anything you think

might help other parents and their children." We took them up on the offer and conducted over a hundred follow-up interviews on the telephone.
When we had specific questions, we conducted minisurveys on the listserv and received intriguing answers that contributed to our data collection.

These parents as well as parents who were not on the listserv but who
received the questionnaire from leaders of child and adolescent support
groups or through our own professional networks and contacts gave us
permission to quote them throughout this book. Their voices and the
voices of their children have pride of place in these pages.

Toward the end of the year we spent writing, we transferred the information from the questionnaires to a database and crunched the numbers.
The data revealed some very disturbing findings about the diagnosis and
treatment of early-onset bipolar disorder. Because of the mixed-symptom
picture of these children—many appear hyperactive and are oppositional
or have obsessive-compulsive and anxiety disorders—most are being
shunted off into these diagnostic groups without the possibility of a bipolar disorder even being considered (despite the fact that most of the children come from backgrounds with mood disorders). Many of these
children were initially diagnosed as having attention-deficit disorder with
hyperactivity (ADHD) and put on stimulant medications; or they were
first seen in the throes of depression with little or no consideration of the
opposite pole of a mood disorder. As a result, a shocking number of children were thrown into manic and psychotic states, became paranoid and
violent, and ended up in a hospital—unstable, suicidal, and in worse
shape than before the treatment began.

We want to state clearly that, given the accumulating knowledge in
the field of research and the reactions of the children in our study, no doctor should prescribe a stimulant or antidepressant drug to a child whose
family history reveals mood disorders without suspecting a "snake beneath the rock." Parents need to be warned of the possibility that these
drugs may wreak havoc on a possible quiescent bipolar gene.

In other words, bipolar disorder should be ruled out before any of the stimulant
drugs or antidepressants are prescribed. Instead, mood-stabilizing drugs such
as lithium, Depakote, or Tegretol should be considered as a first line of
treatment—early on—before episodes become more frequent, and the illness warps the psychological development of a child and destroys the life
of a family.

We cannot imagine how families cope with this illness without an up-to-date resource at their fingertips. It is our fervent hope that this volume will shed new light on the enormous complexities of early-onset bipolar disorder, all the while offering support and intelligent solutions to family members. We also hope that these pages will create a new level of awareness about this illness and inspire further psychiatric research. This, in turn, will ensure more accurate diagnosis, better treatment, and a brighter future for all the children and adolescents suffering with this much misunderstood disorder.

Demitri F. Papolos, M.D.

Janice Papolos

Westport, Connecticut, 1999

Acknowledgments

Throughout the writing of this book, we were privileged to have the encouragement and support of so many people that it is with deep pride and gratitude that we acknowledge them here.

First, we owe the most profound debt to Tomie Burke, the founder of the online support group, BPParents. Several years ago, she created a safe haven on the Internet where parents of bipolar children could come together and share their grief, their struggles, and their triumphs. She was so supportive of this project that she introduced us to her listserv and urged the group to let us subscribe and receive its postings. In so doing, she—and they—opened the private world of the families of bipolar children and gave us the opportunity to write as truthful and compelling a book as possible. This precious community taught us more about heroic parenting, true love, and courage under fire than we could have learned in a lifetime, and we are grateful beyond measure. We would also like to thank all the men and women who filled out our questionnaire, gave us hours of their time on the telephone, and helped us collect invaluable data on the subject of early-onset bipolar disorder. In addition, we wish to thank the many children and young adults who generously discussed their personal experience with the illness and helped us to understand it from their point of view. In order to protect their privacy, we have changed all names and identifying characteristics.

Nine very special women must be mentioned next: Martha Hellander put all of her resources at our disposal, directed us to issues we needed to cover, and supplied us with important books, papers, and contacts. Karen Huckins, Jeanne Landry Harpin, Brenda Souto, Linda DiSantis, and Jennifer Burke made important contributions to these pages. Penny Smith, Linda N., Janice MacDonald, and Barbara Lurie Sand read the early drafts of the manuscript and provided much-needed insight and suggestions.

In our last book, we had the privilege of counting on the great medical expertise of Ross J. Baldessarini, M.D., of Harvard Medical School. His wisdom and keen eye are very much present in this volume also, and we are deeply indebted to him. We would also like to thank Charles Popper, M.D., also of Harvard Medical School, for his pioneering work in the field of early-onset bipolar disorder and for helping us track down some very elusive facts.

The other professionals we wish to acknowledge are: Nancy Austin, Psy. D., Julie Beckett, Deborah Bullwinckle, Trudy Carlson, M.S., Gianni Faedda, M.D., Max Fink, M.D., Shawn Fordham, Victor M. Fornari, M.D., Barbara Geller, M.D., Mark George, M.D., Julie Keys, Paul Kosowsky, L.S.C.W., Shalani Madon, Anna Papadorotheou, Norman Rosenthal, M.D., Andrew Stoll, M.D., Michael Strober, Ph.D., and Stephanie Welch.

We are particularly grateful to Suzanne Faustini, L.S.W., Elizabeth Jester, Esq., and Rosalie Greenberg, M.D., for their time, experience, and guidance.

A special thank-you to Andrew Skrilow, who spent months entering the data and crunching the numbers for us. His work was critical to this book.

Pam Bernstein, our literary agent of thirteen years and cherished friend, jump-started this project and brought it to the attention of editors in the most intelligent way. No two authors ever had a more indefatigable and able advocate. A special thank-you also to Donna Downing of Pam Bernstein and Associates, who was a trusted advisor throughout the project.

We met the team at Broadway Books on what was surely the coldest day of 1998, but we soon found the warmest, most supportive home there. Tracy Behar, our editor and the associate publisher at Broadway Books, should win awards for her insightful editing and responsiveness. We grew to admire her mind and expertise, and we were always grateful for the enormous care she invested in this book. Angela Casey was a pleasure to work with, kept us on track, and was a great source of moral support. Our being Broadway authors is particularly meaningful to us, because its esteemed publisher, William Shinker, originally acquired *Overcoming Depression* for HarperCollins in 1984. He has been the godfather of both these volumes, and we are very grateful for his belief in us then, and now.

We want to say a resounding thank-you to author Victoria Secunda, someone whose work we had long admired. Not only has she become the closest of friends, but she was always there for us, offering unfailing support and wise counsel from the proposal stage to the finished manuscript (even while racing toward her own book deadline). She also talked us through the many anxious moments that come with the writing of any book.

We were most fortunate to have a circle of people who anchored and sustained us and made very special and unique contributions. From the bottom of our hearts we thank Rose Belfiore Albicocco, Nick Granito, Carol Jessemy, Mervyn M. Peskin, M.D., Michael Porder, M.D., Wendy Queen, Nina Schorr, M.D., Irwin Sollinger, Ph.D., Laura and Mark Spector, Robert Shprintzen, Ph.D., Marlene Trotman, Marvin Wasserman, M.D., and Ruth and Alan Winnick.

And finally, we would like to acknowledge our two sons, Alex and Jordy, who tolerated their computer-bound, extremely preoccupied parents with patience and a good-natured humor. We would also like to mention that six-year-old Jordy took it upon himself to man the telephones, telling strangers and salespeople (and, unfortunately, sometimes even teachers): "They can *never* call you back. They have a lot of pages to write." We hope that someday this volume will make them proud.

This book contains general reference information about bipolar disorder in children. It is not intended as a substitute for the advice of a trained medical professional. Readers should not attempt to diagnose or treat their children based on the material contained in this book, but rather should consult an appropriate medical or psychiatric professional before starting or stopping any medication and before implementing any other therapy discussed in this book. The authors and publisher are not responsible for any adverse effects resulting from the information contained in this book.

The
Bipolar
Child

PART I

Diagnosis and Treatment

Voices from the Front

In 1992 Tomie Burke, a young mother in Pullman, Washington, developed a listserv (called BPParents) for parents of children with bipolar disorder. She was motivated to do so because when her six-year-old son first began experiencing the baffling and frightening symptoms of the illness, she searched community and university libraries, bookstores, databases, and Internet pages in her desperate desire to become educated about the illness and to help her child. She found little to check out, purchase, or download.

But eventually she did become extremely knowledgeable about the illness, and she wanted to reach out to other families—to provide information and assure them that they were not alone. She soon had an address on the World Wide Web called Parents of Bipolar Children. The site consisted of a home page, links to information about the disorder, and a guest book where parents could describe how they found the site, note whether they had a boy or girl with a diagnosis of bipolar disorder, and comment a bit about their situations.

The messages left by parents who visited convey a desperate need for information and sheer relief when they discover that they are not alone—that the illness is not uncommon and that it isn't caused by bad parenting. That first year thousands of parents came to the site seeking help for their children.

What is early-onset bipolar disorder, and why is it such a little-known illness? Most people have never heard of the expression, but it is actually psychiatry's phrase for manic-depression that occurs early—*very* early—in life. (Adults who used to be diagnosed manic-depressive are now also referred to as having bipolar disorder.)

Bipolar disorder in children is a neglected public health problem. It is estimated that one-third of all the children in this country who are being diagnosed with attention-deficit disorder with hyperactivity (ADHD) are actually suffering from early symptoms of bipolar disorder. Since close to 4 million children were prescribed stimulants such as Ritalin in 1998, that's over 1 million children who eventually will be diagnosed as bipolar. According to the American Academy of Child and Adolescent Psychiatry, a third of the 3.4 million children who first seem to be suffering with depression will go on to manifest the bipolar form of a mood disorder. Researchers in the field of early-onset bipolar disorder peg that figure closer to 50 percent. In the only large-scale epidemiological study done on the rates of bipolar disorder in adolescence, Dr. Peter M. Lewinsohn and his colleagues examined more than 1,700 high school students in western Oregon, and found that 5.7 percent of this group of adolescents—or ninety-seven students—suffered some form of bipolar spectrum disorder (they met criteria for the "Bipolar Not Otherwise Specified" category we will speak about in the next chapter). Amid all the dry statistics stand several million suffering children, as well as their mothers, fathers, brothers, sisters, and grandparents.

This illness is as old as humankind, and has probably been conserved in the human genome because it confers great energy and originality of thought. People who have had it have literally changed the course of human history: Manic-depression has afflicted (and probably fueled the brilliance of) people like Isaac Newton, Abraham Lincoln, Winston Churchill, Theodore Roosevelt, Johann Goethe, Honoré de Balzac, George Frederic Handel, Ludwig von Beethoven, Robert Schumann, Leo Tolstoy, Charles Dickens, Virginia Woolf, Ernest Hemingway, Robert Lowell, and Anne Sexton.

But until recently, manic-depression was thought to affect people in their early twenties or older. It was not viewed as an illness that could occur among children.

This has proven to be myth. The temperamental features and behaviors of bipolar disorder can begin to emerge very early on—even in infancy.

But because a vast majority of bipolar children also meet criteria for ADHD (and the focus of drug treatment strategies becomes the symptoms of ADHD), the bipolar illness is typically overlooked. As a result, drugs are prescribed to deal only with the symptoms of hyperactivity and distractibility. And, since many, many children initially develop depressive symptoms as the earliest manifestation of the illness, bipolar disorder may again be discounted as the primary diagnosis.

Childhood bipolar disorder can overlap or occur with many disorders of childhood other than ADHD or depression: panic disorder, generalized anxiety disorder, obsessive-compulsive disorder (OCD), and Tourette's syndrome, to name a few. And this mixed-symptom picture can be perplexing and confound diagnosis. Moreover, only in the past few years has bipolar disorder become the focus of research inquiry.

THE ILLNESS IN ADULTS

Bipolar disorder in children presents very differently from how it presents in adults. Adults typically experience a more classical pattern of mood swings. In the manic phase, the person experiences an increased rate of thinking, has surges of energy, and describes him- or herself as feeling more active, creative, intelligent, and sexual than he or she ever thought possible. The need for sleep diminishes as one idea after another bursts into consciousness and the person develops the expectation that he or she will be able to execute all the ideas that are flowing effortlessly into the mind. For many, a mild hypomania (less than manic state) is a period that brims with physical and mental well-being. It is often a time of great creativity.

Unfortunately, this enviable state does not last. A person experiencing the "highs" of manic-depression may make reckless decisions, go on buying sprees, commit sexual indiscretions, or bring financial ruin upon self and family. The mood of someone in a manic state is brittle and irritable; it may shift back and forth quickly, and the person may become very paranoid. If the hypomania escalates into a full-blown mania, the person can lose all touch with reality and become psychotic. In this stage (called stage 3 mania), a doctor may be unable to tell whether the patient is schizophrenic or manic-depressive without having the family history and other information about the patient's previous functioning.

Typically, after the manic energy is spent, the person plummets into the depths of depression. The mind slows down to such a degree that any decision seems almost impossible to make. Some depressed people will experience insomnia and early-morning awakening; others will begin to sleep excessively and yet never feel rested. In addition to mood, energy, and sleep disturbances, a person in a depression may feel bodily pains such as headaches, backaches, and stomach problems.

Some adult patients will feel inordinate amounts of guilt; some will feel irritable, anxious, and hopeless. Depressed patients may feel they deserve only punishment and can become fixed on all the small mistakes they have made in their lives—losing any sense of past accomplishments. In the depths of depression, a person's thinking can become delusional and psychotic.

It is not unusual for adults to experience several weeks of hypomania or mania—very often in the spring or summer months—only to find their energy level ebbing as the days shorten in autumn. Individuals who experience depressions alternating with intense or psychotic manias are referred to as having the Bipolar I form of the disorder. Those who suffer depressions and experience only hypomanic episodes (they never get psychotic or lose total control) are referred to as being Bipolar II. Most adults will have well intervals in between the periods of heightened or lowered mood.

BIPOLAR DISORDER IN CHILDREN

Children rarely fit this recognizable pattern. They have a more chronic course of illness where they cycle back and forth with few discernible well periods in between. Some tend to cycle rapidly (more than four times a year); some cycle within the week or month (and may be called ultrarapid cyclers). Many cycle so rapidly that they fit a pattern called ultra-ultrarapid (ultradian) cycling: They may have frequent spikes of highs and lows within a twenty-four-hour period.

Almost all bipolar children have certain temperamental and behavioral traits in common. They tend to be inflexible and oppositional, they tend to be extraordinarily irritable, and almost all experience periods of explosive rage. They tantrum for hours at a time. Holes get kicked in walls, and parents and siblings and pets can be threatened or hurt.

Bipolar children don't often show this rageful side to the outside world. And because parents don't wish the outside world to see the child in this light, or to learn of their lack of control over the child—most people couldn't possibly imagine what actually goes on anyway—the illness stays behind closed doors as the parents try desperately to find some solutions to the fact that their lives are being turned upside down. As one woman described it: "We feel like we've been thrown into a tornado that is big, black, and powerful."

No one symptom identifies a child as having bipolar disorder, but if hyperactivity, irritable and shifting moods, and prolonged temper tantrums co-occur—and there is a history of mood disorders and/or alcoholism coming down either or both the mother's and father's line—the index of suspicion should be high.

Indeed, our study sample showed that over 80 percent of the children who developed early-onset bipolar disorder had what is known as "bilineal transmission"—substance abuse and mood disorders appeared on both sides of their families.

Perhaps the best way to get a "feel" for what the illness looks like in childhood is to listen to the voices of parents describing the temperaments and behaviors of their children.

Difficulties in Infancy

Many parents recall that their children were different from early infancy. They seemed to sleep erratically and were irritable and difficult to settle:

> From the beginning he slept about four to six hours a night with virtually no naps other than that one span of sleep. This continued until he was four years old.

> He was very fussy, and some nights he did not actually go to sleep until 3:00 A.M. Then he would be up in the morning raring to go.

Many of these babies are referred to as "the wide-eyed babies of the nursery." One mother said that the nurse brought her baby to her after a twenty-four-hour isolation period and said, "Good luck! She's done nothing but cry for twenty-four hours and there was nothing we could do to soothe her."

Author Danielle Steel, whose son Nick Traina had early-onset bipolar disorder and who has written one of the few published accounts of how the disorder evolves from infancy, speaks about her child's surprising lack of a need to sleep in *His Bright Light:*

There was one thing about him that worried me then. He never slept, or not enough, anyway. Long before he was two I came to the realization that I couldn't give him a nap. If I did it meant that he'd be up all night, even long after me, and I work late at night. But he just didn't seem to need much sleep.

Many of the mothers we interviewed remembered their babies excessive activity even in utero. They seemed temperamentally different from their earliest days. Two mothers described it this way:

While my daughter was in the womb, she kicked so hard and so often that I had very little rest . . . much of the time it felt like she was in a fight—rolling and tumbling around inside me and then, when she was born, the nurse gave her a pacifier even though they were not permitted in the nursery. She kept all the other babies up all night with her screaming.

I too noticed signs that this was an extraspirited child. In fact, while I was pregnant, I remember saying, "Uh-oh, the baby is angry again." His kicks would last for an hour as I doubled over in pain toward the end of the pregnancy.

And a mother of twins told us that "at fourteen weeks the sonographer and obstetrician were unable to get a picture of Ian's face and could not sample the amniotic fluid due to 'constant, unpredictable activity.' "

Precociousness

These children seem to burst into life and are on a different time schedule from the rest of the world right from the beginning. Many are extremely precocious and bright—doing everything early and with gusto. They seem like magical children, their creativity can be astounding, and the parents speak about them with real respect, and sometimes even awe:

She was always ahead of her time. She started talking at eight months with the words "kitty cat." She walked at nine months and was speaking in complete sentences by a year. She was writing small novels in the second grade. She acted and danced and sang way beyond her years.

At eighteen months he climbed out of the baby bed in the middle of the night, opened the fridge, got out three dozen eggs (it was Easter time), and proceeded to sit in his booster chair and crack three dozen eggs onto our hardwood floors. (He wanted to bake a real cake—he didn't like the toy mixing bowl I had given him to play with.) After the insurance company quit laughing they did pay to refinish our floors.

Another mother wrote that her son "has never been a child; he always thought like an adult. At the age of four he got very exercised and wanted to know, 'Why *can't* I have a phone in my room?' " Danielle Steel's son, Nick, "developed a passion for disco music at a year. His favorite was Gloria Gaynor singing 'I Will Survive,' and he would dance endlessly as we played records in my room. Our first serious argument came while planning his first birthday party, when he announced he wanted a clown and disco music, strange requests for a one-year-old."

Separation Anxiety

Another behavioral trait often remarked upon is the infant's inability to be separated from the mother. Separation anxiety is often so extreme that mothers can't put the babies down. One mother remembers "cleaning chicken with her in a Snugli"; another hasn't forgotten "vacuuming with her in a sling"; and one mother described being "mauled, with his nails scraping down my chest as he struggled against being withdrawn by his father, who was trying to take him from me so that I could take a shower."

Indeed, this separation anxiety seems to arise long before and persist long after its appearance and disappearance in nonbipolar children. Lillian Hunt-Meeks, the daughter of U.S. ambassador to Austria Swanee Hunt, suffered early-onset bipolar disorder and had this to say about her separation anxiety in an article she and her mother wrote for *Good Housekeeping*:

For as long as I can remember, I was afraid of my mother leaving me. When I was little I would scream and cry every time she went away. Once, I remember, she went to Colorado Springs (just an hour away), and I spent the night at my best friend's house. I cried the whole time. The next day at school I was asked to write a story, and in my five-year-old handwriting scrawled on the title: "When My Mother Left and Went to Colorado Springs."

On the questionnaire that so many parents filled out and sent to us, we would find little notes scrawled in the margins of the pages saying things like "He is never more than a foot away from me"; "If he could crawl back into the womb, he would"; "She follows me into the bathroom; we seem joined at the hip."

Another mother emailed us about the separation anxiety her son was experiencing and had this to say:

> Right now Jamison can't be separated from me—it's like the um- bilical cord grew back! I can't get him out of my room at night. If he falls asleep somewhere else, he ends up there eventually. I've stepped on him in the middle of the night many times. He hides under the bed with only his head sticking out. But he gets so anx- ious, and this relieves some of it.

Actress Patty Duke, who is quite candid about her manic-depression, wrote about separation anxiety in her autobiography *Call Me Anna*. She said: "When I was young, I had a dream, a child's nightmare: that I would be taken someplace away from my mother and never know if I was going to be with her again." She describes holding her mother's hand constantly whenever she was with her.

Night Terrors

Many bipolar children suffer night terrors from which they awaken screaming from fright. Sometimes they cannot even be awakened but re- main in a semiconscious state while they continue to experience some frightening event. Eventually, when they reveal their dreams, what stands out is the content.

They dream of being chased by sharks or monsters, but where typically a nonbipolar child wakes up just before the teeth pierce an arm or a leg, a bipolar child doesn't—the jaws surround the arm or leg, the massive teeth crunch into the skin, and bone and blood fills the water. Their dreams are often filled with blood and gore. As Dr. Charles Popper from Harvard Medical School wrote in an article titled "On Diagnostic Gore in Child's Nightmares":

> As bipolar children talk about these dreams, they report the explicit appearance of blood (not just imagined or inferred, but actually vi-

sualized blood) and descriptions of mutilations of bodies, dismemberment, and the insides of body parts. Their dreams are considerably more affectively intense than regular nightmares.

Dreams of fighting are quite common. In the fighting dreams of children or adults with mere anxiety, a knife may be pulled out and brought into attack, but the dreamer wakes up just before the knife enters the skin or rips the clothing. For bipolar children, the knife goes in, the blood is seen, and the dream may continue at considerable length and with explicit visualization of gore. . . . Where the "newsreel" of a dream story normally stops, the "newsreel" in the bipolar children keeps going.

Dr. Popper explains that "In these individuals, it is as though their unconscious sensors of painful affect are not working, even in their dreams."

Indeed, that may explain why some of these children say such shocking and almost sadistic things during the day. A nursery school director told us the story of a three-year-old boy who one day in the classroom said that "my father is going to come in and put seven knives in your throat." (And this was in response to her asking him to sit down.) Another youngster said to a teacher: "I'm going to put a rope around your neck and pull it till you bleed and your face goes white and your shirt is soaked with blood."

Perhaps the emotionally charged imagery of their nightmares is spilling over to the conscious mind during the day. Whatever the mechanism, these children are dealing with horrifying imagery of bodily threat, dismemberment, and death.

Danielle Steel noted with alarm that her son became "obsessed with Dracula . . . talking about him constantly. . . . At the same time he began drawing pictures of people killing each other, swords drawn, and dripping blood from severed limbs." These drawings, using only black crayons, pencils, and paint, were shown to doctor after doctor, and Ms. Steel was told by doctor after doctor that her son merely had a vivid imagination.

Other parents have told us that their children have never drawn a picture that does not include someone dying; and one mother described her son drawing human figures with huge, Stegasaurus-like blades on their backs.

It is small wonder that these children are afraid to go to sleep and that they need their parents to stay with them all through the night.

Fear of Death and Annihilation

Accompanying these night terrors is a massive fear of death and annihilation. After her name was changed from Anna to Patty for professional reasons, Patty Duke recalls "a fear of death so powerful it precipitated anxiety attacks from the early 1950s to 1983. I was obsessed, truly obsessed with my mortality. All of a sudden the absolute realization of my mortality would hit and I just felt impelled to scream. Sometimes it was what I'd call a bloody-murder scream, sometimes words like 'No! No! No! No!' Inevitably, though, it happened at night, on the way to sleep. I'd scream every night of my life. I was overtaken by abject terror."

Ambassador Swanee Hunt noted something wrong in her daughter and said: "We were baffled by Lillian's preoccupation with death and separation. Even before she could write, the stories she told her teacher were laced with tragedy."

Raging

Nighttime is terrifying for the bipolar child, but daytime becomes something of a nightmare for both the child and his or her family as rages begin to erupt. During these rages, which are typically triggered by a simple parental "no," the child goes into an almost seizurelike tantrum where he or she kicks, hits, bites, punches, breaks things, and screams foul language. This can go on for three hours at a time, several times a day, and can persist through adolescence if the child is not treated.

The child seems to have no control over the rage. One young woman who developed the illness early on told us:

It comes out so quickly; faster than a knee-jerk reaction. It's like electricity shoots through me. It's like being struck with lightning. I feel rage and hurt and need to strike back. It becomes primal—infantile.

I would throw things, smash a couple of frogs between rocks. I was raging all the time—every day, multiple times a day, verbally abusive, nasty, negative, but very careful not to show it to the outside world.

Another teenager described her rage this way:

I used to go to my room and punch the walls and I could not stop crying. The more I would cry, the more I couldn't stop. It was like a dream you can't recover in the morning: You know something bad and worrisome has been a concern somewhere in your brain, but you just can't remember it. Sometimes I felt so bad and would think: Why did I do that? And sometimes I'd actually feel better, like it cleared the air.

An eight-year-old boy explained that "when my moods shift, I am never prepared. It feels all tight around me. During a rage, I feel as though the real me is over on the stairway watching myself, but I'm powerless to stop it."

Indeed, the child seems to go into some kind of trancelike state. The parents describe it as "the look." The child seems to be in his own world, and the pupils of the eyes dilate and the eyes become wild-looking. One woman who was having difficulty describing "the look" said, "I finally came up with a word that fits. It's feral. He looks feral when he rages. Almost like a wild animal that is fighting for its life, territory, whatever. There is a certain shine in his eyes that is almost metallic. He just exudes this primal rage."

We have spoken to parents who haven't bought furniture in years because it all gets broken during one of these "affective storms." Their children are experiencing so much irritability and rage that the parents feel as if they live in a war zone. In Chapter 8 we will discuss some theories as to what is happening in the brain during these seizurelike rages, but on a daily basis parents and siblings are experiencing variations of the following:

Walking on eggshells would have been a treat compared to what life was like at our house. Even looking in her direction was seen as an attack. I was out of a job for a while last fall, and she spent part of every day belittling me—telling me how I was letting the family down by making a career change. The screaming, the foul language, and eventually the violence were devastating to our family.

Another mother described her seven-year-old thus:

He had major, major raging cycles. I'm talking going for several weeks, raging violently, throwing things, attacking me, throwing a chair out the window, going through a knife drawer saying he was going to kill me. I couldn't go to the bathroom, for fear he would hurt himself or me.

Friends, teachers, and the outside world cannot fathom what the parent is talking about (if the parent talks about it at all). But one mother who managed to catch an entire rage on a tape recorder wrote:

Many of our friends and even some of the professionals who work with us have not seen Robby in his full glory. They cannot believe that this sweet, charming, affectionate, and outgoing child could possibly be violent or bipolar. They just assume we are not firm enough with him, or pay too much attention to him.

So I got it on tape from start to finish—the screaming and yelling that he's going to kill me, kill the cats. . . .

Now anytime a friend says: "But he's so wonderful whenever we see him" I can pull out the tape and say, "Have a listen to this."

She went on to say:

How am I to have any kind of work life with this going on every day? It's impossible. After I dropped him off at school, I just had to cry as I have no one to talk to who could possibly understand the terror of living with a child like this.

Sir Isaac Newton's mother understood—even in the seventeenth century. As a youngster, Isaac visited his mother and stepfather and had such a rage attack that, in his own words, he threatened "to burne them and the house over them." He left home for boarding school at the age of ten, but not before terrorizing the household. In his diaries he describes: "Striking many"; "Peevishness with my mother and my sister"; "Falling out with the servants"; and "Punching my sister."

Oppositional Behavior

In addition to the ADHD-like behavior, a significant number of these children exhibit behaviors of, and are diagnosed as having, oppositional defiant disorder (ODD). A child who meets the criteria for ODD typically argues with adults; is negativistic, disobedient, and hostile; and actively refuses to comply with requests made by adults.

But is this oppositionality really a separate diagnosis? Many psychiatrists in the research vanguard view this oppositional behavior as an aspect of the bipolar condition. These children seem incapable of making any transition or of complying with any request made by the parent. Their first reaction to anything is "no."

One father described how oppositional his nine-year-old son had become and told us that when he asked the boy if he wanted to go to the toy store to buy the toy he had been campaigning for, but informed him that they would first stop for pizza and ice cream on the way, his son's first response was "No! I'm not going!"

When presented as surprises, even much-desired experiences can be experienced as threatening—a demand to reset the sequence of already integrated events. Transitions cause stress for these children, and stress causes meltdowns.

Children with bipolar disorder lack the flexibility that allows a smooth transition from one activity to another. In fact, parents soon learn to prepare their children for any transition well in advance so that they can integrate the idea of it.

Because any request or expectation may be viewed as a stressor, these children can become very adept at blocking out anyone else's agenda and become remarkably adept at clamoring for their own. Many parents feel beaten down by this persistence and oppositional behavior. Two women were commiserating with each other on the Internet and wrote:

> My son is another future lawyer—argues and finds some slight difference in semantics to turn things around. I always thought of it as an OCD trait—had to get the last word in no matter what. I picture him as a future "My Cousin Vinny."

To which the other woman responded:

> Ditto for my son. Maybe they could get together and form a company called "Battle Warriors, Inc." Their motto could be something like: "Whether you're right or wrong, we win every battle. Specialists in browbeating all opponents."

Rapid Cycling

Beyond the oppositionality and extreme irritability, the majority of bipolar children cycle rapidly from depression to mania and back again. Some cycle over a period of days; others seem to alternate mood states several times throughout the day. One seventeen-year-old girl, now treated, described it this way:

> My moods shifted constantly throughout the day. I can remember being so so happy, but after a while I wouldn't like it because I knew I would be coming down. It's so rapid. I'd be so happy and an hour later I'd say, "I'm so depressed."
>
> When I crash, I come down so hard, I can't do anything; I can't get up. I'm tired. I just have to sit down. My mom has to force me to go places. No words can describe it. It physically hurts your heart. You're so depressed that you actually feel that you're dying. You feel like you're wasting away—like you have cancer. When I'm depressed, I want to get high [manic], but then I worry about the coming depression. I always get depressed around the beginning to late afternoon. At six or seven I get hyper, happy. Sometimes I get a bad manic period. I feel angry and agitated and I feel I have to punch stuff. I just want to shake things. I have so much energy I feel like I want to jump out of my skin.

Because the mood shifts are so rapid, it is easy to see how children may become trapped in the switch process between depression and mania and develop what is called a *mixed state*. Their internal experience is one of marked agitation, high energy, and constant restlessness. At the same time they feel worthless and self-destructive. While mixed states are not as common in adults unless induced by antidepressant treatment, they are a hallmark of the ultrarapid cycles found in childhood-onset bipolar disorder.

Dr. Barbara Geller of Washington University in St. Louis describes an example of depression and mania—a mixed state—occurring simultaneously in a seven-year-old boy: "He was doing a Michael Jackson imitation at the diagnostic interview but was experiencing suicidal impulses at the same time."

Sensitivity to Stimuli

Many parents describe their children as excruciatingly sensitive to stimuli of all sorts. The mother of one young girl describes her daughter as "very sensitive in the visual realm. She is drawn like a magnet to some designs, colors, beautiful paintings, landscapes, and repelled by others, as strongly as she reacts to odors and tastes. I always try to see the positive in these things—telling her that she would be a good interior or clothing designer, artist, chef, writer, or teacher."

Some bipolar children are so sensitive to stimuli that they cannot tolerate pockets in clothing or labels or collars on shirts. Backpacks must always feel a certain way, and we know children who will stuff them with books to approximate the "right feel" even if there is no homework given and no textbooks are required that day.

We've heard of mothers who've spent whole days shopping for socks that didn't have "nubbies" on the bottom; or for only blue clothing because "that is all my son would wear." Both mothers and fathers could be certified in the "Titration of Shoelaces" because their children have to have their sneakers tied at just the right tension or they can become explosive.

It's as if the arousal system of the child is set at such a threshold that any kind of physical sensation that is not "just right" is extremely irritating and threatens a sense of bodily integrity.

Bipolar children seem to be out of sync. Not only are they bothered tremendously by sensations, odors, and noises, but they seem to have great difficulty making shifts from one context to another. When the demand to do so is made—and it may only be a request to stop watching television and join the family in the kitchen for dinner—he or she may not be able to brook the transition and the change in the state of mood, attention, or motor response required. The child may become easily frustrated and irritable, and a repeated (or eventually heated) demand may provoke the child's angry outburst or rage.

The limbic system (the emotional brain) seems to be involved with the integration of sensory experience, and we will explore this more closely in Chapter 8.

Problems with Peers

We asked parents on our survey to describe their child's relationship with friends. While some children were thought of as "charismatic," "very generous to friends," and "extremely popular," the majority of the respondents (77 percent) reported that their children were having tremendous problems maintaining peer relationships. Some had never been invited to a birthday party or had a sleepover. Many of the children were described as "bossy," "intrusive," "has to have his or her own way or the game is over," or "too overwhelming and aggressive." Sadly, these children want very much to have friends, but they seem to miss the social clues or appreciate social boundaries.

Temperature Dysregulation

In our research, we noticed that parents often mentioned how reactive their children were to cold and heat. These children were often overheated in winter and left the house wearing no coat or gloves. One child slept in a house that was so cold the parents were burrowing under down quilts even as their child kicked off the comforter, saying she was burning hot. Many of these children take their clothes off as often as they can because they are so heat intolerant. Some get red ears or red spots on their cheeks when they make transitions from cold to warm environments. And all foods—soups, teas, milk shakes—must be just the right temperature or they are rejected. (Chapter 8 will also discuss some theories about this pattern of temperature dysregulation.)

Craving for Carbohydrates and Sweets

Another noted difference in children and adolescents with bipolar disorder is their insatiable appetite for carbohydrates and sweets. They may begin hoarding chocolate and cookies in their rooms and consume massive amounts of pasta, cereals, and bread. One mother referred to her daughter as "the Carb Queen from way back."

When we asked a young woman of twenty who had suffered bipolar disorder since childhood if she ever craved carbohydrates or sweets, there was a giggle at the other end of the phone. She asked, "Would you consider a gallon of Breyer's Mint Chocolate Chip every night a craving?"

She went on to tell us that her craving was so strong that she would buy a half gallon and eat it in the car and then go back in the store and buy another one. We asked if she had kept plastic spoons in the car. She laughed out loud and said, "No, I would use my fingers. It was savage."

We know of other girls who pour sugar straight from the box down their throats, or teenagers who drive long distances to get powdered-sugar doughnuts that they consume by the dozen. Many of the girls suffer from co-occurring eating disorders and may become anorexic or bulimic (starving, gorging, and/or purging). Some of the girls (and a smaller percentage of boys) will begin periods of self-mutilation in their teenage years, where they rake their arms with razors, pins, or other sharp objects (see page 44 for more on this).

Children who have bipolar disorder typically have food aversions, sudden demands for certain foods to the exclusion of all others, or notable ingestion habits. A mother from Colorado referred to her son's eating patterns as "snaking" because "he barely eats for days and then devours ungodly amounts of pasta and other carbohydrate foods."

Bedwetting and Soiling

Something also seems to be poorly regulated in the autonomic nervous system of these children. Many wet their beds for years throughout childhood. Other children may smear feces in the bathtub, on walls, or in closets. This enuresis (bedwetting) and encopresis (soiling) is poorly understood.

Impending Mania

Some children cycle so quickly that it's hard to see the switch process from one mood to another; others have a more noticeable transition. At these times, the child may get very goal-oriented. One mother said:

> If he's getting manic, he starts looking for tools or unhooking the computer. If he wants to do something, watch out. Get out of his way, or he'll become very, very angry. You can't set limits. We'll see very up-up-up behavior. He quotes Ren and Stimpy, the cartoon characters, and screams "Happy, happy, joy, joy!" He starts grabbing tools, playing loud music in his room. I don't know when it's going to end . . . could be tonight, could be in a couple of days.

Other parents describe periods of intense silliness—giddy and goofy behavior with a lot of mouthiness, grandiosity, and outrageous comments. The child's thoughts may race. One five-year-old boy told his mother: "My brain feels like it wants to go for a walk ten times . . . up the stairs and down the stairs . . . and again." When this youngster couldn't sleep, he explained: "My brain keeps kicking me out of bed." Dr. Barbara Geller speaks of a child who once told her, "I wish I had a button on my head so I could turn off all these thoughts."

In D. Jablow Hershman and Julien Lieb's book, *Manic Depression and Creativity,* Charles Dickens was described as quite manic in his early teenage years: "He became very sociable, was generally in a humorous mood, and was given to telling jokes and singing comic songs whenever the opportunity offered. His gaiety was so excessive at times as to embarrass school friends. His laughter would become uncontrollable, almost hysterical. He played pranks and acted the clown."

As the manic throttle is pushed, a child may become more and more grandiose. She may think she is the best, the brightest, able to do things no one else can. It may start simply when a student decides he or she can teach the class better than the teacher, or brag about how famous he is going to be someday. A little girl who drew a lot of pictures when she was hypomanic always placed a crown on her head, frequently picturing herself as a queen.

Accompanying this very "up" feeling may be an increased sexuality (hypersexuality). Some mothers report that their boys are always pinching the bottoms of women they meet in the store, or hugging and groping women they know. The phone bill may reveal a number of calls to 1-900 sex lines. A mother from Virginia who filled out our questionnaire commented that her daughter dresses in skimpy clothing when she becomes hypomanic and tries to sit on the laps of her older brother's friends who come over to the house.

Dr. Barbara Geller and her colleagues published an article in 2000 in which they looked at a group of ninety-three children and adolescents with bipolar disorder and found that 43 percent of this group who were manic were also hypersexual.

Often this hypersexuality is viewed by hospital personnel and Child Protective Services as a sign that sexual abuse is taking place inside the home, but it is a symptom of the mood disorder and is present in hypomanic and manic children, as well as hypomanic and manic adults. Dr. Geller reported that less than 1 percent of these hypersexual bipolar children had evidence of sexual abuse in the home environment.

Here is another description of a very hypomanic, hypersexual seven-year-old boy:

He got very silly after dinner—very affectionate with me, and hypersexual at bath time. He said, "I love you, Mommy," trying to kiss me. "Will you lay on top of me. I'm going to rub my penis, can you do it?" After his bath he jumped on top of me trying to give me "long kisses" and telling my husband that he knows a girl who would rub his penis.

The mood and behavior of a child who is becoming manic tends to be *labile*—it shifts dramatically and often. One day can be fairly uneventful; the next day hospitalization may seem imminent as psychotic symptoms appear and violent outbursts occur. This can be very confusing for the family members (and the child), who never know what to expect or how the day will unfold. The following fragments from a mother's journal illustrate this extreme lability of mood in her nine-year-old son.

Twelve Days in May

5/11   Hypomanic, bizarre evening. "I hate me; kill me; Why am I like this?" Very rough with younger brother.

5/12   Good morning, dropped off well at school. Pretty good mood coming off bus, but more defiance in the afternoon. Uneventful evening. Went to bed well.

5/13   Up early, dressed well, good mood but problems on the bus. Kids teasing him. Teacher called and reported very bizarre behavior at school. She also reported a lot of ADHD symptoms—very fidgety, unable to remain seated in the afternoon, cruises around classroom, ran out of classroom, pestering other kids, unable to follow directions, not remaining on task or completing work.

5/14   Teacher reported a great day in school. Good mood after school.

5/15   Good A.M.—off to school well. Very defiant after school. Angered by new doctor. Got very angry in car—punching me, destructive to car, scribbling on dashboard, dumping over trash. Had to be restrained in office—punching, kicking, swearing—settled down at end of meeting and apologized.

5/16   Happy mood in A.M., but doing goofy, impulsive things— squirted water on dad's work shirt, squirted water on table and floor.

Very aggressive after school—threatening me, hitting, increase in defiance. Aggressive toward other students.

5/17   Had a good time with grandparents. Crying a lot in the afternoon.

5/18   "Mixed," very irritable to hypomanic—increase in goal-directed activities, very easily frustrated and angered.

5/19   Good and uneventful day.

5/20   Very irritable in A.M.—threatened father—said: "I'm going to kill you someday." Manic after school—very goal-directed—taking all the tools out of the basement to use up in his room (hammer, sander, drill, staple gun). Very angry when I intervened—very loud, shouting, laughing, singing, dancing, "I don't feel good today. I want to kill myself. When I grow up, I am going to kill myself because being bipolar is bad." Hallucinating in afternoon—auditory and visual: goblin, clown, queen. "I hear the devil, I hear penises in your brain, Mom." Very hyperactive, and not rational. Gave him Risperdal and he went to sleep.

5/21   Hypomanic, happy in the afternoon.

5/22   Woke up laughing—found some needlepoint yarn and needles under the bed. "I'm giving myself a lab test"—trying to stick needles into his arm. Giddy, shouting "hubba, hubba, hubba, howdy, howdy" over and over again, very wound up. Settled down and watched some TV. Pleasant and more normal, but talkative in the afternoon. Easier to please. More irritable after dinner. Fascinated with knives, demonstrated how he would stab a wolf. Very quiet in my lap. He said: "I love you, Mom. You don't love me, you want me to die. I will if you want me to."

Hallucinations

Not all bipolar children who get manic will suffer hallucinations, but many do. Often, if they don't vocalize their thoughts or act very bizarrely, the parents may not even know it is happening. Hallucinations do *not* mean the child is schizophrenic—they are very much a part of the bipolar picture, as we shall see in Chapter 2.

Auditory hallucinations, where the child hears voices or converses with people who are not visible to others, are the most common type of hallucination. The voices are experienced as real to the child and have extraordinary influence over him or her. There may be one voice, or several may be carrying on a conversation. They may simply be overheard by the child, or the voices may make direct statements to the child.

One young woman told us that she hears "hundreds of voices. I feel like my brain is being crushed by the voices." A mother wrote to us and described her daughter having a conversation with a grown man in the living room for about half an hour, and then she snapped out of it and realized no one was there. "She often hears voices of a group of people in the living room, having a conversation." (The girl, eighteen, has now admitted to her mother that she's been hearing these people since she was small but was afraid to tell anyone.)

Another mother wrote about her ten-year-old son's hearing voices and his unique way of making them disappear. She said:

> We have learned that an extra half of a mg of Risperdal, given when the voices are present, will make them go away within ten minutes. On occasions where he could not take the Risperdal, the voices continue for hours. Derek sometimes says the voices don't want us to know about them. He is trying to work out his own cure. Sometimes he gets rid of the voices simply by telling them he is going to take a dose of Risperdal.

Many children also have visual hallucinations—they see things that others don't. One ten-year-old boy described a visual hallucination to his father. He said, "They are one-dimensional and appear flat and static. You cannot see through them, but a tossed pencil will travel through them. You see, Dad, you and the cat are three-dimensional and hallucinations are one-dimensional."

His father then wrote, "Earlier this week he saw one in our living room. It was a man with a knife. He was at first in shock and screaming. Then later he started playing and experimenting further with it to prove all his theories." The visual hallucinations often seem to include satanic figures. One girl was convinced she saw the devil sitting on the mantel of the fireplace in the living room. A boy who had been exhibiting very bizarre behavior began to hallucinate and told his mother that he felt that his head was going to fly off because the devil was hurting him.

Hallucinations are not only auditory and visual. They can involve any of the senses: There are tactile hallucinations (a child feels something touching her) and olfactory hallucinations (a child smells odors that others do not perceive).

Suicidal Ideas

Long before the teenage years, children as young as four, five, six, and seven have suicidal thoughts and have been known to attempt to act on their impulses.

A mother from Texas wrote that her six-year-old son tried to jump out of the car while they were driving over a highway bridge. He said he was going to jump off the bridge and kill himself. Another little boy performed acts of self-mutilation that mimic suicide. He tried to cut his wrists with the wing of a metal toy airplane.

Parents don't know where these children are getting these ideas from. One woman wrote and said, "I was astounded to hear my four-year-old daughter, who had never seen a violent movie or even heard of the concept of suicide, sobbing through the bedroom door that she was going to 'make herself dead' during a horrible tantrum."

Sometimes the children don't make such bold gestures or statements but may ask curiously: "If I jumped off ten stories and opened an umbrella, would I fall?" or "Would you like me to go to heaven with Tucker [their dog] and watch out over all of you?"

A nine-year-old girl who was extremely creative started writing a book one evening. Chapter 6 is entitled "Death," and she says:

> Maybe sometimes your child will say that they will kill themselves. This is something to take seriously. I have poked myself a few times because I get angry and stressed. Sometimes I just don't care about life anymore. I am also really scared.
>
> If your child gets these thoughts, ask the doctor for Zyprexa, or something like that. If this situation ever happens, hold them still until they calm down and stop wanting to kill themselves. Hold them until they feel a part of this world.

A remarkable number of children are feeling these feelings and thinking these thoughts every day throughout the world. It is hard to fathom how they consolidate a core sense of self while struggling through days with moods that are careening from one pole to the other.

Unfortunately, researchers have reported that mood disorders seem to be increasing in incidence among the age group, or cohort, born since 1940. And the age of onset is shifting downward—younger people are being affected. Recently Dr. Raymond DePaulo's laboratory at Johns Hopkins University reported a ten-year earlier age of onset of bipolar illness in affected children compared with their bipolar parent. This trend was noted in the 1980s by Dr. Gerald Klerman at Yale and by Dr. Elliot Gershon and his colleagues at the National Institute of Mental Health. They found that each successive generation of individuals born since World War II appears to have a higher incidence and earlier age of onset of both major depression and bipolar disorder. While there are many theories attempting to explain this "cohort phenomenon," little is actually understood.

Yet there is still cause for optimism.

- Today there are medications that can stabilize the moods of these children, effectively calm the irritability, and stop the raging and hallucinations. New treatments are in the pipeline.
- Research attention is finally being focused on this disorder of early childhood, and groups like the Stanley Medical Research Institute have launched an Early Treatment Initiative in which they are trying to evaluate how early and how best to treat the illness. The Juvenile Bipolar Research Foundation, whose sole focus is the study of early-onset bipolar disorder, was recently launched.
- Consumer advocacy organizations like the National Alliance for the Mentally Ill are using their members to change legislation and fight for equal insurance coverage, medical insurance for the working poor, and better models of treatment for people with brain disorders.
- The Internet has become a vast source of information and support for parents who must deal with this illness and make critical decisions with the treating physicians. No parent with a computer ever has to feel all alone with this illness ever again.

Diagnosed early, and treated appropriately, these children and their families can live infinitely more stable lives. The first step, then, is the diagnosis of the disorder, and it is to this that we turn next.

The Diagnostic Dilemma

When we first met with publishers about this project, one editor listened intently and then asked the following pointed question: "But don't you think that parents will be reluctant to accept this diagnosis? Don't you think they will prefer that their child be labeled ADHD and adopt the 'ostrich syndrome'?"

"You mean bury their heads in the sand?" we replied.

"Yes," came the rejoinder.

It was a legitimate question. But the answers coming back to us on our survey and through our conversations with parents all over the country point to just the opposite reaction. These parents know that something more serious than attention-deficit disorder with hyperactivity is going on. Some who have the illness themselves recognize certain temperaments and behaviors because they either see early versions of themselves in their child, or they may remember all too well one of their family members showing similar traits of the illness. In fact, for many parents who recognize the traits, it is difficult to find a doctor even willing to *make* the diagnosis of bipolar disorder in a child.

The psychiatric profession's wariness about diagnosing early-onset bipolar disorder is a relatively modern phenomenon and requires some explaining. After all, in A.D. 150, Aretaeus of Cappadocia described manic-depressive illness in children younger than twelve; in 1854 the French alienist, Jean Etienne Dominique Esquirol, provided case reports of mania in preschool and prepubertal school-age children; and Emil Kraepelin—the paterfamilias of psychiatric diagnosis—reported mood disorders in children in his famous treatise *Manic-Depressive Insanity and Paranoia,* published in 1921.

But in the 1930s, the Freudian psychodynamic approach to the mind became predominant in the United States, and psychoanalytic theory took the position that a classical depressive syndrome could not occur in prepubertal children. As psychiatrists began to focus on the unconscious motivations of behavior, mood disorders in the young became a neglected issue. In fact, it wasn't until the 1975 National Institute of Mental Health Conference on Depression in Childhood that depression in children was even officially recognized in this country.

The idea that a child could ever suffer mania was almost completely buried, however, when two psychiatrists, E. James Anthony and Peter Scott, published a paper in 1960. In "Manic-Depressive Psychosis in Childhood," the authors detailed criteria for early-onset mania that were so stringent they literally guaranteed that the diagnosis of juvenile manic-depression would be a rare one indeed.

One of Anthony and Scott's criterion cautioned a clinician *not* to make the diagnosis of mania unless he or she found an illness so severe that it required "inpatient treatment, heavy sedation, or electroconvulsive therapy (ECT)." But they went even further: They reviewed the literature of reported cases of mania in children between the years 1884 and 1954, and, applying their criteria, they uncovered only twenty-eight cases of alleged manic-depression in young children. While this study was done quite some time ago, it contributed to the prevailing attitude that bipolar disorder was rare in childhood.

DIFFICULTIES OF DIAGNOSIS

Diagnosis in psychiatry is a problem. After all, there are no lab tests that conclusively pinpoint a diagnosis, there are a host of overlapping symptoms (especially in children's disorders), and each person experiencing an illness expresses it through the unique filter of mind and temperament. The psychiatrist's main diagnostic instruments are the patient's report of symptoms, observable behavior, family history, and clinical course of the disorder.

Distinguishing between normal behaviors and pathological ones in a young child is even more challenging for a number of reasons: The span of time in a young life is insufficient to establish a course of illness; developmental factors are in full play; and a child's often nonstop motion, lack of impulse control, difficulty tolerating frustration, and vivid imagination are a part of the typical, everyday picture.

If you then consider that mood disorders in children *may* have a developmental evolution of symptoms—separation anxiety, night terrors, distractibility, poor attention, restlessness and hyperactivity followed by obsessions, defiant and contentious behaviors, finally culminating in a very rapid-cycling course with irritable or mixed mood states—it is no small wonder that children are often misdiagnosed, or plastered with a literal alphabet soup of diagnostic labels: attention-deficit disorder with hyperactivity (ADHD), obsessive-compulsive disorder (OCD), oppositional defiant disorder (ODD), conduct disorder (CD), generalized anxiety disorder (GAD), and so on.

Yet a correct diagnosis is vital to a child's well-being, for it is the proper diagnosis that guides the treatment and—equally important—prevents the child from being placed on medications that can considerably worsen the course of the disorder.

The most recent diagnostic criteria established by the American Psychiatric Association (APA) are delineated in the fourth edition of the *Diagnostic and Statistical Manual of Mental Disorders,* the *DSM-IV.* These criteria are used to determine psychiatric diagnoses in children and adults.

What Does the *DSM-IV* Say About Children and Mood Disorders?

In the *DSM-IV,* mood disorders are divided into depressive disorders and bipolar disorders. Children are mentioned, but they are to be diagnosed basically according to the adult criteria. (And this is where the problem begins.) The criteria that must be met before a diagnosis of a major depressive episode can be made are as follows (our comments appear in italics).

CRITERIA FOR MAJOR DEPRESSIVE EPISODE
A. Five (or more) of the following symptoms have been present during the same two-week period and represent a change from previous functioning; at least one of the symptoms is either (1) depressed

mood, or (2) loss of interest or pleasure. Note: Do not include symptoms that are clearly due to a general medical condition, or mood-incongruent delusions or hallucinations.

1. Depressed mood most of the day, nearly every day, as indicated by either subjective report (e.g., feels sad or empty), or observation made by others (e.g., appears tearful). Note: In children and adolescents, can be irritable mood.

2. Markedly diminished interest or pleasure in all, or almost all, activities most of the day, nearly every day (as indicated by either subjective account or observation made by others).

3. Significant weight loss when not dieting or weight gain (e.g., a change of more than 5 percent of body weight in a month), or decrease or increase in appetite nearly every day. Note: In children, consider failure to make expected weight gains.

4. Insomnia or hypersomnia *(sleeping excessively)* nearly every day.

5. Psychomotor agitation or retardation nearly every day (observable by others, not merely subjective feelings of restlessness or being slowed down).

6. Fatigue or loss of energy nearly every day.

7. Feelings of worthlessness or excessive or inappropriate guilt (which may be delusional) nearly every day (not merely self-reproach or guilt about being sick).

8. Diminished ability to think or concentrate, or indecisiveness, nearly every day (either by subjective account or as observed by others).

9. Recurrent thoughts of death (not just fear of dying), recurrent suicidal ideation without a specific plan, or a suicide attempt or a specific plan for committing suicide.

B. The symptoms do not meet criteria for a Mixed State *(where a patient displays symptoms of mania and depression every day during at least a one-week period).*

C. The symptoms cause clinically significant distress or impairment in social, occupational, or other important areas of functioning.

D. The symptoms are not due to the direct physiological effects of a substance (e.g., a drug of abuse, a medication) or a general medical condition (e.g., hypothyroidism).

E. The symptoms are not better accounted for by bereavement; i.e., after the loss of a loved one, the symptoms persist for longer than two months, or are characterized by marked functional impairment, morbid preoccupation with worthlessness, suicidal ideation, psychotic symptoms, or psychomotor retardation.

The criteria that must be met before the diagnosis of a manic episode can be made are as follows:

CRITERIA FOR MANIC EPISODE

A. A distinct period of abnormally and persistently elevated, expansive, or irritable mood, lasting at least one week (or any duration if hospitalization is necessary).

B. During the period of mood disturbance, three (or more) of the following symptoms have persisted (four if the mood is only irritable) and have been present to a significant degree:

1. Inflated self-esteem or grandiosity.
2. Decreased need for sleep (e.g., feels rested after only three hours of sleep).
3. More talkative than usual or pressure to keep talking.
4. Flight of ideas or subjective experience that thoughts are racing.
5. Distractibility (i.e., attention too easily drawn to unimportant or irrelevant external stimuli).
6. Increase in goal-directed activity (either socially, at work or school, or sexually) or psychomotor agitation.
7. Excessive involvement in pleasurable activities that have a high potential for painful consequences (e.g., engaging in unrestrained buying sprees, sexual indiscretions, or foolish business investments).

C. The symptoms do not meet criteria for a Mixed State.

D. The mood disturbance is sufficiently severe to cause marked impairment in occupational functioning or in usual social activities or relationships with others, or to necessitate hospitalization to prevent harm to self or others, or there are psychotic features.

E. The symptoms are not due to the direct physiological effects of a substance (e.g., a drug of abuse, a medication, or other treatment), or a general medical condition (e.g., hyperthyroidism). Note: Maniclike episodes that are clearly caused by somatic antidepressant treatment (e.g., medication, electroconvulsive therapy, light therapy) should not count toward a diagnosis of Bipolar I Disorder.

Although the inclusion of childhood mood disorders in the *DSM-IV* could be seen as a major advance, thoughtful clinical investigators are beginning to realize that bipolar disorder in childhood presents in a very different pattern—one that often bears little resemblance to classical cycles of mania and depression as they are expressed in adulthood. For instance, children have more irritable moods with explosive outbursts, and their cycles of mania, hypomania, and depression are far more rapid than the typical adult presentation.

Which brings us to one of the major problems of the *DSM-IV* criteria as they apply to children: the fulfillment of the duration criteria. *DSM-IV* specifies that a mood episode (either manic or depressive) must last for a specified period of time. For instance, duration criteria for the diagnosis of a hypomanic episode requires a "distinct period of persistently elevated, expansive, or irritable mood lasting throughout *at least four days*" (italics ours). Yet a significant proportion of early-onset bipolar children (some estimates are as high as 70 percent) have a form of the condition that is marked by frequent mood and energy shifts that occur *several times within a day.*

For a depressive episode, the *DSM-IV* duration criterion is even more demanding: The manual requires at least a two-week period with five or more depressive symptoms. Therefore, by definition, an individual who has rapidly shifting mood states of less than the required duration cannot be formally diagnosed as having a bipolar disorder.

A separate and distinct category, code number 296.7—Bipolar Disorder Not Otherwise Specified (NOS)—was established to include disorders with bipolar features that do not meet full duration criteria. This category allows individuals who have a very rapid alternation of manic and depressive symptoms, but who do not meet minimal duration criteria, to be identified within the bipolar spectrum. While most children with bipolar disorder fit within this category, it still is not an accurate description of the condition as it presents in childhood.

It is becoming clear that bipolar disorder in children requires its own criteria. However, at this time, the APA has no plans to publish a revision until after the year 2010.

This leaves researchers in an extremely difficult position: When they propose studies on children with bipolar disorder, either they cannot use *DSM-IV* criteria and must describe these children as having "manialike symptoms," or they must modify other diagnostic instruments in order to continue with their work. Dr. Barbara Geller's team at Washington University in St. Louis has modified a version of the KIDDE-SADS (a structured diagnostic interview developed by the late Dr. Joaquin Puig-Antich), which is more sensitive to the cycling patterns that are most commonly observed in childhood bipolar disorder, such as ultra-ultrarapid (or ultradian) cycling.

It is hoped that the use of this new diagnostic instrument in future research studies will help to establish a more accurate picture of childhood-onset bipolar disorder. But, in the meantime, it is good for both clinicians and family members to keep in mind that the *Diagnostic and Statistical Manual* was not handed down at Sinai; it was always a tentative working system of classification that was intended to be changed and refined as it kept pace with new developments in psychiatry.

MEDICAL CONDITIONS THAT CAN MIMIC MOOD DISORDERS

Even if the clinician begins to suspect a possible bipolar disorder, he or she must, as the *DSM-IV* cautions, rule out any medical conditions that can mimic or masquerade as depression or mania. The following list shows such conditions, which range from hormonal disorders and neurological syndromes to malignancies and diseases of the blood.

HORMONAL AND METABOLIC DISORDERS
Cushing's disease
Diabetes
Hyperparathyroidism
Hyperthyroidism
Hypoglycemia
Hypothyroidism
Wilson's disease

INFECTIOUS DISEASES
AIDS
Hepatitis
Influenzas
Mononucleosis
Syphilis
Viral pneumonias

NEUROLOGICAL DISORDERS
Kleine-Levin syndrome
Temporal lobe epilepsy

BLOOD DISEASES
Acute intermittent porphyria
Iron-deficiency anemia

METAL INTOXICATIONS
Manganese
Mercury
Thallium

NUTRITIONAL DISORDERS
Pellagra
Pernicious anemia

CANCERS
Central nervous system tumors

GENETIC DISORDERS
Asperger's syndrome (can be comorbid with bipolar disorder)
Velo-cardio-facial syndrome

OTHER DISEASES
Chronic fatigue syndrome
Lyme disease

Almost all of these medical conditions can be ruled in or out by physical examination coupled with appropriate clinical laboratory tests. There-

fore, it is extremely important that the diagnosing physician take a personal patient and family medical history as well as request that the child have a complete physical exam and certain blood tests, including thyroid function studies. Only then should a primary mood disorder—one that is not secondary to or caused by a primary medical condition—be diagnosed.

Once a comprehensive medical workup has been done, the physician needs to elicit a complete family history of possible psychiatric illness and substance abuse. The substance abuse factor is an important piece of the puzzle because it has been shown that a significant number of individuals with bipolar disorder abuse alcohol and drugs. It is thought that many of these individuals are self-medicating (calming the agitation or sleep problems with alcohol or sustaining a high with cocaine), or that the two illnesses—bipolar disorder and substance abuse—are highly comorbid (they occur together). There is some thought now that a person with bipolar disorder is extremely vulnerable to addiction. Dr. Barbara Geller once advised, "If you see substance abuse, suspect bipolar, and if you see bipolar, suspect substance abuse."

Until definitive blood or other tests can confirm a psychiatric diagnosis, nothing can replace an informed diagnostician who understands how this illness manifests itself in childhood and who understands how important the family history is. (Chapter 3 discusses how to find a good physician.)

THE FIRST DIAGNOSTIC DILEMMA: THE UNIPOLAR VERSUS BIPOLAR DISTINCTION

It is not uncommon for the initial episode of childhood-onset bipolar disorder to present as major depression. But as clinical investigators follow the course of the disorder in children, they have observed a significant rate of switching to bipolar symptoms.

In 1994 Dr. Geller published a study on a group of seventy-nine prepubertal patients suffering from depression. These children were followed for a two- to five-year period. Within two years, 32 percent of these children had switched into mania. In 2001, a follow-up study of seventy-two of the original seventy-nine prepubertal children was reported in the *American Journal of Psychiatry.* The mean age of these children was then about twenty, and 48.6 percent of them had been rediagnosed with some form of bipolar disorder. (If children with ADHD had not been excluded from the study, the rates would no doubt have been even higher.)

It may be that a depression manifested very early in life is the first salvo in the evolution of an illness that can progress to bipolar disorder, particularly after exposure to antidepressant medications.

Because it is a known fact that antidepressant treatment can induce hypomania, mania, rapid cycling, and mixed states—often accompanied by severe aggressive or violent behaviors in those who have an as-yet-unexpressed predisposition to bipolar disorder—it is extremely important that all parents and physicians be alert to the possibility that the child may indeed be bipolar.

What are the possible predictors of a switch from a major depressive disorder to a manic-depressive disorder? In our survey, some of the common symptoms that preceded a bipolar course were depressions marked by a craving for sweets and carbohydrates, prolonged and aggressive temper tantrums, lethargy, oversleeping, separation anxiety, self-consciousness with others, and phobic anxiety.

Does this mean that a child should never be treated with an antidepressant? Even if a physician thinks there is a strong likelihood of a latent bipolar gene and is circumspect about initiating antidepressant treatment, the risk/benefit to the child needs to be considered. In Chapter 4, when we discuss medications, we'll outline some treatments and precautions for the child whose first episode is a depressive one.

COMORBIDITIES: DISORDERS THAT CAN OCCUR SIMULTANEOUSLY WITH BIPOLAR DISORDER

Rarely does bipolar disorder in children occur as a pure entity by itself. Rather it is often accompanied by clusters of symptoms that—when observed at certain points in a child's life—suggest other psychiatric disorders, such as attention-deficit disorder with hyperactivity, obsessive-compulsive disorder, oppositional defiant disorder, conduct disorder, or Tourette's syndrome.

The questions researchers are attempting to resolve are:

1. Does bipolar disorder occur simultaneously with other psychiatric disorders, making it possible for a child actually to have three or four diagnoses?
2. Are these clusters of symptoms that suggest distinct disorders merely early precursors on a developmental continuum that eventually expresses itself as full-blown bipolar?

3. Are all these symptoms merely a more apt description of early-
   onset bipolar disorder?

The truth is no one knows for certain. And until research can provide
clarification, parents are going to have to tolerate a great deal of diagnostic ambiguity; for surely they will come up against a few of the following
comorbid diagnoses.

The Great Debate: Does the Child Have ADHD, Bipolar Disorder, or Both?

Perhaps the greatest source of diagnostic confusion in childhood bipolar
disorder is that its symptoms overlap with many of the symptoms of
attention-deficit disorder with hyperactivity. At first glance, any child
who can't sit still, who is impulsive, inattentive, easily distracted, or emotionally labile is more likely to receive a diagnosis of ADHD than bipolar disorder. (In our survey, 93 percent of the children met *DSM-IV*
criteria for attention-deficit disorder with hyperactivity.)

The *DSM-IV* criteria for attention-deficit disorder with hyperactivity
include:

DIAGNOSTIC CRITERIA FOR ATTENTION-DEFICIT DISORDER
WITH HYPERACTIVITY
A. Either (1) or (2):
(1) Six (or more) of the following symptoms of inattention have persisted for at least six months to a degree that is maladaptive and inconsistent with developmental level:

Inattention
(a) Often fails to give close attention to details or makes careless
mistakes in schoolwork, work, or other activities.

(b) Often has difficulty sustaining attention in tasks or play activities.

(c) Often does not seem to listen when spoken to directly.

(d) Often does not follow through on instructions and fails to finish schoolwork, chores, or duties in the workplace (not due to oppositional behavior or failure to understand instructions).

(e) Often has difficulty organizing tasks and activities.

(f) Often avoids, dislikes, or is reluctant to engage in tasks that require sustained mental effort (such as schoolwork or home-work).

(g) Often loses things necessary for tasks or activities (e.g., toys, school assignments, pencils, books, or tools).

(h) Is often easily distracted by extraneous stimuli.

(i) Is often forgetful in daily activities.

(2) Six (or more) of the following symptoms of hyperactivity-impulsivity have persisted for at least six months to a degree that is maladaptive and inconsistent with developmental level:

Hyperactivity
(a) Often fidgets with hands or feet or squirms in seat.

(b) Often leaves seat in classroom or in other situations in which remaining seated is expected.

(c) Often runs about or climbs excessively in situations in which it is inappropriate (in adolescents or adults, may be limited to subjective feelings of restlessness).

(d) Often has difficulty playing or engaging in leisure activities quietly.

(e) Is often "on the go" or often acts as if "driven by a motor."

(f) Often talks excessively.

Impulsivity
(g) Often blurts out answers before questions have been com-pleted.

(h) Often has difficulty awaiting turn.

(i) Often interrupts or intrudes on others (e.g., butts into conversations or games).

B. Some hyperactive-impulsive or inattentive symptoms that caused impairment were present before age seven years.

C. Some impairment from the symptoms is present in two or more settings (e.g., at school [or work] and at home).

D. There must be clear evidence of clinically significant impairment in social, academic, or occupational functioning.

E. The symptoms do not occur exclusively during the course of a pervasive developmental disorder, schizophrenia, or other psychotic disorder and are not better accounted for by another mental disorder (e.g., mood disorder, anxiety disorder, dissociative disorder, or a personality disorder).

Part of this bias toward making the ADHD diagnosis is the overlap of symptoms between the conditions. In fact, Drs. Janet Wozniak and Joseph Biederman of Harvard Medical School found that 94 percent of a sample of forty-three children with mania met *DSM-IIIR* criteria for attention-deficit disorder with hyperactivity. Also, mindful of Anthony and Scott's incredibly stringent criteria for making the diagnosis of bipolar disorder, it just seemed sensible that "when one hears the clatter of hoofbeats on the roof, one looks for horses and not for zebras."

But now, realizing that there is a large population of children suffering with mood disorders, how would a clinician determine whether the problem is ADHD or a mood disorder?

According to Dr. Charles Popper, who has written extensively on the issue of distinguishing between ADHD and bipolar disorders: "All of the features of ADHD can be seen in mood disorders at times, so *ADHD is a diagnosis reached only after ruling out a mood disorder.*" In his article entitled "Diagnosing Bipolar vs. ADHD: A Pharmacological Point of View," he lists several distinctions between the two diagnostic groups and brings great clarity to this diagnostic confusion. With permission, we quote them here:

1. Destructiveness may be seen in both disorders but differs in origin. Children who are ADHD often break things carelessly while

playing ("non-angry destructiveness"), whereas the major destructiveness of children who are bipolar is not a result of carelessness but tends to occur in anger. Children who are bipolar may exhibit severe temper tantrums during which they release manic quantities of physical and emotional energy, sometimes with violence and physical property destruction. They may even exhibit openly sadistic impulses.

2. The duration and intensity of physical outbursts and temper tantrums differs in the two disorders. Children who are ADHD usually calm down in twenty to thirty minutes, whereas children who are bipolar may continue to feel and act angry for up to four hours.

3. The degree of "regression" during angry episodes is typically more severe for children who are bipolar. It is rare to see an angry child who is ADHD display disorganized thinking, language, and body position, all of which may be seen in angry bipolar children during a tantrum. Children who are bipolar may also lose memory of the tantrum.

4. The "trigger" for temper tantrums is also different. Children who have ADHD are typically triggered by sensory and emotional overstimulation, whereas children who have bipolar disorder typically react to limit-setting, such as a parental "no."

5. The moods of children who have ADHD or bipolar disorder may change quickly, but children with ADHD do not generally show dysphoria (depression) as a predominant symptom. Irritability is particularly prominent in children who are bipolar, especially in the morning on arousal. Children with ADHD tend to arouse quickly and attain alertness within minutes, but children with mood disorders may show overly slow arousal (including several hours of irritability or dysphoria, fuzzy thinking or "cobwebs," and somatic complaints such as stomachaches and headaches) upon awakening in the morning.

6. Disturbances during sleep in children with bipolar disorder include severe nightmares or night terrors, often with themes of explicit gore and bodily mutilation.

7. Children who are bipolar often show giftedness in certain cognitive functions, especially verbal and artistic skills (perhaps with verbal precocity and punning by age two to three years).

8. The misbehavior in children with ADHD is often accidental and

usually caused by oblivious inattention, whereas children with bipolar disorders intentionally provoke or misbehave. Some bipolar children are described as "the bully on the playground."

9. The child with ADHD may engage in behavior that can lead to harmful consequences without being aware of the danger, whereas the child with bipolar disorder is risk seeking.

10. Bipolar children tend to have a strong early sexual interest and behavior.

11. Children with ADHD usually do not exhibit psychotic symptoms or reveal a loss of contact with reality, whereas children with bipolar disorder may exhibit gross distortions in the perception of reality or in the interpretation of emotional events.

12. Lithium treatment generally improves bipolar disorder but has little or no effect on ADHD.

But the problem of diagnosis is even *more* complicated. Because many children meet full criteria for both disorders—ADHD and bipolar—some psychiatrists and researchers (but not all) have begun to talk about the two disorders as comorbid, or co-occurring. Indeed, in a recent study conducted by Drs. Wozniak and Biederman, they documented that the parents and siblings (the first-degree relatives) of manic children not only had increased risk for mania and ADHD but these two conditions occurred together in those same relatives. Their report of a 16 percent rate of bipolar disorder among relatives of bipolar-ADHD cases indicates that co-occurring bipolar-ADHD is highly familial.

Other researchers disagree strongly with the concept that these children have two co-occurring disorders and point to an excessive amount of misdiagnosis. Still others think that attention-deficit disorder with hyperactivity may be, for many, an early stage on a developmental path that culminates in a full-blown bipolar disorder.

Obsessive-Compulsive Disorder

Many parents who answered our survey and a significant number of parents writing on the BPParents listserv note that their children have mood disorders as well as unambiguous symptoms of obsessive-compulsive disorder.

Children with OCD have recurrent and intrusive thoughts of impending harm that can be allayed only by some compulsive act. They feel com-

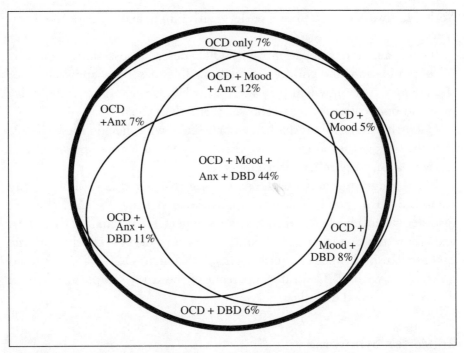

Comorbidity of Juvenile Obsessive-Compulsive Disorder. *Anx,* any non-OCD anxiety disorder; *DBD,* disruptive behavior disorder; *Mood,* mood disorder; *OCD,* obsessive-compulsive disorder.

pelled to perform repetitive acts or rituals to ward off the discomfort and anxiety they experience, but these acts can cause the child shame and embarrassment as well as make it hard to get out of the house and go about a typical kid's day.

Some examples of repetitive acts designed to reduce the anxiety and keep a dreaded event from occurring include: placing objects just right; touching things a self-specified number of times; checking behaviors, such as checking to see that the doors are locked over and over again; flicking the lights on and off; or turning the sink or shower faucets to the hot and cold settings a prescribed number of times. Some children count or repeat phrases over and over; other children compulsively pick at their skin.

Anyone who saw Jack Nicholson portray a man suffering with OCD in the film *As Good As It Gets* watched him turn the deadbolt on his front door to the left and to the right quickly and repetitively each time he entered his apartment and assiduously avoid cracks on the sidewalks of New

York. He always carried plastic cutlery with him to avoid germs in restaurants.

Indeed, a majority of patients with OCD describe obsessions about dirt or contamination, and children as well as adults describe handwashing or showering rituals in which they wash their hands over eighty times a day or spend hours attempting to shower themselves clean.

Many children explain that they don't know why they do these rituals, that they know they are senseless. Still, they feel a sense of pressure, and the action partially relieves the anxiety.

In the diagram that follows, one can see that juvenile OCD is highly comorbid with mood disorders, oppositional defiant disorder, conduct disorder, attention-deficit disorder with hyperactivity, anxiety disorders, and Tourette's syndrome. Although this study of 217 children at the McLean Hospital/Massachusetts General Pediatric OCD Clinic focused on children with OCD, a full 69 percent of the study sample also carried diagnoses of mood disorders.

Tourette's Syndrome

A percentage of children with bipolar disorder manifesting OCD symptoms also bear the diagnosis of Tourette's syndrome. This is almost certainly a physical disorder of the brain that causes involuntary movements (motor tics) and involuntary vocalizations (vocal tics). A child with motor tics may exhibit eye blinking, facial grimacing, nose scrunching, shoulder shrugging, head jerking, and hand movements. Common vocal tics include throat clearing, grunting, sniffing, making loud sounds, or saying words. A much smaller group of children exhibit copralalia—they use obscene or other socially inappropriate words. According to the *DSM-IV,* a child can be diagnosed with Tourette's only if "both multiple motor and one or more vocal tics have occurred at some time, but not necessarily at the same time."

An excellent book on this subject is edited by Tracy Haerle and is called *Children with Tourette Syndrome: A Parents' Guide.*

Oppositional Defiant Disorder and Conduct Disorder

Many bipolar children also meet criteria for oppositional defiant disorder (ODD) and conduct disorder (CD), and vice versa. What do these behaviors look like?

Oppositional Defiant Disorder

Oppositional defiant disorder as defined by the *DSM-IV*:

> A recurrent pattern of negativistic, disobedient, and hostile behavior toward authority figures that persists at least six months and is characterized by frequent occurrence of at least four of the following behaviors: arguing with adults, actively defying or refusing to comply with requests or rules of adults, deliberately doing things that will annoy other people, blaming others for his or her own mistakes or misbehavior, being touchy or easily annoyed by others, being angry and resentful, or being spiteful and vindictive.

One mother on the listserv wrote, "At one school my son went to this year, he had a list of the rules that he was taking back and forth with him. When I asked him why he was keeping them with him, he said he needed to make sure he broke them all!"

Conduct Disorder

A child with ODD can infuriate adults; a child with conduct disorder is cause for great concern. Many clinical investigators have observed that some youngsters with bipolar disorder have expressed serious delinquent and antisocial behaviors, including burglary, stealing, and vandalism. Other behaviors may include bullying and intimidating people, intentionally destroying property, and using weapons such as baseball bats, broken bottles, knives, or guns with the intention of causing someone serious harm.

In 1989 Dr. Stan Kutcher and colleagues, who are now at Dalhousie University in Halifax, examined the comorbidity of conduct disorder in a group of ninety-six adolescent inpatients. Nineteen of this group had a primary diagnosis of bipolar disorder; and the remaining seventy-seven individuals had been diagnosed with other primary psychiatric conditions. Dr. Kutcher and colleagues reported that while 27 percent of their entire sample had conduct disorder, 42 percent of the bipolar subgroup were also given a secondary diagnosis of conduct disorder.

In 1995 Dr. Maria Kovacs and Myrna Pollock, M.S.W., confirmed the strong association between bipolar disorder and conduct disorder in their study of twenty-six bipolar youths. In this group, eighteen were found to have had conduct disorder at some point in their lives, yielding a 69 percent lifetime comorbidity rate.

Some of the questions researchers are trying to answer are:

1. Are conduct disorder symptoms directly associated with bipolar disorder as a co-occurring diagnosis (therefore implying that they are inherited together)?
2. Are these defiant and oppositional behaviors expressed primarily during full episodes of mania or hypomania (implying that these behaviors are motivated by the mood disorder)?

Kovacs and Pollock found that more than half of their sample, or 54 percent of the entire bipolar group, had overlapping mania or hypomanic episodes with conduct disorder.

But apparently these conduct disorder behaviors can occur before or after the manifestation of bipolar symptoms. By determining the age of occurrence of conduct disorder in their bipolar subjects, Kovacs and Pollock found that, for eleven of the eighteen youths, conduct disorder appeared prior to the first episode; for seven subjects, conduct disorder occurred subsequent to the first episode of mania or hypomania. The study populations are too small to come to any definite conclusions, but it is clear that clinically these disorders are commonly linked.

To add to the confusion, both bipolar disorder and conduct disorder have been found to co-occur with ADHD. *Until we know more about the underlying causes of child psychiatric disorders, no diagnosis should be discounted because another disorder is present.*

Dr. Joseph Biederman, when speaking at the 1997 International Conference for Child and Adolescent Psychiatry in Toronto, said, "There is a group of children whose entire clinical picture of conduct disorder may evaporate if you treat the manic symptoms."

Girls Who Binge and Cut: Bulimia and Borderline Personality Disorder

A subgroup of young women with bipolar disorder are diagnosed with co-morbid eating disorders, particularly bulimia, a condition in which one binges and then purges what one has eaten. In addition, substance abuse seems to be a part of the clinical picture, and a fair number of these adolescent girls have a history of cutting or scratching themselves with knives or razors.

These girls commonly report periods of unbearable agitation and irritability. Some of them attempt to calm themselves by using alcohol and drugs—they self-medicate; others attempt to stop this continuous state of depression and agitation by cutting or scratching their arms or legs with razors and knives, or burning their thighs with lighted cigarettes.

One young woman talked very openly about her self-mutilating behavior. She described it thus:

> I dig into my heels with my nails and rip layers and layers of skin off. While I'm doing it, I'm not thinking. I feel as though there's an animal rage inside me—it's like a super-electrically charged thing . . . like voltage. And when I see the blood, I stop feeling this horrible rage and come out of this state.

Chillingly, another girl described this feeling as "being trapped inside her body with a snarling and snapping wolf."

One theory about these self-mutilating behaviors is that a powerful impulse to discharge aggression is counterpoised against the individual's attempt to inhibit that impulse. The tension created by these conflicting forces builds to an unbearable pitch, and the tension is relieved by physical pain directed toward the self. This discharge of aggression and the concomitant activation of the pain pathways could act as a cathartic release, but no one really understands what exactly is happening and why hurting oneself resolves the problem temporarily.

Many doctors, upon hearing of self-mutilating behavior, begin to suspect a diagnosis of borderline personality disorder. Someone given this diagnosis typically has a history of unstable and tempestuous interpersonal relationships, impulsive behaviors, frequent displays of temper, marked shifts of mood with the moods lasting hours or days, identity confusion, feelings of emptiness, and "frantic efforts to avoid real or imagined abandonment."

Dr. Hagop Akiskal at the University of California at San Diego has always conceived borderline personality disorder as a part of the mood disorder spectrum. He feels it is closely linked to bipolar disorder, perhaps a subclinical manifestation. He and his colleagues, then at the University of Tennessee College of Medicine, reported a study of one hundred patients diagnosed as having borderline personality disorder. In this group, almost half (forty-five) were also found to have some form of mood disorder. Fifty-seven of these one hundred young women had substance abuse problems.

Follow-up data further supported the close kinship of borderline disorders to mood disorders. Of the one hundred patients, twenty-nine developed unmistakable major depression with melancholic symptoms, eleven had brief hypomanic episodes, four others had psychotic mania, and eight developed mixed states.

Autistic Spectrum Disorders and Bipolar Disorder

There is a group of children who fit somewhere within the autistic spectrum, but if one looks closely, one can see a pattern of intense shifts in mood, irritability, and sleep loss. In many cases, the autistic behaviors are so dramatic that the possibility of a bipolar comorbidity is often overlooked.

The *DSM-IV* groups autistic disorder, Rett's disorder, childhood disintegrative disorder, Asperger's disorder, and pervasive development disorder not otherwise specified (NOS) under the umbrella category of Pervasive Developmental Disorders, or PDD. When the shorthand diagnostic label "PDD" is given to a child, it typically stands for PDD-NOS, not the general category of Pervasive Developmental Disorders.

The essential characteristics of a Pervasive Developmental Disorder are: impairments in social interaction, imaginative activity, verbal and nonverbal communication skills, and a limited number of interests and activities that tend to be repetitive.

Children diagnosed with autistic disorder have a moderate to severe range of communication, socialization, and behavioral problems. It is estimated that about 50 percent of children with autism have some kind of mental retardation, but there are also high-functioning autistic children.

Children diagnosed with Asperger's disorder have general language, but not social or reciprocal language. This means that they have adequate language skills in terms of vocabulary and grammar, but they fail to catch the subtleties of conversation, such as humor or irony, and their language does not mold and modify according to responses and cues from the person with whom they are conversing. These children also develop restrictive, repetitive patterns of behavior, interests, and activities, but it is not unusual for children diagnosed with Asperger's disorder to have average or above average intelligence.

The inclusion of a diagnostic category of PDD-NOS within the *DSM-IV* complicates things because this is a diagnosis that is given when there is a "severe and pervasive impairment in the development of reciprocal social interaction or verbal and nonverbal communication skills, or when stereotyped behavior, interests, and activities are present, but the criteria are not met for a specific Pervasive Developmental Disorder . . ." This description is not all that helpful and it's difficult to grasp when a child has PDD-NOS or autistic disorder. No doubt the *DSM-IV* will change some of these categories and focus on the fact that this is a spectrum disorder, but this is not due to be published until after 2010. In the meantime, the categories as they are presently defined are bound to confuse parents.

In 1988, George Robert DeLong, M.D., of Duke University, one of the first pediatric neurologists to study the interface between autistic spectrum disorders and bipolar disorder, published a paper in which he reported a very high incidence of mood disorders among family members of children with autistic spectrum disorders. He reported on the family histories of fifty-one children with autistic spectrum disorders and found that twenty-three of the fifty-one children had a family member with manic-depression (first- and second-degree relatives were examined). The incidence of bipolar disorder was 4.2 percent, about fivefold greater than that expected in the general population, and the highest incidence was in the families of the children who had Asperger's syndrome. There could be some relationship between mood disorders and Asperger's syndrome.

In 1994, Dr. DeLong reported the results of another study of forty children with autistic spectrum disorders and examined their family histories. Twenty-nine of the families had a history of manic depression.

How common is it that a child diagnosed with one of the pervasive developmental disorders is found to have a comorbid bipolar disorder? While there has been no formal study, Edwin H. Cook, M.D., Professor of Psychiatry and Pediatrics at the Department of Psychiatry at the University of Chicago, feels that "based on my experience, my best guess is that 10 percent of the children with autistic spectrum disorder have a bipolar comorbidity." Dr. DeLong feels this may eventually turn out to be higher (more in the 35 percent range).

Because several studies have shown that children in the autistic spectrum have benefited from antidepressant medications, it is important to look carefully at the family history of a child so diagnosed, and also to look for any pattern of cycling, marked irritability, and disinhibition before prescribing these drugs. There is a high-potential risk for inducing increased cycling or switching in a child who may have both an autistic spectrum disorder as well as a bipolar vulnerability.

Dr. Cook reported that he sees a number of children who are on the autistic spectrum, have bipolar symptomatology and also obsessive-compulsive disorder. "These children are very hard to treat," he said, "because the use of antidepressants that would treat the OCD symptoms are so dicey."

Only family genetic studies that delineate specific subgroupings of autistic spectrum disorders will help us sort out this comorbidity. However, doctors and parents should know that this comorbidity exists (and perhaps in greater numbers than we know) and rule out the possibility of a comorbid bipolar disorder before initiating treatment with medications. In other words, it would be important to first treat a cycling disorder with mood stabilizers and perhaps an atypical antipsychotic and to be wary of antidepressant-induced cycling.

Psychosis: The Schizophrenia Bugaboo

Psychotic symptoms—such as delusions (fixed irrational beliefs) and hallucinations (voices and visions) *can occur during both phases of a bipolar disorder.*

The nature of delusional ideas may vary with the mood state. When manic, a child can exhibit grandiose delusions. The child may feel that he or she can teach better than any teacher in the school, or become convinced that he can "beat Michael Jordan at his game" following the first after-school basketball game. When depressed, a child's delusional ideas tend to bear more guilty or morbid content. For example, a young girl felt that she was so terrible and worthless that every time her mother answered the phone, she was sure it was the director of an orphanage making plans for her to be sent away. The delusions can be unshakable.

Auditory and visual hallucinations—hearing voices or seeing things that aren't there—are not uncommon in bipolar disorder. The nature of the auditory hallucinations may vary according to the mood state. For example, a six-year-old boy experiencing mania was prompted by a voice to fly from the top of the jungle gym. Sometimes the voices are threatening: A young woman told us that she used to hear the voice of a man telling her she would die at 6:30 in the morning. She would spend the nights up and alone, waiting until the hands of the clock swept past 6:34, signifying that she could let down her guard and start breathing calmly again.

Visual hallucinations can be interesting or terribly frightening. One teenage girl told her mother she saw cowboys in her room dressed in red. A young boy was very paranoid and saw one of his mother's porcelain figurines moving around the room and glaring at him. Quite a few other children report seeing bugs all over the room and desperately try to prove to their parents that the bugs really do exist.

In addition to auditory and visual hallucinations, children can experience olfactory hallucinations (they smell things that other people don't) and tactile hallucinations (they feel something touching their skin).

It is terrifying for a parent to watch reason fly from a young mind. The fear that a child is becoming "schizophrenic" looms large, and the specter of madness and locked asylums can leave a parent virtually paralyzed.

There is a long and tragic history to the assumption that anyone experiencing delusions or hallucinations is schizophrenic, and a discussion about this should help ground a parent or relative when dealing with a child who is delusional or hallucinating.

The History of the Differential Diagnosis of Schizophrenia and Manic-Depression

In the beginning of the twentieth century, Emil Kraepelin drew strict boundaries between manic-depressive psychosis and dementia praecox (an early name for schizophrenia). But in 1911 the Swiss physician Eugen Bleuler reversed this line of thought and described a concept of schizophrenia that was so broad it diagnosed as schizophrenic a large group of patients that Kraepelin would have certainly called manic-depressive.

In 1960 a German psychiatrist named Kurt Schneider composed a list of symptoms that he felt strongly suggested a diagnosis of schizophrenia. His symptoms of "first rank" included auditory hallucinations, hallucinations of touch, the feeling that thoughts are being inserted into one's mind or that one's thoughts are being broadcast, and the feeling that all of one's actions are under the control of others. Accepting these criteria, psychiatrists—and particularly American psychiatrists—began to diagnose anyone experiencing even short-lasting delusional, bizarre, and psychotic thinking as schizophrenic.

But in 1973 Drs. Gabriele Carlson and Frederick Goodwin began to refute these diagnostic practices when they reported that there seemed to be three stages of mania. And in the third, and most extreme stage, patients did indeed experience hallucinations, bizarre beliefs, and paranoia. Drs. Carlson and Goodwin knew that these patients would have been diagnosed as schizophrenic if they hadn't appeared clearly manic both earlier in the course and later as the episode was resolving.

Dr. Harrison Pope of Harvard Medical School's McLean Hospital in

Belmont, Massachusetts, also began to home in on this diagnostic problem. He reviewed twenty studies and found that so-called schizophrenic symptoms occurred among 20 to 50 percent of patients with extremely well-validated cases of manic-depressive illness.

In 1977 he and Dr. Joseph Lipinski joined forces to write what has become a landmark article in the psychiatric literature. It was titled "Diagnosis in Schizophrenia and Manic-Depressive Illness: A Reassessment of the Specificity of 'Schizophrenic' Symptoms in the Light of Current Research," and it argued forcefully that psychosis and schizophrenia are *not* synonymous. They cautioned psychiatrists to look first and foremost at the family history and to look at the patient's functioning before the onset of illness, his or her response to treatment, and the eventual outcome.

These illnesses tend to breed true. If the family history reveals manic-depression, depression, or alcoholism, it is unlikely that the patient is schizophrenic. (Naturally a parent has to remember that Aunt Jane may have been labeled a paranoid schizophrenic because that was diagnostic tradition at the time. It was not necessarily the truth of her condition.)

Any teenager who is seen by the medical profession in a full psychotic episode may initially be suspected of drug use or of a schizophrenic break, because both of these causes for psychosis tend to appear first in that age group. Parents will need to understand the whole picture and gather any and all family history facts to ensure the correct diagnosis. (See the discussion about piecing together the family history in the next chapter.)

Parents with a child who is experiencing psychosis or extreme paranoia may also hear the term "schizoaffective" during the diagnostic evaluation. This is a term used when the patient seems to manifest a confusing mix of symptoms that straddle the boundaries of both schizophrenia and mood disorders. These children may meet the criteria for depression or mania, but their delusions and hallucinations are not related to the disordered mood—they are "mood incongruent," and they persist beyond the resolution of the mood disorder.

While the third revised edition of the *DSM (DSM-IIIR)* created an intermediate disease category for the schizoaffective diagnosis, *DSM-IV* returned schizoaffective disorder to the categories of schizophrenia and other psychotic disorders. It lists two subtypes, the bipolar type and the depressive type, and it requires that delusions and hallucinations last for a minimum of two weeks in the absence of prominent mood symptoms.

This remains a very controversial diagnosis. Whether schizoaffective disorder is a variant of schizophrenia, a variant of mood disorders, a mixture of the two, a transitional state between schizophrenia and a mood disorder, or a heterogeneous syndrome including different conditions is unknown at this time.

Still, many psychiatrists view schizoaffective disorder as a variant of mood disorders because the family studies of patients who meet criteria for schizoaffective disorder bipolar type reveal a higher incidence of bipolar disorder, almost identical to that of the families of pure bipolar patients.

The Big Picture

It is obvious that the diagnosis of mood disorders in children is extremely complex. While the perplexing questions raised by the frequency of comorbid diagnoses cannot be resolved at this time, researchers have begun to define a syndrome that encompasses symptoms of a number of childhood psychiatric disorders but also has unique features of its own.

Ranging from "very common" to "less common," the symptoms and behavioral traits that have been consistently observed in children with early-onset bipolar disorder include:

VERY COMMON
Separation anxiety
Rages and explosive temper tantrums lasting up to several hours
Marked irritability
Oppositional behavior
Rapid cycling (frequent mood swings, occurring within an hour, a
    day, or several days) or mood lability
Distractibility
Hyperactivity
Impulsivity
Restlessness/fidgetiness
Silliness, giddiness, goofiness
Racing thoughts
Aggressive behavior
Grandiosity
Carbohydrate cravings
Risk-taking behaviors
Depressed mood
Lethargy

Low self-esteem
Difficulty getting up in the morning
Social anxiety
Oversensitivity to emotional or environmental triggers

COMMON
Bedwetting (especially in boys)
Night terrors
Rapid or pressured speech
Excessive daydreaming
Obsessional behavior
Compulsive behavior
Motor and vocal tics
Learning disabilities
Poor short-term memory
Lack of organization
Fascination with gore or morbid topics
Hypersexuality
Manipulative behavior
Extremely bossy behavior with friends/bullying
Lying
Suicidal thoughts
Destruction of property
Paranoia
Hallucinations and delusions

LESS COMMON
Migraine headaches
Bingeing
Self-mutilating behaviors
Cruelty to animals

A discussion recently took place over the Internet when a mother wrote that a child psychiatrist to whom she had taken her very young son was reluctant to make a diagnosis of bipolar disorder, despite the fact that the child had separation anxiety and periods of marked irritability and temper tantrums and was threatening to slice off his older sister's ears with a knife. In addition, the boy's father had been diagnosed with bipolar disorder.

The doctor did not want to "label" the child with a diagnosis of bipolar disorder until it was absolutely necessary. Instead, he focused on the boy's attentional difficulties, prescribed Ritalin, and advised a conservative "wait-and-see" approach.

Members of the BPParents listserv expressed a strong reaction to this psychiatrist's opinion and recommendations, and there were many postings in response. Our feelings lie closest to those of the mother who wrote in to vigorously protest this strategy and counseled:

> You need the diagnosis because it explains so much of the emotional and behavioral experiences of the child, and it guides the appropriate treatment and helps avoid the use of medications that could worsen the course of the illness. An accurate and early diagnosis allows the family to develop plans for the future, to make better decisions, and to obtain better services. It also helps families form relationships with other families who are experiencing the same problems so that they don't feel so alone and so that they can share information and solutions with each other.

The fact that the diagnosis even appears "optional" speaks to the complexity of this disorder in children, to its overlapping and evolving symptoms, and to its evanescent nature. (There are weeks and even months when these children are, to quote one mother, "on a good roll," further confounding the diagnostic investigation.)

But let us say this very clearly: *There are serious risks to delaying diagnosis and treatment.* We can't quite imagine what it must be like for a child to experience overwhelming and almost atomic rage several times a day triggered by a simple "no" from a parent or even by the loud chewing of a sibling at a dinner table. We can only guess how a child responds internally to a sea of angry, disapproving faces surrounding him or her due to out-of-control and oppositional or defiant behavior. And there is something known as kindling, or sensitization.

Some years ago Dr. Robert Post of the National Institute of Mental Health advanced the idea that initial periods of cycling may begin with an environmental stressor, but if the cycles continue to occur unchecked, the brain becomes kindled or sensitized—pathways inside the central nervous system are reinforced, so to speak—and future episodes of depression, hypomania, or mania will occur by themselves (independently of an outside stimulus), with greater and greater frequency.

Perhaps the most important reason for early intervention and treatment is the fact that this can be a lethal illness. Suicide rates for bipolar disorder have been estimated to be as high as 15 percent. Failed suicide attempts are higher still.

Dr. Joseph Biederman made a plea for early diagnosis and intervention when speaking to an overflowing audience at the 1998 National Alliance for the Mentally Ill Conference in Washington, D.C.

He said:

In many cases, there is a ten-year gap between the onset of symptoms and intervention. Once you have ten years of anything unchecked—from a car to your teeth, to some rampant psychopathology—I would propose this is the equivalent to having metastatic disease ten years later. The problem could be different if the diagnosis were made at the beginning . . . and effective treatments were deployed. . . . It is possible that the prognosis could be very different than the one we see at the end of the line once these children reach adult psychiatry's shore.

Childhood is such a fleeting time and so much must be consolidated within a growing person: ego development, social and academic skills, biological and psychological maturation. . . . Every day counts. There is no time to waste.

Since the entire future of the child as well as the family rests on the proper diagnosis of the disorder and the extremely competent psychopharmacological management of it, we spend the next chapter exploring how one might go about finding a diagnostician/clinician who is adept at recognizing early-onset bipolar disorder and at initiating medication trials with the aim of stabilizing the child. In the chapter following that, we discuss the medications used to accomplish just such stabilization.

How to Find Good Treatment

In our survey and in direct interviews, we asked parents how they initially understood their child's early symptoms and behavioral difficulties. The answers that came back to us were varied. Many parents blamed themselves and criticized their own parenting skills. "We thought we weren't firm enough," they wrote; or "Maybe we weren't always consistent." (Sadly, their relatives and even people in the street joined the chorus and gave plenty of unsolicited, often very hurtful advice.)

First-time parents, with no basis for comparison, were slower to recognize how atypical their child's behavior was. One woman said: "This was my first child and I assumed there are all different kinds of temperaments, but I thought: Wow! I got one on the other end of the spectrum. This is absolutely exhausting."

Over half of the parents thought their child was hyperactive. One mother joined a support group for parents of ADHD children, but soon noticed that her child's problems were of a completely different magnitude: "The more I talked with the other parents, the more I realized that they weren't dealing with the same behaviors I was," she told us. "Their kids weren't raging for hours a day, trying to strangle their parents, or experiencing such rapid mood shifts. Something more than ADHD was going on here."

Sooner or later, as the symptoms become more severe and disruptive, the family has to seek professional advice and find a name for the problem. And here's where things get complicated.

Ideally, a child psychiatrist should diagnose and treat a child or adolescent. A child psychiatrist is a medical doctor who has completed two or three years of an adult psychiatric residency and two additional years of a child psychiatry fellowship program.

But there is a nationwide shortage of child psychiatrists. Fewer than 6,500 practice in the United States, and locating a child psychiatrist in the states of Alaska, Arkansas, Idaho, Missouri, Mississippi, Montana, Nevada, Vermont, West Virginia, and Wyoming presents a particular problem: Each of those states has fewer than thirty child psychiatrists; Wyoming has just four.

Even if a parent is able to locate a child psychiatrist close to home, the treating clinician *must* have a view of childhood psychiatric diagnosis that is informed by the latest research findings in childhood bipolar disorder. If not, it is likely that the focus of attention will be on one of several potentially co-occurring or alternative diagnoses such as ADHD, obsessive-compulsive disorder, or oppositional defiant disorder, and the primary symptoms of bipolarity may be overlooked or misdiagnosed. And as we've mentioned in earlier chapters, trials of stimulants and antidepressant medications are likely to be prescribed, potentially complicating or worsening the course of the bipolar disorder.

In the event that a child psychiatrist (with expertise in mood disorders) is not available, an adult psychiatrist with a broad background in mood disorders and an interest and history of treating children and adolescents may be a suitable alternative. A pediatric neurologist may also be suitable for the psychopharmacological treatment because pediatric neurologists have significant experience with the anticonvulsant medications that are fast becoming the first line of treatment for juvenile bipolar disorders.

Parents whose children had been seen by a number of child psychiatrists were very emphatic about what constituted a good doctor. They advise looking for someone who:

- Has an expertise in mood disorders, who is strong in psychopharmacology, and who keeps up with (or better yet, is involved in) the latest research with regard to bipolar disorder.
- Isn't convinced that he or she knows all the answers (too many variables with symptoms and meds at a young age).
- Communicates and does not talk over one's head, keeps the jargon

to a minimum while educating the child and family, responds to questions openly, and has an empathic understanding of what the family is going through.

- Listens well, takes subtleties into account, and returns phone calls in a timely manner.
- Is aggressive—taking too much time to give a diagnosis and initiate treatment hurts the child and the family—and is not afraid to initiate new medication trials to achieve stabilization.
- Wants to work along with the family, not blame them.
- Understands how traumatic a hospitalization is for the family and stays in close contact during this time. Even a message on the answering machine would be a big comfort.
- Is willing to wage a battle with the managed care companies to see to it that the child gets all the care he or she needs. Is also willing to speak with the school or come to the IEP meeting (see Chapter 10) to ensure that the child gets the proper modifications in the program and best education.
- Values parental input and has a good rapport with the child.

How to Find a Doctor

Most pediatricians are familiar with the child psychiatrists in the area and may be able to direct you to a good one. Or, if there is a university-affiliated teaching hospital nearby, you can call the division of child psychiatry and ask to speak to the senior fellow, admissions director, or clinical director, and then tell the person that you are looking for the names of child psychiatrists who have an expertise in treating bipolar disorder in children and adolescents.

The Resources section on page 420 includes the telephone numbers of the nation's two leading patient support groups. The patients and family members who belong to these organizations have had firsthand experience with many of the psychiatrists in your area and are often in a good position to steer you toward a competent physician. Naturally, if you're enrolled in a managed care program, you will be referred to someone on its panel. (This does not assure you a competent referral.)

The Internet may be your best ally in this quest. The Child and Adolescent Bipolar Foundation has message boards where parents often post requests for "pdocs" (their term for child psychiatrists and psychologists) in their geographical area, and two or three people always write back with details about the doctors with whom they are familiar. (The website is www.bpkids.org. Information there will also tell a parent how to subscribe to the listserv.)

Because the diagnosis is so critical, some parents seek out evaluations at major teaching hospitals that have clinics well known for their pioneering work in early-onset bipolar disorder. There are a handful of such clinics in the United States and Canada and we've listed the most prominent ones, along with their medical directors:

Boston, Massachusetts: Massachusetts General Hospital, Pediatric Psychopharmacology Unit, Wang Building, Room 725, 15 Parkman St., Boston, MA 02114; (617) 726-2725; Dr. Joseph Biederman, director.

Chicago, Illinois: Rush-Presbyterian–St. Luke's Medical Center, 1725 W. Harrison St., Suite 955, Chicago, IL 60612; (312) 942-5592; Dr. John Zajecka, director.

Cincinnati, Ohio: Pediatric Bipolar Program at Children's Hospital Medical Center of Cincinnati, 3333 Barnet Ave., Cincinnati, OH 45229; (513) 558-0956; Drs. Robert A. Kowatch and Melissa DelBello, directors.

Cleveland, Ohio: The Stanley Research Center, Case Western Reserve University; University Hospitals of Cleveland, Department of Psychiatry, 11100 Euclid Ave., Cleveland, OH 44106; (216) 844-3881; Dr. Robert L. Findling, director.

Columbus, Ohio: Division of Child and Adolescent Psychiatry, The Ohio State University, 1670 Upham Dr., Columbus, OH 43210-1250; (614) 293-8235; Dr. Mary Fristad, director.

Dallas, Texas: Pediatric Bipolar Disorders Program, Children's Medical Center of Dallas, 6363 Forest Park, Dallas, TX 75390; (214) 648-4419; Dr. Russell Scheffer, director.

Halifax, Nova Scotia, Canada: Mood Disorders Clinic, Department of Psychiatry, The IWK-Grace Health Sciences Center, Halifax, NS, Canada; (902) 428-8375; Dr. Vivek Kusumakar and Dr. Stan Kutcher, directors.

Los Angeles, California: Adolescent Mood Disorders Program, UCLA Neuropsychiatric Institute, 760 Westwood Plaza, Los Angeles, CA 90024; (310) 825-5730; Dr. Michael Strober, director.

New Hyde Park, New York: Long Island Jewish Medical Center of the Albert Einstein College of Medicine, 269-01 76th Ave.,

New Hyde Park, NY 11040; (718) 470-8444; Dr. Vivian Kafantaris, director.

Philadelphia, Pennsylvania: Children's Hospital of Philadelphia,
Department of Child and Adolescent Psychiatry, 34th Street and
Civic Center Blvd., Philadelphia, PA 19104-4399; (215) 590-
7573; Dr. Elizabeth Weller, director.

Pittsburgh, Pennsylvania: Child and Adolescent Bipolar Services
(CABS), 100 North Bellefield Ave., Bellefield Towers, #612,
Pittsburgh, PA 15213; (412) 624-CABS or (877) 851-CABS:
Drs. David Axelson and Boris Birmaher, directors.

Richmond, Virginia: Virginia Treatment Center for Children, Division of Child and Adolescent Psychiatry, Virginia Common-
wealth University, 515 N. 10th Street, Richmond, VA 23298;
(804) 828-3129; Dr. Bela Sood, director.

Stanford, California: Stanford Pediatric Mood Disorders Clinic,
Stanford University School of Medicine, 401 Quarry Road, Stanford, CA 94305; (650) 723-5511; Dr. Kiki Chang, director.

St. Louis, Missouri: Washington University Child Psychiatry
Clinic at Children's Hospital, Montclair Building, 24 South
Kingsway, St. Louis, MO 63108; contact person: Linda Bosslet,
(314) 286-1740; Dr. Barbara Geller, director.

Stony Brook, New York: Division of Child and Adolescent Psy-
chiatry, State University of New York at Stony Brook, Putnam
Hall-South Campus, Stony Brook, NY 11974; (631) 632-8850;
Dr. Gabrielle Carlson, director.

After giving a diagnosis and initiating a trial of medications, the specialist may be willing to consult with a local child psychiatrist or pediatric neurologist and oversee the course of treatment by phone or email.

PARENTS' ROLE IN GETTING GOOD TREATMENT

The reality is that it can be difficult to get good treatment. There is confusion in the field of child psychiatry and no broad consensus about juvenile mood disorders. Thanks to the work of some pioneering researchers,
the picture of bipolar disorder in early childhood is becoming clearer, but
the diagnosis is by no means widely accepted.

Because the family history is one of the most important pieces of the puzzle, some knowledge of a parent's, grandparent's, aunt's, or uncle's tempera-

ment, behaviors, and reactions to life's events and psychiatric hospitalizations can contribute very useful information to the process of diagnosis.

It is incumbent on the mother and father of the ill child to search
within his and her family of origin for evidence of bipolarity. And this is
not always easy. For one thing, diagnosis was not very accurate a generation or two ago; for another, stigma and shame forced families to hide a
problem and present as normal a face as possible to the community. A
parent may have to push hard against this reluctance to reveal the family
psychiatric history and may even have to travel to interview family members who can help fill in the blanks.

Next, a few of the many possible behaviors, reactions to life events, or
temperaments that may be suggestive of a bipolar illness in a family
member:

- Your father's father was an alcoholic and seemed very withdrawn
  at times. But he was the life of the party and larger-than-life at
  other times.
- Aunt Sarah had a "nervous breakdown." She was hospitalized and
  received shock therapy.
- Uncle Mike was notorious for his temper. His family walked on
  eggshells around him.
- You remember your mother vacuuming at three o'clock in the
  morning and staying up all night cleaning the rest of the house.
  She was often irritable. She planned huge holiday parties and then
  spent a great deal of time in bed suffering an overwhelming fatigue and lassitude, "recuperating from her efforts."
- Your father crisscrossed the country with unrealistic ideas for
  making a lot of money. Multiple financial crises, even bankrupt-
  cies, may have been the result.
- You remember your mother spending a lot of time in bed after the
  birth of a baby. She cried a lot and found it difficult to get dressed,
  even months after the child was born.
- Two of your uncles were diagnosed "paranoid schizophrenic."
- Your mother's brother was a big gambler.
- There were suicides in the family.

Beyond the family history, the parents need to provide detailed information about the symptoms and behaviors of their own child. The following checklist was included in our questionnaire. If a parent

photocopies this and fills it out, it should be a great help to the diagnosing clinician.

Once you've received a referral to a physician, you simply make a phone call. Just give your name, mention the doctor or individual who referred you, and tell the psychiatrist you would like to schedule an appointment for him or her to see your child for a consultation. Unless the child psychiatrist asks you for it, this is not the time to go into great detail or have a lengthy conversation—all of that will be handled in the consultation session.

SYMPTOM CHECKLIST							
	AGES						
SYMPTOMS AND BEHAVIORS	0–2	3–5	6–8	9–11	12–13	14–16	17–19
1 Bedwetting							
2 Night terrors							
3 Temper tantrums							
4 Excessive worry about harm befalling parents							
5 Excessive distress when separated from family							
6 Extreme clinging behavior							
7 Repeated complaints of physical symptoms							
8 Has marked changes in appetite							
9 Often has cravings for carbohydrates or sweets							
10 Periods of extreme sadness							
11 Elevated or irritable mood greater than 1 hr/day							
12 Elevated or irritable mood greater than 6 hrs/day							
13 Elevated or irritable mood greater than 2 days							
14 Depressed mood greater than 1 hr/day							

Symptom Checklist

		AGES						
	SYMPTOMS AND BEHAVIORS	0–2	3–5	6–8	9–11	12–13	14–16	17–19
15	Depressed mood greater than 6 hrs/day							
16	Depressed mood 1–2 days in duration							
17	Depressed mood greater than 2 days in duration							
18	Has suicidal thoughts often							
19	Has cut self with sharp instrument							
20	Has made suicide attempt							
21	Has difficulty getting to sleep at night							
22	Often awakens in the middle of the night							
23	Frequently oversleeps							
24	Has decreased need for sleep							
25	At times has very fast speech							
26	Thoughts race/has many ideas at once							
27	Has wide swings in mood							
28	Often does not seem to listen when spoken to							
29	Often takes excessive risks							
30	Is easily distracted by extraneous stimuli							
31	Has periods of inflated self-esteem or grandiosity							
32	Has engaged in unrestrained buying sprees							
33	Often blurts out answers to questions							

SYMPTOM CHECKLIST							
				AGES			
SYMPTOMS AND BEHAVIORS	0–2	3–5	6–8	9–11	12–13	14–16	17–19
34 Has difficulty engaging in playful activities							
35 As a newborn, extremely irritable and difficult to settle							
36 Is extremely sensitive to sensory stimuli							
37 Often has difficulty organizing tasks							
38 Often loses things necessary for tasks							
39 Often is reluctant to engage in tasks							
40 Often fidgets with hands or feet							
41 Often leaves seat in classroom							
42 Often has difficulty waiting turn							
43 Often interrupts or intrudes on others							
44 Demonstrates an inability to concentrate at school							
45 Frequently attempts to avoid school							
46 Illicit drug use							
47 Alcohol use							
48 Migraine headaches							
49 Speech difficulties (specify) _____							
50 Panic symptoms—marked anxiety attacks							

SYMPTOM CHECKLIST							
		AGES					
SYMPTOMS AND BEHAVIORS	0–2	3–5	6–8	9–11	12–13	14–16	17–19
51 Excessive anxiety or worry (apprehensive expectation)							
52 Anxiety causes impairment in social functioning							
53 Fear of closed spaces							
54 Fear of animals							
55 Fear of heights							
56 Fear of crowded places							
57 Hears voices							
58 Paranoid thinking							
59 Bizarre behavior (specify) _____							
60 Recurrent anxiety-producing thoughts or impulses							
61 Repetitive mental acts (counting, repeating words silently)							
62 Frequent and repetitive checking behavior							
63 Frequent and repetitive hand-washing							
64 Tics: recurrent stereotyped movements or vocalizations							
65 Frequently lies							
66 Has deliberately engaged in fire setting							
67 Is frequently mischievous							
68 Often bullies, threatens, or intimidates others							
69 Often initiates physical fights							

Symptom Checklist							
				AGES			
SYMPTOMS AND BEHAVIORS	0–2	3–5	6–8	9–11	12–13	14–16	17–19
70 Has deliberately destroyed others' property							
71 Has broken into someone's house							
72 Often lies to obtain goods or favors							
73 Often stays out at night against curfew							
74 Has run away from home overnight at least twice							
75 Is often truant from school							
76 Often loses temper							
78 Often argues with adults							
79 Often defies or refuses to comply with rules							
80 Often blames others for his or her mistakes							
81 Is often touchy or easily annoyed by others							
82 Is often angry and resentful							
83 Has fear of social or performance situation							
84 Increased sexual interest							
85 Increased sexual behaviors							
86 Other _____							
87 Other _____							
88 Other _____							
89 Other _____							

THE CONSULTATION

We asked child psychiatrist Rosalie Greenberg, who practices in Summit, New Jersey, how she conducts a diagnostic consultation, and she said:

> I typically need three to four sessions to completely evaluate a child. The first session, I see only the parents. I want to get a very detailed presenting history, a birth and developmental history, a medical history (did the child ever have encephalitis, mononucleosis, seizures? could something organic be going on?), and, very important, the family history. I see the parents alone because I want no distractions, and I don't want parents talking about the bad behavior of the child or possible suicides in the family in front of the child.
>
> At the second session, I meet with the child alone, and talk with him or her, all the while observing the child's affect, activity level, and thought process. I also talk with the child's teacher or previous therapist. If I think it's important, I may ask for some psychological testing. In the third session, I meet with the parents and the child and watch the child's interaction again, in a now more familiar setting.
>
> If I suspect a mood disorder and I want to try the child on medications, I first ask the parents to schedule a complete physical exam for the child, including a complete blood battery, an electrocardiogram [ECG], urinalysis, thyroid function tests, and possibly an electroencephalogram [EEG]. Once I see the results of the physical exam, I decide on the medication trial. I then inform the family why that drug or drugs were chosen; what laboratory tests, if any, will be required while the child is taking it; and what the short- and long-term side effects might be. I also try to answer all of their questions.

We asked Dr. Greenberg how she talks with a child about a psychiatric illness and the idea that the child may need to take medications for a protracted period of time. She told us:

> If I'm talking to a young child, I say something like: "Danny, you're sad that things aren't much fun. You get very cranky and mad, and you do things that make you feel badly afterward. I'm going to give you a medicine that will make you less sad and mad, and help you do better in school and get along better with your family and

friends." (Interestingly, most of the young children only want to know if the medicine tastes bad.)

She continued:

> If I'm talking with an adolescent—say a sixteen-year-old—the conversation is very different. I may say: "You get mood swings, ups and downs. It's a part of your chemistry, but the medicines will help you. Do they fix things? No, *you* fix things. But they will help you do it."

Dr. Greenberg has a frank discussion with an adolescent about staying up late or taking any drugs or alcohol. She explains how all of these lifestyle decisions can contribute to a worse course of the disorder. In Dr. Greenberg's experience, teenagers don't want to know too much. They are frightened and often upset at the thought of being different from their peers, so she limits the information and discusses things only when the patient is ready.

When we asked her about the course of treatment, she said:

> In the beginning phases of treatment, I stay in very close contact with the parents because I need to know how the child is tolerating the medications, and I tend to see the child once a week. Once the child is stabilized, I can see him or her less frequently, but I always think family therapy, and often individual therapy for the child, is a part of good medical treatment, and I discuss this with the parents and make a referral to a psychologist or family therapist who understands the disorder in children.

Medicines address certain problems, but a host of psychological problems are caused by the early onset of a mood disorder, and we discuss therapy later in this chapter. We just want to remind parents that psychological treatment is important. Many issues beyond medications need to be worked through for the child and for the child in the context of the family.

HOW TO JUDGE A DOCTOR'S ABILITY TO DIAGNOSE AND TREAT BIPOLAR DISORDER IN CHILDREN

Family members have every right to inquire about the physician's orientation and clinical views, and questions such as "Do you strictly adhere to

DSM-IV criteria?" or "Are you aware of the clinical studies done by Drs. Barbara Geller and Joseph Biederman describing the nature of the symptoms and how it differs from adult bipolar disorder?" or "What is your view about the existence of comorbid conditions like ADHD, oppositional defiant disorder, and anxiety disorders with bipolar disorder?" will reveal the orientation and his or her level of knowledge and expertise.

If the doctor mentions that most children who have bipolar disorder cannot be diagnosed according to current diagnostic criteria, and he or she knows that the duration of cycling is much shorter in children, and then treats this form of the condition as a bipolar disorder anyway, the parents should breathe a sigh of relief. If there are comorbid syndromes such as ADHD, ODD, OCD, and if the doctor views the treatment and stabilization of the bipolar disorder as the primary initial goal, the parents are halfway home.

Other clues into the doctor's experience level are how the doctor formulates a treatment plan when there are two coexisting conditions—one of them ultrarapid bipolar disorder and the other ADHD (stabilize the mood disorder first and then cautiously add low-dose stimulants); how experienced the doctor is in using mood stabilizers; how frequently the psychiatrist prescribes lithium, Depakote, Tegretol, Trileptal, or Lamictal, and how comfortable she or he is about trying newer medications. Naturally, the doctor should always explore the family history when making the diagnosis.

Parents should feel that the doctor welcomes an open dialogue and views the parents as collaborators on the treatment team. The doctor should want to teach the parents, should encourage them to chart their child's illness and course of treatment (see Chapter 5), and should not feel threatened when the parents do their own research. The parents should trust their gut instincts about a doctor.

PSYCHOLOGICAL THERAPIES

As Dr. Greenberg mentioned, an ideal treatment program has the child seeing the child psychiatrist once a week throughout the diagnostic process or when the child is cycling, and less frequently once the child is stabilized. An adjunctive family therapy or individual psychotherapy for the child is also recommended, and a group for adolescents with bipolar disorder can be greatly beneficial.

Many families who recognize the need to address the psychological issues for the child and themselves seek out less expensive mental health professionals such as psychologists, social workers, or nurse practitioners to conduct the therapy. The child psychiatrist then manages the medical aspects of the treatment on a less frequent basis.

However, the professional who manages the psychotherapeutic part of the treatment must have a solid understanding of early-onset bipolar disorder, its course, and its medical treatment (and understand the side effects of the medications) in order not to misinterpret some of the child's behaviors. For example, a child's fatigue and phlegmatic behavior may be an early side effect of a medication rather than a symptom of depression, or both factors—depression and medication side effects—may be contributing to the picture. Granted, it's hard to tease apart moods and behaviors that arise from temperament and the flux of childhood life from those propelled by an impending episode of illness or its treatment (especially with children who have rapid mood shifts), but a child is best served when all things are considered, and this requires a comprehensive view of the child and the disorder.

Therapy for children with bipolar disorder is pretty much uncharted territory, but Dr. Nancy Austin, who practices in New York City, treats a number of bipolar children. We asked her to describe some of the particular ways she works with them. She told us:

> First of all, a therapist has to understand the level of discomfort that is going on inside the bodies of these children. I tend to focus initially on the body experience of the child, because irritability and anger may be a response to this. Children often can't verbalize the internal experience of changing mood states, but I find they will symbolically represent it.
>
> For instance, I had one little girl who repeatedly started each session by adding to a collection of rubber bands and attaching them to each other and to items in the room. The whole place looked like a spider's web. She showed me what it felt like to be inside her head: She couldn't get out. If she stepped there, she would fall through; if she stepped here she would be trapped. She was always "getting caught" in her weblike structure.

Dr. Austin knows that these kids are experiencing something terrifying for which they initially have no words, and therefore the shifting body experience can only be expressed in metaphor. In play or verbal expression via storytelling, Dr. Austin looks for the underlying mood state. She also focuses on the way the child takes in and expresses things. If the stimulation or demand is too great, the child and therapist adjust the therapy so the child's unique moment-to-moment experience of his or her world (in the therapy room) is shared by both.

Dr. Austin has adapted tools that were developed by Dr. John March from Duke University in his cognitive-behavioral approach to obsessive-compulsive disorder in children and adolescents. One tool that is particularly helpful is the image of a thermometer, which allows the child to indicate the intensity of an event that typically causes irritability and rage—such as frustration with homework, getting up and ready for the bus in the morning, dealing with shoelaces that are not tied tightly enough, or going into a store and not being allowed to buy every toy he or she wants.

"We discuss what upsets them," says Dr. Austin. "We talk about the temper tantrums." She and the child find ways of recognizing and then talking about the child's experience of shifting inner states. Only then can she help the child to recognize behaviors that scale back the intensity of a tantrum, and help him or her to de-escalate. Once they've identified how to do that—and it may be deep breathing, quiet time, watching a familiar video, or taking a bath—she helps the parent-child team facilitate strategies that get the anger into a more manageable range.

Dr. Austin also helps the parent and child see how differently each of them is viewing a tantrum. For instance, on the scale from one to ten, a parent may experience his or her child as having a tantrum of incredible intensity: Often the parent views it as a "nine or a ten" and yet the child sees it as a "six or seven." "At this point the parents' nerves are shot," says Dr. Austin. "They experience something akin to a posttraumatic stress response, and they begin to assume that nothing will change. But when the parent successfully contributes to a scaleback, the parent begins to develop renewed hope about the enormously challenging task of parenting a bipolar child, and the parent is able to stay calmer and experience less anger and upset. I help the parent understand what the child is experiencing at the moment and intervene at the first sign of a tantrum. When there is improved attunement between parent and child, full-blown tantrums decrease."

A critical part of the therapy is working with the parents together and helping them to understand each other's actions. It is not uncommon to hear a husband complain to his wife: "You baby him. You indulge him in everything." But once the diagnosis is made, and it is understood what is going on inside the child, both parents may come to realize that the child needs this kind of attention and attunement. The father may come to realize that his wife is actually doing heroic parenting. Significant reduction of the tension and contention between parents is helpful to them and to all their children.

Dr. Austin also helps the parents identify which one is strong in which areas so that one can spot the other, support the other, but not ask the other to do what he or she does not do best. At some point, one of them will be so worn down that the other has to take over. When one spouse can help the other to stay calm, home life can be less traumatic. Parents can then regain their sense of competency as parents.

Dr. Austin feels strongly that the entire team—the parents, the prescribing physician, the school personnel, and the therapist—should be collaborating, and the therapist can facilitate an ongoing discussion.

It is not easy to find a therapist who has such an understanding of the internal states of a bipolar child. Trying to give a synopsis of all that goes on in such a complicated therapy is near impossible, but parents might be well served to think of elements that are present in Dr. Austin's work to ensure that a therapist is attuned to the rapidly shifting inner mood states of bipolar children and to the special problems they and their families face.

Costs

How much would treatment with any of these different professionals cost? As of this writing, typical fees per session are:

Psychiatrist	$140–$200
Clinical psychologist	$90–$160
Social Worker	$75–$120

A comprehensive evaluation by a medical expert in child bipolar disorder may cost in the neighborhood of $1,000. Neuropsychological testing, which scores and defines the child's cognitive strengths and deficits, perceptual strengths and difficulties, and abstract reasoning abilities, with a full emotional functioning component may require up to nine hours of time and cost anywhere between $2,000 and $3,000. Parents should expect a detailed written report suitable for school and therapeutic purposes (some run from five to fifteen pages long) and a parent feed-back session.

OTHER TREATMENT OPTIONS

The National Institute of Mental Health and the Stanley Medical Research Institute (SMRI) are conducting research in the area of early-onset bipolar disorder, and they are funding a number of diagnostic studies and clinical trials that recruit volunteers from around the country. A call to the NIMH at (301) 443-4513 or to the SMRI at (305) 571-0760 will inform a parent of ongoing studies that may cost the family little or nothing for expert diagnosis and treatment. Another organization solely devoted to research into early-onset bipolar disorder is the Juvenile Bipolar Research Foundation. The foundation sponsors research that is conducted through a consortium of medical schools, notably Yale, Albert Einstein College of Medicine, Cornell, and SUNY-Purchase. For information about ongoing studies, go to http://www.bpchildresearch.org.

Some of the clinics mentioned earlier in this chapter may have an ongoing study that would accomplish the same thing, closer to home.

PARENTS AS SHERLOCK HOLMES

In this chapter, we've tried to warn parents how difficult it is to obtain proper diagnosis and good treatment for a child with bipolar disorder. Parents are going to have to work hard to assemble as clear a family history as possible, take a close unvarnished look at their child's behaviors, become educated about this disorder so that they can discern which doctor they should trust for the diagnosis and treatment, and try hard to seek out a therapy that addresses the many issues that affect the child and the family members. If parents know what they need and want, they have a better chance of finding it and maximizing the benefits to their child and the family as a whole.

Prescriptions for Treatment

A few weeks before we sat down to work on this chapter, we got a call from a couple we had known for many years. Laura and Alan were living on the West Coast and had heard through other friends that we were writing this book. They had a young son named Matthew, who was living a tortured existence. Laura and Alan detailed the grim facts of Matthew's behaviors over the past few years. He had rages that went on for hours; he was very destructive, and though he was in a small therapeutic school, his parents kept receiving notes from the teacher reporting very disturbing events. Once Matthew tried to destroy the classroom and kicked a window out of its frame. Many days he was so out of control that Laura and Alan were called and asked to pick him up. Some days they kept him home because his behavior was just too erratic.

Laura and Alan trudged the route from doctor to doctor, and Matthew was finally diagnosed with ADHD. (Bipolar disorder was discussed, but Matthew was adopted and there was no family history. Also, one doctor told them that the diagnosis could not be made until Matthew reached puberty.) Matthew was put on a stimulant and an antidepressant, but within a few weeks he began experiencing visual hallucinations at night, begging Laura to see all the bugs and snakes that were crawling on his bed. He was about to be hospitalized when he was taken off these medications and actually had a few weeks on a good roll, his mother explained.

But the cycles continued, and "family life" was something that happened only for other families (or so they thought). Laura sent us her journals of these years, and they are extremely painful to read. In a series of telephone conversations, we discussed the importance of early diagnosis and intervention and mentioned that although Matthew was still young, the clock was ticking, and early childhood was coming to an end. Laura replied in a broken and grief-struck voice: "This hasn't been a childhood, this has been a horror show." Demitri suggested a mood stabilizer, and their doctor on the West Coast initiated a medication trial of Depakote.

And so, as we spent the week organizing this chapter, it seemed particularly meaningful that we received a letter in the mail from Laura. We held our breath as we sat down and opened it. Afterward, neither of us said anything for a minute or so. With Laura's and Alan's permission we reproduce part of it:

Dear Demitri and Janice:

Alan and I have been meaning to call to give you the miraculous details of Matthew's progress, and we will, but in the meantime, a short note to tell you what a fantastic change we are seeing in Matthew.

He is so much more even-keeled, so cheerful, cooperative, reasonable. His sense of humor has come out of hiding, and he actually jokes about things. The *darkness* is gone.

Of course he still tends to be impulsive and to overreact angrily to certain things, but these reflexes are fewer and he recovers much more quickly. For the first time we can see a real willingness and ability on Matthew's part to change his behavior. He's doing so well that we're even thinking of bringing him back to district school in the near future. It's just too good to be true . . .

Toward the end of the note, Laura repeated something her son, now nine years old, said to her after six weeks on a mood stabilizer and *off* stimulants and antidepressants: "Mommy, I'm going to ask God if he can please let me keep feeling this way."

It is possible for a child to be rescued from all that rage, aggression, and anxiety. There is, however, no way to know exactly which medication will work for any individual child. It is very much a trial-and-error procedure, and it may take multiple medication trials until the right drug or combination of drugs is found. (It is not uncommon for children with early-onset bipolar disorder to require a combination of two mood-stabilizing drugs to achieve stability.) All of the drugs have side effects—they will be detailed in the pages that follow. Many side effects are bothersome only in the beginning of treatment and disappear once the body grows accustomed to the medication. Some persist throughout the period the child is taking the drug. The hope is (and it is not an unreasonable one) that, as attention is paid to this disorder of early childhood, newer and safer drugs with fewer side effects will be coming through the pipeline.

Most of these medications have only recently begun to be used in children, and not many studies of their use in childhood exist. Many are not even approved by the U.S. Food and Drug Administration for use in children, and double-blind placebo-controlled studies are only now being mounted or completed. Many psychiatrists are simply adapting what they know about the treatment of adults to the pediatric and adolescent population.

Foremost in a parent's mind must be the risk/benefit of any medication. While a few parents answered a question on our survey saying that they fought the use of drugs and that medicating a child made them "uneasy," the overwhelming majority of mothers and fathers said that they were relieved to know there was something that could help lift their child out of a "nightmare" and into a more naturally paced life.

In the pages that follow, we will explore all the psychiatric treatments for early-onset bipolar disorder. Before we do, however, we want to state bluntly, right up front, that *antidepressants and in many cases stimulants given without the benefit of a mood stabilizer (possibly even with the protection of a mood stabilizer) can cause havoc in a child suffering from a bipolar condition, increasing anxiety states, potentially inducing mania, more frequent cycling, and increases in aggressive outbursts and temper tantrums.* In our study, over 80 percent of the children given antidepressants of all kinds became agitated, or more aggressive, paranoid, or psychotic. Many were hospitalized.

Mood stabilizers are the mainstays of treatment of a bipolar disorder. People often ask if one mood stabilizer is better than another and how do physicians make the choice for the first trial. The truth is, no studies have shown any of the medications to be superior to the others. In fact, lithium may be better in the maintenance part of treatment than any of the other drugs. Everything depends on the child's unique and individual reaction (and, of course, on the doctor's expertise in prescribing and titrating dosages).

Lithium, Tegretol, and Depakote are three mood stabilizers that require blood levels, and parents of needlephobic children can easily envision the struggle ahead with these medications. But one of these may work best for their child and parents should know about a product developed in Israel called Emla. It is an anesthetic available by prescription that can be administered to a child's arm about an hour before the blood draw. One five-gram tube costs about $12.50 and is good for one or two blood draws. There is a five-tube kit that costs about $45. Some insurance companies will pay for the prescription; some won't. But if Emla helps the child deal with the uncomfortable situation at the lab, then it is priceless to the child and parent.

MOOD STABILIZERS

Lithium

Lithium is a naturally occurring alkaline substance that exists in trace amounts in the human body, in plants, and in mineral rocks. It has been used as a medication at different times throughout history. Over 1,800 years ago, the Greek physician Galen formulated a treatment for mania by bathing patients in alkaline springs and by having them drink the water. (It is thought that they were lithium springs.) In 1817 August Arfwedson, a young Swedish chemist, inserted lithium into the chemists' periodic table as the lightest of the alkali metals. He christened his new element lithium, from the Greek word for stone, *lithos.*

From the 1840s to the early 1900s, and for some years after that, lithium was touted as a cure for such maladies as gout, epilepsy, diabetes, sleeplessness, and even cancer. It was never all that effective, but something about the drug prompted its resurrection every few decades.

In the late 1940s, lithium chloride was prescribed as a salt substitute for patients with heart or kidney disease and who required a low-sodium diet. And this time the use of lithium was a disaster. It was discovered—too late—that lithium exchanges for sodium in the body. If a person is salt-depleted, it competes with sodium and rises to toxic levels in the body and brain. Some people suffered lithium poisoning; several people died.

In what surely must be the worst timing in history, a psychiatrist named John Cade, far away in a primitive laboratory in Australia, stumbled upon the true value of lithium. The year was 1948.

Dr. Cade had a hunch that people became manic when there was too much uric acid in their bodies. He decided to test out his hypothesis by injecting uric acid into guinea pigs. In order to control the potency of the uric acid, it had to be put into a soluble form so that it could be diluted. And what solution did he choose? Lithium salts.

The guinea pigs, notably excitable in the Cade laboratory, became extremely calm and impassive once they were injected with the solution. Perhaps the animals simply became toxic, but seeing their "calm," Dr. Cade ran upstairs to the ward and injected ten manic patients, six schizophrenic patients, and three patients diagnosed as melancholic with the lithium solution. In the *Medical Journal of Australia,* on September 3, 1949, John Cade reported:

W.B., a male, aged fifty-one years, had been in a state of chronic manic excitement for five years, restless, dirty, destructive, mischievous, and interfering, had long been regarded as the most troublesome patient in the ward. His response was highly gratifying. From the start of treatment on March 29, 1948, with lithium citrate, he steadily settled down and was enjoying the unaccustomed surroundings of the convalescent ward. . . . He remained perfectly well and left the hospital on July 9, 1948, on indefinite leave with instructions to take a maintenance dose of lithium carbonate, five grains twice a day. . . . He was soon back working happily at his job. However, he became lackadaisical about his medicine and finally ceased taking it. His relatives reported that he had not had any for at least six weeks prior to readmission on January 30, 1949, and was becoming steadily more irritable and erratic. He ceased work just before Christmas. On readmission to hospital he was at once started on lithium carbonate, ten grains three times a day, and in a fortnight had again settled down to normal. . . . He is now (February 28, 1949) ready to return to home and work.

This seminal article reported ten case histories demonstrating the profound effect of lithium on manic patients, but Cade's monumental discovery failed to garner any attention. The lithium poisonings in America made lithium a word akin to "thalidomide," and the great potential for its usefulness was buried under the weight of negative public opinion and government restrictions.

But a Danish psychiatrist named Mogens Schou, who became the world expert on the use of lithium in psychiatry, clearly understood the magnitude of its importance and was not about to let this drug retreat to the back shelves of the pharmacy. His brother apparently suffered severe mood swings for many years and yet became well stabilized on lithium. After studying more than 150 patients using double-blind study methods (neither the doctors evaluating the results of the "medicine" given nor the patients taking the medicine know if the patients are taking a placebo or the active drug), Schou was convinced that lithium worked not only for the treatment of mania but also to prevent recurrence of the cycles in either direction. He began to campaign for its use in 1957, and, slowly, other countries began to use lithium for the treatment of manic-depression. In America, however, the Food and Drug Administration (FDA) restricted its use to small experiments only.

After many clinical studies and the determination of Drs. Samuel Gershon, Nathan Klein, and Ronald Fieve to reignite interest in a medication they saw as so life-saving, the FDA partially lifted the nonapproved status of lithium and allowed doctors to prescribe it for the treatment of acute mania. But it was not until 1974 that the FDA finally approved its status as a prophylactic medication—one that acted to prevent future episodes of mania. To date, millions of people have lived normal lives thanks to John Cade's serendipitous discovery.

How Does Lithium Work?

While there are unequivocal data proving that lithium works in adults, no one is sure how it exerts its effects, or why it works preventively in both mania and depression. It is known that lithium affects a complex biological system called the phosphatidyl inositol cycle inside many types of cells. This cycle is referred to as a "second messenger" system that relays and amplifies signals from neurotransmitters, hormones, and other molecules. Apparently lithium inhibits or dampens down the activity of the pathway, which may be overactive in both mania and depression, but much remains unknown at present.

How Well Does Lithium Work for Children?

In adults, lithium is considered to be the gold standard for the treatment of bipolar or cyclic mood disorders. An estimated 70 to 80 percent of bipolar patients have a positive therapeutic response to it. But the group of patients who have been described as "rapid cyclers" (those who have four or more cycles in a one-year period) were thought not to do as well on lithium as they do on other mood stabilizers, such as Depakote or Tegretol.

Since children typically have a rapid-cycling condition, and many children cycle several or more times in a twenty-four-hour period—they are called *ultradian* cyclers—there was a question about lithium's effectiveness in the pediatric population. However, despite the rapid cycling, many children do have an excellent response to the drug or to its use in combination with another mood stabilizer.

Very important, there is newly emerging evidence from the research literature that lithium has a strong and possibly unique effect against suicidal behavior in people with bipolar disorder. Apparently this is not true of the other mood stabilizers. According to Dr. Ross J. Baldessarini from Harvard Medical School, "If the antisuicidal effects of lithium are not shared with other mood-altering agents, this may be due to the cerebral serotonin-enhancing properties of lithium, properties that are not known to be associated with anticonvulsants."

Lithium has also been shown to be neuroprotective and this will be discussed in some detail in Chapter 9.

Determining Dosages

Before lithium can be prescribed for a child, a complete medical history is taken and a physical exam is performed. Some routine lab work such as simple blood tests and a urinalysis are ordered. Because lithium is almost entirely eliminated from the kidneys, tests of kidney function are done before the lithium therapy begins and at regular, approximately four- to six-month, intervals after that. A psychiatrist will also ask that tests of thyroid function be obtained since lithium can occasionally cause goiter (a treatable and reversible enlargement of the thyroid gland) or a decrease in thyroid function (hypothyroidism). Blood tests of the levels of thyroid hormones (T3 and T4) and thyroid-stimulating hormone (TSH) are typically performed prior to initiation of treatment and annually thereafter.

Children will have to have periodic blood tests in order to determine the lithium concentrations in their blood. In order for lithium to be effective, its concentration in the blood must be held within a specific range: Too low a level is ineffective, but too high a level can be toxic. Maintenance therapeutic levels for children typically range from 0.8 to 1.2 mEq/liter.

At the beginning of lithium treatment, blood levels are monitored five to six days following each increase in dosage, but once the level of the drug has stabilized in the body, blood levels typically are obtained every four to six months.

The blood sample needs to be drawn approximately twelve hours after the last dose and before the child takes the next dose. Because a blood sample taken soon after a dose can be misleading, parents are going to have to time the trip to the lab carefully.

A liquid form of lithium citrate is available, which is helpful for young children who can't swallow pills, and there are other choices of lithium formulations. Most are 300 milligram immediate-release lithium carbonate tablets or capsules, but 150 and 600 milligram tablets and capsules are available also. The drug is immediately absorbed and, as a result, can produce relatively high peak blood levels. For this reason, a divided dosage regimen is prescribed—often three or four times a day.

Several pharmaceutical companies produce different forms of release designed to minimize this sawtooth pattern of lithium levels in the blood. For instance, Lithobid R is a slow-release form of lithium that flattens the peak blood levels. The drug is released slowly enough that the blood level peak occurs approximately four hours after ingesting the medicine.

Another of these release designs is Eskalith CR, a sustained release formulation. The lithium is embedded in a nondigestible carrier that delays absorption even longer, as much as twelve hours after the child takes it. This allows the drug to be given less frequently, perhaps only once a day, but some children complain of lower abdominal cramps or diarrhea, perhaps because of this delayed absorption in the gut.

The following chart identifies a typical lithium-carbonate dosing schedule for children under twelve years of age.

WEIGHT (pounds)	DOSAGE (MG)			
	7 A.M.	12 noon	6 P.M.	Total Daily Dose
Less than 55	150	150	300	600
55–88	300	300	300	900
88–110	300	300	600	1,200
110–132	600	300	600	1,500

Source: Adapted from "Lithium Dosage Guide for Prepubertal Children" by Elizabeth B. Weller, Ronald A. Weller, and Mary A. Fristad, *Journal of the American Academy of Child Psychiatry* 25 (1986): 92–95.

If a dose of lithium is missed, the next dose should *not* be doubled. It is much safer to skip a dose than to double the next one.

Lithium is rapidly absorbed into the bloodstream and carried to all body and brain tissues. As mentioned, the medication is eliminated almost entirely by the kidneys. Sodium is also excreted by the kidneys in competition with lithium, and if there is sodium depletion in the body, lithium will be retained in its place. The possible buildup of lithium could result in toxicity. Therefore, a normal sodium balance is needed to ensure a reliable lithium balance. This means that patients must avoid taking diuretics and eating low-sodium diets, or the prescription should be adjusted downward. Also, parents should be aware that any severe loss of fluids, such as that caused by fevers, vomiting, and diarrhea, even dehydration on very hot days, can cause lithium levels to rise in the bloodstream to potentially toxic levels. In such situations, the doctor should be called and the child should be given fluids such as Pedialyte or Gatorade. Likely the doctor will request that a lithium level be taken and that the daily dose of lithium be lowered—perhaps even stopped—for the duration of the illness.

Signs of Possible Lithium Toxicity
Elevated levels of lithium in the blood can be severely intoxicating, brain damaging, or even fatal. However, parents should understand that what could be a subtherapeutic level for one child could be toxic for another. While rare, it has been reported that toxicity can occur at levels lower than 0.8mEq/liter. Therefore, parents should take careful note of the following signs of lithium toxicity:

Fatigue	Coarse or worsening hand tremor
Sleepiness	Unsteady gait
Confusion	Tremor of the lower jaw
Muscle weakness	Muscle twitches
Heaviness of limbs	Nausea, stomachache, diarrhea
Slurred speech	Ringing in the ears (tinnitus)

Some of these symptoms could be caused by other illnesses or, in adolescents, abuse of alcohol or street drugs. No matter what a parent suspects, the child should not be given any more lithium and the doctor should be contacted immediately. A blood test to check the lithium blood level should clarify the picture, and if necessary, the dosage can be adjusted.

Side Effects of Lithium

Most young people tolerate lithium very well if it is carefully dosed and monitored. In fact, because their kidneys are so efficient, they excrete lithium quickly and often need doses similar to those prescribed for adults in order to maintain adequate levels in the blood for maintenance therapy.

Lithium is nonsedating and nonaddictive. Most of the side effects are both harmless and easily dealt with. The following side effects can occur as lithium therapy is instituted, but typically subside in a few days as the body adjusts to the medication:

EARLY SIDE EFFECTS
- Nausea, vomiting, diarrhea, abdominal distress
- Headache
- Excessive thirst (polydipsia) and frequent urination (polyuria), and bedwetting (nocturia)

These side effects usually can be dealt with by adjusting the dosage or raising the dosage more slowly, or changing the schedule of dosing.

OTHER SIDE EFFECTS
- Hand tremor. An active tremor of the hands is uncommon in children and adolescents taking lithium, but if it does occur, often it can be counteracted with small doses of propranolol (Inderal) or by lowering the dosage of lithium.
- Weight gain. Most children and adolescents will gain weight on lithium, probably five to ten pounds in the first year, sometimes even more. There is some speculation about lithium's anti-insulin effect on carbohydrate metabolism, but some weight gain can be attributed to the thirst that lithium can cause and a child's tendency to quench that thirst with soda or fruit juices, which are highly caloric. Low-calorie sodas or water will reduce the amount of weight gain. Many people in support groups have reported that increased exercise also can combat the problem of weight gain.
- Acne. Teens especially may experience the eruption or worsening of acne on the face, neck, shoulder, or back, but this can be treated with typical anti-acne therapies (but not Accutane, as this can cause depression).
- Hypothyroidism. A condition in which the thyroid gland becomes underactive and enlarges. Should a child report feeling cold, tired, slow, experience muscle aches, hair loss, menstrual changes, or an unusual

weight gain, the doctor should be alerted and thyroid function studies be performed. Problems with the thyroid can be treated easily and effectively with synthetic hormone replacement therapy, such as Synthroid or Levothroid. Selenium, such as that provided in a multivitamin like Centrum Silver, may help counteract any hair thinning or loss.

• Cognitive problems. Lithium has been reported to cause short-term memory problems; rarely, some children talk about feeling "spaced out." However, these problems seem to be dose-related.

Are There Long-Term Side Effects to Lithium Therapy?

It is natural to think of the long-term side effects of any medication therapy that may continue for years. When lithium was first prescribed, there was some fear of kidney damage due to long-term treatment. But in 1984, the Consensus Development Conference of the National Institute of Mental Health concluded that, with the exception of possible thyroid problems, there are few significant permanent risks from long-term lithium therapy. However, in children it is wise to watch closely their kidney and calcium levels as well as their bone development.

Although lithium can be fatal in overdose, it is the only medication that has been proven to lower the risk of suicide. For this reason alone, lithium should be considered a potential first-line treatment for bipolar disorder in children and adolescents.

Lithium Interactions with Other Drugs

The following chart details the interaction of lithium with other over-the-counter and prescription medications as well as with other psychotropic medications such as Tegretol, Depakote, and the antipsychotic drugs:

INTERACTIONS OF LITHIUM WITH OTHER DRUGS

LITHIUM MAY INTERACT WITH	RESULTING IN
Nonsteroidal Anti-inflammatory Drugs	
Ketorolac (Toradol)	Increased lithium level
Ibuprofen (Advil)	
Indomethacin	
Naproxen (Aleve, Naprosyn)	
Phenylbutazine	

INTERACTIONS OF LITHIUM WITH OTHER DRUGS

LITHIUM MAY INTERACT WITH	RESULTING IN
Antibiotics	
Erythromycin	Increased lithium level
Metronidazole	
Spectinomycin	
Tetracycline	Reports conflict as to tetracycline's increasing or decreasing lithium levels
Bronchodilators	
Aminophylline	Significantly increased lithium excretion
Theophylline	
Antihypertensives	
Clonidine	Decreased antihypertensive effect
Cardiac Medications	
Ace inhibitors	Increased lithium level, increased potassium
Calcium channel blockers (verapamil, etc.)	Possible increased rate of lithium excretion
Quinidine	Decreased lithium effect, possible cardiac conduction effects may be potentiated by lithium
Diuretics	
Thiazides	Increased lithium concentration, decreased potassium
Indapamide	Increased lithium level
Potassium-sparing agents (amiloride, etc.)	Increased lithium concentration
Insulin and Oral Hypoglycemics	Increased glucose tolerance (careful monitoring of glucose levels is necessary)

INTERACTIONS OF LITHIUM WITH OTHER DRUGS

LITHIUM MAY INTERACT WITH	RESULTING IN
Anticonvulsants	
Carbamazepine (Tegretol)	Increased carbamazepine toxicity unless doses of both drugs are modified
Divalproex (Depakote)	Possible decreased lithium level
Neuroleptics	Increased risk of neurotoxicity, tardive dyskinesia
Sodium Bicarbonate	Decreased lithium effect

The Need for Caution When Discontinuing Lithium Therapy

Lithium treatment is associated with an approximately sevenfold reduction of suicide attempts and fatalities in bipolar patients. However, Drs. Ross J. Baldessarini and Leonardo Tondo and colleagues recently reported that discontinuing lithium rapidly after long-term maintenance therapy led to sharp increases in suicidal risk. The risk increased twentyfold in the first twelve months than at later times, but was only half as great following slow discontinuation (fifteen to thirty days versus one to fourteen days). These researchers recommend gradually discontinuing mood-stabilizing medicines whenever possible, perhaps over several months.

Antidepressants should *not* be used during this time.

OTHER MOOD STABILIZERS

In the 1970s, some studies conducted in Japan by Dr. Teruo Okuma showed that a drug introduced for the treatment of temporal lobe epilepsy, carbamazepine (Tegretol), can be an effective treatment for acute mania and work to prevent future episodes of bipolar illness. A team at the National Institute of Mental Health led by Drs. James Ballenger and Robert Post, using placebo-controlled double-blind conditions in a study of adult patients, reported data that supported these claims.

Shortly after that, studies about another anticonvulsant, valproic acid (Depakene), or its more commonly used salt form, divalproex sodium (Depakote), showed great promise in the treatment of patients who did not respond to lithium or who were in the difficult-to-stabilize categories of rapid cycling or mixed states.

Today a number of anticonvulsant medications are being evaluated in the treatment of bipolar disorder: Tegretol, Depakote, Neurontin (gabapentin), Lamictal (lamotrigine), Topamax (topirimate), and Gabitril (tiagabine). Trileptal (oxcarbazepine) has been recently released in the United States and has become rather widely prescribed in the past year. Of these only Depakote has been approved for the treatment of mania in adults. This renders the other anticonvulsants "off label." Although they are being used quite frequently in the treatment of bipolar disorder, they are not specifically approved for use as mood stabilizers at any age. And only lithium has been approved for the treatment of mania in children under sixteen. Parents should understand that paradoxical reactions have been observed with anticonvulsant mood stabilizers, particularly in very young children between the ages of two to seven. A paradoxical reaction is a reaction that is opposite of what the drug is expected to cause. For example, it may stimulate rather than calm.

We will list all drugs initially with their generic and brand names. Generic refers to the scientific, noncommercial name for the chemical compound and off-patent trade manufacturing; trade names are the names the drug companies choose for marketing purposes. We list both initially and then use whichever name is more commonly used by the lay public. (Beginning on page 137 we will discuss brand-name and generic versions of the same drug.)

Depakote

We'll start with Depakote (divalproex sodium) because it's an antimanic anticonvulsant frequently prescribed for children.

Getting Started on Depakote

Before a child is started on Depakote, he or she needs a medical examination to gauge liver function, blood cell and platelet counts, and serum iron concentration. These tests contribute to the safe use of Depakote and, when repeated, provide information to help the prescribing physician evaluate how the body systems are affected by the medication.

Depakote is supplied in 125, 250, and 500 milligram tablets or capsules, and a capsule that can be opened and sprinkled on ice cream or applesauce or some other food a child likes. There is a red liquid syrup called Depakene.

While children can be started on a test dose of 125 mg and adolescents on 250 mg, the doses are gradually increased to obtain a daily target dose of between 1,000 and 1,200 mg. Once this is reached, a blood level is taken and the dosage increased until the serum levels are within the 70 to 100 microgram per milliliter of serum (mcg/ml) range. The blood levels should not be measured until the child has been on a stable dosage for about six days. It takes this long to ensure that a steady state has been achieved (when the amount of the drug ingested equals the amount excreted in a twenty-four-hour period). Many children respond best at levels between 80 to 90 mcg/ml, but some require levels of 100 to 125 mcg/ml to achieve adequate symptom relief.

Never give a child a double dose of the drug if a dose is forgotten. If it is within four hours of the regular dosing time, the child should take the dose. If it is close to the hour of the next allotted dosing time, the forgotten dose should be skipped.

A parent should begin to see improvement in the child within two to three weeks of attaining a therapeutic serum level; the maximal clinical response may occur six to eight weeks after the steady-state serum levels are reached.

Blood tests should be taken in the morning, twelve hours after the last dose. Once an appropriate therapeutic level is attained, blood levels need be taken every three or four months in the early stages of mood stabilization.

Side Effects of Depakote

Many of the side effects of Depakote disappear as the body becomes adjusted to the medication. Drowsiness, indigestion, nausea, and vomiting sometimes occur, but these side effects may subside in a week or two. Taking the Depakote with meals may diminish the nausea. A thinning or loss of hair has been reported, but usually resolves over time, and the use of a multivitamin with zinc (15 milligrams) and selenium (50 mcg) often can prevent this from happening.

Not all children gain weight on Depakote, but many do. Some children experience what is referred to as "Depakote hunger" for a few weeks after treatment starts; some continue eating (gorging, actually) at such fantastic rates that some mothers have made lists of the food consumed in a few hours. One log was particularly specific and included: five packets of instant oatmeal with tons of sugar on top, four potatoes, two cheeseburgers, two pieces of chicken, one hamburger bun, one piece of coffee cake, sixteen ounces of grape juice, and twenty ounces of Mountain Dew.

This hunger may be caused by a direct effect that Depakote has on the hypothalamic centers that regulate satiety. It does not happen to everyone, but it should be anticipated, and low-calorie snacks and drinks as well as an increased daily exercise schedule should be planned. Topamax, a newer anticonvulsant, used in low doses (25 to 75 mg) may counteract this ravenous appetite.

A very rare side effect of Depakote is liver toxicity. Most cases of this potentially fatal side effect involved children under the age of one who were taking the drug for a seizure disorder. Liver function studies should be done before treatment starts, several times over the first year of treatment, and annually thereafter. The signs of liver toxicity can be nausea, vomiting, fatigue, weakness, swelling in the ankles, jaundice (yellowing of the eyes or skin), or easy bruising. If these signs appear, the medication should be stopped and the parent should call the doctor immediately.

Another rare side effect, but one which all parents and caretakers should be alert to, is pancreatitis—an inflammation of the pancreas. In July 2000, the manufacturer of Depakote, Depakene, and Depacon added a black-box warning to its labeling of this medication. To quote: "Parents and guardians should be warned that abdominal pain, nausea, vomiting, and/or anorexia can be symptoms of pancreatitis that require prompt medical evaluation." The abdominal pain is usually severe pain in the upper abdomen that moves to the back and is accompanied by nausea.

Should a parent note any of these symptoms, he or she should call the doctor immediately, state up front that the child is being treated with Depakote, and inquire about a possible case of pancreatitis. The doctor should order an ultrasound and/or CT scan of the pancreas to determine if it is swollen or inflamed (a blood test of pancreatic enzymes is not totally predictive).

Pancreatitis caused by a medication typically resolves with the stopping of the drug, but a parent and a doctor must act quickly as it can rapidly progress to a lethal condition. Pancreatitis can develop early in treatment, or after years of use.

Depakote Interactions with Other Drugs

Certain drugs should not be taken in combination with Depakote. They include:

Barbiturates
Phenytoin (Dilantin)
Phenobarbital
Carbamazepine (Tegretol)
Lamotrigine (Lamictal)
Alcohol (Depakote and alcohol may produce central nervous system depression)
Note: Caution is suggested with aspirin because the interaction of aspirin and Depakote may cause higher Depakote levels.

Parents of a daughter prescribed Depakote will hear about (and need to know the entire story of) the reports of polycystic ovary disease in young epileptic women treated with Depakote before the age of twenty. In 1993 Dr. Jouko Isojärvi in Finland studied menstrual disturbances in 238 young women treated with anticonvulsants—either Depakote or Tegretol—for epilepsy before the age of twenty. Of the twenty-nine women taking Depakote, twenty-three were followed, and ten (or 43 percent) of the twenty-three developed polycystic ovary disease. At first it looked like the culprit was the anticonvulsant, but after following these patients for three years, some new facts came to light.

It seems as if the majority of these young women were severely obese. And since obesity can lead to increased insulin levels, and high levels of insulin promote the ovarian production of testosterone, and testosterone can produce polycystic ovary disease, it seems more likely that the problem begins with severe obesity. No nonobese women taking Depakote developed polycystic ovary disease.

If parents are at all worried about this, their daughter could have a yearly gynecological exam to ensure that all is well.

Tegretol

Another anticonvulsant, Tegretol (carbamazepine), has acute antimanic effects and also acts to prevent future episodes of illness in bipolar adults. Moreover, Tegretol has been established to have anti-aggressive properties, something that might make it particularly useful for children with frequent rage attacks.

In 1992 an open pilot study conducted by Dr. Vivian Kafantaris and her colleagues at Long Island Jewish Hospital treated ten children between the ages of five and ten who had symptoms of explosive aggressiveness. Five of the ten had taken lithium and it had not been effective, but on Tegretol, nine of the ten experienced a significant reduction in explosiveness and aggressiveness. The European literature has many reports of the use of Tegretol to treat children and adolescents, but there are no placebo-controlled studies.

Despite the fact that there are no controlled studies in children, almost twenty nonblinded studies and five double-blind placebo-controlled studies in *adults* showed Tegretol to be effective in acute mania. (Seventy percent of all the patients had an excellent response.) So, clinically, it is often considered as an alternative to lithium in the younger population who need mood stabilization.

Getting Started on Tegretol

Before starting on Tegretol, a child needs a medical evaluation, and blood tests to evaluate liver function, blood cell and platelet counts, and iron concentration. A child between the ages of six and twelve is typically started on a dose of 100 mg twice daily (or 50 mg four times daily if the liquid is used). The dose may be increased weekly by increments of 100 mg with a daily target dose of 400 to 800 mg and a blood level of 6 to 12 mcg/ml.

Patients older than twelve years usually start treatment with doses of 200 mg twice daily; the dose is increased weekly by increments of 200 mg. The usual daily maintenance dose is 800 to 1,200 mg with the same therapeutic blood levels established for adults with epilepsy. The drug is supplied in 200 mg tablets, 100 mg chewable tablets, and a liquid suspension or in an extended release form, Tegretol XR.

Because Tegretol activates certain enzymes in the liver, and this causes the drug itself and many others to be metabolized faster, the serum Tegretol level may drop somewhat after the first month of treatment, requiring increased doses based on blood levels. Blood tests are needed more frequently in the beginning of treatment and every three months or so afterward. The blood should be drawn twelve to fourteen hours after the child's last dose, usually in the morning before the first dose of the day.

If a dose is forgotten, and less than three hours have elapsed since the dosage time, the child should take it. If more than three hours have elapsed, the child should skip that dose and resume taking the medication at the next regularly scheduled time. In other words, do *not* double the dose.

Always store this medication away from sources of heat and out of direct sunlight, and never store it in a bathroom cabinet because humidity may cause it to lose one-third or more of its effectiveness. The tablets can absorb the moisture, harden, and become less soluble and less well absorbed when taken. The Food and Drug Administration recommends that during humid weather, Tegretol be dispensed in limited amounts and in moisture-proof containers.

Side Effects

The most common side effects of Tegretol are dizziness, drowsiness, unsteadiness of gait, nausea, headaches, rash, double vision, and confusion. Many of these side effects—if they occur—don't last beyond the first week or so of treatment, and can be curtailed by lowering the dose. If the treatment is begun at low doses, and the doses are raised in small increments, many of them may not occur at all.

There have been some reports of bone marrow suppression (aplastic anemia) with Tegretol. While very rare, this is a life-threatening condition. Therefore, it is good medical practice to have a red blood cell count weekly at first and again if the patient starts to develop any bruisability or chronic infections.

What are the signs of aplastic anemia? Photosensitivity (the skin's extreme sensitivity to sunlight), easy bruising, fever, sore throat, and purple spots on the skin. Should *any* of these symptoms appear, the Tegretol should be stopped immediately and the doctor called. After the first few months on Tegretol, the risk of aplastic anemia is reduced.

Tegretol Interactions with Other Drugs

Tegretol interacts adversely with some other drugs, as shown in the list below.

INTERACTIONS OF TEGRETOL WITH OTHER DRUGS

Increased Tegretol Levels and Toxicity Produced by:
Diltiazem
Erythromycin (and similar agents)

Fluoxetine (Prozac)
Fluvoxamine (Luvox)
Isoniazid
Nefazodone (Serzone)
Propoxyphene (Darvon and others)
Sertraline (Zoloft)
Triacetyloleandomycin
Verapamil
Viloxazine

Decreased Tegretol Levels Produced by:
Primidone (Mysoline)
Phenobarbital
Phenytoin (Dilantin and others)

Tegretol Diminishes Effects of:
Barbiturates
Benzodiazepines
Corticosteroids (decreases levels and therapeutic response to
    steroids)
Dexamethasone
Dicumarol
Ethosuximide (Zarontin)
Neuroleptics (decreases blood level)
Oral contraceptives
Phenytoin (decreases levels of both drugs)
Pregnancy tests
Theophylline
Thyroid hormone (decreases thyroid levels)
Tricyclic antidepressants
Valproate (Depakote)
Warfarin

Parents should be aware that there have been some problems with the
generic versions of carbamazepine—they tend to be less well formulated
than the brand-name drug, Tegretol. The generic versions also seem to be
less well absorbed, and there have been reports of some of the tablets
falling apart. If carbamazepine is prescribed, it would be wise to use
Tegretol.

Young women taking birth control pills should understand that Tegretol interferes with the contraceptive ability of the pills. (It accelerates their normal breakdown and makes them less reliable.)

In the past few years, some newer anticonvulsants have begun to be used as mood stabilizers in adults, and studies are now beginning in the pediatric population. While controlled clinical trials are only in the early stages, these novel anticonvulsants are being used clinically in adolescents and, in some cases, in children. So, without the benefit of substantial data, we'll discuss what is known about Trileptal (oxcarbazepine), Neurontin (gabapentin), Lamictal (lamotrigine), Topamax (topiramate), and Gabitril (tiagabine).

Trileptal

Trileptal (oxcarbazepine) is an anticonvulsant launched in this country in February 2000 (but used in the European pediatric epilepsy population since 1990). Its use in bipolar children is just being evaluated, but it seems to be quite effective for some children, it requires no systematic blood draws, and it does not cause weight gain, liver toxicity, or aplastic anemia.

Trileptal (oxcarbazepine) is an analogue of Tegretol. An analogue is structurally similar to another compound, but differs slightly in its composition (such as replacing one atom by another atom of a different element).

Someone in the Ciba-Geigy labs in Switzerland played around with the Tegretol (carbamazepine) compound and added one oxygen atom to the top of the middle structure. What a difference an oxygen atom can make: Whereas Tegretol oxidizes in the body into an active metabolite called 10/11 epoxide, Trileptal rapidly converts in the body to 10-monohydroxide derivative (MHD). Tegretol is a very effective mood stabilizer for bipolar disorder, but it seems that the 10/11 epoxide metabolite is responsible for some of the major problems that can occur with the drug, most notably the activation of certain enzymes in the liver which cause the Tegretol itself to be metabolized faster so that the serum Tegretol level may drop during treatment.

In contrast, the principal metabolite of Trileptal (MHD) has little effect on liver enzymes, so that its own serum levels remain fairly constant. Moreover, unlike Tegretol, it is less likely to increase the elimination of many other drugs.

Because of its different metabolism, Trileptal is much less likely to cause the rare cases of aplastic anemia we referred to in the Tegretol section above. In addition, liver toxicity occurs rarely with Tegretol, but is unknown with Trileptal.

How Well Does Trileptal Work in Bipolar Disorder?

Several studies have evaluated the effectiveness of Trileptal in acute mania. In 1983, Dr. Hinderk M. Emrich of the Max Planck Institute in Munich performed a double-blind, placebo-controlled study in adults using oxcarbazepine, and found an average change of 50 percent in the mania scales was achieved by this medication. As a consequence of these findings, Ciba-Geigy of Basel organized two multicenter studies using the drug. One compared oxcarbazepine with the antipsychotic drug haloperidol (Haldol). After two weeks, both treatments (haloperidol and oxcarbazepine) were about equally effective in the fifty-eight-patient study, on the basis of decreasing mania-scale scores.

Another international study compared the antimanic effects of oxcarbazepine to lithium. Again, after a two-week period, the drugs were found to have about equal efficacy for the treatment of acute mania.

In May 2001, at the American Psychiatric Association's annual conference, Dr. Michael Reinstein of Rush Medical Center in Chicago presented a poster in which he compared Trileptal to Depakote in the treatment of mania in adults and found them to be indistinguishable in both efficacy and tolerability of side effects.

How well does Trileptal work as a maintenance medication? To date, no drug but lithium has been approved for the prevention of episodes of mania in bipolar disorder, and none is approved for preventing episodes of bipolar depression specifically. Nevertheless, Tegretol and Depakote are used routinely for these purposes and often do the job well. We have only anecdotal information about prevention of episodes and future stability with the use of Trileptal and more studies are needed to assess the medication—especially for children.

Getting Started on Trileptal

Before starting on Trileptal, it is wise for a child to have baseline blood tests and serum electrolyte panels. Because a drop in sodium blood levels (hyponatremia) can occur in 3 percent of those taking Trileptal, a baseline lab test should be done on all patients before the drug is started, and children with sodium levels below 135 mEq/liter should be watched more closely. Hyponatremia is rare in children, but teenagers who may ingest diuretics surreptitiously for weight loss are at risk and this should be explained to them at the beginning of treatment.

Symptoms of hyponatremia include a reduction in urination, headache, confusion, tiredness, and if very severe, seizures and coma. It can be treated easily and it is recommended as a general practice that every fourth drink should be a sodium-containing one such as milk or Gatorade. Milk has 125 grams of sodium in an eight-ounce glass, and Gatorade has 115 mg of sodium in an 8.45-ounce juice box.

After the initial lab work, there are no blood levels that need to be done when taking Trileptal (a great boon for needle-phobic children and their parents). There is a blood level that can monitor the serum level of MHD (monohydroxide derivative), but the clinical value of this measurement is uncertain. At this point the blood test might be useful to ensure that an adolescent is taking the medication—more of a measurement of compliance, whereas dosing is better guided by clinical response and tolerability by individuals.

Trileptal is supplied in 150, 300, and 600 mg tablets, scored so that they can be cut in half. In addition, there is a lemon-flavored oral suspension for children who have difficulty swallowing tablets. The liquid preparation must be shaken well before given to a child. It is supplied at a concentration of 60 mg/ml, or 300 mg per 5 ml teaspoon.

Children are typically started at 300 mg per day—in divided doses—150 mg in the morning; 150 mg approximately twelve hours later. The dosage is then raised every six or seven days in increments of 300 mg (again, the 300 mg increases are best divided into two-a-day half doses) with a target dose of approximately 900 to 1,200 mg (some children may require as much as 1,500 to 2,400 mg).

The drug reaches a steady state, or stable, concentration in the bloodstream after about four doses or within two days. One mother whose eleven-year-old was cycling wildly throughout the day—despite his being on Clozaril and Zyprexa—wrote of her son's experience with Trileptal: "At about three weeks, as his dose was 900 mg, we began to see the amplitude of his mood swings diminish. At six weeks and 1,200 mg, the cycling practically stopped. Since no other medication was added at this time, we're sure the Trileptal smoothed out the cycling pattern."

This young man had been on the medication for a few months, as of this writing, and continues to do well, but only time will tell if the drug is effective as a long-term mood stabilizer.

Side Effects

The most common side effects that may occur early in treatment with Trileptal are sleepiness (somnolence), headache, dizziness, double vision, ataxia (unsteadiness), vomiting, rash, and abdominal pain. Most of these side effects—should they occur—recede as the body adjusts to the drug in a few weeks. We have heard of a case of sun sensitivity caused by the drug (not surprising because Tegretol can cause this also). Trileptal causes little if any weight gain.

Interactions of Trileptal with Other Drugs

Although Trileptal has less risk of drug-to-drug interaction than Tegretol, it can increase the rate of elimination, and reduce the effectiveness of some drugs—notably oral contraceptives and one calcium channel blocker, Felodipine. Trileptal may be safely combined with Lamictal, Depakote, and lithium, as well as with antipsychotic and antidepressant medications.

In conclusion, we'd like to quote child psychiatrist Boris Rubinstein of Columbia University's College of Physicians and Surgeons in New York City. He said: "I feel that Trileptal may turn out to be a particularly useful drug for children—especially the difficult-to-assess four-year-olds who present with ADHD and a lot of aggression. If these are budding bipolar children, I would feel comfortable starting with Trileptal. Unlike stimulants and antidepressants this option would not exacerbate a possible bipolar disorder."

Studies in the planning stages will tell us more about this promising new mood stabilizer. Meantime, Trileptal is FDA-approved as an add-on anticonvulsant for children age four and older.

Neurontin

Neurontin (gabapentin) is an anticonvulsant drug that seems to have few side effects except for some fatigue, dizziness, ataxia (unsteady gait), and tremor, and it can be used safely with other medications often needed by a patient with bipolar disorder. It does not cause weight gain. Recent studies in adults have found Neurontin to be ineffective as a mood stabilizer, however it may have some value as an anti-anxiety agent.

A therapeutic dose seems to be between 900 and 1,800 mg a day, and it must be given in divided doses, three times a day using 300 to 400 mg capsules.

There have been several reports of Neurontin-induced mania in the psychiatric and epilepsy literature, and a number of children have become activated and aggressive on the medication (but this paradoxical reaction can happen with any of the drugs).

Lamictal

Lamictal (lamotrigine) is an anticonvulsant medication that seems to have several advantages: It is frequently effective for controlling rapid-cycling and mixed bipolar states, and it seems to work in the depressed phase of bipolar disorder. (The other mood stabilizers work against acute mania and prevent future episodes of mania and depression but are not truly effective against current depression.)

Studies to confirm this antidepressant effect of the drug are going on now at twenty different medical centers across the nation. The first report of a double-blind placebo-controlled study was published by Dr. Joseph Calabrese at Case Western Reserve University and his colleagues in February 1999. This multicentered study evaluated Lamictal treatment of Bipolar I depression and found that 200 mg a day in adult patients was significantly effective against the depression.

A second study by Dr. Calabrese and his group published in November of 2000 concluded that Lamictal was effective as a monotherapy over a six-month period, particularly for patients who had the Bipolar II form of the disorder.

Most people tolerate the drug well, but the side effect profile includes gait disturbances, dizziness, headaches, nausea, blurred vision, and sleepiness. A patient is most likely to experience these side effects for a few days after a dosage increase, but they tend to disappear as the body adjusts. The drug does not cause weight gain.

Perhaps the side effect of greatest concern is rash. The risk of rash is greatest in the first eight weeks of treatment. A rash is also more likely to develop when the dosing schedule starts too high or is increased too rapidly (start low and go slow is the pertinent phrase here), or when Lamictal is prescribed with Depakote, a practice that was common early on until the problem became apparent. There have been many reports of people breaking out with mild rashes—similar to a slight sunburn—or with a total body rash that resembles a severe case of poison ivy. If a rash occurs, the doctor *must* be notified immediately. Usually the rash clears up after ceasing to take the drug (and a patient can even resume the drug later and no rash will occur), but in rare instances the rash is associated with a life-threatening syndrome known as Stevens-Johnson syndrome, or the more deadly toxic epidermal necrolysis. These are severe and sometimes fatal allergic reactions to an infectious disease or a drug. Stevens-Johnson syndrome is typically an abrupt onset of rash accompanied by high fever and complete exhaustion (prostration). The eyes may become puffy and blisters may appear around the mouth. It is often misdiagnosed as chicken pox; toxic epidermal necrolysis resembles more of an extensive burn with painful lesions.

Stevens-Johnson syndrome can also be caused by sulfa drugs, penicillin, and anticonvulsants—especially Dilantin (phenytoin). The syndrome seems more likely when Lamictal is given with Depakote or Depakene, which can double Lamictal blood levels. This particular combination of drugs may produce the vulnerability for Stevens-Johnson syndrome. Presently, the FDA has placed Lamictal on black label: It is not to be given to children under the age of sixteen.

However, new reports confirm that starting Lamictal at lower doses and titrating the doses with more gradual increments significantly decrease the risk of rash. Dr. N. Earl and his colleagues examined a database of more than 10,000 adult patients with epilepsy or bipolar disorder who were treated with Lamictal. Twenty-eight percent of this group had serious rashes, of which eleven (0.10 percent) had Stevens-Johnson syndrome and none had toxic epidermal necrolysis. When they looked at the 5,798 patients who were treated with the more conservative dosing guidelines now recommended by the manufacturer, the incidence of Stevens-Johnson syndrome was 0.05 percent. This study should indicate that—with conservative dosing—more patients should be able to use Lamictal, with a decreased likelihood of a serious problem.

We spoke to the mother of a sixteen-year-old girl who had asked her daughter's doctor to initiate treatment with Lamictal. He was wary and warned her of the dire side effect of Stevens-Johnson syndrome. This mother was a registered nurse, had read the literature on the drug, and knew her daughter, Mariana, had been on every class of medication except the monoamine oxidase (MAO) inhibitors (a type of antidepressant). She also knew that Mariana had been suicidal all summer and was in a very fragile state. Time was running out. Her child's life was in the balance, and the threat of death by suicide was infinitely greater than the chances of a problem with Lamictal. (Her last update informed us that Mariana had been stable on the drug for eight months. While she is still experiencing some activation in the early evenings, her mother told us that the drug has been a miracle for her. "She's the best she's ever been," she reported.)

Lamictal is supplied in 25, 100, 150, and 200 mg tablets. It is also available in 5 and 25 mg chewable tablets for children.

If Lamictal is prescribed for an adolescent, it is started at 12.5 mg once a day (usually in the morning) and *very slowly* raised—every 6–7 days—by 12.5 mg. A target dose of 75 to 100 mg a day may be effective, but sometimes as much as 225 mg is required.

Some patients feel the antidepressant or antimanic effects early in treatment, but a significant improvement usually takes about three or four weeks.

The following table lists Lamictal's interactions with other drugs and alcohol.

Lamictal Interactions with Other Drugs and Alcohol

LAMICTAL MAY INTERACT WITH	RESULTING IN
Depakote (divalproex sodium) Depakene (valproic acid)	A doubling of the plasma level of Lamictal. In some patients, the level of Depakote is decreased.
Tegretol (carbamazepine)	Increased plasma level of Tegretol and its metabolites. In turn, Tegretol lowers the concentration of Lamictal in the blood.
Zoloft (sertraline)	Increased plasma level of Lamictal
Phenobarbital and Primadone	A significant lowering of the plasma level of Lamictal (approximately 40 percent)
Alcohol	An increase in the severity of Lamictal side effects

Topamax

Topamax (topiramate) is an anticonvulsant drug chemically unrelated to any other anticonvulsant or mood-stabilizing medication. It seems to work to control rapid-cycling and mixed bipolar states in some patients who have not responded well to Tegretol or Depakote, but because it was approved in this country only in the last week of 1996, it is not yet established whether the drug offers long-term prevention from cycling. No studies of the drug's use in children have been reported, but it is being prescribed for young people nevertheless.

What makes this drug of particular interest is that it causes no weight gain (in fact, some people lose weight on the drug).

An initial dose of 25 milligrams is given once or twice a day and increased by 25 to 50 mg every week. When Topamax is prescribed as an add-on drug with other anticonvulsants, a target dose of 150 to 200 milligrams is often enough for mood stabilization, but some children will require higher doses, even up to 400 milligrams a day.

The side effect profile includes: sleepiness (for many people it is simply too sedating), fatigue, dizziness, vision problems, speech problems, unsteadiness, nervousness, nausea, memory problems, and cognitive dulling in an estimated 20 percent of patients. Many of these side effects are most noticeable the few days after a dosage increase and then often fade away as the body adjusts. Some people notice the antidepressant or antimanic effects early in treatment, but significant improvement may take up to four weeks.

While no interaction between Topamax and lithium has been noted, Topamax may increase the blood levels of phenytoin (Dilantin) and decrease the effectiveness of birth control pills. Depakote and especially Tegretol have the ability to lower the blood levels of Topamax.

In the fall of 2001, the FDA and the manufacturer strengthened the label of Topamax, warning of the possibility of eye problems—specifically secondary angle closure glaucoma in pediatric and adult patients taking the drug.

The signs of the condition would be occular pain or decreased vision. The treatment would be discontinuation of the medication. As of August of 2001 there were twenty-three reported cases—mostly with adults—but children should have regular eye checkups and, every six months, a screening for glaucoma.

Gabitril

The anticonvulsant Gabitril (tiagabine) has been FDA-approved for the treatment of convulsive disorder in adolescents but is now being used in patients with bipolar disorder as well. Not a great deal is known about its effectiveness yet, but anecdotal reports show it to work for some children who have not responded to the other mood stabilizers.

The maximum recommended daily dose of Gabitril is 32 mg, and, again, the medication should be started at low doses and increased slowly—only weekly—until a good response is noted or the dose reaches 32 mg.

The side effect profile may include dizziness, fatigue, and an unstable gait. Like Topamax, there may be drug-to-drug interactions, and no medications should be taken without checking with the child's doctor.

Calcium Channel Blockers

Calcium has long been linked to mood dysregulation. It is thought to play a role in the underlying biological basis of bipolar disorder. Calcium plays an important role as a "second messenger" in a wide variety of cellular mechanisms, from gene regulation to electrical activity and neurotransmitter release as well as regulation of circadian rhythms. Low and high calcium levels in the blood have been observed to produce irritability, anxiety, maniclike states, and psychosis. There is evidence to support the idea that both lithium and a group of drugs called calcium channel blockers exert some of their therapeutic properties on the illness through a direct effect on calcium metabolism. Calcium channel blockers act primarily by decreasing the inflow of calcium through cell membranes. This group of drugs, which includes verapamil (Calan, Isoptin), nimodipine (Nimotop), and isradipine (DynaCirc), has recently received attention as potential mood stabilizers for the treatment of acute mania, ultra-ultrarapid cycling, and recurrent depression in adults. A number of small double-blind placebo-controlled studies and many case reports have found significant improvement in some adult patients treated with calcium channel blockers, primarily verapamil.

Among this group of drugs, several—including nimodipine—have shown great promise in the prevention of migraine headaches and a related syndrome known as cluster headaches. (Some studies found a 90 percent reduction of symptoms after one to two months of treatment.)

Both conditions are not uncommonly reported in patients with early-onset bipolar disorder, particularly adolescent females with twenty-four-hour cycling patterns.

The most common side effects caused by calcium channel blockers are due to excessive vasodilation. These effects may be experienced as dizziness, low blood pressure and headaches, facial flushing, nausea, and pins-and-needles sensations in the arms and legs. In addition, swollen ankles may occur in a small group of patients, but this is usually dose-related. These side effects are usually benign and may subside over time.

It is important to point out that grapefruit juice inhibits an enzyme in the gut that breaks down calcium channel blockers and can lead to a three- to fourfold increase in blood levels of this class of drugs. Therefore, grapefruit juice should not be consumed by an individual taking a calcium channel blocker.

Verapamil
Verapamil has been the most frequently studied channel blocker. Effective doses for the treatment of acute mania in adults have ranged between 160 to 480 mg a day. It is supplied as 40, 80, 120, and 240 mg (extended release) tablets.

Nimodipine
Nimodipine (Nimotop), another calcium channel blocker, is similar to verapamil but has several characteristics that make it unique in its class. It is more fat soluble; therefore, it crosses the blood-brain barrier more easily than the other calcium channel blockers and is more easily taken up into nerve cells. It was these features that prompted a group at the National Institute of Mental Health led by Dr. Peggy Pazzaglia to conduct a preliminary controlled trial of nimodipine to determine its effectiveness in adult patients with the rapid-cycling variant of bipolar disorder. Patients were started on 90 mg a day in three divided doses of 30 mg each and gradually increased to 360 mg a day. In the eight patients who completed the study, nimodipine was associated with a significant reduction in the magnitude of mood swings, and marked improvement was observed in several patients with ultrarapid cycling (the form most commonly seen in childhood-onset bipolar disorder).

Unfortunately, nimodipine's difficulty in administration (three to four times daily, one to two hours before or after meals) and extreme costliness (approximately $500 a month) make its regular use almost impossible. It would be a drug to try only if all other mood stabilizers failed, or if the patient suffers from co-occurring cluster headaches or migraines.

Isradipine

Isradipine (DynaCirc), currently used as an antihypertensive, has similar effects and properties as nimodipine; however, it can be administered in a sustained-release form and is much less expensive. To date there are only anecdotal reports of its effectiveness in the treatment of mood disorders.

What Constitutes an Adequate Trail of a Mood Stabilizer? At What Point Do You Move on to the Next?

In attempting to tackle these questions, we need to point out several things:

1. Reports from many clinical researchers indicate that a combination of two mood stabilizers are often necessary to achieve symptom remission. Therefore, partial response does not mean that the first drug tried is of no value.
2. If antidepressants have been administered prior to the trial of a mood stabilizer (between one week to three months), or are prescribed at the same time, it will be difficult to judge the effectiveness of the mood stabilizer. Antidepressants are destabilizing for the majority of children with bipolar disorder. While some clinicians believe that high doses of mood stabilizers will buffer the activating effects of antidepressants, this still needs to be established by clinical trials.

Now the question becomes, how long should a child be kept on a mood stabilizer before it is determined that another choice might better be instituted? Although it has not been objectively established, a reasonable time period to continue a mood stabilizer once a high therapeutic level has been established (and this can take weeks to months), would be between five and six weeks.

A decision has to be made by a physician, the parents, and the child if the drug has any beneficial effects. If so, it might be wise to add another mood stabilizer for increased stability. If not, the drug should be tapered slowly and another trial should be initiated.

ANTIPSYCHOTIC MEDICATIONS

Despite the wide use of mood stabilizers, antipsychotic drugs are also useful in the treatment of bipolar disorder. They may be prescribed periodically for some children during manic states, particularly when they may be experiencing delusions or hallucinations and when rapid control of mania is needed; or they may be a long-term component in the maintenance treatment of children or adolescents. Emerging evidence is suggesting that a combination of a mood stabilizer and one of the newer "atypical" antipsychotic medications may be required for adequate mood stabilization and to control rage and aggression, as well as any psychotic symptoms. They are often prescribed for children to treat the symptoms of Tourette's syndrome.

Listed below are the traditional as well as the newer antipsychotic drugs. Although the newer antipsychotic drugs such as Risperdal (risperidone), Zyprexa (olanzapine), Clozaril (clozapine), Seroquel (quetiapine), and Geodon (ziprasidone) produce fewer motoric side effects than the traditional antipsychotics, the newer drugs are expensive (some may cost between $2,000 to $4,000 a year), have other potential side effects, and may not work for every child. We will discuss the traditional antipsychotic drugs and their side-effect profiles first.

COMMON ANTIPSYCHOTIC MEDICATIONS

GENERIC	BRAND NAME
Traditional Antipsychotics:	
chlorpromazine	Thorazine
fluphenazine	Prolixin
haloperidol	Haldol
molindone	Moban
perphenazine	Trilafon
thioridazine	Mellaril
thiothixene	Navane
trifluoperazine	Stelazine

COMMON ANTIPSYCHOTIC MEDICATIONS

GENERIC	BRAND NAME

Newer Antipsychotics:

clozapine	Clozaril
olanzapine	Zyprexa
quetiapine	Seroquel
risperidone	Risperdal
ziprasidone	Geodon

Parents should understand that there is up to a fiftyfold difference in the milligram potency (antipsychotic effect per mg) of each drug but no difference in the efficacy per dose given clinically. Naturally, there is a correspondingly large variance in the doses that are prescribed by physicians. For instance, because Haldol (haloperidol) is forty to fifty times more potent than Thorazine (chlorpromazine), a child given 100 mg of Thorazine would be given only 2 mg of Haldol.

The antipsychotic drugs are typically prescribed in tablet or liquid form and are taken once or twice a day. Two of the drugs—fluphenazine decanoate (Prolixin Decanoate) and haloperidol decanoate (Haldol Deconate)—can be given as a long-acting injection that lasts from two to four weeks.

Children seem to be more sensitive to the movement disorder side effects we will discuss below, and they may need lower mg/kg doses than adults do. As with the anticonvulsant medications, paradoxical reactions have been observed with antipsychotic medications in some young children.

Side Effects of Traditional Antipsychotic Drugs

Dr. Ross J. Baldessarini from Harvard Medical School, one of the foremost experts on psychotropic medications, says that "the antipsychotic agents are among the safest drugs available in medicine." This is not to say that they don't cause side effects and that some of the side effects aren't upsetting and uncomfortable. Early side effects of an antipsychotic drug are constipation, blurring of vision, drowsiness, nasal congestion, and dry mouth. These typically fade as the child adjusts to the medication.

Movement Disorders

Also common (but terribly upsetting to a child experiencing them and a parent observing them) are the movement disorders: dystonic reactions and akathisia. These are known as *extrapyramidal* effects, and they are more commonly seen with the high-potency antipsychotics such as Thorazine, Haldol, and Navane. These movement disorders are treatable and reversible, and are defined as follows:

• *Dystonic reactions.* These are involuntary muscle contractions that cause uncontrolled and alarming movements of the face, neck, tongue, and back and an uncontrolled rolling of the eyes. Boys are at greater risk for dystonic reactions. All of this can be counteracted in minutes with an anti-Parkinson drug such as Cogentin (benzotropine) or Artane (trihexyphenidyl).

• *Akathisia.* This is a feeling of internal and external restlessness. A child may be incapable of sitting still and may feel a sensation of discomfort akin to anxiety or agitation. This side effect is often mistaken for anxiety or agitation or an increasing aggressiveness rather than a side effect of the medication, but a parent should listen carefully to the child describe how he or she is feeling and call the doctor. Inderal (propranolol) or clonidine sometimes helps counteract this truly horrible feeling.

These two movement disorders can be dealt with in a number of ways: The dose of the antipsychotic can be lowered, an anti-Parkinson drug can be added to the drug regimen prophylactically (some doctors prescribe Cogentin, Artane, or Benadryl along with the antipsychotic drug to prevent or treat dystonia), or the child can be switched to another class of antipsychotic drug. Generally, the more sedation an antipsychotic causes, the less chance that the child will be bothered by movement abnormalities. And, as we mentioned, the newer antipsychotic drugs cause less of this.

• *Akinesia.* This is characterized by stiffness and diminished spontaneity of gestures, physical movement, and speech. Again, Cogentin and Artane counteract this.

• *Tardive Dyskinesia.* Another worrisome side effect of antipsychotic drugs is "late-appearing abnormal movements" called tardive dyskinesia. TD, as it is called, is more typically a problem in elderly patients taking traditional antipsychotics continuously for many years, but it is characterized by involuntary facial grimacing, lip-smacking, chewing and sucking movements, cheek puffing, and wormlike movements of the tongue and fingers and toes. The patient may also experience sudden and purposeless movements of the arms and legs or writhing movements of the body. (This is seen more often in boys.) TD is not painful but is disfiguring, and a spontaneous remission is most likely in children once the child is no longer taking the medication. Parents should *not* just discontinue the antipsychotic abruptly, however. They should consult with the psychiatrist and perhaps even a neurologist specializing in movement disorders.

Although children seem to be less vulnerable to tardive dyskinesia than elderly patients, there are ways to minimize the risk. A child should be put on the lowest dose necessary to control the psychotic symptoms, and the doctor should regularly attempt to reduce the dose. The child should be closely watched for any signs of TD.

While there are little data available, the antipsychotic drug Moban (molindone) seems to cause fewer movement disorders than some other antipsychotics.

Other Side Effects
• *Menstrual changes* in young women have been reported, as have *breast discharge* in both sexes as well as a diminished sex drive.
• *Weight gain.* Children and adolescents can gain a great deal of weight on antipsychotic medications (especially young women, and this is a major factor in noncompliance). The only antipsychotic that doesn't seem to cause weight gain is molindone (Moban), and this drug may be particularly helpful for a bipolar child because, in small doses, it seems helpful in treating conduct disorder.
• *Sun sensitivity.* Parents need to know that a child is likely to develop a sensitivity to the sun while taking antipsychotic medications (especially low-potency ones). Children may burn very easily. Therefore, children's activities in full sun should be limited, and a sun screen with a high SPF—15 or higher—and with protection against UVF and UVB light—should be applied and reapplied often.
• *Neuroleptic malignant syndrome.* Neuroleptic malignant syndrome is a now-rare but life-threatening side effect of antipsychotic medications that is poorly understood. The patient can become severely rigid and may have a high fever, rapid heart rate, labored breathing, and sweating, and a blood test may show irregularities.

This syndrome constitutes a true medical emergency. The medication should be stopped immediately at home, and the child should be admitted to the hospital. There cardiac monitoring, fever control, and fluid maintenance will be administered, and Dantrium (dantrolene) or Parlodel (bromocriptine) will be given.

Many people might ask: Who would expose their child to such a symptom profile? Well, it all goes back to risk/benefit. The chances are that the movement disorders and TD may not appear, but certainly psychosis, severe rage, and mania are malignant for a child. Psychosis untreated gravely imperils a child.

Fortunately, the newer antipsychotic medications seem less likely to produce tardive dyskinesia and the acute movement disorders.

Newer Atypical Antipsychotic Medications

Since 1990 newer antipsychotic medications have begun to be used in this country, in both adults and children. They are clozapine (Clozaril), risperidone (Risperdal), olanzapine (Zyprexa), quetiapine (Seroquel), and ziprasidone (Geodon).

They are considered "atypical" because they have relatively lower risks of acute extrapyramidal symptoms (the movement disorders spoken of on page 106 and tardive dyskinesia).

Clinical experience with childhood bipolar disorder patients suggests that the atypical antipsychotic agents may accomplish things and target symptoms the mood stabilizers don't. The atypicals may benefit children who have prolonged rage attacks, psychotic symptoms, mixed-irritable moods, and possibly very rapidly cycling mood, all of which are commonly associated with early-onset bipolar disorder and may require different forms of treatment than are usual in adults.

Clozaril

Clozaril (clozapine), the first atypical neuroleptic to be marketed, was hailed as revolutionary because it produced no dystonia, little akathisia or Parkinsonian syndrome movement symptoms—the extrapyramidal symptoms we described earlier. Its ability to produce tardive dyskinesia or neuroleptic malignant syndrome is very low. Clozaril can, however, cause sedation, profound weight gain, seizures in a small percentage of patients, diabetes, and drooling or excessive salivation.

In the first years of prescribing Clozaril, doctors thought it produced agranulocytosis—a disease in which the bone marrow stops producing neutrophilic white blood cells. With biweekly monitoring of the blood, however, there have been fewer than ten cases in the United States. If the white blood cell count begins to drop and the medication is stopped, the patient's blood returns to normal.

This frequent taking of blood makes Clozaril somewhat less than ideal as a treatment for children, and today, children with early-onset bipolar disorder who require antipsychotic medication are more commonly prescribed Risperdal (risperidone) and Zyprexa (olanzapine).

Risperdal

Risperdal (risperidone) is prescribed for a number of reasons. It not only treats psychotic symptoms, but—very important—the drug seems to calm the rages these children often experience. And it works rather quickly, sometimes within hours.

Very low doses of this medication are somewhat less likely to produce the extrapyramidal side effects that the more traditional antipsychotics can cause. Risperdal does have side effects, however. Sedation can be a problem, and weight gain can be extremely troubling: One nine-year-old girl gained thirty-five pounds in four months, but children have been known to gain even greater amounts of weight. We've heard parents complain of drooling and urinary incontinence (a leaking of urine, actually). Less common side effects include nausea, dizziness, headache, and a runny nose.

A child is typically started on a dosage of 0.5 mg, increasing the dose until symptom relief is achieved, or until the onset of sedation. Many children do well on 1 to 2 mg a day; some children experiencing acute mania require higher doses.

Zyprexa

Although Zyprexa (olanzapine) was introduced in 1996, much remains to be learned about this drug. It seems to be effective for psychotic symptoms, and it may decrease them within hours of taking the drug, but the full benefit usually takes several weeks.

The main side effect is weight gain, and it too can be considerable. Zyprexa can cause tardive dyskinesia, but the risk is lower than with most traditional antipsychotic drugs.

Children usually take 5 to 15 mg of Zyprexa in an acute manic state. As a maintenance drug, 2.5 mg to 5 mg is often sufficient.

Seroquel

Seroquel (quetiapine) may prove especially useful since it appears to produce far less weight gain at lower dosage ranges (50–150 mg) than its cousins, Clozaril, Risperdal, and Zyprexa.

Although there was some initial concern about cataracts and high-dose Seroquel treatment, there is less so now. Still, it is prudent to have baseline and follow-up eye examinations if long-term usage is contemplated.

Geodon

Geodon (ziprasidone) is the newest atypical neuroleptic on the market, and is of particular interest to parents of bipolar children because it causes little if any weight gain. The medication has a mild SSRI-like activity versus serotonin uptake, however, and can induce an odd kind of over-arousal (this may be seen at lower doses and not higher doses; however, a number of parents have written to us about anxiety and maniclike reactions to the drug).

Geodon's major risk is that it has at least weak direct cardiac depressant effects (seen in the EKG as a slowing of repolarization, and hence the prolongation of the QTc interval). This cardiac depressant effect is not unlike that of some of the older tricyclic antidepressants and even the antipsychotic drug Mellaril, all of which were more dangerous in this regard. Good medical practice would follow EKGs in children throughout the time spent on Geodon. A baseline measurement of serum potassium and magnesium would also be wise.

The most common side effects are sleepiness and nausea, orthostatic hypotension, and rash.

Geodon is supplied in 20, 40, 60, and 80 mg capsules. A child is typically started on an initial daily dose of 20 mg, twice a day, and increased every few days to a level of 80 mg, twice a day (160 mg daily). Some patients in clinical trials have taken as much as 200 mg a day and some experts believe that at least 80 mg a day is required for an antipsychotic benefit.

Atypical Antipsychotics as the Only Treatment for a Bipolar Child?

The popularity of the newer atypical antipsychotics for childhood bipolar disorder is growing rapidly, and we have now heard of a number of cases where these drugs are prescribed alone, as the major, or only treatment offered. Usually this practice involves medications such as Risperdal, Zyprexa, Seroquel, Clozaril, or Geodon. If studies of combinations of atypical antipsychotics with antimanic-mood stabilizing agents are limited, those involving monotherapy with an antipsychotic agent in children are practically nonexistent.

One mother whose son's psychiatrist placed him on Zyprexa as a monotherapy for his newly diagnosed bipolar disorder wrote us and asked: "Is my child being used as a guinea pig?"

Some thoughtful and experienced clinicians are using this approach, and find that it can be quite helpful for some young patients in certain situations. Dr. Maurizio Tohen and his team at Eli Lilly laboratories have been studying Zyprexa (olanzapine) and have reported on its mood stabilizing effect. When we spoke with him he said that Zyprexa not only worked on the manic and psychotic symptoms, but was also effective on the depressive symptoms of mixed states or the depressive aspects of acute mania. That statement may be a bit bewildering, but manic states are not just a constant high with grandiose and activated thought, speech, and behavior. Often in adults, and very commonly in children, mania is interlaced with a rapidly shifting mood (mood lability), irritability, sadness, sleeplessness, anxiety, and agitation.

Dr. Tohen hastened to add that his study did not demonstrate a therapeutic effect in acute depression, nor a long-term mood-stabilizing effect on all phases of manic-depressive illness, though he indicated that such studies are being mounted.

In 1995, Drs. Gianni Faedda and Ross Baldessarini and their colleagues published an important review, entitled "Pediatric-Onset Bipolar Disorder: A Neglected Clinical and Public Health Problem." In it, they made a strong point that juvenile mania often includes psychotic features and a good deal of agitation and aggression, possibly more so than in adolescent or adult forms of the illness. They also emphasized evidence of the tendency toward an admixture of manic and depressive-dysphoric-irritable elements in children—more than in adults—and a common lack of a clean, episodic course, or very rapid fluctuations of mood and behavior in bipolar children.

Since agitation is a principal component of mixed manic-depressive states, it should come as no surprise that the atypical antipsychotic medications have a special place in the treatment of pediatric bipolar disorder.

Risperdal, Zyprexa, and Seroquel can calm the agitation, anxiety, rage, and hostility, as well as diminish psychotic symptoms such as hallucinations and delusions.

So there is some rhyme and reason here, based on the nature of juvenile bipolar illness for some doctors to use these medications as a first line of treatment. They are easy to administer and blood drawing to determine serum levels of the drugs are not necessary.

But—ease aside—do these treatments do the job and are there any negatives associated with them?

Some Negatives

As with lithium and with some anticonvulsants, two words come to mind when discussing the downside of most of the atypical antipsychotics: weight gain. Not every child gains weight on these medications, but many do, particularly with Clozaril, Zyprexa, and Risperdal. And when they do, it can be astonishing. The mother whose son was placed on Zyprexa wrote this to us: "He has put on eight pounds since Friday and it's continuing." Since we received her email on Tuesday, we wrote back to make sure we were talking about a four-day period. "Yes," she shot back through cyberspace. That's two pounds a day and climbing.

The atypical antipsychotics cause more weight gain than most of the conventional antipsychotic medications. Dr. Tohen told us that the weight gain seems to be greater in children than in adults and that the younger the child the greater the risk, but it is unclear why. Since weight gain usually appears right away in children, as it did in the little boy mentioned above, one can assume it will continue and consider alternative treatments. It is unknown why people gain weight (and so much of it) but it is hypothesized that the drugs' effects on the part of the hypothalamus that regulate satiety may be the root cause. Some clinicians will even mix Zyprexa with Risperdal and particularly with Seroquel in order to limit weight gain, and there are promising observations of a weight-limiting effect of the novel anticonvulsant Topamax. The dose range for the appetite-suppressant effects of Topamax is usually between 50 to 75 mg, and this is best administered at night, given the drug's secondary sedating properties.

The histamine receptor blocker Axid (nizatidine), whose primary indication is for the treatment of stomach and intestinal ulcers, has been found to counter weight gain associated with Zyprexa. A sixteen-week study of 132 patients treated with Zyprexa taking 300 mg twice daily of

Axid gained significantly less weight (6.08 pounds) than a control group taking a placebo (12.5 pounds).

Some clinicians report that the potential benefit of this countermeasure occurs only when Axid is administered at the beginning of treatment with the atypical antipsychotic (and some child psychiatrists report using 150 mg twice a day). Studies will have to be done to shed real light on the benefits and risks of the use of Axid.

All hopes have been on Geodon for its weight-neutral property, but clinical reports of its effectiveness in children with bipolar disorder are equivocal at best, and anecdotal reports suggest that Geodon carries a greater risk for activation of these children than the other atypicals.

Side Effects Beyond Weight Gain

There is anecdotal evidence and a few case reports in adults that Risperdal and Zyprexa have been associated with the induction of mania or mixed states. This may be because the atypical antipsychotics have an antiserotonin (5-HT2) receptor-blocking effect and thus are mood elevating. (We have seen and heard of an induction of mania in children and a few adolescents, and it is something parents should be aware of. This tends to happen more frequently in children younger than eight.)

Finally, there are a series of general medical, metabolic problems that are being increasingly reported in association with clozapine as well as the newer antipsychotics. These include new-onset, type II (noninsulin-dependent) diabetes mellitus, changes in lipid metabolism and blood concentrations, sometimes severe and persistent elevations of prolactin and other hormonal imbalances, and a range of adverse cardiovascular effects that include low blood pressure and abnormal functioning of the heart. The long-term implications of such adverse effects are not known, particularly for youngsters who may need to remain on such medication for decades to come. Moreover, we are just starting to be concerned about the potential individual and public health implications of such effects, which threaten to be at least as problematic as tardive dyskinesia and the extrapyramidal symptoms of the older drugs.

It is recommended that prior to the institution of treatment with any atypical neuroleptic—particularly if long-term use is contemplated—a set of baseline measures should be taken. These include measurements of weight, fasting blood glucose, glycosylated alpha 1c hemoglobin, and blood lipids. Children should be retested periodically (every four to six months) during treatment, and those children who experience significant weight gain or have a family history of diabetes should be monitored especially closely.

In general, children tend to break down and eliminate most drugs more rapidly and efficiently than adults and elderly persons. That tends to protect them from drug side effects. However, there is both laboratory and clinical evidence that children are more sensitive to antipsychotic drugs than adults, and require much smaller doses. As the optimal dosing with the newer antipsychotic drugs is worked out, it is wise to start with low doses in children. For example, daily doses of Risperdal of 0.25 to 2.5 mg, 2.5 to 5 mg of Zyprexa, and less than 200 mg of Seroquel may suffice. Hopefully, such doses may also limit side effect risks.

Until their safety and efficacy both in the acute and the maintenance phases of treatment are proven, the use of the atypical antipsychotics as a monotherapy is not yet justified, except in select cases where a child cannot tolerate therapeutic doses of a mood stabilizer.

BENZODIAZEPINES AND OTHER MEDICATIONS FOR SLEEP AND MANIA

Benzodiazepines

There is a definite place for the benzodiazepines—particularly the potent agents Klonopin (clonazepam) and Ativan (lorazepam), and Restoril (temazepam)—in the treatment of adults with bipolar disorder. These drugs help to put a brake on acute mania or hypomania. In addition, the benzodiazepines decrease activity in brain arousal systems and can diminish anxiety, agitation, activity, and promote standard sleep. Benzodiazepines are used most commonly as adjuncts to mood stabilizers such as lithium, Depakote, or Tegretol, and with antipsychotic medications in acute mania.

In prepubertal children, it has been observed that this class of drugs can produce paradoxical effects—they can be disinhibiting rather than calming. Therefore, their use may be more limited in this population. Nevertheless, the low threshold for anxiety these children have and their commonly comorbid anxiety disorders make these drugs useful under certain circumstances. If a decision is made to use benzodiazepines, good medical practice would be to start with low doses and watch carefully for any signs of disinhibition.

Because there is often a daily pattern in mood and energy (particularly in children who cycle within the day), it is not uncommon for a child to experience increased activity, agitation, anxiety, irritability, and aggressive behavior from the late-afternoon hours well into the evening. Their thoughts may race, they may become distractible and have difficulty concentrating (thus complicating any completion of homework), and they may find it nearly impossible to settle down. A benzodiazepine given in the late afternoon may preemptively stop this arousal from reaching a certain pitch.

Benzodiazepines not only reduce the number of awakenings these children experience throughout a night, but they also exert an effect on the architecture of sleep. They can decrease the time spent in stages 3 and 4 of slow-wave sleep. This may be particularly advantageous to children who are bipolar; a decrease in stage 4 sleep is accompanied by a reduction in the night terrors commonly experienced by these children.

Despite the benzodiazepine's shortening of stage 4 sleep and rapid-eye movement (REM) sleep, the net effect is usually an increase in total sleep time. And it is recognized that enhanced sleep can improve mania.

The question that arises about the benzodiazepines is: Do they cause dependency? There is always the risk, and there are definitely withdrawal effects, so a child should always be tapered off the drug slowly.

Which of the benzodiazepines should be prescribed and when? If the child is experiencing increased activation and restlessness and racing thoughts that begin and escalate from early evening to bedtime, and the child has difficulty going to sleep (but once asleep, sleeps through the night), Ativan might be prescribed just prior to the period of activation and again shortly before sleep. If on the other hand, the child has trouble getting to sleep and is also experiencing interrupted sleep, Restoril forty-five minutes before bedtime would be a better choice.

The side effects of the benzodiazepines include sedation, drowsiness, and decreased mental acuity.

Clonidine

Clonidine (Catapres) is used to treat high blood pressure in adults but is often used to treat children with tic disorders, ADHD, pervasive developmental disorders, and aggression. It is often prescribed for bipolar children who have comorbid ADHD or Tourette's syndrome, or who have difficulty sleeping at night. Although clonidine is an excellent hypnotic agent, there have been anecdotal reports of this medication causing depression in children. Therefore, children with bipolar disorder who are prescribed clonidine should be watched very carefully for this adverse effect.

Tenex

Tenex (guanfacine) is another adult blood pressure medication that appears to be less sedating than clonidine and to have more of an effect on attentional difficulties.

Tenex is supplied in 1 mg tablets, and most children are started on one half a tablet twice a day. The side effect profile includes irritability, fatigue, confusion at higher doses, and, rarely, agitation. Because clonidine can cause mood swings in bipolar children, there is speculation as to whether Tenex does as well, as they are in the same class of drugs. If a child seems unstable or irritable and he or she is taking Tenex, its use should be examined. Like clonidine, it should never be discontinued abruptly because of the risk of rebound hypertension.

Omega-3 Fatty Acids

Ever since Dr. Andrew Stoll and his colleagues at Harvard University published provocative findings about the greater stabilization of rapidly cyling adult bipolar patients with the supplementary use of high doses of fish oils (the majority of patients were on traditional mood stabilizers), a large percentage of parents have opted to add omega-3s to their children's regimens of pills and capsules.

Omega-3 fatty acids are essential fatty acids and they are called that because though they are crucial for growth and development, they cannot be manufactured in the body, but must be consumed through the diet we eat or from the supplements we swallow.

There are two families of essential fatty acids: omega-6 fatty acids and omega-3 fatty acids. The omega-6s are found in common vegetable oils such as corn, safflower, sunflower, and cottonseed; omega-3 fatty acids are found in the tissues of oily fish such as mackerel, anchovies, herring, and salmon, and in green leafy vegetables, canola oil, flaxseed, and walnuts.

While omega-6 fatty acids are distributed throughout the body, the omega-3 fatty acids are needed in the brain to an extraordinary degree. In fact, the major structural component of the brain and its cells is fat and water. The dry weight of the brain is 60 percent fat.

A Closer Look at Omega-3s

There are three important omega-3 fatty acids:

LNA—Alpha-linolenic acid
EPA—eicosapentanoic acid (pronounced EE-ko-sa-pehn-ta-No-ic acid)
DHA—docosahexaenoic acid (pronounced do-ko-sa-HEX-eh-noic acid).

LNA is a shorter chain omega-3 that comes from walnuts, flaxseed, canola oil, and other green leafy vegetables. LNA can be converted— sometimes inefficiently—into the longer chain EPA and DHA molecules.

EPA and DHA, the longer chain essential fatty acids, come primarily from the tissues of certain fish, and the fish get them—in the wild—by eating the chloroplasts of plants. Only the chloroplasts of marine and freshwater algae produce high quantities of long-chain omega-3 fatty acids. And these are eaten by small aquatic animals and shrimp, which are in turn eaten by larger fish, which are in turn eaten by humans (if they eat fish!). Only wild fish, not farmed fish, have large quantities of essential fatty acids in their tissues.

The Fish Connection to the Increasing Rates of Depression and Bipolar Disorder

Something has been going on since 1945: The rates of depression have increased world wide, and the age of onset is shifting downward—younger people are being affected. This trend, called "the cohort phenomenon," was noted in the 1980s by Drs. Gerald Klerman, Myrna Weissman, and Elliot Gershon, who found that each successive generation of individuals born since World War II appears to have a higher incidence and earlier age of onset of both major depression and bipolar disorder.

While there are many theories attempting to explain this striking increase, one of them points to the increase in our diets of sources of omega-6 oils (corn and soy as two examples), and the corresponding marked decrease in omega-3 fats (this has not been proven, however).

The association between depression and the types of fats we consume was made when Joseph R. Hibbeln of the National Institute of Health examined the consumption rate of omega-3 in countries around the world. In an important paper published in 1998 in the British journal *The Lancet,* he reported that the rates of depression were lower in countries that consumed a lot of fish. He found that the rates of depression could actually be predicted based on fish consumption.

A year after this association had been established, Dr. Andrew Stoll and his colleagues published the first double-blind placebo study that examined what happens when bipolar patients had their medications supplemented with high doses of fish oils (it should be noted that eight of the thirty were not on medications of any kind).

The thirty patients were divided into two groups, and one group got a placebo of olive oil capsules; the other nine grams of pharmaceutical-quality EPA and DHA fatty acids. While the study was designed for a nine-month period, a preplanned preliminary analysis of the data found a significant discrepancy between the placebo control group and the omega-3 fatty acid group; the patients on the placebo relapsed or failed to improve, while the patients taking the omega-3 supplements experienced dramatic recoveries.

Why might this be? To paraphrase Dr. Stoll in his book *The Omega Connection:* When a neurotransmitter binds to a receptor, the receptor sets in motion within the cell a series of chemical processes known as signal transduction, amplifying the original signal and ultimately altering the activity of the cell. We know that mood stabilizers inhibit signal transduction.

He goes on to write that "inhibiting signal transduction in bipolar disorder would be analogous to building a dam across a raging river, quieting the downstream waters."

Lithium and the anticonvulsants inhibit signal transduction . . . so too do omega-3 fatty acids.

A Host of Questions

Since the Stoll findings were published and received a lot of media attention, a number of parents have placed their children suffering with bipolar disorder on fish oil supplements. Some parents report a difference in their children's behaviors: They seem less explosive, calmer, and their moods appear more stable. One mother whose very young child was given only omega-3s said: "He went from a ten in severity to a two."

Another mother wrote that her daughter was stabilized on lithium, but at age thirteen she began taking 1 gram of an enriched EPA omega-3 product in addition to the lithium. "She's gained a higher level of stability than we've ever seen before," the mother reported.

But questions about this treatment abound: How many grams of

omega-3s a day must a child ingest (in addition to many pills and capsules of prescription medications)? Which brand should children take?
And (most confusing), what ratio of EPA to DHA is optimal?

We turned to David Horrobin, M.D., a neuroendocrinologist in Scotland who is a pioneer in lipid metabolism, and who has been researching
and reporting on essential fatty acids for over two decades.

First we told him that many parents want to know how they are supposed to get their children to swallow so many capsules of omega-3s (they
are extrapolating from Dr. Stoll's study which gave 9 grams of omega-3s
to the patients with bipolar disorder)?

Dr. Horrobin responded that he could answer dosing questions only
about unipolar depression and schizophrenia because he and his research
team had conducted dose-ranging studies with pure ethyl EPA looking at
1 gram, 2 grams, and 4 grams per day. In schizophrenia the optimal dose
was 2 grams per day with 4 grams giving less benefit. In depression, the
optimal dose was 1 gram, with 2 grams and 4 grams giving less benefit.

In other words, there were diminishing returns when giving higher
doses—*in those two illnesses.*

Then we raised the question about the amounts of EPA and DHA in
each capsule. What should they be? And why, if the brain is constructed
mostly of DHA, is the impression growing that pure EPA, or ratios high
in EPA compared to DHA, may be preferable? (This has also not been
proven in bipolar disorder.)

Dr. Horrobin answered that the impression of EPA's greater impression
is derived from the conclusions of three studies in depression and schizophrenia which compared placebos to an EPA-rich oil and a DHA-rich oil
and found that the EPA preparation was effective, but the DHA preparation was not. In some studies, mixed EPA/DHA preparations were effective, however.

So ratios of EPA versus DHA (or whether the supplement should be
pure EPA) are unknown and the answers will have to await future studies. We do know that each child responds differently to different brands
and different EPA and DHA ratios, so it behooves a parent to try more
than one brand if the first produces little effect.

So What's a Parent to Buy?

Omega-3 supplements abound in every health food store and even in su-
permarkets. We will direct parents to a few companies who manufacture
pharmaceutical-grade omega-3 fatty acids. When looking to choose a

brand, always look at the source of fish oil. Those made from anchovies and sardines are less likely to incorporate mercury and other contaminants such as PCBs as they are lower on the food chain. Parents should also understand that a 500 mg capsule is much smaller than a 1,000 mg capsule. This is important to know if a child has difficulty swallowing pills. In alphabetical order, some brands to examine are:

COROMEGA takes fish oils and delivers them in a creamy, pudding-like orange-flavored emulsion that is packaged in a squeeze pak (think Go-Yurt). There are no pills to swallow and blended with orange juice it's almost Smoothie-like.

Each packet contains: EPA: 350 mg; DHA: 230 mg; plus vitamin C, E, and folic acid. Three packets would give a child over a gram of EPA (although we still don't know what a child needs). Sold at Stop and Shops across the country, go to www.oilofpisces.com for more information.

KIRUNAL capsules are manufactured by Dr. Horrobin's company in Scotland and are Emerson Ecologics (www.emersonecologics.com or 1-800-654-4432). The capsules are 500 mg. Four capsules provide 420 mg of EPA and 140 mg of DHA.

NORDIC NATURALS' Pro DHA is a 500 mg capsule that is strawberry flavored. Each capsule provides 250 mg of DHA and 150 mg of EPA, with small amounts of vitamins E and C for freshness. Their Pro EPA is a lemon-flavored 1,000 mg capsule that provides 450 mg of EPA and 100 mg of DHA. Go to www.nordicnaturals.com for more information, or call 1-800-662-2544.

OMEGABRITE offers 500 mg capsules. Three capsules provide 1,125 mg of EPA and 100 mg of DHA. Go to www.omegabrite.com, or call 1-800-383-2030.

What are the Downsides of Omega-3 Supplements?
There seems to be the smallest possibility of mania induced by omega-3 supplements. We have read of six cases to date. Interestingly, five of the six occurred with EPA-enriched products (much higher doses of EPA than DHA), but there is some impression among researchers that mania

would more likely occur with a DHA-enriched product. Again, there are many questions and very few answers.

Fish oils should not be used by people allergic to iodine or those who are using blood thinners or anticipating surgery. It is recommended that fish oils be taken with supplements of antioxidants to prevent the oxidation of the extra omega-3 oils going into the body; 400 IU (international units) vitamin E and 600 mg vitamin C should take care of this.

Parents should understand that flaxseed oil is not equivalent to omega-3, and some patients have experienced hypomania on it.

ANTIDEPRESSANT THERAPIES

While antidepressant medications, and in particular the selective serotonin reuptake inhibitors (SSRIs) such as Prozac, Zoloft, and Paxil, and the atypical antidepressant Wellbutrin, have found widespread and popular acceptance for the treatment of unipolar depression, anxiety, and panic disorders, their use in children and adolescents has been established only recently.

The SSRIs, Wellbutrin, and the older tricyclic antidepressants can be miracle drugs for children suffering from nonbipolar depression, incapacitating obsessive-compulsive disorder, and anxiety disorders, but for those children who carry an inherited vulnerability for bipolar disorder, the rose can hide thorns.

Reports from both the adult and child literature document that individuals with bipolar disorder who have been treated with antidepressants during depressive episodes may have a significant risk of switching into mania or hypomania. In addition, antidepressants have been reported to increase the frequency of cycling. There is considerable concern in the field that the introduction of antidepressants may cause an earlier onset and possibly more virulent course of the illness. In 1998 Demitri Papolos, M.D., and his colleagues reported on twenty-five adult ultrarapid and ultra-ultrarapid cycling patients, as well as patients who cycled four or more times a year—all of whom had had childhood or adolescent-onset bipolar disorder. Of these patients, over 90 percent retrospectively reported increased cycling on exposure to all classes of antidepressants.

In addition, our survey of 120 children revealed that over 80 percent of those who were taking an antidepressant switched into mania or psychosis or became very activated, aggressive, and even violent.

Some did well for weeks or even months before a deterioration in behavior became evident. ("It seemed like a miracle, he was so happy," said one mother of an eight-year-old boy. "Then he began to think that he could fly and flew off the playground's jungle gym and broke his hand." After trying to smash his younger sister in the head with his casted hand a week later, he was hospitalized in a psychotic state.)

We have heard of and seen variations of this story with hundreds of children who are bipolar. Even Wellbutrin (bupropion), a mild stimulant antidepressant unrelated to the SSRIs and thought to be less likely to induce hypomania or mania in adults, can produce both mania and increased cycling.

Therefore, the use of antidepressants for children with known bipolar disorder, or even for children who initially show symptoms of depression only (but who may have a family history of bipolar disorder), must be considered highly risky and potentially harmful.

For children who are currently being treated with an antidepressant, parents and physicians should ask themselves: Has the child been *unstable*—despite the protection of a mood stabilizer? If the answer is yes, then the use of an antidepressant should be suspect and perhaps the child should be slowly withdrawn from it.

And this is where doctors and parents find themselves between a rock and a hard place. While many children cycle through depressed states very rapidly, for some children depression is the predominant pole of the illness, and they linger in depressed states for agonizing periods of time. Some retreat to their rooms, or move from the bed to the sofa and back. All outside activity ceases. This behavior is excruciating not only for the child but for the parents watching him or her as well. There is also the risk of suicide.

It is so tempting to want to use an antidepressant and watch that child's life take shape again. But if antidepressant medications are ultimately so destabilizing, the price may be very high. So then the questions become: What do you do about the depressions, and are there any other options?

There may be several:

- If the child is over sixteen, Lamictal (lamotrigine) is a unique mood stabilizer that appears to have antidepressant properties.
- If the depressive episodes have a seasonal component, or if, as is often

the case, the child is manifesting an increased need for sleep and a marked craving for sweets and carbohydrates, then phototherapy (treatment with bright lights) may be a useful adjunct to mood stabilizers.

- Despite all negative media connotations, electroconvulsive therapy (ECT) may be the most beneficial alternative in the battle against depression and mood instability. Later in the chapter we'll discuss a study that showed that young people who had ECT had had beneficial results from the treatment, and it should not be overlooked as a treatment option.

So, would you ever want to use antidepressant medications? In some instances, where comorbid obsessive-compulsive symptoms interfere significantly with the child's daily functioning (and behavioral treatments have failed) and mood stabilizers and antianxiety drugs or behavioral desensitization approaches do not produce relief, an appropriate approach to treatment may be low doses of an SSRI such as Luvox (fluvoxamine) plus increased levels of the mood stabilizer.

If an SSRI *is* used, a rule of thumb is that once the medication produces an antidepressant effect that is sustained for several weeks, attempts should be made to *slowly* reduce and discontinue the drug. To put it another way: The less exposure a bipolar child has to antidepressant treatment, the better.

For all these reasons, we start the discussion of antidepressant therapies with nondrug interventions, such as light therapy and electroconvulsive therapy, mention the new and experimental therapy of repeated transcranial magnetic stimulation (r-TMS), and finally move on to the SSRIs, such as Prozac, Zoloft, Paxil, the atypical drug Wellbutrin, and others.

Light Therapy

Light therapy (phototherapy) was originally studied for its effects on seasonal affective disorder (SAD). This syndrome was characterized by Dr. Norman Rosenthal and his colleagues at the National Institute of Mental Health when their studies revealed that some patients became very sluggish, irritable, and depressed as the days grew shorter in the fall. They began to sleep excessively, binge on carbohydrates, and withdraw from social activities. But come spring and the lengthening of the photoperiod (the hours of light in the day), these patients experienced new energy and found their moods returning to normal or slightly elevated levels. (It is now pretty well accepted that these patients are bipolar with seasonal depressions and hypomanias.)

Dr. Rosenthal found that sitting these patients in front of a bank of high-intensity, full-spectrum (all wavelengths—like sunlight) lights for certain periods of time in the morning or the evening lifted the depressive symptoms, and most of the patients felt better. When the light treatments were stopped, a number of patients relapsed.

Today it is understood that the pineal gland—the gland that secretes melatonin—receives information about light from special nerve pathways, and the secretion of melatonin may provide the link with depression. Melatonin is a sleep-inducing hormone, produced in the dark, which appears to depress mood and mental agility. Melatonin secretion is at its highest levels in the winter. Serotonin (long associated with depression and suicide) is actually a precursor of melatonin.

It seems that the timing of circadian rhythms varies in relation to mood in a predictable way in rapid-cycling patients. Specifically, the phase of temperature, the excretion of a metabolite of norepinephrine (MHPG), and melatonin secretion all occur earlier in the day in a hypomanic state than in the depressed state. Bright light can shift the phase of circadian rhythms, with morning light shifting the rhythms to an earlier time and evening light delaying them. Manipulating these phase shifts could treat the depressed phase of the illness.

Dr. Ellen Leibenluft and her colleagues at the National Institute of Mental Health conducted a small pilot study on nine rapid-cycling patients and found that midday light—between the hours of 12:00 and 3:00 P.M.—improved the symptoms of a number of the patients. There is reason to believe that midday light treatment may prevent phase shifts in the normal nightly rhythm of melatonin release. Midday light seems to increase the potency of the signal that melatonin gives to areas in the central nervous system. By increasing the amount of melatonin released *at a particular time,* you make it more difficult for other influences to delay or advance the rhythm of melatonin secretion.

Studies in rapid-cycling children are now being conducted, and we spoke with Dr. Norman Rosenthal about the administration of light therapy in children and adolescents. We started discussing the light boxes that a parent can purchase to begin light treatment.

According to Dr. Rosenthal, "A suitable light box is usually a metal fixture approximately two feet long and one and a half feet high. It contains ordinary white fluorescent lightbulbs set behind a plastic diffusing screen, which houses a film that filters out most of the ultraviolet [UV] rays from the bulbs."

Typically, the light emitted from these boxes is 10,000 lux in intensity, but Dr. Rosenthal mentioned that the eyes of children under the age of eight have greater sensitivity to light; thus, for them, less intense light sources should be used—for example, 2,500 lux. (Lux is a unit used to measure the intensity of light. Indoor light levels range from 200 to 700 lux; outdoor light levels on a sunny spring day range from 2,000 to well beyond 10,000 lux.)

A box that can be angled is best so that the light fixture can be positioned at an angle toward the eye and more light can enter. A child should sit approximately one to three feet from the light source and look up for a few seconds to the light every minute or so. A child can play video games in front of the light, watch television, or read. The treatment may take only fifteen minutes a day, and if there is any activation or hypomania, this timing can be scaled back. Dr. Rosenthal said it would take approximately two weeks to see a full response to the lights.

But how is a rapidly cycling child going to receive fifteen minutes of treatment between the hours of 12:00 and 3:00 P.M. on a school day? Well, this depends on how much a parent wants to keep this noninvasive intervention going (and whether the parent can afford two light boxes). One can be stationed at home for weekends and nonschool days, and one might be placed in a resource room or some area of the school where the child could go for fifteen minutes and do schoolwork while glancing into the light. (Since 3 to 4 percent of school-age children may suffer from SAD, the school might be willing to purchase a light box, or several parents could buy one together for their children's treatments.)

Dr. Rosenthal and Dr. Susan Swedo at the NIMH and Drs. Martin Teicher and Carol Glod at McLean Hospital in Massachusetts studied light therapy and dawn simulation together and found that the combined treatment worked well to reverse the depressive symptoms *and* helped the children get up in the morning.

Parents of a child with bipolar disorder can tell you how terribly difficult it is to awaken his or her child in the mornings for school. The children seem almost in an anesthetized state (some doctors refer to it as "sleep drunkenness") and no amount of coaxing, noisemaking, or screaming can get them up. One boy actually asked his mother to throw a pitcher of ice water on him in the morning. Then he instructed his mother to just jiggle the pitcher with the ice on the following mornings and his Pavlovian fear reaction would make him get out of bed. (The thought of a mass of wet bedding did not appeal to her, and she found the icy water treatment a bit sadistic, so we can't report if this self-styled method works or not.)

Dawn simulators seem much kinder and perhaps more scientific. This is a small electronic timer that can be plugged into an ordinary bedside lamp with a 60- to 100-watt-intensity bulb. It can be programmed to create an artificial dawn lasting between sixty to ninety minutes. In other words, if your child has to get up at 6:30 to make the school bus, the timer should be set at 5:00 or 5:30 A.M.

How does this work if the eyes are closed? we asked Dr. Rosenthal. "No one is really sure, but it may be that the eyes are particularly sensitive during the predawn hours and may be capable of responding to even the very small amounts of light that are transmitted through the child's closed eyelids." He added: "It may be that some phase-shifting is going on also."

There are quite a few light box manufacturers, and we will mention three here:

Apollo Light Systems Inc.
Orem, Utah
1-800-545-9667
http://www.apollolight.com

Northern Light Technologies
Montreal, Canada
1-800-263-0066
http://www.northernlight-tech.com

The SunBox Company sells both sunboxes and dawn simulators
Gaithersburg, Maryland
1-800 LITE-YOU (548-3968)
http://www.sunboxco.com

Light boxes cost between $200 and $500. A dawn simulator costs between $100 and $200. Some companies will rent you the box to see if it works and, if you buy it, deduct the rental fee from the total cost. Also, insurance companies may pay for the box if the child's doctor writes a letter detailing its medical necessity.

Electroconvulsive Therapy for Children

It's hard to imagine that a treatment that involves the distressing image of an electrical current passed through one or both hemispheres of the brain could result in a dramatic change in mood and energy, but, in fact, ECT as a treatment for depression, psychosis, suicidal impulses, and intractable mania is unsurpassed by any other treatment in psychiatry. It has evolved into a safe option, one that works. And it bears little resemblance to the way it was performed in the 1940s, from which came sadistic fictional characters such as Nurse Ratched in Ken Kesey's *One Flew Over the Cuckoo's Nest.*

In fact, ECT is especially safe for pregnant women who probably should not take drugs for depression or mania throughout the gestation period. But is it a safe option for children and adolescents? Won't the seizures "damage" a developing brain? According to case reports and reviews, apparently not. In 1990 Drs. Mark W. Bertagnoli and Carrie M. Borchardt published a review of the use of ECT in 151 children and adolescents ages five to nineteen years in which 67 percent of the children improved.

ECT is usually given to a child or adolescent three times the first week and twice each week thereafter for a total of six to nine or fifteen to twenty completely painless treatments. The number of treatments depends, of course, on the clinical response.

The child is put to sleep with a very short-acting barbiturate, and then the drug succinylcholine is administered. This medication temporarily paralyzes the muscles so that they do not contract during treatment and cause fractures. An electrode is then placed above the temple of the non-dominant (usually right) side of the head, and a second is placed in the middle of the forehead (this is called unilateral ECT); or one electrode is placed above each temple (this is called bilateral ECT). A very small current of electricity is passed through the brain causing a seizure. The child breathes pure oxygen through a mask, and the heart is monitored by an electrocardiogram (ECG) while the seizure activity is monitored by an electroencephalogram (EEG).

Since seizure thresholds in adolescents are notoriously low, the first treatment should be given at the minimum energy level; only if the seizure is not adequate should the energy be increased. Since adolescents develop tolerance quickly, the third or fourth treatment may call for increased energy. The child wakes up ten to fifteen minutes after treatment.

It is not unusual for a child to have a headache upon awakening, some muscle aches, confusion, and disorientation, and perhaps some nausea, but these side effects typically clear up within an hour or so of the treatment. The child will probably have no memory of the period surrounding the treatment, and studies in adults have found that experiences up to three weeks prior to the first treatment may not be consolidated in memory. We do know that unilateral ECT causes less immediate memory impairment than bilateral placement. With unilateral treatment, the individual usually experiences less confusion and disorientation after the seizure. However, there remains a question as to whether unilateral is as effective as bilateral treatment. Experts agree that in adults, memory losses may persist for up to several months posttreatment.

How Does ECT Work?

To this day, no one is sure how ECT works. Animal research shows that it enhances dopamine sensitivity, reduces the uptake of serotonin, and activates the systems in the brain that use norepinephrine. It definitely seems to increase the amount of the major inhibitory neurotransmitter, gamma amino butyric acid (GABA), and thereby increase inhibitory tone in the central nervous system. But much remains unclear about ECT's mechanism of action.

How Do Patients Feel About ECT?

A study done in England almost twenty years ago reported on interviews with seventy-two consecutive adult patients treated with ECT. Some of the questions asked were: "Were you frightened by the procedure?" "Were you angered by the experience?" "Would you ever have ECT again?"

Fifty-four percent of the sample said they considered a trip to the dentist more distressing. Many praised the treatment, and 81 percent said they would have ECT again.

Repeated Transcranial Magnetic Stimulation (r-TMS)

In Mozart's opera *Cosi Fan Tutte,* the young maid Despina dresses as a doctor and pretends to revive the two heroes who lie "dead" on the floor. She (he) brings forth a huge magnet and, with a grand flourish, bids everyone present to witness the remarkable curative powers of his great new invention. Sure enough, the heroes do rise to sing again.

The opera takes place in eighteenth-century Naples, but researchers from the National Institute of Mental Health, from Yale Medical School, from Germany and Israel, and from as far away as Tasmania are currently talking about a possible new treatment for depression using a coiled magnet aimed at the left prefrontal cortex of the brain.

Researchers at the NIMH wondered if magnetic waves could be used to speed up the motor nerve pathways in patients suffering with Parkinson's disease and found that some of the patients became less depressed.

Naturally there is great enthusiasm for a treatment that seems to have few side effects beyond an occasional headache, does not require anesthesia, and causes little or no discomfort, but much remains to be learned about this experimental therapy.

The treatment involves a patient sitting in a lounge chair while a small but powerful coiled electromagnet is placed on the scalp. This creates a strong magnetic field that passes through the skull. When this rapidly changing magnetic field encounters the brain's nerve cells, it causes an electric current that depolarizes them—in other words, the nerve cells fire.

The eight-inch coils in the electromagnet must be water-cooled because the electricity generates heat; and the patient wears ear protection because the treatment is noisy.

The patient receives forty stimulations in two seconds, and this is repeated twenty times. One patient described it as painless but a little like "having Woody Woodpecker on your head."

Dr. Mark George at the Medical University of South Carolina has transferred his research from the NIMH and is completing studies that show the treatment to be safe and effective.

Six open and three double-blind studies have all found that the treatment can be effective in depression, but many questions remain. For instance, what are the parameters of the treatment, how often must it be conducted, and how long do its effects last? The early studies with adults are giving the treatment five times a week for two weeks. It has been used with a very small number of adolescents, and Dr. George and his colleagues are now gathering data to show the FDA so that it can be used with adolescents (and eventually with children).

Apparently, some of the bipolar adult patients had excellent responses to r-TMS—it reduced their depression, and only one of the nine became slightly hypomanic. No mania was induced in any of the bipolar adult patients.

As we write, the machines needed to conduct treatment cost about $30,000, but these costs are going down, according to Dr. George, and he doesn't expect the treatments to be extremely expensive. He is hoping that the machines will be FDA-approved within two years.

Repeated transcranial magnetic stimulation therapy for depression is intriguing, without a doubt, and unlike Despina's little trick, it is backed by scientific evidence and measurement. Cautious optimism is advised.

Newer Antidepressant Drugs

Imipramine was discovered in the late 1950s, and it and other tricyclic antidepressants are named after their three-ring chemical structure. These drugs are effective against depression, but they have largely been displaced by the newer selective serotonin release inhibitors (the SSRIs), and atypical drugs such as bupropion (Wellbutrin), venlafaxine (Effexor), and mirtazapine (Remeron), which have a more benign side effect profile and are extremely difficult for patients to overdose on. The SSRIs and the other newer antidepressants are just as effective against depression as the tricyclic antidepressants, but their common side effects include:

- Sleepiness
- Insomnia
- Agitation
- Nausea
- Diarrhea
- Dry mouth
- Sexual dysfunction (Wellbutrin and Remeron do not cause this)

All SSRIs—Prozac, Zoloft, Paxil, Luvox, and Celexa—can produce withdrawal hypomania, and therefore need to be tapered slowly during the discontinuation period. For instance, if a child is taking 20 mg of

Paxil, then perhaps the medication should be reduced by 5 mg every five to ten days. If agitation, panic, or sleep problems follow the reduction, the tapering process should be lengthened and perhaps a benzodiazepine should be prescribed for that period of time. This is especially important with Paxil, Luvox, and Effexor because of their shorter half-lives.

Newer Antidepressants and Their Effects on Liver Enzymes

Prozac, Zoloft, Paxil, Luvox, Serzone, Effexor, and Celexa, to varying degrees, inhibit one or another of the liver enzymes that metabolize other medications. These enzymes are known as cytochrome P-450 isoenzymes, and their inhibition can result in increased circulating levels of medications listed in the chart. Note that Celexa weakly inhibits P-450 isoenzymes, so it is best to talk to a child's doctor before the child takes any prescription medications.

ANTIDEPRESSANT INHIBITION OF CYTOCHROME P-450 ISOENZYMES

PROZAC	ZOLOFT	PAXIL	LUVOX	SERZONE	EFFEXOR
phenytoin (Dilantin)	phenytoin	TCAs, anti-	theophylline,	carbamazepine	TCAs, anti-
diazepam (Valium)	diazepam	psychotics,	caffeine, TCAs,	alprazolam	psychotics
hexobarbital	hexobarbital	type 1C anti-	tacrine	triazolam	type 1C anti-
methobarbital	methobarbital	arrhythmics,		terfenadine	arrhythmics,
tolbutamide	tolbutamide	codeine,	carbamazepine	astemizole	codeine,
propranolol (Inderal)	propranolol	beta blockers	alprazolam	cigapride	beta blockers
			triazolam	(Propulsid)	
TCAs, anti-	TCAs (weak),	alprazolam	terfenadine		
psychotics,	antipsychotics,	(weak)	astemizole		
type 1C anti-	type 1C anti-				
arrhythmics,	arrhythmics,				
codeine,	codeine,				
beta blockers	beta blockers				
carbamazepine	carbamazepine				
(Tegretol)	alprazolam				
alprazolam (weak)	triazolam				
(Xanex)	terfenadine				
triazolam (Halcion)	astemizole				
terfenadine (Seldane)					
astemizole (Hismanal)					

Tricyclic Antidepressants (TCAs)

Tricyclic medications are still prescribed, and side effects of these drugs include:

- Sedation (drowsiness or sleepiness)
- Anticholinergic effects (dry mouth, blurred vision, constipation, difficulty urinating, increased heart rate, delirium)
- Orthostatic hypotension (light-headedness or dizziness when rising quickly from a sitting or lying position)
- Weight gain

The less commonly reported side effects of the tricyclic antidepressants are:

- Skin rash
- Sweating
- Tremor
- Altered orgasmic function

The anticholinergic side effects of the tricyclic antidepressants require some explaining. In addition to enhancing norepinephrine or serotonin transmission in order to combat depression, these drugs unfortunately also block the acetycholine receptors at the salivary glands (causing dry mouth) and at the iris of the eye (causing blurred vision). These drugs also affect the systems that regulate the contractions of the intestines and the bladder (causing constipation and urinary retention).

It is important to bear in mind that these side effects may decrease as the body adjusts to the medications.

When Should a Child Be Treated with an Antidepressant?

We thought it might be a good idea to explore several scenarios illustrating when and if a child with bipolar disorder should be exposed to an antidepressant.

A nine-year-old child is brought by her parents to a psychiatrist's office. She appears withdrawn, melancholic, and complains of feeling tired. She has been oversleeping and has sweet and carbohydrate cravings. The family history reveals that her alcoholic father has an explosive temper, and her maternal grandmother had been treated with ECT.

Since a high preponderance of bipolar adolescents and adults have a similar profile of "atypical symptoms" (fatigue, oversleeping, and carbohydrate cravings) when they become depressed, this triad should be considered a risk factor for a bipolar vulnerability.

Given the risk factors on both maternal and paternal sides of the family and the "atypical" symptoms of depression that are classically found in bipolar disorder, and based on our current state of knowledge, this child would have a high risk of mania and the onset of rapid cycling if exposed to antidepressant treatment.

Prescription: The first intervention might be to start bright light treatment in the morning or midday coupled with a dawn simulator set an hour in advance of the usual time of current morning awakening. If the depressive symptoms are unabated after two to three weeks of treatment, what are the options? Because ECT is not typically used in nine-year-olds, it is an unlikely choice. Therefore, in preparation for the likelihood of starting the child on antidepressant treatment, a mood stabilizer such as lithium, Trileptal, or Depakote should be introduced until a therapeutic level is reached, at which point an antidepressant medication such as bupropion (Wellbutrin) can be prescribed. If Wellbutrin is deemed necessary, it should be started at a low dose—either 18.25 mg or 37.5 mg, and then the doctor and parents should wait seven to ten days to observe whether this low dose has an effect, or whether it is activating. If it is neither activating nor effective at that dose, it should be raised incrementally by 18.25 mg every seven to ten days.

This is not the standard method of dosing in the field, however. Generally it is common practice to start treatment as high as 100 mg and increase the dose to 200 or 300 mg over a three-week period. But clinical experience in treating children with bipolar disorder has suggested that this higher dosing pattern is more likely to induce such adverse effects as manic induction, increased cycling, and even psychosis, despite the presence of a mood stabilizer.

The parents of a ten-year-old boy take him to a psychiatrist for an evaluation because they are concerned about their son's severe obsessive-compulsive symptoms, hand washing, and showering. He washes his hands approximately fifty times a day, and they are chafed and reddened. He has had several previous episodes of depression and has been increasingly irritable with pronounced temper tantrums, racing thoughts, and difficulty sleeping at night. He says that unless he goes to sleep with a radio or television turned on in his room he becomes extremely fearful. His mind is filled with thoughts that something terrible will happen to his parents as well as to him.

The boy tells the doctor that in the past few months his mood goes up and down. Sometimes he's happy; sometimes he's sad. Some days he awakes filled with energy and feels really good. Then he gets really down on himself and doesn't know why.

His father has been diagnosed with bipolar disorder and his mother with recurrent depressions. She has had periods of bulimia. The boy had been diagnosed with obsessive-compulsive disorder and separation anxiety disorder.

Although the OCD symptoms are the primary concern of the boy and his parents, the fact that the father has a bipolar disorder and the mother a recurrent mood disorder, coupled with the boy's current mood and anxiety symptoms, should raise concerns about the likelihood of a bipolar disorder evolving.

Prescription: Beginning treatment with a mood stabilizer would be a prudent first step in the treatment plan.

Once adequate therapeutic levels have been reached, and the boy reports feeling more even-keeled and his sleep has improved, it is important to reassess the nature and intensity of the OCD symptoms. If they persist, behavioral treatments that can reduce obsessive-compulsive symptoms, especially with the addition of an antianxiety medication such as gabapentin (Neurontin) or clonazepam (Klonopin), might be the next step.

If these treatments fail to bring relief, adding an SSRI such as Luvox (fluvoxamine) may be the next most likely treatment.

A fifteen-year-old young woman comes to a psychiatrist's office with her parents and complains of a loss of energy, down mood, and wanting to sleep long hours. She also tells the doctor that she has been consuming large quantities of mint chocolate chip ice cream every day and cannot stop herself.

These symptoms began in early September, and she recalled that the same set of symptoms had occurred in each of the previous two years in late autumn and continued through the early spring. In fact, she typically experienced improvements in energy and mood throughout the spring and summer months. Then, in mid-August of this year, she became extremely active, stayed out late at night, and grew argumentative and oppositional when her parents tried to set a curfew.

As mentioned, many individuals with bipolar disorder commonly experience regular seasonal episodes. The pattern of fall depressions and spring-summer hypomania is one of the most common and has been termed seasonal affective disorder (SAD).

Prescription: This fifteen-year-old would be best treated with bright light therapy during the fall and winter months. Her behavior, activity level, sleep/wake cycle, and mood state in the summer months should be monitored for hypomania. If this pattern continues, a mood stabilizer such as lithium carbonate or Tegretol should be considered.

Stimulants

Attention-deficit disorder with hyperactivity (ADHD) is a behavioral disorder that appears to have a strong genetic component and to involve dysregulation of the norepinephrine and dopamine neurotransmitter systems. ADHD is characterized by inattention, impulsiveness, and hyperactivity. These behaviors, which may appear at home, at school, or in other social situations, are generally worse in situations requiring sustained attention; as a result, academic underachievement is a frequently associated problem.

Although the onset of ADHD usually occurs before the age of four, it is most commonly diagnosed when a child enters school. Four percent of school-age children are said to be affected, and it occurs six times more often in boys than girls.

The majority of individuals who have pure ADHD respond to an adequate trial of one of the four available stimulants: dextroamphetamine sulphate (Dexedrine), methylphenidate hydrochloride (Ritalin), and pemoline (Cylert), and a combination of dextroamphetamine and levoamphetamine (Adderall). An extended-release methylphenidate (Concerta) is now available.

But a child who has bipolar disorder will also manifest the cardinal symptoms of ADHD (inattention, impulsiveness, and hyperactivity). And as we discussed in Chapter 2, it is not unusual for these symptoms to be early manifestations of bipolar disorder or for a child to carry a dual diagnosis: It appears as if he or she has both disorders concomitantly.

Distinguishing whether a child has pure ADHD, bipolar disorder, or both is complicated. (See Chapter 2 for a complete discussion of the differential diagnosis.)

One might ask: How could a simple trial of a drug that is so commonly prescribed and that wears off in a number of hours be detrimental to a child's well-being? Out of seventy-three children in our study who were diagnosed initially with ADHD and subsequently treated with stimulant medications, 65 percent were thrown into manic or depressed states or became psychotic on these drugs.

A recent report by Dr. Melissa DelBello and her colleagues at the University of Cincinnati College of Medicine evaluated thirty-four adolescents who were hospitalized for mania. Using a retrospective chart review and interviews with the parents and the adolescents themselves, the researchers systematically determined the age of onset of the bipolar disorder and the pharmacological treatment history.

Although this was a small sample, they found that the adolescents with bipolar disorder who had a history of stimulant exposure prior to the onset of the bipolar disorder manifested the bipolar illness at an earlier age than those without prior stimulant exposure. Additionally, bipolar adolescents treated with at least two stimulant medications had a younger age of onset compared with those who were treated with only one stimulant medication.

Why might this be so? Stimulants directly increase the release of the neurotransmitters dopamine and norepinephrine. Both of these neurotransmitters have long been implicated as associated with bipolar disorder. Indeed, one theory with a significant body of evidence suggests that an increase in dopamine and norepinephrine transynaptically results in a switch into mania. Therefore, the use of stimulants on a daily basis, potentiating an excess release of these neurotransmitters, could interact with a genetic predisposition for bipolar disorder, perhaps precipitating an earlier onset of the illness.

While stimulants may positively address attentional issues, they may also negatively affect other areas of the brain such as the amygdala. Dopamine pathways in the amygdala have been known to directly influence the modulation of aggression.

As yet, there is no consensus in the field and no established guidelines in the pediatric psychopharmacology literature regarding either the use or witholding of stimulant drugs. However, the following clinical scenarios should give families pause before pursuing treatment with stimulant drugs:

- There is a strong family history of bipolar disorder.
- Prolonged temper tantrums and mood swings are present along with symptoms of inattention, impulsiveness, and hyperactivity.
- The child is oppositional and defiant.
- The child appears to have better behavior at school and a marked deterioration of behavior in the home.
- The child is explosive and manifests aggressive behavior toward parents and siblings.
- The child has severe separation anxiety, night terrors, and a fascination with gore and mayhem.

When some children who appear to have both bipolar disorder and attention-deficit disorder with hyperactivity are treated with a mood stabilizer, they suffer much less distractibility, inattention, impulsive behaviors, and hyperactivity. (In these cases, it would seem that the "ADHD" symptoms were merely part of the bipolar disorder.) However, other children experience mood stabilization yet continue to have attentional problems. Now the question becomes: Is it safe to give them stimulant medication after a therapeutic level of a mood stabilizer has been achieved?

A number of clinical investigators have reported anecdotally that the addition of stimulant medication to a regimen of one or more mood stabilizers, for the purpose of treating residual attentional problems, can be effective. However, recent private conversations with other investigators who are engaged in treatment trials in bipolar children and adolescents have raised concerns about this practice, particularly with high doses of stimulants. The children *seem* to tolerate lower doses without untoward effects. However, long-term studies have not been conducted that would allow any conclusions about long-term stimulant use in bipolar children.

This is a particularly important area for controlled clinical trials, and until such studies are completed, the clinical treatment of the ADHD aspect of bipolar disorder will remain unclear.

Are Generics Just as Good?

Once the doctor and the parents agree to try a child on a medication, or a combination of medications, the physician writes the prescription(s) and the parent troops off to the pharmacy to have them filled. But the first question the pharmacist will ask is: "Do you want the generic or brand-name version of the drug?"

In the cases of Depakote (divalproex sodium), Neurontin (gabapentin), Lamictal (lamotrigine), Risperdal (risperidone), or Zyprexa (olanzapine), and so on, there is no generic version. They are all under patent. But for many older drugs, including Tegretol (carbamazepine), Klonopin (clonazepam), Haldol (haloperidol), Mellaril (thioridazine), and others, there are generic equivalents that are usually much cheaper, and managed care companies would prefer you to use the generic formulations.

Most people assume that a generic version of a drug is identical to a brand-name drug, merely minus all the exorbitant advertising in glossy magazines and trade journals. They also reason that the generic companies don't have the enormous expense of maintaining the huge sales staff known as detail men (many of them are women) who visit doctors at their offices and attempt to get them to dispense their drugs.

But while generic versions are cheaper to produce (after all, the generic company did not spend the $500 million it takes to develop a drug today), the FDA does not require generic drugs to be carbon copies of the brand-name drugs.

The active chemical ingredients must be the same, and the strength, the route of administration, and the dosage form (tablet versus capsule) must be identical. But the FDA allows other variations: The inert ingredients such as binders, fillers, color, and flavoring can differ, and often the manufacturing process itself is distinct from that of the brand-name drug. However, the generics must be shown to be "bioequivalent" to the brand-name drug. They must deliver the same amount of active ingredients into the patient's bloodstream in the same amount of time as the brand-name medication. (Incidentally, brand-name drugs are subject to the same bioequivalency tests as generics when their manufacturers reformulate them.)

Parents should know that many brand-name manufacturers package their own brand-name drugs as generics so as not to lose market share to their generic competitors, and that almost 80 percent of the U.S. generic drug production is done by brand-name firms in modern manufacturing plants.

At this point, most of the mood-stabilizing medications (except for lithium and carbamazepine) are under patent, as are many of the antipsychotic medications typically prescribed for children with bipolar disorder. For instance, there is no generic version of Risperdal, Zyprexa, or Seroquel. Lithium—even in its slow- or sustained-release forms—is rather inexpensive, but of the drugs that do have generic versions, should a parent opt for the generic or the brand name?

Because there's been some problem with carbamazepine (the generic version of Tegretol), it might be best to use Tegretol. It might also be wise to begin treatment of any other medication with the brand-name drug, and if the child has a good response, the generic can then be considered.

The major problem with generic prescriptions is that a pharmacy may buy from different suppliers from time to time (or a parent may fill a prescription at a different pharmacy whose drugs are supplied from a different manufacturer). Since no two drugs are able to be superimposed perfectly (nor are they supposed to be), blood levels may change, behavior and side effects may change, and all of this will be problematic for the child and the family. If the child is switched from a brand-name to a generic drug, or from one generic to another, and the parents note adverse effects or behavioral changes, it's a good idea to check the blood levels about two weeks after the change is made to ensure that proper levels are maintained.

Of course, a patient may have no choice about generic versus brand-name decisions if the managed care company decides that a drug is too expensive and does not list it on the company's formulary (its list of approved drugs). In such cases, the parent can pay for the brand-name drug him- or herself or agree to try one of the drugs that is covered. (These tend to be the older, cheaper medications.) All parents should check their insurance company's drug formulary and discuss its latitude with the psychiatrist before a decision is made about prescriptions.

So, understanding all of this, let us close this section by pointing out that everyone should comparison shop for medications. The same medication in three drugstores in the same neighborhood can have three very different prices. Also, purchase the largest-size tablet or capsule available, consistent with the dosage prescribed. A patient taking 1,000 mg of Depakote a day would pay less for two 500 mg tablets than for four 250 mg tablets.

Sometimes a child needs half of a tablet for his or her dosing regimen, and parents spend a lot of time with pills flying through the air as they try to cut them. One mother cleverly joked that she is "preparing for her next life as a diamond cutter in Amsterdam." Inexpensive cutters are available that catch all the pieces, and some pharmacies will compound the smaller doses in tablet or capsule form (to the specifications of the prescribing physician) and ship them overnight, anywhere in the country. Naturally, this will be more expensive. Check with your local pharmacy for a referral.

What If a Family Can't Afford Prescription Medications?

Many psychotropic drugs are extremely expensive and many of the pharmaceutical companies have special programs to assist parents who can't afford the medications their children need. The treating physician typically has to fill out a form to apply for free medications, but the website called http://www.NeedyMeds.com lists most of the meds and gives the manufacturers' contact numbers, program guidelines (including how much a family can earn in a year and still qualify for the program), and directions for the doctors initiating the enrollment. This website makes it easier for both parents and doctors.

HOW TO GET A CHILD TO TAKE A MEDICATION

All of us have stories about our attempts to give balky children medication, and some of us still have stains on rugs and furniture where the medicine was spit out or the spoon was knocked out of a frustrated parental hand. So, how, we wondered, do you get a medication into a child who is smack in the middle of a rage or who refuses to take it?

We asked this question of many parents and got a variety of answers. Some parents bribed their child if he or she was not raging. The toy-for-spoonful trade can be effective but quite expensive. One mother told us that she simply said to her child: "You have a choice: You can take this now or we can go to the hospital where they can give you a shot." She said that usually earns her more cooperation.

One mother on the BPParents listserv wrote that: "He is on 1,000 mg now and doing much better, especially with the rages! He must be able to tell a difference, because he doesn't give me a hard time about taking his meds anymore."

We were quite taken with one father's idea: He and his wife take their vitamins, blood pressure pills, and other medications together when their daughter takes her medications so she doesn't feel she's doing anything out of the ordinary.

In Chapter 12 we discuss the particular problem of teens on medications and how to deal with it.

Drugs to Be Avoided by Children with Bipolar Disorder

The following prescription and over-the-counter drugs and even herbs can cause hypomania, mania, mixed states, rapid cycling, or increased aggression in children who are bipolar:

- Beta blockers (such as propranolol). These drugs can induce depression. (Sometimes they are needed with an antipsychotic medication, however.)
- Caffeine. It acts on certain second messenger systems that may contribute to activation and arousal. (See the section on cyclic AMP, pages 228–29, in Chapter 8.)
- Imipramine or desipramine used to treat bedwetting. (The nasal spray desmopressin [DDAVP] seems to be safe.)
- Nitrous Oxide (laughing gas used at dentists' offices).
- Steroids, particularly cortisol derivatives. Even topically applied agents, such as hydrocortisone 1 percent, if applied to richly vascularized areas such as the scalp, the hands, or the face, have been known to induce hypomania. Parents should try to ensure that their child has reduced exposure to poison ivy, oak, and the like—any rash necessitating the use of steroids. (However, steroid use for the treatment of severe asthma may be essential as asthma is a life-threatening illness. The pediatrician and psychiatrist should be in close communication during the time of steroid treatment and during the weaning-off period.)
- St. John's wort or Ginkgo biloba. St. John's wort has several active ingredients that can activate a bipolar child.
- Sudafed (or any medication with pseudoephedrine). It acts on the noradrenergic system, increasing norepinephrine and therefore increasing arousal and anxiety states.

Dealing with the Disillusionment of a Failed Medication Trial

It is highly unlikely that the doctor will hit upon the right drug and dose right away for every child. What works for one child may fail miserably for another or produce intolerable side effects. Unfortunately, psychopharmacology is still very much of a guessing game, guided by experience and perhaps good luck. Many, many parents have had to deal with their hopes being dashed when their child doesn't respond, responds poorly, or is unable to tolerate the side effects of the medication or medications. During the search period (which can last quite a while), the child and the family become deeply distressed and demoralized. As one mother graphically put it, "I think if all of us at once flushed all the medications that didn't work or caused too many side effects, we would back up the sewer systems."

Therefore, we thought it might be helpful to quote from parents who've been through many medication trials and who have finally happened upon the right regimen for their child.

I won't go through the gory details, but suffice it to say "been there, done that." We tried over ten different medications in varying combinations with zero luck. Then last spring we were put in a study for the drug _____.

Within four weeks my son was a different person. Actually, he was coming back to being the kid we always thought he could be. I'm happy to report that he is back in public school and though we still have our "moments," we are actually getting to the point where we get angry at him for all the normal stuff (like: "get your feet off the sofa!") without feeling like we are taking our lives in our hands.

The medication part can take some time. Doctors throw the dice, come up with some combination, and finally see some results. For example, the Depakote helped Alicia, but when the lithium was added, it helped a bit more, and so on and so on. She has been on nine meds. Then when you start doing combos, sometimes you don't know what has worked and what you might possibly remove. Some things put them on the ceiling; some on the floor. Finding the middle ground takes time. Just when you think you have found it, your kid grows a few inches, puts on a few pounds, etc. Hang in there!

Everyone responds so differently to meds. I believe you have to keep trying and "turning over all the stones" with the meds. I have found it helpful to keep a journal, especially when trying new meds, to note behaviors, etc. I have also compiled a list of all the meds he has been on and the doses, the effects, and so on. We are up to twenty-four meds in three years! The list is very helpful to look back on.

Fortunately, we found a combination of meds and he is doing quite well now.

We thought it appropriate to close this chapter in much the way we opened it: with one more story of a child who feels and behaves well now, who is once again capable of smiling and participating in life, in family life, *and in her childhood*—all due to treatment with the proper medication.

After years of tantrums and misbehaviors that only another bipolar parent could understand, Micaela has finally been placed on medication that is making a huge difference.

A while ago, my husband went to Micaela's weekly doctor appointment. He said to the doctor: "We can't stand it anymore. We can't live with her. You have to do something. It's been five years. You have to help us."

His upset was so great that the doctor finally agreed to try something different. (She hadn't, to this point, agreed with the diagnosis of bipolar disorder that two previous psychiatrists had given.) She tapered the existing med (an SSRI) and then started Micaela on Lithobid a week later.

The first week on Lithobid was awful. The SSRI had finally left her system and the lithium hadn't kicked in. Then a powerful change began to take place.

The child was transformed. She can wait for things now. We can say "no" to her. She can accept disappointment. She has stopped teasing and tormenting her sibs. She has been getting along with her sister. They even asked to go back to sharing a room. A month ago, her sister Anna (age nine) was saying that she wished she lived with another family because she hated Micaela so much she would give up living with the rest of us just to get away from her.

Micaela is sweet and loving and funny. She asked me yesterday if she could help me fold the laundry. She came home an hour early last night from a neighbor's house because it got to be "too much" for her (the noise, excitement), and she was attuned to herself enough to know she couldn't take it anymore.

Her behaviors were *not* part of her personality. She was *not* suffering from "middle-child syndrome." She was *not* trying to get more attention focused on herself. My husband and I are *not* bad parents. She was ill, and after many years, countless hours of anguish, many lost friendships, months of lost learning and schoolwork, a lifetime of heartache, she is better.

It's not perfect. She wigs out a little at night. We also have her on risperidone, and we moved the dosing time from bedtime to 5:00 P.M., which helps. We're thrilled with the 80 to 85 percent that we have her "normal." We'll gladly take the small percentage of time when she's her "old" self. She has no side effects to the medications. She remains bubbly and chipper.

I am so grateful for what has happened. I will take it as it comes and not dare hope that this will last a lifetime. But I now have hope and I now have proof that I have a wonderful child who was trapped in a prison of her illness. Seeing her like this makes it all worthwhile, and I am so thankful that we never gave up as we were tempted to so many times.

I hope this will give a lift to someone who may be struggling at this point and wondering if there will ever be an end in sight. Don't give up the fight!

Charting the Course of the Disorder

Typically, a doctor might see a child suffering with bipolar disorder once a month or less. Parents, however, live with the child twenty-four hours a day. Parents dispense the medications, observe and deal with side effects, and are privy to (and sometimes the target of) all the behaviors and moods of the child. They *must* be viewed as partners of the treatment team—the on-site experts who contribute all the vital information to the treating physician and therapists.

While many parents keep a written journal noting their child's behaviors, sleeping patterns, daily stressors, and so on, a more graphic representation—a cycle chart—is invaluable to the doctor making the diagnosis and prescribing the medications as well as to the therapist conducting the psychotherapy and to the parents themselves.

WHY IS A CYCLE CHART SO IMPORTANT?

A cycle chart is a chronological account of changes that occur within the day, from day to day, week to week, and through the course of the year. It helps to determine the cycle length and the nature of the episodes. Recording a child's variations in mood and shifts in energy over time in the form of a simple continuous graph provides a visual display of the course of the illness and brings into focus the specific symptoms and behaviors that define the condition. A cycle chart can help determine if the child is a rapid, ultrarapid, or ultra-ultrarapid cycler; if the child is in a mixed state; or whether periods of depression or mania dominate the clinical picture. The chart also helps determine whether the medications the child is taking are working to stabilize his or her mood or are worsening the symptoms and increasing the cycle frequency. In addition, a chart can guide decisions concerning maintenance treatment. It can identify periods of heightened vulnerability when a breakthrough episode is more likely to occur (for example, many children experience greater periods of depression in the fall and become more activated in early spring), so that the doctor knows when to modify or augment the medication regimen or increase the frequency of therapy sessions.

Creating a Cycle Chart

One chart often used in research studies is the Kiddie-Life Chart method, available free of charge from the National Depressive and Manic Association at (800) 82-NDMDA; www.ndmda.org. Some parents find this chart rather complex, so we present a simpler method that captures the most important information. The type of chart used is less important than the fact that some regular records are kept. This section describes how to develop and use a cycle frequency chart.

Because many bipolar children cycle so rapidly, and have cycles within cycles, it becomes necessary to plot symptoms and behavioral changes to be able to view these daily variations, as well as longer-duration episodes. Not only can there be cycles within cycles, but changes may occur on a seasonal basis. Each chart is constructed to accommodate daily information collected over monthly periods, so that each day, each week, and each month can be reviewed over time.

A sample chart that may be photocopied and enlarged for personal use is included here. The chart is divided into five separate categories: sleep, medications, anger, energy, and mood. There is a separate row to record the days of the month. For girls, this row can be used to record the days of their menstrual cycles as well as their premenstrual days. Additionally, one row (the "stressor" row) should be set aside to make notations for stressful or anxiety-producing events, such as separations, trouble at school, losses, embarrassments, or rejections, whether they are real or perceived.

Mood	Energy	Anger	Medications	Sleep
			List starting doses for each	

Mood chart grid with column headers: Mood, Energy, Anger, Medications (List starting doses for each), Sleep.

Energy scale markings: 0, -2, -3, -4, -5

Anger scale markings: 30 min., 40, 50, >50, STRESSOR

Mood scale: -3 -2 -1 0 +1 +2 +3 +4 +5

Sleep legend:
- Sleep Awakenings ●
- Night Terrors ▲
- Sleepwalking ⌇
- TOTAL HOURS SLEPT
- TIME ASLEEP–TIME ARISE
- DAY

Sleep time markings repeated per row: 10 12 1 2 3 4 5 / 7 10 12 3 6 10 12

Sleep

Bipolar children commonly report difficulty getting up, sleepiness, low energy, and poor concentration in the morning, with gradual increases in energy and initiative as the day goes on. Late afternoon and evening frequently bring a marked increase in energy levels, and the mood can become elated or irritable—or both—as bedtime approaches.

These children have a natural inclination to delay sleep later and later into the night, as mental functions become more active. (The daily pattern may vary in intensity depending on seasonal change or, for girls, on the menstrual cycle.) It is important to record whether the child is experiencing racing thoughts and increased arousal levels, because there is growing evidence that sleep loss may induce or intensify episodes of mania or hypomania in predisposed individuals.

Dr. Thomas Wehr and his colleagues at the National Institute of Mental Health have reported that the majority of a group of depressed, rapid-cycling bipolar patients switched into mania or hypomania the day after they were deprived of sleep *for one night.* The results of sleep deprivation experiments strongly suggest that the insomnia caused by mania, in turn, exacerbates or sustains mania. In this way, sleep loss arising from a variety of causes (including that caused by jet travel through time zones) could set in motion a hypomanic or manic episode that becomes self-perpetuating. This possibility underscores the importance of monitoring the sleep/wake cycle and of intervening with the appropriate sedative medication to preserve a regular cycle. Depending on the degree of activation, any of a number of drugs may be prescribed to put a brake on the hypomanic symptoms and to induce timely sleep.

Documenting any changes that occur in the sleep cycle can be helpful in the early recognition of cycle onsets (see top section of chart). The daily sleep period is recorded as the previous night's sleep, and the box to be filled in is divided in half, the section above the midline intended to record the occurrence of any sleep disturbances. There are three to choose from: sleep awakenings, night terrors, and sleepwalking. These can be signified by specific symbols (for example, for sleep awakenings, a filled in circle; night terrors, a triangle; and sleepwalking, a jagged vertical line), which can be added to the chart according to the time they occurred, between 10:00 P.M. and 5:00 A.M. The time spent sleeping can be noted on the bottom portion of the section; this should reflect the time elapsed from when the child first falls asleep to the time when the child gets up in the morning (for instance, 10:00 P.M. to 7:00 A.M. = 9 hours). Decreases or increases in the amount of sleep may signal an impending episode; longer sleep intervals may precede depression, and shorter sleep intervals, hypomania or mania.

Medications

It is not uncommon for doctors to try a bipolar child on a variety of medications until his or her mood is stabilized. Careful and consistent documentation of the dosages and duration of these trials as well as the side effects experienced provides the treating psychiatrist with critical information. The medication time line offers a review at a glance of what has and has not worked. It also indicates whether the levels were adequate or the trials of sufficient duration.

The names of drugs that the child is taking should be listed with the starting doses for that month noted in a separate section. Then plot the times the child takes each medication; the numbers on the table reflect morning, late morning, midday, afternoon, evening, and bedtime administration.

The upper part of each daily medication box is used for any change in dosage or in time of administration that occurs over the course of treatment, as well as for recording the blood levels of the drug (the parent should get these levels from the doctor). For example, as shown in Samantha's chart, page 157, where each column represents two days, a child who was previously taking 500 mg of Depakote (two 250 mg doses at 10:00 P.M.) is gradually increased by 250 mg increments over six days by the addition of 250 mg at 7:00 A.M. on days 3 and 4 and again on days 5 and 6. The final increase on day 7 was added at 10:00 P.M. to avoid daytime sedation. By carefully charting medication dosage changes, the improvement in symptoms or the development of side effects are more directly attributable to a specific change over time.

Anger: Temper Tantrums and Rages

Frequent and prolonged temper tantrums associated with aggressive, and sometimes violent, behaviors are among the most common features of early-onset bipolar disorder reported by parents. Recording the frequency and duration of these episodes can be a useful barometer in helping to diagnose the illness and determine the effectiveness of mood-stabilizing medications.

In the third section of the chart, "Anger," is recorded—both the extent or degree of temper tantrums or rage attacks and the duration of an episode. One of four stepwise peaks can be chosen, and in the lower section the time duration for each episode is recorded (30-, 40-, 50-, or > 50-minute periods).

Many parents report that stimulants and antidepressant drugs of all classes intensify these episodes and that their use is often associated with an increased frequency of cycling. Whether this happens is extremely important to establish for each child.

Noting any changes in the cycling pattern or in the rate and duration of temper tantrums would help the parents and the doctor know whether these drugs are detrimental to the child. Similarly, determining whether there is a reduction in symptoms following the slow withdrawal of these medications would serve the same purpose.

Energy—From Lethargy to Hyperactivity

It is not unusual for a child to experience frequent, sudden, and dramatic energy switches within a single day. It may be difficult for children to think about and express clearly in words these variations in their energy and activity levels without the use of a metaphor that captures some intrinsic quality of these changes. We have found the simple analogy of five mountains and five valleys to be extremely helpful in determining their energy levels.

Questions such as: "Did you have so much energy that you could have climbed mountain number 1, 2, 3, 4, or 5?" Or, "Did your energy level drop into the valley, and how deep into the valley did it drop?"; and "How quickly did these changes occur?" will often engage them, and allow them to choose more easily between eleven graded levels (0 to +5 or 0 to −5), and to record them along a continuum. Parents record the number of switches from low- to high-energy states within the day in the small rectangle that appears in the top right-hand corner of the daily energy box (see page 147).

SEVERETY LEVEL	TYPE OF MOOD AND SYMPTOMS	FUNCTIONAL IMPAIRMENT
Level+1 to +2	Increase in energy Increase in activity Enthusiastic, more social	Minimal or none Performance may improve in some areas Functions well at school and home
Level+3	Elated or irritable Hypertalkative Insistent and overinvolved Decreased need for sleep	Difficulty with goal-directed activity Feels productive but may not be (starts many projects without finishing)
Level+4	Grandios and/or tantrums Marked periods of increased energy Flights of ideas, racing thoughts Increased sexual interest/activity Impulsive or reckless behaviors	Gets in trouble at school or with family Cannot focus attention Others comment about behavior Poor judgment
Level+5	Feels invincible, challenges authority Explosive, angry, potentially violent Excessive energy, driven, reckless Hallucinations and/or delusions	Needs close supervision Unable to function at school, major conflicts at home Bizarre behaviors, in trouble with the law Requires hospitalization
Level −1 to −2	Periods of mild sadness or melancholy Sluggish, complains of low energy in the morning Feels bored	Minimal or no impairment Have to push to arise in the morning
Level −3	Depressed moods, feels hopeless Tearful, anxious, irritable Decreased energy, concentration, increased sleep	Extra effort needed to function and sustain interest Difficulty performing tasks Attentional problems at school
Level −4	Unable to enjoy things, appetite disturbance Marked loss of energy, very slowed down Socially withdrawn, isolated Irritable, agitated	Much extra effort needed to function Significant impairment in school and at home Misses many days at school
Level −5	Unable to care for self, very agitated, pacing, suicidal Marked impairment of short-term memory Morbid and/or paranoid delusions	Not in school; in bed much of time Requires hospitalization

Adapted from the Stanley Foundation Bipolar Network Early Intervention Initiative Survey.

Mood

The final section of the chart is for entering variations in mood during the course of the day. Because of the rapid fluctuations that are common with the disorder, two and possibly three recordings would be ideal to document the often dramatic changes in mood states observed between morning and evening. Objectively determining changes of mood within oneself is not easy for anyone and may be more problematic for a child when mixed symptoms predominate, or when there are many rapid switches throughout the day. The chart on page 151 provides sample descriptors for each state. Each descriptor is linked with a numerical value, 0 to +5 and 0 to −5, denoting types of symptoms, degree of functional impairment, and severity level.

EXAMPLES OF CHARTING

The following charts are examples of two patients: one with childhood-onset bipolar disorder and another whose mood swings started in early adolescence.

Keith

When Keith's parents first went for a consultation, they told the psychiatrist that their ten-year-old son had been experiencing a number of symptoms for at least several months, beginning in the late fall. They described a persistent fatigue and lack of energy, difficulties getting him out of bed in the morning, and struggles over getting him to dress for school. Keith had multiple physical complaints, and his parents could see his general lack of initiative and irritable and depressed moods, often culminating in explosive bursts of anger. They also noted that the irritability seemed to be more prominent at night and that Keith was beginning to experience difficulty getting to sleep.

Keith's teachers reported that he was fidgety, that he often seemed to be daydreaming, and that he appeared unable to concentrate or sustain interest in classroom activities.

Because of the prevailing depressive symptoms, the diagnosis of major depression was made, and Keith was started on one of the newer antidepressants in the first week of January with an increase in dosage after two weeks. Clonidine was added at night as Keith had more trouble getting to sleep at night. About fourteen days later, Keith's parents noted that his activity and energy level improved and that he seemed to have more initiative. His teachers reported improved concentration with school assignments and in the classroom. At the same time, however, his mood became more irritable—particularly in the late afternoons and evenings. The flashes of anger that had previously been short-lived became more pronounced, and on one occasion Keith smashed his fist into a wall. Along with this late-evening irascibility, he became more agitated and distractible and was having more difficulty getting to sleep. During this period Keith described himself as feeling very nervous and angry, and his parents described an increase in both oppositional defiant and social withdrawal behaviors, which raised the level of family tension significantly.

The psychiatrist prescribed an additional dose of clonidine in the late afternoon. This caused Keith to become more sedated, and he was able to fall asleep more easily at bedtime, but his sleep was fitful and he had many awakenings. One morning, after a night of poor sleep, Keith told his parents that he felt "hyper" and that his thoughts were "speeded up." His temper tantrums became explosive and prolonged and his thinking became paranoid as he became increasingly threatened by the thought that wolves were going to devour him in the night.

Because of the emergence of delusional thoughts, the doctor prescribed 2 mg of Risperdal at bedtime. Keith began to sleep through the night, and gradually the paranoid thinking resolved. When the antidepressant was withdrawn he stopped having explosive rages but continued to show rapid shifts in mood with wide variations between low energy and depression in the morning and irritability and high energy in the evening every day for another two weeks.

Keith's chart over eight weeks, had it been constructed, would have looked like the charts on pages 154 and 155. The data have been averaged over a month's period on the charts with each column representing the average over four days of entries.

Three months later, in May, after another period of sleepless activation possibly occasioned by the change of seasons, Keith again suffered pronounced temper tantrums and rages. This time the doctor started him on lithium carbonate.

After reaching a blood level of 0.9 mEq/liter, Keith's rapidly fluctuating mood and energy swings became muted, and the Risperdal and clonidine were gradually tapered and discontinued.

This turbulent nine-month period could have been avoided had an ear-

Keith's chart—1st 4 weeks

Mood	Energy	Anger	Medications — List starting doses for each	Sleep

Energy scale: 0+1, 0-2, 0+3, 0-4, 0+5

Anger: 30 min. 40 50 >50 · STRESSOR

Mood scale: -5 -4 -3 -2 -1 0 +1 +2 +3 +4 +5

Medications:
- Paxil 10 mg. 1x daily
- Clonidine 0.5 mg. 1x daily

Sleep legend:
- Sleep Awakenings ●
- Night Terrors ▲
- Sleepwalking ⋛

TOTAL HOURS SLEPT
TIME ASLEEP–TIME ARISE
DAY

DAY	TOTAL HOURS SLEPT	TIME ASLEEP–TIME ARISE
1–4	8 1/2	10:00 pm — 7:30 am
5–8	8 1/2	10:00 pm — 7:30 am
9–12	8 1/2	10:00 pm — 7:30 am
13–16	8 1/2	10:00 pm — 7:30 am
17–20	8 1/2	11:00 pm — 8:00 am
21–24	6 1/2	11:30 pm — 6:00 am
25–28	6 1/2	11:30 pm — 6:00 am

Sleep hour scale: 10 12 1 2 3 4 5 / 7 10 12 3 6 10 12

Mood	Energy	Anger	Medications *List starting doses for each*	Sleep

Keith's chart — 2nd 4 weeks

Column headers (Sleep section): Sleep Awakenings ● / Night Terrors ▲ / Sleepwalking Ƶ / TOTAL HOURS SLEPT / TIME ASLEEP–TIME ARISE / DAY

Anger: 30 min. 40 50 >50 / STRESSOR

Medications: Paxil 10 mg. 2x daily / Clonidine 0.5 mg. 1x daily / Risperdal 2 mg. 1x daily

DAY	TOTAL HOURS SLEPT	TIME ASLEEP–TIME ARISE
1–4	5 1/2	11:30 pm – 5:00 am
5–8	5 1/2	8:30 pm – 6:00 am
9–12	7	11:00 pm – 6:00 am
13–16	7 1/2	10:30 pm – 6:00 am
17–20	7 1/2	10:30 pm – 6:00 am
21–24	7 1/2	10:30 pm – 6:00 am
25–28	8	10:30 pm – 6:30 am

lier diagnosis of bipolar disorder been made and a mood stabilizer started as the first measure of treatment. Instead, the antidepressant, while initially helping Keith's depressive moods and improving his concentration, caused a significant activation in arousal and increased his raging, leading to sleeplessness and rapid shifts of mood as well as paranoid delusions.

Unless bipolar disorder is placed high on the list of possible diagnoses when a depressive episode first appears, and unless there is an objective record of the time course of symptoms during a medication trial, a switch into hypomania or mania can occur and the course of the illness can worsen.

Samantha

Samantha was initially brought to a psychiatrist by her parents at age fourteen when they became aware that she was smoking marijuana and when they could no longer control the physical fights that increasingly erupted with her younger sister. Previously shy and retiring, Samantha's relentless demands and uncharacteristically provocative behaviors had turned their home into a battleground. She was regularly breaking her nighttime curfew and was testing every parental limit.

At first, her parents chalked up this dramatic change in behavior to adolescent rebellion, but as her responses to their pleas for self-control were met with ever-increasing angry outbursts alternating with periods of sullen withdrawal, they sought family counseling with a psychologist. The family began three unproductive months of trying to talk through the problems that had developed in the household. The treatment focused on efforts to understand Samantha's anger at her sister and the oppositional and defiant behaviors directed toward all authority figures.

One day, after being rejected by a boyfriend for another girl in her class, Samantha could not stop crying, became inconsolable, and later that night made a suicide gesture by superficially cutting her arms with a nail file. Frightened and confused, Samantha's parents brought her to the emergency room of the local hospital, where she was interviewed by a psychiatrist who diagnosed her as having a borderline personality disorder. He prescribed 1 milligram of Risperdal a day to treat her agitation and advised that she be seen three times a week in individual psychotherapy and enrolled in a substance abuse program at the day hospital.

Samantha attended the day hospital unwillingly, stopped taking the

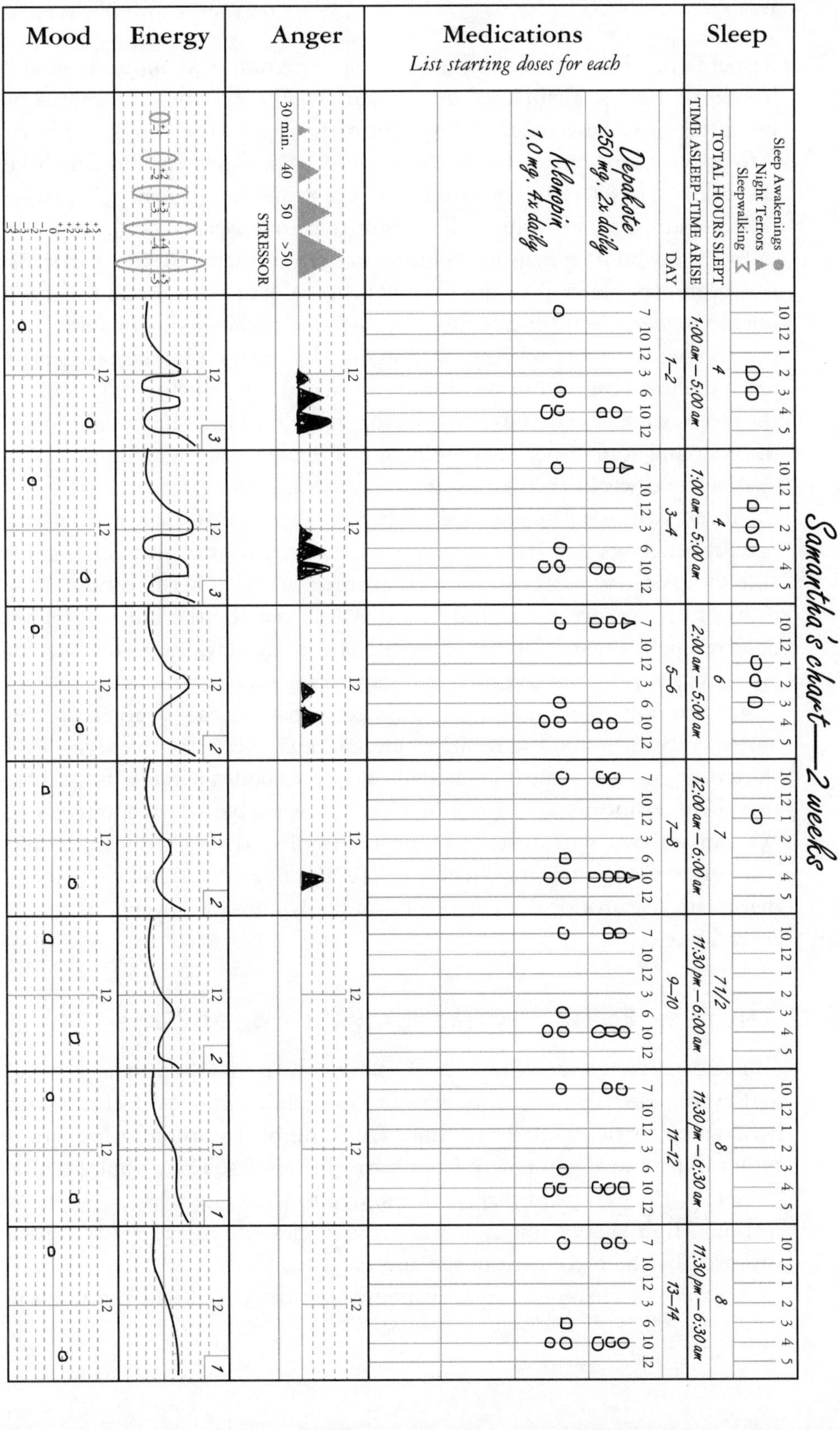

Samantha's chart—2 weeks
Mood
Energy
Anger
Medications
List starting doses for each
Sleep
Sleep Awakenings
Night Terrors
Sleepwalking
TOTAL HOURS SLEPT
TIME ASLEEP–TIME ARISE
DAY
Depakote 250 mg. 2x daily
Klonopin 1.0 mg. 4x daily
30 min. 40 50 >50
STRESSOR
1–2
3–4
5–6
7–8
9–10
11–12
13–14
1:00 am – 5:00 am
1:00 am – 5:00 am
2:00 am – 5:00 am
12:00 am – 6:00 am
11:30 pm – 6:00 am
11:30 pm – 6:30 am
11:30 pm – 6:30 am

Risperdal, and was soon skipping the day program, staying up later and later at night, and again breaking her curfew. Finally, when confronted by her father after he smelled the odor of marijuana in the house, she burst into an hour-long tirade, broke three windows in her room, and destroyed the television set that her sister had been watching. The police were called, and she was involuntarily committed to a psychiatric unit.

In the hospital, Samantha confided to the psychiatric resident that she had been experiencing severe swings in mood and energy and had been unable to sleep well for five months. She also acknowledged having racing thoughts, flights of ideas, and grandiose beliefs. On the psychiatric unit, she was observed to be highly distractible and unable to sit still in the afternoon and evenings. The doctor in the hospital diagnosed bipolar disorder and started her on a regimen of Depakote and Klonopin.

After two weeks in the hospital, Samantha became less irritable, and the mood swings subsided considerably. As the oppositional, defiant, and rageful behaviors that had characterized her early course resolved, she was able to go on day passes and was discharged home to her family. A daily chart of her two-week hospital stay that was kept by the nursing staff is depicted here. Again, for the purpose of visual display, the recordings for two days have been averaged and collapsed into each column.

For the first four nights in the hospital, Samantha's sleep record revealed early insomnia and multiple awakenings. Her activity/energy level shifted dramatically during the day, and her moods switched frequently from tearful outbursts, to giggling elation or irritable argumentativeness. We can see that within several days of sleeping through the night and reaching a therapeutic level of Depakote, she began to stabilize, and the disruptive features of the condition gradually subsided over a period of several weeks.

ANOTHER FORM OF CHARTING: THE MOOD TREE

The Mood Tree, developed by Rosalyn Newport-Olsen, is a personal and customized graphic representation of a child's moods, feelings, and actions at a particular point in time. This tangible communication tool is rather like a board game with Colorform-like apples. These apples can be chosen by the child and placed on the tree to illustrate what he or she is feeling. High energy states, as well as low ones and mixed states can be captured by the placement of the apples.

A parent or therapist can then photocopy the board and compile the copies in a binder, thus producing an easily-read record of the child's mood swings and feelings, and also an illustration of the effects of a particular medication trial.

The Mood Tree not only lets the child be an active participant and helps him or her put a name to feelings, it allows the child to feel understood by the parent or therapist. The Mood Tree is available in a child or adolescent version for $39.95. Order online at www.moodtree.com or call (850) 386-3455.

We cannot emphasize how important this systematic collection of information from parents and children is to the clinical evaluation of mood disorders in childhood and adolescence. Retrospective and prospective measures of mood and energy cycles, sleep disturbances, and the recording of stressors that may impact on the condition are critical to diagnosis and to an understanding of the variable and often unpredictable course of the illness, and guide the media and psychotherapeutic treatment recommendations.

Equally important, the conversation facilitated by the charting methods demonstrates to a child how deeply concerned his or her parents are and how much they want their child not to hide these frightening and uncomfortable symptoms or to bear this burden alone.

PART II

Inside the Brain and Mind

The
Genetic Aspects
of Bipolar Disorder

R arely does a person speak of only one family member with depression or manic-depression. More often two or more relatives are affected, as these illnesses tend to run in families. That these illnesses are passed down through the generations was recognized long before we understood the nature of genes and the genetic code. Among the first to remark on this heritable tendency was Emil Kraepelin, the father of modern psychiatry. Kraepelin was a German physician who spent countless hours with the mentally ill, carefully noting their symptoms and the course of their illness. He observed that of his patients who suffered from manic-depression, over 80 percent had positive family histories. In 1921 Kraepelin reported on nine hundred patients and found that the greatest frequency of initial attacks of the illness occurred between the ages of fifteen and twenty.

Today's bipolar children tend to experience the first episode of illness ten years earlier than their parents. Several studies have confirmed that in every generation following World War II, there is a higher incidence and earlier age of onset of both bipolar and recurrent depressive illness. And it is anticipated that in the coming decades, a lifetime hazard of a broad spectrum of mood disorders will occur that is greatly in excess of the rates observed in previous generations.

Although there is no clear explanation for this so-called cohort effect, genetic researchers have begun to explore the possibility that this increase in disease severity, coupled with a decrease in the age of onset in succeeding generations, may be due to a known inheritance pattern within families called "anticipation."

An example of how anticipation works can be found in Huntington's chorea, the disease that took the life of folksinger Woody Guthrie. The gene for this incapacitating neurological illness has been mapped to the upper portion of chromosome 4. While there are a variety of patterns within the genes, those genes that mutate and have a successively repeating number of sequences through the generations lead to a progressively earlier and more severe expression of the illness. The parent who transmits the defective gene for Huntington's chorea may have fewer than forty repeats and have no symptoms of the illness, but in the process of transmitting the gene to offspring, the repeat sequences increase in number, causing disease onset in each successive generation to be earlier and with a greater severity. A small study by Drs. Melvin McInnis and Raymond DePaulo and their colleagues at Johns Hopkins University School of Medicine in Baltimore point to the possibility that anticipation may be at play in bipolar disorder, but many genetic studies will have to be mounted to confirm or refute this finding. Multigenerational families with many brothers and sisters in each generation would be needed to conduct such research. Where would one find such families? Right here in this country with the Old Order Amish of Lancaster, Pennsylvania.

THE AMISH STUDIES

Dr. Janice Egeland of the University of Miami School of Medicine has been conducting an important and imaginative study with a group of people who dress in plain clothes and live much as they did when they first came to America in the eighteenth century.

In many ways the Amish community provides a living laboratory for all genetic research. They are a well-defined, closed population, numbering some twelve thousand people, with little migration into or out of the community. They are able to trace their ancestry back to thirty original progenitors, and they keep extensive geneologic records. Very important, the couples marry young in life and the community encourages a very high birth rate, thereby allowing genetic researchers to study large and multigenerational families.

Because of a long-standing trusting relationship with Dr. Egeland, the

Amish have been extremely cooperative with her and colleagues from Yale University and the National Institute of Mental Health. These scientists have long been engaged in a landmark study on the genetic basis of bipolar disorder. The DNA of the Amish families who have bipolar disorder running through the generations have now been immortalized at the NIMH. The clinical records and follow-up studies—as well as the genetic material mined from this unique population—has resulted in a national treasure trove that will continue to provide a wealth of information about bipolar disorder for years to come.

Readers will be especially interested in the study in which the children of Bipolar I parents are being observed over time. The researchers have made a surprisingly discordant finding: Data from the first completed interviews of two hundred at-risk children suggest a different symptom presentation than the one depicted by recent research findings in the non-Amish population at large.

First of all, few Amish children who go on to develop bipolar disorder are reported to have the same early comorbid conditions. For example, separation anxiety, symptoms of attention-deficit disorder with hyperactivity, and oppositional defiant behaviors are uncommon. While anger dyscontrol and bossiness are frequently present in the Amish bipolar children, the degree and intensity of these symptoms seem markedly tempered.

The regularity and simplicity of the Amish lifestyle, characterized by consistent social values, a philosophy of nonviolence, strong family and community kinship structures, and a proscribed daily, weekly, and monthly schedule centering around the church provide focus and structure to the social world. The absence of electricity weds the Amish to the natural daily and seasonal light/dark cycles, and—in comparison to the ordinary American child—introduces a complete buffer to overstimulation.

These social and environmental buffers may modify many behaviors that could reach their extreme pitch in families that do not have such defined social and religious values and cannot provide such consistent boundaries.

NATURE VERSUS NURTURE

So this brings us to the age-old question: What part does the inheritance of genetic material ("nature") contribute to early-onset bipolar disorder, and what part does the environment ("nurture") play in this form of the illness? In order to disentangle the subtle strands of heredity from environmental influence, scientists turned to the classic methods of examining the nature/nurture controversy—twin and adoption studies.

Identical twins develop when a single fertilized egg splits in two. Therefore, these sibling pairs are genetic carbon copies of each other. When a trait is wholly genetic, then if one partner of an identical twin pair develops an illness, the other twin would develop it also. Their "concordance rate"—the rate of similarity—would be 100 percent.

Seven twin studies gathered from five countries examined the rates of mood disorders for identical twins and pegged the combined concordance rates at 76 percent. However, nearly all these twin pairs were raised in the same homes, so the issue of nature versus nurture remained unresolved.

Scientific researchers then looked at identical twins raised apart from each other. They examined twelve pairs of identical twins adopted away from each other at birth and found that eight of the twelve pairs—or 67 percent—were concordant for major depressive or bipolar disorders. These data suggest that there is indeed a genetic component at play but that the disorder is not wholly genetic. Environmental factors must be interacting with the genetic trait in some way.

BIPOLAR DISORDER AND ALCOHOLISM

Perhaps the differences in the presentation of the illness early on in the Amish and non-Amish children may be accounted for by more than simply the "gentler" way of life and greater social structure that exists in the Amish community.

Alcoholism and substance abuse are rare conditions in the Amish. In comparison, alcoholism in combination with bipolar disorder in the general population seems to be quite common—particularly where early-onset bipolar disorder is concerned.

Dr. Richard Todd and colleagues at Washington University in St. Louis found increased rates of mood disorders and alcoholism among the adult relatives of seventy-six prepubertal children who were initially diagnosed with major depressive disorder. All of these children were followed over two to five years by Dr. Barbara Geller. Within this period, almost 30 percent of these children progressed from depressive to Bipolar I or Bipolar II disorders. The rates of alcoholism were higher in adult relatives of bipolar children (20.3 percent) than in relatives of those children diagnosed with depression only (12.3 percent). Follow-up studies in this latter group of children now being conducted by Dr. Geller will likely yield important information.

As we transferred information from our questionnaires to coding sheets to enter the findings in a database, we were struck by a consistently recurring pattern: In the majority of the children who had been diagnosed with bipolar disorder before the onset of puberty, the family histories revealed mood disorders and/or alcoholism coming down both the maternal *and* paternal sides. When the data were analyzed, it showed that over 80 percent had this unique "bilineal transmission."

Now that the bipolar/alcoholism link is being studied in the families of children with early-onset bipolar disorder, the question arises: Could the same heritable tendencies predispose one family member to bipolar disorder, another to alcoholism, and a third to the combination of the two? And, if this is so, does environmental influence play a presiding role in this difference in expression, does some other genetic variable play a modifying role, or both?

Again, we can look at the Amish families. Since there is virtually no alcoholism among the Amish, and therefore none in the bipolar families, could this fact account for the different presentations of the disorder in Amish and non-Amish children? This hypothesis could provide the impetus for an interesting cross-cultural study to examine the genetic and environmental forces at play in early-onset bipolar disorder.

The last fifteen years have seen huge advances in the field of molecular biology, and scientists has been probing at the level of the cell and inside the stuff of life itself—DNA. To make the next section a bit easier, we need to review some terminology.

GENETICS 101

DNA molecules exist in the nucleus of all cells. However, the DNA molecules don't just float around willy-nilly; they are organized into genes within strands of materials called chromosomes. Genes transmit specific hereditary characteristics by specifying the structure of proteins or by controlling the function of other genetic material. It is through the templates of DNA—the genes—that all cellular activities of the body are precisely coordinated and continuously maintained.

A child inherits one complement of twenty-three chromosomes from her mother and one complement of twenty-three chromosomes from her father. Human cells contain two copies of each of twenty-two autosomal (nonsex) chromosomes and two sex chromosomes. (For example, girls have two X chromosomes; boys have an X and a Y.) Parents, children, siblings, and nonidentical twins share approximately 50 percent of each other's genes, and grandchildren share some 25 percent of their grandparents' genes.

What we actually inherit from the combined parental library of DNA are the instructions for the construction and maintenance of the physical body. This includes the development of the all-important organ, the brain, and its ongoing biological processes that guide the organization of information, memory, and emotional expression.

Each of the genes that occurs at a given location or address on the chromosome is called an allele. There may be variations of each allele that, when inherited in particular combinations, produce physical differences as well as differences in behavioral responsiveness to the environment. When Gregor Mendel studied peas in the 1850s, he discovered the inheritance patterns of various traits. Today we know that a variation in allele patterns determines the physical characteristics—the peas are either smooth or wrinkled.

In human terms, when both parents carry the same allele for a given gene, and they transmit those two identical alleles (genes) to their children, their children are considered *homozygous* for that gene. When the parents transmit two different alleles, the individual is said to be *heterozygous.* Since the gene is related to the expression of a specific trait—say, hypothetically, overreaction to stressful events—*homozygosity* for this allele could confer a more heightened response to stressors. Just as variations in our genetic makeup determine differences in weight, height, coloring, and blood type, subtle variations in coding for the protein molecules (the DNA) that sustain these regulatory processes can result in individual differences in behavior and emotional responsiveness to stimuli from the environment. The combination of these genetic parameters, altered by environmental influences over time, is referred to as the *phenotype.*

Behavior is a new frontier for molecular biology. The greatest discoveries are yet to be made in this area. Making genetic associations to human behavior and temperament is the most complex area of study in molecular genetics. Studies of human twins suggest that genes contribute measurably to certain psychological traits, such as the tendency to have irrational social fears. Identical twins reared together have a much higher concordance for this trait than fraternal twins.

Could the transmission of a combination of genes that predispose to alcoholism from one parent and genes that predispose to bipolar disorder from the other produce offspring with a greater likelihood for the symptoms of earlier-onset bipolar disorder as well as a form with unique behavioral and temperamental features and a future tendency to become alcoholic? Any attempt to answer this question would require a massive undertaking involving the recruitment of thousands of related subjects, extensive diagnostic testing, and the capacity to scan the entire genome with DNA probes. These kinds of studies have been funded and are under way, but for the most part they are predicated on looking for the influence of single genes linked to a *DSM-IV*–defined psychiatric illness. Only recently have methods for examining multiple gene effects incorporating features of temperament with major disease phenotypes been contemplated.

What Kinds of Genetic Studies Have Been Done So Far, and What Have They Revealed?

In order to screen the genome, researchers began to conduct what are called "linkage studies." They assumed that if a gene for bipolar disorder resided close to a gene that was already known, the two traits would be inherited together. Originally they looked at known genetic markers—color blindness and blood types. No case could be made.

But linkage studies really got under way when molecular biologists developed a remarkable technique for probing the genome using recombinant DNA. The researchers produced DNA in the laboratory and found that if they could manufacture a piece of synthetic DNA that happened to match a segment of the natural DNA, the two pieces would stick together. Probing with the synthetic DNA, they saw that the chromosomes are studded with interesting variations. Each variation is unique to a particular point on a specific chromosome in an individual's cells. These variations have been named restriction-fragment-length polymorphisms (RFLPs or "riflips" for short).

By using the RFLP probes, geneticists are mapping the human genome. They have been searching the blood cells of families who have different kinds of inherited diseases. In the case of bipolar disorder, if a specific variation is present primarily in people who have the illness, it might be assumed that the RFLP is close to a gene that is somehow involved with the manifestation of the disorder. To put it another way, if a marker—an RFLP—can be found that shows that it segregates with the disorder, a gene involved with that disorder is probably located close to that particular marker.

For some time it was thought that bipolar disorder might be a one-gene illness. One gene was thought to be missing (deleted), or mutated. In 1987 Dr. Egeland's team, probing the Amish family cell-lines with RFLP techniques, reported findings that seemed to link bipolar disorder to a dominant gene on the short arm of chromosome 11. The Amish pedigree they searched consisted of eighty-one individuals, nineteen of whom were affected with bipolar disorder. Unfortunately, follow-up work on the original Amish pedigree yielded two new diagnoses of bipolar disorder, which reduced the evidence for linkage to nonsignificance. An extension of the original pedigree also failed to replicate the original result.

Since this disappointing lack of replication in the Amish studies, a number of research groups have reported linkage to other chromosomes. Dr. Nelson Freimer and colleagues screened the members of two large Costa Rican families vulnerable to bipolar disorder and found linkage to chromosome 18. This is the third group to find linkage to chromosome 18: In 1984 Dr. Wade Berretini of Thomas Jefferson University in Philadelphia and his colleagues at the NIMH linked the disorder to that chromosome, as did Johns Hopkins researchers led by Dr. Colin Stine in 1995. However, these three linkage reports on chromosome 18 encompass nearly the entire chromosome. They are, in essence, all over the map, the linkages widely dispersed and quite distant from each other. Therefore, they do not necessarily provide independent confirmation.

As molecular genetic studies progress, bipolar disorder is looking more and more like a multiple-gene disorder, or at least like one with a single important genetic mutation (perhaps several different single important mutations), modified by other variations in the genetic makeup, greatly influenced by interactions with the environment.

If this current view is correct, contemporary linkage studies—including the large family pedigree approach—will not succeed in identifying linkage because they can detect only major gene effects in which one gene is largely responsible for a behavioral disorder. This suggests the need for molecular biology strategies that can detect DNA markers that account for small variations of behavior. Testing such a view would require jettisoning criteria specified in *DSM-IV* for diagnosing bipolar disorder and instead attempting to determine whether linkage exists between a related group of behavioral traits common to bipolar disorder—for example, rapid switches in mood and arousal states, pronounced tendency to retain and experience extreme separation anxiety throughout life, craving for sweets and carbohydrates, or the lack of a capacity to modify or stop certain repetitive behaviors and thoughts. This quite different view of the problem would change the question from "Which gene(s) is associated with a common group of symptoms?" to "Can a gene modify a rather specific group of behaviors that have some developmental program and are associated with bipolar disorder?"

Although the entire genome has not been screened for linkage with bipolar disorder, it is conceivable that there are no genes of major effect to be found, despite clear evidence for genetic influence demonstrated in twin and adoption studies. Newer linkage methods, such as sib-pair analysis, which do not depend on mode of inheritance assumptions, can detect genes of somewhat smaller effect. However, these methods still depend on the model that a single gene explains most of the genetic effects on the trait.

CHILDREN WITH VELO-CARDIO-FACIAL SYNDROME

Although well-known genetic diseases such as cystic fibrosis or sickle-cell anemia are caused by the mutation of individual genes (with little effect from other genes or from the environment), the most common illnesses—among them cancer, heart disease, and many psychiatric disorders such as bipolar disorder—appear to be influenced by multiple genes. And, to one degree or another, their expression is influenced by the environment. The process of deducing the causes of these common illnesses is one of the most daunting ever faced by medicine.

Another living laboratory that is also providing clues as to where the genes for bipolar disorder may reside is a group of children with velo-cardio-facial syndrome (VCFS for short). The syndrome was characterized by Dr. Robert Shprintzen in 1978, and children with VCFS suffer a variety of anomalies: nasal speech (usually cleft palate), cardiac problems, learning disabilities, and a characteristic facial appearance that includes a vertically long face, a long nose with a widened nasal bridge, small ears whose uppermost sections are overfolded, long tapering fingers, narrow "squinting" eyes, and a flat facial expression. Our studies at the Albert

Einstein College of Medicine have found that more than 90 percent of VCFS children over the age of twelve have some form of bipolar disorder. Unraveling the specific effects of the loss of genetic material in VCFS may provide important clues in understanding the genetic basis for childhood-onset bipolar disorder.

VCFS, a relatively common congenital disorder, is estimated to affect 1 in 2,000 to 1 in 3,000 children. Approximately 85 percent of patients with VCFS have a mutation on the short arm of chromosome 22. Actually, in genetic terms, this type of mutation is called a microdeletion, because approximately thirty genes are missing from one of the two complementary chromosomes.

Mutations are not always a negative occurrence. To a large extent, evolution depends on mutations that alter existing genes to create in their place new gene variants. However, if a gene sustains a mutation such that it no longer encodes a needed protein, or if, as is the case in VCFS, an individual has lost half of the complement of genes on a particular chromosome, disease may result.

Psychiatric Illness in VCFS

Within a few years after they identified VCFS, clinicians at the Center for Cranio-facial Disorders at Montefiore Medical Center of the Albert Einstein College of Medicine began to observe several common temperamental features in these children. They were oversensitive to specific sensory stimuli, particularly thunder and lightning and repetitive mechanical noise. In addition, a number of these children were reported to have certain psychiatric disorders, including attention-deficit disorder with hyperactivity (ADHD), separation anxiety disorder, cyclothymia (shorter and milder mood swings), and obsessive-compulsive disorder.

The first follow-up study of forty-four adolescent VCFS patients who were identified when they were children revealed that over a third of the patients sixteen years of age or older had severe psychiatric disorders. As this cohort of VCFS children reached adolescence, approximately 30 percent developed psychotic symptoms.

In a mixed group of twenty-five VCFS children, adolescents, and adults, Demitri Papolos and his colleagues found that 68 percent (seventeen of the twenty-five) met *DSM-IV* criteria for some form of bipolar disorder. Looking back over their histories, nine of twenty-five met criteria for attention-deficit disorder with hyperactivity. In this group of VCFS patients, the average age of onset for bipolar disorder was twelve years, while evidence of cyclothymia or dysthymia (low-level, chronic depression) was retrospectively reported as early as age nine. In general, for those diagnosed with childhood bipolar disorders, disturbed sleep with night terrors often preceded the appearance of rapid mood swings.

Their mood swings, rapid but not excessively low or high, then went on to become frank episodes of mania or hypomania. At full onset, six patients had ultra-ultrarapid cycling. In addition to ADHD, many of these children were diagnosed with oppositional defiant disorder and anxiety disorders (including separation anxiety disorder, avoidant disorder, and obsessive-compulsive disorder) prior to the manifestation of significant mood and energy cycling.

Remarkably, these patients were showing the same developmental pattern of symptoms that we were later to observe in the bipolar children in our study. These studies reveal some tantalizing clues about bipolar disorder. Could one or more of the thirty genes that are deleted on one of the complementary pair of chromosome 22 contribute to the development of a bipolar disorder? Or do genes that reside in the same commonly deleted region in VCFS patients modify the condition in the general population?

The Candidate Gene Approach and Velo-Cardio-Facial Syndrome

One of the genes on the commonly deleted region in VCFS patients codes for the enzyme catechol-O-methyltransferase (COMT). This enzyme breaks down three important neurotransmitters—norepinephrine, dopamine, and epinephrine—all of which have been implicated in mood disorders for many years. The allele pattern for COMT has three variations, depending on the alleles inherited from the parents. If "H" stands for high activity and "L" stands for low activity, then the allele variation that codes for an enzyme that is very active is called COMT HH; another of the variations codes for an enzyme that is moderately active and is called COMT HL; and the third variation codes for an enzyme that has a very low activity rate is known as COMT LL.

Drs. Herbert Lachman and Demitri Papolos and colleagues at the Albert Einstein College of Medicine examined the DNA of the VCFS patients—specifically at the undeleted chromosome 22—and homed in on the parents' allele patterns for COMT. They found that 100 percent of the VCFS patients diagnosed with the ultra-ultrarapid-cycling form of bipolar disorder had the low-activity allele on the solitary undeleted chromosome. (Naturally, all of them are missing the COMT allele on the chromosome that is deleted.)

Prompted by these intriguing findings and supported by a research award from the National Alliance for Research on Schizophrenia and Depression, they then examined twenty-five non-VCFS adult patients who were bipolar and who had been rapid cyclers from the time of onset. (Almost all of these patients began their course of illness in childhood. Some were rapid cycling, some were ultrarapid cyclers, and some were ultra-ultrarapid cyclers).

The investigators found that the frequency of the COMT L (the low-activity allele) was significantly higher in the individuals who had the ultra-ultrarapid-cycling form of the disorder. This finding has now been independently confirmed by a team at the University of Cardiff in Wales. This variant of the COMT allele may represent a modifying gene that predisposes to ultra-ultrarapid cycling, the cycling pattern most commonly seen in children.

Additionally, several recent studies have now found that COMT LL is strongly associated with aggressive and violent behavior as well as adult alcoholism. It is interesting and potentially very important that the same genetic variation that leads to a decrease in the rate of breakdown of three neurotransmitters—norepinephrine, dopamine, and epinephrine—is associated with two cardinal features of childhood-onset bipolar disorder—ultrarapid cycling and aggression—and one comorbid feature of the adult form of bipolar disorder, alcoholism.

To further investigate these findings, Dr. Maria Karayiorgou and fellow researchers at Rockefeller University in New York City performed a fascinating experiment: They knocked out the COMT gene in a group of mice and watched to see if there were any behavioral changes. They found that the mice had a significant increase in aggressive and anxious behavior. It is hoped that future studies examining the relationship between variations in the COMT genotype and specific temperamental traits associated with childhood-onset bipolar disorder and alcoholism will provide a more complete understanding of how a particular allele pattern contributes to temperamental variation in the context of psychiatric illness.

TEMPERAMENT

To talk of a child's temperament is to refer to his or her mode of emotional response. A tricky concept to capture in words, Dr. Richard Alpert (Baba Ram Das), formerly a professor of psychology at Harvard University, described temperament well as "the characteristic phenomena of an individual's emotional nature, including his susceptibility to emotional stimulation, his customary strength and speed of response, and the quality of his prevailing mood." To some extent, temperament is genetic and heritable.

Perhaps bipolar children inherit a basic set of temperamental traits, such as easy arousability, separation and social anxiety, shyness or inhibition prompted perhaps by an overreactive stress response, as well as problems modulating sensory experience. All of these temperamental traits could contribute to the development of rejection sensitivity, avoidant and oppositional behaviors, sleep disorders, and the other features of a bipolar condition.

One important line of research inquiry has been to ask the question: To what degree does temperament correlate with a predisposition for psychiatric illness? Drs. Joseph Biederman, Jerrold Rosenbaum, and Jerome Kagan and colleagues at Harvard University have found that parents of shy and inhibited children have higher rates of a particular anxiety disorder—panic disorder with agoraphobia. But the correlations do not explain the underlying genetic causes of human anxiety disorders.

While psychological traits such as fearfulness and extroversion run in families, it is difficult to dissect the genes away from the contributions of the environment in the formation of these traits. Looking for a gene variation that magnifies or diminishes behavioral and physiological reactions to the environment might be particularly difficult without the correct strategy and the necessary tools of observation.

By combining genetics with new methods in the study of animal behavior, researchers are now exploring the interface between nature and nurture in animals. In a fascinating experiment, investigators released individual mice into a large unfamiliar space lit by glaring klieg lights. Some of the mice explored the new and highly stimulating environment with few fearful responses. Others, however, froze in terror at the new and overstimulating environment and defecated in fear. How much an animal explores an environment known to be frightening to it and its rate of defecation combine to determine the trait of emotionality. Yet Jonathan

Flint of the Institute of Molecular Medicine in Oxford, England, and his coinvestigators, John Defries and Allan Collins of the University of Colorado at Boulder, have found that three genes (actually, the areas where the genes are thought to reside) contribute to almost all the genetic variety of the trait of emotionality in rodents.

If we were trying to define the temperament of children with early-onset bipolar disorder, we might choose the following set of traits and characteristic behaviors: emotional sensitivity, sleep/wake and activity-rhythm and mood disturbances, sensitivity to daily and seasonal changes, oppositional and socially avoidant behavior, and anger dyscontrol. How could a genetic variation that affects a specific biological system combine with environmental influence to produce this predictable set of behavioral characteristics?

Let's hypothesize that a coding variation in the DNA of an enzyme that promotes an unusually broad oscillation in some specific physiological process—let us say, thermoregulation (the body's capacity to generate and dissipate heat)—could, in combination with other modifying factors, produce more pronounced daily and seasonal variations in energy. Individuals who inherited this genetic trait could be predisposed to sleep/wake reversals, which in turn bring wide mood oscillations and potentially wide daily variations in arousal and attentional states. What would such a variation lead to at the level of social and interpersonal behavior? How would such individuals adapt to their social milieu?

Many permutations in personality or temperament might evolve as a result of effects on these behavioral rhythms, and they would depend on environmental influences. If a person with these traits were thrown into a high-energy state yet sufficiently buffered by regular time and social boundaries, such a genetic trait could promote prolific and even unrelenting dedication to work. Alternatively, this same genetic trait could promote brief, high-energy and elevated or irritable mood states, punctuated by frequent and more sustained low-energy states with depressive moods leading to oppositional or avoidant behaviors, especially if no consistent social support existed for that individual.

"WHAT ARE THE CHANCES THAT OUR NEXT CHILD COULD HAVE THE ILLNESS?"

Advances in molecular biology will no doubt shed much light on the causes of early-onset bipolar disorder, but parents of these children are desperate for answers to some more immediate concerns: They want to know: "If we have the risk factors [the positive family history, perhaps linked to alcoholism], what are the chances that any of our other [or future] children will onset with the illness?" This is an extremely difficult question to answer.

The likelihood of developing bipolar disorder is many times greater in relatives of patients with mood disorders than in the general public (although the illness can, and often does, skip a generation). Overall, researchers have observed that a first-degree relative (parents, siblings, or children) of a bipolar patient has a 13 to 35 percent risk of developing a mood disorder of any type. The offspring of two ill parents have at least double the risk for mood disorders in comparison with the offspring of one affected parent. Likewise, it has been consistently reported that the risk for an individual to develop mood disorders increases significantly if both a parent and a sibling are ill, in contrast to an individual with *either* an ill parent or sibling.

The chart that follows is merely a general guide for the risk to various relatives. It is important to remember that there is considerable variation in reported risk figures among investigators as a result of differences in methods and diagnostic criteria used in the various studies. In addition, the chart does not include the influence of alcoholism, which, as discussed earlier, appears to confer a greater risk for early-onset forms of bipolar disorder.

RELATIVE	BIPOLAR PATIENT (%)
Identical twin	70
Fraternal twin	15–25
Offspring of one ill parent	15–30
Offspring of two ill parents	50–75
Sibling	15–25
Second-degree relative	3–7
General population	1

GOOD NEWS: PROTECTIVE GENES

This chapter has shown that there is strong evidence for a genetic component in the susceptibility to develop bipolar disorder. But we need to point out again that multiple genes probably are involved in the disorder, each with an additive effect.

In 1998 some provocative findings were reported—again from Dr. Egeland's Amish family pedigrees. She and her team identified chromosomal locations that harbor genes that seem to protect against the manifestation of bipolar disorder. This means that even if a family is loaded with mood disorders, and a child inherits the set of genes that cause the disorder, if he or she also inherits the "wellness" gene or genes (one is thought to be on chromosome 4), the child may never manifest the illness.

Meanwhile, if parents are aware of the existence of genetic risks, they can observe thoughtfully and be ready to intervene early in the life of their child. They also can ensure that their child is not placed on antidepressants without mood stabilizers and attempt to establish regular sleep/wake patterns and social structure in their households. It is hoped that the time is coming when a better understanding of what is happening on the level of the genes will bring new and better medications targeted at the primary biological dysfunction and producing minimal side effects.

The Psychological Dimensions

When Melissa and her husband discovered she was pregnant, they were overjoyed about having their first child. As she began to feel the frequent kicks and movements within, Melissa would chuckle to herself and talk about the "Ninja Baby," a nickname that would come to haunt her as Eric grew older.

"The doctor did not need to give him a tap on the bottom, because he was delivered screaming like a banshee," Melissa recalled. "On the night the nurse first brought him to me, he howled so loudly that he woke up every newborn on the wing, and after that never seemed to be able to get to sleep easily."

Melissa was sure that the bright lights and the activity level in the nursery were overstimulating him, and once she got him home, she would be able to settle him. Eric took to nursing with a voracious suckling instinct, yet he was hard to satisfy and unusually fussy. He was also extremely colicky and a poor and erratic sleeper. Rarely able to sleep for more than four hours, he seemed to have no schedule and did not sleep through the night until he was fourteen months old. When Melissa would try to put him down, or if her husband Tom offered to take him, Eric would struggle so much against leaving her chest, his nails would dig into her skin.

By the time he was a toddler, Melissa began to notice that everything in the house ended up in pieces on the floor. Regardless of where he was or who he was with, Eric always seemed to take up the whole room. At nine months, a very embarrassed nursery school director took Melissa aside to ask if she and her husband would mind if he were moved up to the toddler nursery, as he was bulldozing over all the other children in the room. When he started nursery school, he was easily the most difficult child in the class. Melissa and Tom would share their concerns with friends, family, or the pediatrician, but the usual response was to pass remarks on the difference between boys and girls.

In preschool the problems became even worse, as Eric had a hard time staying in his seat and remaining attentive to his work. Shortly after the family moved to Delaware, Eric started kindergarten. He seemed all right at first, but the problems of staying in his seat and remaining focused continued. Outside of school, the behavioral problems increased. One day, after Melissa refused to buy him candy, Eric ran out of the grocery store and attempted to run across the street. A few times he attacked her—hitting, kicking, and biting. Once, when sent to his room for a time-out, he opened the second-story window, knocked out the screen, and threatened to jump. Later he told his mother that he thought he could fly.

EARLY SYMPTOMS AND BEHAVIORS

Melissa's story of Eric's early development underscores a number of the most commonly reported early features of children who are later diagnosed with bipolar disorder. From the beginning of her account, we are struck by the high levels of motor activity, the high state of arousal, the volubility of his crying, the sleep disturbance, and the pronounced difficulties in separating from his mother. Also obvious is Eric's impulsiveness, aggressiveness, and grandiosity.

From its earliest manifestation in infancy, often long before the advent of what are considered the cardinal symptoms of mood swings, certain temperamental features and common behavioral responses to environmental triggers arise as precursors in a significant number of children. These temperamental features interact with social experience to shape the child's ability to be and engage in the world and to form behavioral responses, thereby influencing nearly every aspect of the child's development.

If we define these early symptoms and behavioral traits that appear to persist over time, we will be better able to explore the likely impact of their interaction with the major developmental stages of childhood and to learn how these factors may shape the formation of enduring personality characteristics.

Because of the continuing controversy over how early-onset bipolar disorder is defined by the fields of child psychiatry and psychology, and because, until recently, it was thought that the condition was exceedingly rare in childhood, no longitudinal studies that examine the early evolution of symptoms and behaviors have been available to clinicians.

Children Who Are Easily Startled and Aroused

Many children who have bipolar disorder are highly excitable, have problems integrating sensory experience, and clearly have difficulties regulating their level of mental and physical arousal. They have difficulty getting to sleep at night, experience an unusual degree of motor restlessness, and have rapid and prolonged periods of emotional excitability as well as high rates of anxiety symptoms. Frequent bouts of anxiety can be abruptly triggered by any number of stimuli or demands. In early childhood, thunder and lightning, vacuum cleaners—almost any sound that threatens to break or dominate sensory and attentional focus—can induce high levels of arousal and anxiety. By any current definition, these traits are examples of a tendency toward high arousability.

Arousal States in Infancy

A great deal happens in the first year of the life of an infant, and emotional development starts at the beginning. Through constant interaction with the mother, early social responses and behaviors begin to evolve. We now know that the influence of a select set of experiences in the first year extend far into the future and alter, in some mysterious way, the structures and processes that will emerge in the three-, four-, and five-year-old. To understand the potential behavioral disturbances of early childhood and the evolution of the personality, the defining events of the first weeks and months of infancy must be understood.

Of primary importance is the capacity to manage frustration and to settle into calm states that allow for easy transitions between the several stages of an infant's sleep and arousal states. Recently studies have found that the degree of control an infant has over the range and variation of these states is the best predictor of cognitive and social performance at eighteen months.

An infant progresses through various states of consciousness linked to different levels of central nervous system arousal during the day and night, ranging from deep and light sleep states, to semiconsciousness, then to a very alert state, on to fussy, and then to inconsolable crying. Aroused, alert, and active to quiescent, inattentive, and passive—an infant's early existence consists of transitions back and forth between these states.

The length of sleep cycles (rapid-eye movement [REM] active and non-REM deep sleep) typically changes with maturation. In a full-term infant, sleep and waking occur approximately in four-hour cycles. Within these cycles a baby is in deep sleep for forty-five to fifty minutes and then rouses to become active but remains in light sleep. After a certain period, the infant settles back down into deep sleep. A lack of regularity in these cycles may signal problems in the maturation of the nervous system, particularly in those components that regulate shifts from one state of arousal to another and the timing functions of the transitions from sleep to wakefulness.

Learning to sleep for longer than a four-hour period involves learning how to cope with transitions from REM-active into non-REM deep sleep. It is a complex process that requires the capacity to reach a state of calm and remain in that state for an extended period. For this to happen, the infant's nervous system must be mature enough to tune out stimuli from the environment without waking up. In order to sleep beyond these three- or four-hour cycles, babies must develop reliable behavioral patterns that serve to comfort them when they are trying to move from light sleep into a deeper sleep. Babies who are able to manage these transitions for themselves when frustrated or overstimulated during the day are also more likely to learn patterns necessary for nighttime sleep.

A hereditary predisposition to become aroused easily, leading to internal states that produce motor restlessness (fidgetiness), would certainly tend to counter this natural developmental process. We have already noted the frequent reports of difficulty settling and the irregular and shortened sleep patterns in children who later develop bipolar disorder. The sensitivity to sensory stimulation and overreactive startle responses in these children may be related to the difficulty they seem to have in keeping themselves from falling off to sleep and also waking at short intervals each time they come up to REM sleep. Many of these children have "restless leg syndrome" where their legs flail around during sleep.

Arousal and Relaxation

Seen from the outside, the newborn appears to move from a state of relative calm and well-being to intense distress, to the ready intake of milk with blissful satisfaction, to the ebbing of distress, and a return to ease, calm, and well-being. In hunger, the distress soon becomes a generalized discomfort that overtakes the whole body with crying and thrashing about. With nursing the whole body relaxes. It is these states of generalized arousal and heightened anxiety, followed by relief, that characterize the diffuse pleasure and anxious distress of the newborn.

Rooting and sucking are the most reliable activities of newborn babies. When the mother offers a breast or bottle and touches a newborn's cheek, the baby will turn his or her head repeatedly, then gobble the nipple firmly in the mouth. Infants have been observed to suck in a regular pattern of bursts and pauses. Bursts seem to be sequenced in groupings of five to twenty-four sucks per burst. The interval between bursts is a time of rest and recovery as well as a time in which information is processed. Dr. T. Berry Brazelton, founder of the Child Development Unit at Boston Children's Hospital, has suggested that these pauses are important in the early mother-child relationship, since mothers use them to stimulate the infant to return to sucking.

Dr. Brazelton has noted that mothers tend to look down to talk to and jiggle their babies when they pause between bursts of sucking. Infants, in turn, come to anticipate these responses, and over time, the mothers' shaking of the breast actually prolongs the pause as the infants become alert yet relaxed and attend to the signals given by their mothers.

In exchange for these regular pleasurable interactions with the mother, the infant begins to postpone the immediate need to satisfy hunger and perhaps takes the first steps toward acquiring the capacity to regulate need and manage frustration. This patterning may provide one of the earliest experiences of self-other boundary formation and the development of an internal stimulus barrier, foreshadowing the capacity to postpone immediate gratification and to take turns in exchange for the pleasures of social contact with others.

Many mothers of bipolar children commented in their descriptions of early infancy that rooting and suckling behaviors were intense, persistent, and often brooked no interruption. Clearly such patterning, lacking rest and recovery pauses, might displace one of the earliest and most fundamental aspects of bonding and affiliative behavior between mother and child and could contribute to the difficulty in the maturation of natural strategies for managing overaroused states and to subsequent difficulties in initiating social interaction.

HABITUATION: MANAGING THE SENSORY WORLD

The infant's waking life centers around continuous attempts to achieve sensory and emotional homeostasis. Habituation—the ability to appropriately modulate arousal induced by internal or external sensory experience—is a protective response, a closing down of the nervous system against too much stimulation from the outside. It is essential to newborns' capacity for survival, helping them deal with potentially overwhelming demands on their immature sensory systems. The steady hum of an air conditioner eventually fades away and is lost, until it is switched off and the hum suddenly becomes conspicuous by its absence. Infant studies have found that when presented with a series of bright lights, babies first startle, then gradually respond less and less. The motor responses eventually cease. The increases in heart and respiratory rate that occur after the initial bright light stimulus eventually decreases. The infants begin to breathe deeply and steadily until they appear to go into a deep sleep.

The habituation response can be initiated by auditory, visual, or tactile stimuli. A balance between the capacity to become alert, and evaluate and assess a new stimulus and the capacity to withdraw interest through inhibition of sensory systems is a critical regulatory function for human survival, and one that may be poorly modulated in children with bipolar disorder.

Studies of an infant's behavioral responses to stimulation—for example, the degree to which a newborn turns away or approaches a stimulus—have found that these early coping responses can evolve into defensive styles such as psychological avoidance, denial, or confrontational modes in later years. An abundant literature on startle and fear responses in animals confirms the biological and hence genetic basis for these temperamental differences.

NIGHT TERRORS IN BIPOLAR CHILDREN

A significant number of children in our study reported wakening in the night with bloodcurdling screams. One mother wrote to us and described her toddler's sleeping hours thus: "My son gets up many times throughout the night, crying, screaming, and thrashing his body. Sometimes his eyes are closed and you can't wake him due to a hypnoticlike state he seems to be in."

When a child is experiencing a night terror and actually remembers it, he or she later reports dreams that are extremely threatening. The content has to do with some predatory person or animal chasing them, or terrible fears of abandonment such as a parent being killed. Some adults who suffer them and seem to have greater recall speak of ceilings and walls pushing down on them, and others report snakes and spiders slithering and crawling all over the bed or room.

Since other features of bipolar disorder indicate that these children have very low thresholds for arousal (they are easily provoked to anger, easily excited, they have low thresholds for anxiety, and are easily overstimulated by external and internal stimuli), it is not surprising that they experience these physiological states of overarousal during sleep.

In fact, in a study of the relationship between parasomnias (night terrors), sleepwalking, confusional arousals, restless leg syndrome, bedwetting (enuresis), teeth grinding (bruxism), and psychiatric illness in a very large sample of adults, Dr. Maurice Ohayon and his colleagues at the Phillipe Pinel Research Center in Montreal reported a strong association between the adults who experienced night terrors and those diagnosed with bipolar disorder and depression comorbid with anxiety.

In order to discuss night terrors, we need to explain the architecture of sleep and the way night terrors differ from nightmares, for night terrors are not happening during the dreaming sector of sleep—the rapid-eye movement (REM) sector—but apparently in the deepest stage of non-REM sleep, or in some transitory state in between.

The Typical Architecture of Sleep

Normally throughout the night a person experiences two kinds of sleep that alternate rhythmically. One is called rapid-eye movement (REM) sleep, during which most dreaming takes place; the other (not surprisingly) is called non-REM.

As we wrote in *Overcoming Depression,* 3rd edition:

Non-REM sleep has a four-stage development plan as revealed by electroencephalogram (EEG) sleep studies. Stage 1 is the light sleep that begins the night and from which a sleeper may be easily awakened. The brain waves are small and fast. After about a half an hour, the sleeper slips deeper into sleep as stages 2, 3, and 4 of non-REM sleep progress. EEGS of stage 3 reveal larger and slower brain waves. Stage 4 brain waves are large, slow, and regular. This is the deepest period of sleep.

After approximately ninety minutes have passed, a brief period of REM sleep appears (the eyeballs can be observed moving rapidly beneath the eyelids), only to be followed by one of the non-REM stages. A pattern develops in which the REM and non-REM sleep phases alternate with each other, cycling back and forth in a remarkably periodic ebb and flow. Later on in the night, REM sleep asserts itself for longer periods of time. Apparently the sleep cycle oscillates on a ninety-minute time frame. The first ninety-minute cycle might consist of eighty-five minutes of non-REM sleep and five minutes of REM; by the time the fourth cycle rolls around, it might consist of sixty minutes of non-REM and thirty minutes of REM.

But all is not always so regular. As Drs. Mark W. Mahowald and Carlos H. Schenck of the Minnesota Regional Sleep Disorders Center at the University of Minnesota Medical School have written: "The rapid oscillation of states or the inappropriate intrusion of elements of one state into another may result in the appearance of parasomnias, which are particularly apt to occur during the transition periods from one state to another. Given the large number of neural networks, neurotransmitters, and other state-determining substances that must be recruited synchronously, and given the frequent transition among the three states of being, it is surprising that parasomnias do not occur more frequently."

Although people dream during the REM stage of sleep and can usually remember a nightmare or bad dream if it occurs at that time, a child or adult experiences a night terror commonly in stage 4 (and possibly 3) of the non-REM period. It has been supposed that the mind is void during the deeper stages of non-REM sleep, but this may not be true. A person having a night terror will moan, cry, scream, and bolt upright in apparent terror. The heartbeat can be as fast as 160 to 170 beats per minute, which is excessively fast. These rates are similar to those seen in severe panic attacks.

A night terror can last anywhere from five to twenty minutes and though the child's eyes may be open, he or she is still asleep and—typically—inconsolable. A parent should not yell at the child and startle him or her, but make reassuring and soothing sounds and make sure that no glass objects are anywhere near the bed area. Also, halogen or hot lamps could be dangerous with a panicky child thrashing about, so keep the light low and away from the child's body and bedding. Take care to lock or blockade windows that are near the bed (but ensure that another window exit is available in the event of fire).

One mother wrote to us and chillingly described her five-year-old daughter's night terrors. Note the child's degree of panic as well as the imagery of blood and dismemberment:

> In the last few months she has had some very upsetting dreams, with details of children in the school playground that have been stabbed, and seas of blood on the ground. She came into my bedroom to tell me this, dripping with sweat and heart racing. I struggled to calm her down and didn't succeed as she got so worked up she vomited on the bed.
>
> Other dreams include a decapitated man with blood coming from his neck and his head lying on the floor talking to her. We've heard about giant moles rumbling under the ground of her classroom, and apparently this mole was choosing which table of kids he was going to come up and gobble up.

This may explain why children with bipolar disorder seem fixated on blood and knives and always seem under threat. Something is overaroused in the amygdala—the part of the brain that governs "fight or flight." While researchers such as Jonathan Winson, author of *Brain and Psyche: The Biology of the Unconscious,* have suggested that REM sleep preparations were for the formulation of strategies for dealing with local predators (to rehearse and ready the system), this primitive survival mechanism is overstimulated in these children and, trapped in transitory states from one stage of sleep to another, they are suffering horribly. Is it any wonder that these children are so often in combative and irritable modes and that they are terrified of going to sleep at night?

We are concerned about the effects such parasomnias are having on the psychological development of these children. The rate and frequency of night terrors and nightmares and the nature of the highly disturbing content which seems referable to fight-or-flight mechanisms seems coupled with many of the behavioral problems these children have. Many of the behaviors are congruent with "fight": oppositional, defiant, argumentative, defensive, behaviors; while other behaviors are more consonant with "fright": anxious, fearful, withdrawn, and phobic. The disturbances in sleep may be contributing to the disturbances within the psyche, or reinforcing them on a nightly basis.

What would induce a more typical, less-threatening sleep pattern? No one has studied this in youngsters, but practitioners suspect that a drug like clonazepam (Klonapin) may help because of its capacity to reduce stage 4 sleep. A number of parents who wrote to us about this issue said that the night terrors seemed to diminish with the use of an atypical antipsychotic medication such as Zyprexa or Risperdal, but only sleep studies will indicate proper treatment and abatement of this harrowing symptom of nighttime overarousal.

SEPARATION DISTRESS

Our study of 120 children with early-onset bipolar disorder revealed that over 60 percent had some pronounced degree of separation distress, often preceding any other diagnosable psychiatric symptoms. These children expressed great fearfulness and anxiety about the loss of their parents, exaggerated worries about harm befalling their parents, and excessive anxiety when separated from family members.

Many had extreme clinging behaviors. Mothers have told us that they felt as if they and their child were "joined at the hip." They often had to clean the house carrying the child in a sling. One woman said, "If he could crawl back into the womb, he would."

Anxiety and separation distress along with easy arousability, hyperactivity, and distractibility and an exaggerated tendency to overreact to situationally related stress make these children more likely to express avoidant and oppositional behaviors. Taken together, these features represent some of the most pervasive and enduring psychological determinants of the condition.

SENSORY PROCESSING DEFICITS AND OBJECT CONSTANCY

In bipolar children, well-modulated sensory processing that would provide for fluid transitions between varying states of attention and arousal seems to be lacking. A child who is unable to adequately buffer environmental stimuli will often experience overstimulation. For such a child, it would be quite difficult to sustain attentional focus.

In order for a young child to separate successfully from the mother, an image of the mother must be internalized. "Object constancy" is a term applied to describe the mental process of holding an image of another in conscious awareness long enough to endow it with emotional meaning and to sustain the idea and feeling of a positive, protective source of comfort. It may be that in the bipolar child, the deficits mentioned earlier produce a developmental delay in this psychological function of object constancy. This delay may combine with other factors to set off a reverberating alarm, signaling an almost primal fear at the times of separation from the mother as well as during transitions to unfamiliar settings. Being able to sustain the image of the mother when physically separated from her could become a herculean task.

Dr. Margaret Mahler, the person most associated with a full exploration of infant-mother differentiation, observed that in the progression from a so-called symbiotic phase, where the child is totally dependent on the mother for nutrients and nurturance, to separate functioning, the toddler seems to show two modes or poles of self-orientation. Interest and curiosity about his own body and its functions represents the landmarks of one pole; interest in the mother represents the other.

In infancy, a child's states of well-being and discomfort center more around the presence or absence of the mother. The child psychoanalyst and pediatrician D. W. Winnicott counsels that "at this stage, it is necessary to think of the infant not just as a person who gets hungry, and whose instinctual drives may be met or frustrated, but rather as an immature being who is all the time on the brink of 'unthinkable anxiety.' " For a newborn, this kind of "unthinkable anxiety" is kept at bay by the vitally important function of the mother and her capacity to empathize with her baby—to know what her baby needs and to calm states of high arousal.

This "unthinkable anxiety" is well illustrated by a night terror that occurred over and over again between the ages of four and eight, described by a twelve-year-old boy who had recently been diagnosed with bipolar disorder. He recalled: "I was in a space suit, and I would start floating out there all by myself, and all of a sudden, I would start screaming at the top of my lungs, but no one is there to hear me."

This dream imagery of being locked in a space suit in the vastness of the universe, with no experience of external boundaries, with no possibility of human contact, and the terror of absolute isolation and abandonment, clearly captures the fear of annihilation that many children with this disorder report.

Similar to the newborn, whose experience of inner and outer self and other are not easily or consistently distinguished, children with bipolar disorder often have self and other boundary issues, which—for many— seem to persist long into adolescence and adulthood.

STAGES OF RAPPROACHMENT

The period that extends from about the ninth to about the eighteenth month and coincides with what psychoanalyst Phyllis Greenacre termed the child's "love affair with the world" is a primary stage of ego development. The child begins to acquire upright, free locomotion as well as what the pioneer in child development, Jean Piaget, regarded as the beginning of representational intelligence. During this period of rapid development of motor skills and cognitive development, most children have major periods of exhilaration or at least relative elation. These functions absorb so much of the child's energy and attention that the junior toddler appears for a while relatively independent of the mother. But as the child achieves success in these areas, an increasing awareness of separateness develops, and the need for mother's acceptance and renewed participation reasserts itself as the so-called rapprochement stage begins.

How does the child's sense of self-awareness and independence from the mother develop? The child's expanding awareness of the mother as a different entity creates the necessity for him to begin to establish a new form of relationship with her and to negotiate the loss of the familiar symbiotic relationship. It is at this critical juncture that separation anxiety arises, signaling that the child has developed a concept of a separate and differentiated self and that a new developmental pathway has been established. The child then begins to move in two directions, with halting steps forward toward autonomy and regressive pulls backward toward dependency.

What if the development of some critical physiological function, such as habituation, lags behind its normal developmental trajectory? And what if this lag produces a tendency to overrespond to novel stimuli? With the age-appropriate demands for independent functioning, the child would no longer be protected by the mother's capacity to dampen arousal states, and deficits in habituation responses likely would pose a significant and terribly upsetting problem for the child.

The type of emotional response provided by parents of children with such deficits—whether generous, supportive, empathic, and accepting, or refusing, rejecting, withholding, demanding, critical, and punitive—will exert a significant modifying influence on future emotional development.

Mahler suggests that during the rapproachment stage, the main forces that need to be balanced are the child's wishes for continued gratification through contact and reunion and his knowledge of and anxiety over repeated brief separations from the mother. Two typical patterns of behavior—closely following or shadowing the mother and then fleeing from her with the expectation of being chased and enfolded into her arms—indicate the toddler's desire for reunion. Side by side with this wish is a fear of being reingulfed. How this critical phase of establishing a sense of separateness from the mother is negotiated is thought to be of enormous consequence for future psychological and emotional development. According to Mahler, it is a mainspring in humans' eternal struggle against fusion and isolation—the beginning stage of establishing boundaries between self and others.

Could this natural stage of psychological and emotional development be impinged upon by some genetically endowed physiological traits that shape sensory experience? For example, how would a child's emotional and psychological development be affected by an extreme sensitivity to stimulation, and/or low threshold for anxiety and arousal, or an early, excessive motor activity? The answers to these questions could have far-reaching implications for our understanding of the psychological features and treatment needs of children with bipolar disorder and may also point to specific forms of intervention that might have special value in the early treatment of the condition.

Thus it appears that children with bipolar disorder have a behavioral predisposition that leads to a greater tendency to startle as well as difficulties settling as infants. Some progress to pronounced separation anxiety during the rapproachment stage, and most—if not all—experience a heightened response to stress. Later, establishing and sustaining peer relationships in childhood becomes a major obstacle in emotional development, as shyness, social withdrawal, or oppositional behaviors begin to emerge in full force. Social avoidance, social phobia, and panic attacks, all frequently associated with bipolar disorder throughout life, may be predictable outcomes as these children reach the shores of adolescence and adulthood.

HIDDEN REGULATORS OF ATTACHMENT AND
SEPARATION BEHAVIOR

Dr. Myron Hofer and his colleagues at Columbia University in New York City performed a compelling series of experiments using a well-established experimental model: the separation paradigm in animals. They began to focus on a change in behavior that occurred in rat pups after four to eight hours of separation from their mothers. The rat pups became hyperactive.

To explore the regulatory processes of the mother-infant interaction, they attempted to selectively supply aspects of the mother's presence. For example, they found that by simulating the body temperature of the mother, her touch, or olfactory cues, the level of motor activity after separation from the mother lessened substantially. This led the researchers to propose that the mother herself provides a combination of signals that act together to exert a long-term control over infant behavioral responsiveness. Furthermore, since much evidence exists that the neurotransmitters norepinephrine and dopamine may mediate generalized behavioral activity in animals, and since these neurotransmitter systems are most involved with motor activity and attention, they asked whether, by her presence, the mother was directly regulating specific brain neurotransmitter systems and thereby affecting the pup's levels of behavioral arousal and motor activity.

The researchers then decided to see if drugs that prevent the accumulation of norepinephrine and dopamine would prevent the development of hyperactivity in separated pups. And that is precisely what they found. A small dose of reserpine given at the time of separation entirely prevented the development of hyperactivity during the ensuing hours of maternal deprivation. Since reserpine is known to prevent the accumulation of these neurotransmitters at nerve terminals in the brain, the researchers concluded that sustained interaction with the mother normally depletes norepinephrine and dopamine to a moderate degree in rat pups. The loss of interaction with the mother would cause the concentration of these neurotransmitters to rise in the brain, and the pups would become behaviorally hyperresponsive.

From the work of Myron Hofer and others we now know that in animals, the regulatory interactions with the mother serve to maintain high levels of physiological functions in the infants' systems during normal conditions. For example, interaction maintains the infants' heart rate and oxygen consumption at ordinary levels. In addition, interaction with the mother dampens other activities: behavioral reactivity, arousals during sleep, and suckling. See infant separation responses on chart below.

INFANT SEPARATION RESPONSES

BEHAVIOR	PHYSIOLOGY
Acute ("protest" phase, lasting minutes to hours)	
Agitation	Increased heart rate
Vocalization	Increased cortisol
Searching, inactivity	Increased catecholamines
Chronic (slow-developing "despair" phase, lasting hours to days)	
Decreased social interaction, play	Decreased body weight
Mouthing, rocking	Sleep disturbance
Hyporesponsiveness or hyper-responsiveness	Decreased rapid-eye movement, increased arousals
Decreased or variable food intake	Metabolic
Postures and facial expressions of sadness	Decreased core temperature
	Decreased oxygen consumption
	Cardiovascular
	Decreased cardiac rate, increased vascular resistance
	Increased ectopic beats
	Endocrine
	Decreased growth hormone
	Immunologic
	Decreased T-cell activity

Source: Reference for each response is given in Hofer, 1984. (Reproduced with permission from *Psychosomatic Medicine* [1975], 37, 245–264. Baltimore: Lippincott, Williams & Wilkins.)

Persistent and severe separation anxiety in a child is a signal that successful negotiation and completion of this critical phase of psychological

and emotional development is in jeopardy and that perhaps some underlying biological process is impaired. While individual variability does occur, the broad outline and even some of the details are surprisingly similar
for different species. It is tempting to think that since proximity to the
mother is a clear emotional regulator that produces varying degrees of
arousal and separation distress in all mammalian species studied, warmth
provided by her body may be one of the important links to emotional
arousal in infancy.

As Dr. Hofer has suggested, this early postnatal period might be considered as "extrauterine gestation," in that the infant's heart rate, respiratory rate, and endocrine status are under subtle but pervasive maternal
control. What is of particular interest about this model is the implication
that the way in which maternal behavior and infant physiology interact is
reciprocal and largely dependent on the infant's stage of development.

WHAT TO DO ABOUT SEPARATION ANXIETY

In almost all instances, the mother is most affected by the child's powerful attachment demands; but as the child's exclusive desire for her com-
panionship begins to rule the roost, others in the family also will be
affected. Some fathers may be entirely excluded from this intense relationship and viewed by the children as intruders. Mothers who remain
identified with the role of satisfying the child's needs are easily drawn into
perpetual motherhood. They too find it hard to separate, particularly if
they have inherited a bipolar disorder or temperament and their own fears
of separation and abandonment fuse with those of the child.

There are no formulas for dealing with these particular problems, but
it is abundantly clear that managing the separation anxiety in the child
and becoming aware of its effects on the family should become a primary
therapeutic goal in the clinical treatment of the condition. Each mother
and each family will handle this problem differently. Their reactions will
be shaped in large measure by their experiences as children, parented by
mothers who may or may not have had the illness themselves.

Crucial is helping the child who experiences this level of fear and terror to understand that the sense of imminent loss of control (by becoming isolated from the mother) is not based on reality. But how do you do
this? Again, there are no formulas. Mothers have always cuddled,
swathed, swaddled, and rocked their babies to quiet and calm their distress, and mothers of bipolar children find themselves engaged in these ef-

forts, working overtime. They need to help the verbal child to grasp the range and intensity of his feelings—anxiety and anger as well as elation and depression—and to express these feelings openly on a regular basis. Any exercise that helps a child to label feelings and talk about them in play gives order, definition, and a feeling of self-control that would counter the prevailing tendency to believe that feelings are overwhelming and unmanageable—a tendency likely to impede emotional growth and maturation.

EFFECTS OF GENETIC PREDISPOSITION ON BEHAVIOR

If applied to humans, Hofer's model of a continuous dynamic interaction between infant and mother that itself acts as a modifying influence or buffer on the infant's central nervous system arousal functions is intriguing. It leads us to focus not only on the importance of mothers' parenting styles with children but to wonder how genetic influences that may confer a decreased capacity to break down brain catecholamines might influence the early developmental stages of ego maturation during the separation and individuation phase.

Could this commonly observed tendency of behavioral hyperresponsiveness to separation from the mother in animals and in humans be affected by a diminished capacity to break down brain catecholamines, such as in those individuals who inherit two copies of the low-activity catechol-O-methyltransferase (COMT) gene (see page 173)?

Interestingly, several recent studies have confirmed that the inheritance of two copies of the COMT low-activity gene, which confers a three- to fourfold lower level of activity of the enzyme, is strongly associated with ultra-ultrarapid cycling, the most common form of cycling in childhood-onset bipolar disorder.

How might such an inherited predisposition manifest itself developmentally? If being apart from the mother produces an expectable increase in the release of norepinephrine and dopamine (as per Hofer's animal model), but the child's genetic endowment leaves him or her with a diminished ability to break down the rising brain levels of these neurotransmitters, susceptibility for pronounced and prolonged separation distress could result.

Increased motor activity and restlessness as well as pronounced separation anxiety are frequently reported as early occurring features of childhood-onset bipolar disorder. In fact, Margaret Mahler's observations of human mothers and infants led her to propose that if the maturational spurt of locomotor activity takes place simultaneously with a lag in the child's emotional readiness to function separately from the mother, "organismic panic" may result. This state of panic would not be readily discernible because the preverbal child cannot communicate it. If each attempt at separation and reattachment is suffused by high degrees of fearfulness, increased arousal, and high states of anxiety—all disruptive states—and these are relieved only by continuing close proximity to the mother, an intense emotional attachment will likely ensue.

The normal phenomenon of active wooing and pleasure in sharing with the mother could turn into a repetitive, coercive, aggressive pattern of manipulation. Shadowing of the mother then becomes a desperate appeal to ward off the anticipated anxiety of overstimulation. In this state, toddlers have been observed to aggressively exclude any other goal-directed activity or substitute comforting by any person other than the mother. Clearly, a sense of mastery and autonomy could not develop if such anxiety were to persist. Thus a critically important transitional phase of individual social development would be arrested. And it would not be surprising that interactive play, sharing, and the acquisition of the language of interpersonal experience would be delayed. Each of these features was commonly reported in our survey of parents of children with early-onset bipolar disorder.

WILLIAM'S STORY

We have spent a good deal of time examining and trying to underscore some of the earliest behaviors and tendencies in children with bipolar disorder, and have speculated on some of the possible consequences on psychological development. The following account of William further illustrates the impact of the condition on the development of psychological defense mechanisms that evolve in these children.

William, age twelve, was referred by his psychotherapist for a diagnostic consultation. He was described as a gifted young boy who had an exceptional talent for mathematics and science and a strong self-esteem regarding these abilities. He was an avid reader who demonstrated intense and prolonged concentration playing computer games. While he loved to read and was enthused by science and mathematics, he was also very distractible, would lose his school equipment, and would overreact when teased by classmates. If he perceived their teasing as an insult, his mother said, "He would go to war, couldn't let it go, and would force a conflict." At these times he became quite volatile. Yet at other times he could be quite charming and often mischievous.

At age seven, William's social studies teacher reported that he was often squirming and fidgeting in his seat as well as disrespectful of rules and to authority figures at school. She viewed him as not achieving up to his potential and noted that he was melancholic, became easily bored, or lacked motivation. Yet at other times he could be a cheerful and engaging youngster who was excited by classroom discussions. These latter moods could easily escalate, and he would begin talking loudly and in a boisterous manner, sometimes using funny voices or offering nonsensical responses. On these occasions, William appeared to think he was smarter than the other students and refused to share the same assignments, regarding himself as special and entitled to a more individualized program of study.

William's oldest sister had been diagnosed at age twenty-five with rapid-cycling bipolar disorder and had periodic rage attacks. William's maternal grandmother had been hospitalized and treated with electroconvulsive therapy, and two paternal uncles were in treatment programs for alcoholism.

William had met all the normal milestones for motor and language development. While he toilet trained on time, he had a history of bedwetting and daytime wetting and soiling, which continued until the age of nine. He also experienced night terrors and had severe separation anxiety during early childhood until the age of nine.

He was noted by his teachers to have trouble reading social cues and was often in physical fights. William's parents reported that his oppositional behavior began to escalate during the first-grade year, whereas before that time he was viewed as being an "easy kid." His mother reported that he began to refuse to stop playing computer games at night and then would get to sleep late and have trouble waking up for school the next morning.

Concerned about these changes in their son's behavior, William's parents arranged for psychological testing, which revealed confusion about his emotional life and intense aggressive impulses. William's need to develop rigid defenses to ward off constant perceived threats from the environment (anything that portended of bodily harm or emotional abandonment) had become a predominant feature of his mental life. William's responses on the Children's Thematic Apperception Test (see

Chapter 11) were particularly disturbing. Eight of the nine stories he created involved death and dying and were filled with bizarre and gruesome content. They revealed anxious fantasies about losing his parents and were heavily laden with sadistic, aggressive elements as well as fears of bodily harm, physical mutilation, and emotional separation and loss.

William scored poorly on tests that used familiar pictures of real-life social situations and required careful attention to visual detail to find missing features in pictures, suggesting significant problems in the ability to decode social cues.

During a psychiatric evaluation he recounted many times of being picked on and fighting with older siblings and peers. He described feeling in a state of almost constant fearfulness—always threatened and feeling vulnerable to outside attack. Because he had difficulty distinguishing social cues, he would often misinterpret social advances for hostile intrusions into his private space, especially when outside of familiar contexts where he otherwise might feel secure or protected.

During the evaluation, William described two personas that evolved over time to respond to his experience of an ever-threatening environment:

> It's like I have two minds, one for living and one for fighting—like two different organisms with two different sets of logic, and they seem to have no connection to each other. When my fighting self, William Fight, takes over, he is unscarable, invulnerable. No bully can scare him. When I feel frightened, William Fight takes over and immediately begins to consider strategic options and the appropriate weapons of choice.

He described an encounter with a peer at school, who, according to William, brandished a knife. William Fight immediately chose an X-acto knife and prepared to throw it.

William was also afraid of being either physically or sexually abused at night, while asleep, and slept with a long stick at his bedside, saying, "If anyone intrudes in my space, I wake up immediately, alert, and prepared to do battle." When in "Fight" mode, William would experience a lot of energy and imagined fighting four or five other kids simultaneously. During these periods, he stated, "I get a rush of energy and I think really clearly."

William Fight was also, he thought, the source of his creative ideas. Says William, "He'll give me thoughts about medical technologies, antiterrorist activities, guns, missiles, space ships, and computer games."

He first recalls experiencing these intense aggressive feelings at around age seven, interestingly when the oppositional defiant behavior was originally observed by parents and teachers. At age twelve he described becoming easily fearful, then angry and volatile, sometimes four to five times within a day. Typically this would occur when he perceived others as picking on him or when surprised by some new situation or event. His sensitivity to social rejection, humiliation, disappointment, and loss was profound.

At other times when not feeling threatened, William would switch over to his second self, William Live. He explained that William Fight lets William Live do things that only have to do with happiness and that William Live is very optimistic. "He even thinks I still may be able to go back to being normal."

During these periods, William described feeling silly, goofy, giddy, and elated, and would become mischievous, develop fast, pressured, and loud speech, often saying things that were nonsensical and that others found odd. These periods, like the irritable, angry periods, could last for minutes or hours, and would occur many times within a day. William also volunteered that he had a very high level of energy and was often able to do with four to five hours of sleep on a regular basis. Although he would sleep deeply ("I'm able to sleep through fire alarms"), when he arose in the morning he was fully alert and aroused.

It is obvious that William has the common developmental sequence of signs, behaviors, and symptoms that are consistent with the diagnosis of early-onset bipolar disorder: separation anxiety; bedwetting and soiling; rapidly shifting irritable moods alternating with periods of elation; avoidant and oppositional behaviors; distractibility; angry aggressive rages; and, alternatively, a grandiose and self-deprecatory self-image; an abbreviated sleep cycle; and morbid concerns of death, dying, and mutilation.

Profound fears of loss and separation, the difficulty in adequately modulating intense emotions of elation, irritability, and the aggressive and sadistic impulses, coupled with discrete deficits in visual-motor integration (in the area of attention and executive memory, and in the capacity to decode social cues accurately) have placed significant obstacles in the way of the maturation of more adaptive coping skills that would lead to autonomous self-esteem regulation and the possibility of positive and sustaining peer relationships.

To cope with these intense impulses, emotions, and fears of abandonment and bodily harm, which can become magnified by the accumulated experience of the "perceived sense" of constant danger and threat from the environment, an inflexible, rigid defensive style often develops.

William's two personas, then, can be viewed as efforts to organize in thought, feeling, and behavior the intense mood and energy states—the hallmarks of untreated childhood bipolar disorder—that dominated his mental life. The irritable, angry, aggressive, and sadistic impulses that occur periodically throughout the day—often induced by perceived threat or slights—and the silly, goofy, giddy periods of elation are also a function of the ultra-ultrarapid cycling pattern typical of the condition.

Oppositional Behavior and Defiant Attitudes

Just as William displayed oppositional behaviors toward authority figures, our survey revealed that oppositional behavior and defiant attitudes toward parents were high on the list of associated features of early-onset bipolar disorder. Confirmation of this observation comes from preliminary findings reported by the Stanley Foundation Childhood-onset Bipolar Disorder Consortium, showing that 80 percent of the children and adolescents they studied met *DSM-IV* criteria for oppositional defiant disorder.

Usually appearing between the ages of six and eight, this aspect of the condition poses significant challenges for parents and educators who must contend with the unreasonable demands, refusals, and the unprovoked rigidity that commonly occur in these children.

Psychological theory suggests that oppositional behavior is defensive in nature and arises out of an attempt to maintain control when stressful experience threatens personal autonomy or judgment. Children who are striving to feel safe when the world around them feels threatening, who are distractible, who have difficulty switching from one activity to another, who are easily aroused by novel stimuli, or who frequently misrepresent the intentions of others are prime candidates to use oppositional behavior to protect themselves and establish some semblance of control in the world. They try to accomplish this by constantly standing their

ground—admitting no new stimuli, no changes, and no transitions—
with absolute resolve.

Such intensity of conviction might be tolerated if it were attached to
some important value, but a struggle of this proportion can ensue over a
parent's request to come to the dinner table. The combination of intensity and inflexibility that these children bring to social interactions cannot help but produce conflict with parents, siblings, friends, and
educators. But from the point of view of a bipolar child, this is an adaptive response. Any request to change or to transition from one place to another is perceived as a stressor and then quickly transformed into a threat.
Anxiety levels rise, and when the parent persists and reinforces some necessary priority, such as "You've got to get up now so you have enough
time to get dressed and have breakfast before the school bus arrives," anxiety over this regular daily separation arises and tips the scales toward
stubborn opposition.

It is as if these children are responding to a pressing inner emotional
directive that is signaling red alert and whose switch is easily triggered.
Since the children have little capacity to stop, reflect, and interrupt this
alarm, they meet change with oppositional and defiant behaviors that
eventually can crystallize as formidable defensive postures. Resistance
from the outside simply raises the pitch.

The constant exercise of oppositional and stubbornly defiant behaviors
in interactions with others, while personally and socially maladaptive,
serves the greater goal of preserving self-identity. Ultimately, however,
the continuation of this behavior draws greater and greater negative attention, further isolating these children from others, narrowing their social experience, and limiting the possibilities for healthy interactions that
might serve to provide a greater sense of mastery, self-control, and self-
esteem.

Over time, children who constantly dig in their heels and refuse to listen to parents and whose behavior alienates potential friends feel negatively about themselves and are more isolated and more fearful. In
adolescence these behavioral tendencies can consolidate as defense mechanisms and gradually become enduring features of the personality. Such
behaviors, typically experienced as disobedience and disrespect, elicit
consistent negative responses from parents and the larger social world,
further eroding an already fragile sense of self-esteem. Oppositional behavior and defiant attitudes combine with a strong inclination to take

risks and easy addictability to psychoactive drugs, such as marijuana and cocaine, rendering adolescence a minefield waiting to detonate the illness.

When children feel threatened by something they cannot contain or control, opposition to the source of that feeling can provide a sense of immediate relief that some pressing need will not be extinguished or forever lost. Frequent refusals to accept the legitimacy of a parental "no" can be viewed as the bipolar child's inadequate effort to establish some absolute boundary—some anchor that holds time still and everything else constant.

ANXIETY, NEGATIVE EMOTIONS, AND THE FEAR OF LOSS OF CONTROL

Current developments in cognitive and emotion theory suggest that anxiety plays a central role in negative emotions, such as anger, rage, and irritability. Growing evidence indicates that early experience with diminished control may foster a mind-set likely to interpret or process events as out of one's control. Persistent anxiety of imminently losing an attachment to the mother, easy distractibility, motor restlessness, and bedwetting are common in boys with childhood-onset bipolar disorder. Such a set of symptoms occurring daily in the life of a child could be expected to cause high levels of anxiety; over time, the child could tend to interpret events as being out of control. When combined with frequent misrepresentations of the intentions of others, anger, rage, and irritability in a child might be a final common behavioral pathway.

When children continuously experience aggressive and explosive outbursts and prolonged temper tantrums, they are certain to feel even more of a loss of control. This leads to a poor sense of mastery over a host of cognitive, bodily, and emotional functions. In these children arousal, attention, motor behavior, and emotional responses are all subject to erratic regulation, which reinforces a feeling of threat to personal autonomy and self-integrity.

IMPULSIVE BEHAVIOR

As children mature, they become increasingly capable of manipulating objects and events symbolically, thereby becoming free of concrete dependency on them. Jean Piaget spoke of the development of intelligence as always moving toward increased spatial and temporal distance between the individual and the environment. And although young children cannot inhibit impulse expression very well, over time they become increasingly capable of interposing thought and reflection between impulse and action, which allows them to delay action and attune to the demands or requirements of the social situation.

Children with bipolar disorder have difficulty postponing gratification, taking turns, waiting on others, or holding back an impulse to talk first or have it all. This sets the stage for frequent conflict with others, sadly restricting the possibilities for the adaptive and maturing experiences of sharing, appreciation, and empathy.

DISTRACTIBILITY AND INATTENTION

All of the behaviors and symptoms that occur in attention-deficit disorder with hyperactivity were also reported in our survey of early-onset bipolar disorder—at very high rates. A significant majority of children had five or more of the primary symptoms, including difficulty sustaining attention and effort (distractibility), lack of attention to details, difficulty following through on tasks or instructions, motor restlessness, difficulty waiting one's turn, and interrupting or intruding on others. Children with early-onset bipolar disorder have deficits in a crucial set of thinking skills that are most often referred to as "executive functions."

Specifically, executive functions include cognitive skills such as the ability to shift efficiently from one mind-set to another and the ability to organize and plan strategically. This kind of planning includes the anticipation of problems and the formulation of goals in response to problems. Deficits in working memory—information stored and accessible in short-term memory—and the ability to separate one's emotions from one's thoughts interfere with these executive functions.

The ordinary demands of the child's life are fraught by the constant perceived dangers of loss of emotional control and anxiety over change. We know from recent research studies that the capacity to assess information, plan reactions smoothly, adhere to social rules, and evaluate what is and what is not a threat varies with the degree of individual control over arousal and its effects on attention and social memory (reflection on past experience). If a child who is easily aroused has difficulty separating emotion from thought, cannot regulate angry impulses, and selectively feels the need to defend against a perceived threat or rejection, there are few behavioral alternatives available; these imperatives dictate an expectable response such as opposition, anger, or rage.

CONCLUSION

During early development, human beings learn to substitute the exclusive caring that is provided by parental figures with attachment to others. Gradually humans attempt to establish mastery over the environment, developing varying and unique styles of adaptation that provide in adult life the individual distinction we call character or personality.

Along the way a child must meet a variety of developmental challenges; he or she learns how to walk, to modulate emotion and response to stress, to organize memory, to establish psychological defenses. Each stage has its issues, however, and many things can go awry. Whether it be the separation-individuation stage of infancy, the learning and peer-relatedness of childhood, or the struggles over dependence and autonomy that come to prominence in adolescence, the individual temperament of the child plays a large role in how each stage is negotiated.

As we have described, children with bipolar disorder appear to have pronounced deficits in modulating arousal states and sensory responses to the environment from an early age. Not surprisingly, their reactions to stressful or novel stimuli lead to high levels of anxiety and deficits in negotiating social boundaries as well as to problems with separation and attachment and to persistent difficulties in sustaining stable peer relationships.

Because of the high degree of arousability and sensitivity to physical and environmental stimuli, these children may need to make more dramatic and often more extreme adaptations to social contexts. They tend to be more rigid and inflexible in response to parental rules and requests—their reactions may be driven primarily by natural attempts to safeguard themselves from overstimulation and to protect against a pervasive fear of losing control. Yet, paradoxically, they may also be bold, adventurous, and uninhibited—driven toward the pursuit of stimulation that brings physical pleasure and/or intellectual or creative satisfaction. These latter tendencies, when channeled appropriately and with sufficient discipline, have produced some of the greatest scientific and artistic achievements in the history of humankind.

All of these states of increasing or diminishing arousal are regulated by central nervous system processes in reaction to bodily and environmental demands. Since neuroscience has delineated the basic characteristics of the arousal system, disturbances in levels of arousal can be reliably traced to particular regions of the brain, innervated by known neurotransmitter and neuropeptide pathways. It is to these systems that we turn next.

What Causes
This Condition?

Parents watching a child smile one minute, turn tyrannical the next, then hurl obscene phrases at family members, and finally escalate into explosive tantrums may look to appease the child for a time and feel tremendous anger and confusion. Sooner or later, after relentlessly examining their own parenting skills and attending class after class to improve them, these parents are going to ask themselves: "What on earth could be going on inside this child's brain?"

What indeed.

To address this question, we begin by focusing on brain/behavior relationships that seem most relevant to the clinical description of the illness. We explore the most recent findings from psychiatric and behavioral neuroscience research, and we provide the background information necessary to examine the hypotheses being advanced to explain the underlying biological basis of the condition.

We believe that genetic information inherent in our cells unfolds in the context of the internal and external environment and that certain vulnerability genes predispose to disturbances in the regulations of emotion and behavior.

In this chapter we also examine the overall workings of the brain and its multiple circuits and their interactions and how these interactions play into behavior. And we examine the neurotransmitter and neuropeptide systems that influence arousal, anxiety, stress, fear, aggression, attention, reward, sleep, and body temperature regulation, and the biological timing functions of these systems. In addition, we look at the interacting functions of the limbic and neuroendocrine systems and their known effects on the organization of behavior.

TOWARD A NEW DEFINITION OF THE SYNDROME

A newer definition of early-onset bipolar disorder, which builds on earlier views but is further informed by more recent clinical and family genetic studies, might be as follows:

1. Marked variations in mood and energy that are characterized by abrupt, rapidly alternating levels of arousal, emotion, excitability, and motor activity, typically, with four variable mood states of differing duration and severity: mirthful (silly, goofy, giddy, elated, overly optimistic, grandiose); angry (irritable, aggressive, violent, paranoid); depressed (withdrawn, bored, overly pessimistic, sad, or dysphoric), and anxious (worrying, ruminative, fearful, obsessive, compulsive, agitated).

   a. Hypomanic or manic episodes are often associated with elated, euphoric, or irritable mood states; flight of ideas; diminished need for sleep; increased energy and activity; and decreased appetite.

   b. Depressive mood states are often associated with loss of interest in previously enjoyed activities; decreased sense of self-esteem; slowed speech; paucity of thought; increased need for sleep; decreased energy; psychomotor retardation; and sweet and carbohydrate cravings.

   Mood, energy, and arousal states (environmental reactivity) often exhibit regular diurnal variations. These daily patterns are typically manifest by low energy and irritable mood states in the morning and excessive energy with hyperactivity, and greater mood lability and arousability, in the late afternoon that intensifies over the course of the evening into the night.

   Seasonal change may be associated with a lengthening or shortening of this two-phased daily pattern. Typically, periods of lower energy levels are more pronounced and of longer duration in the fall/winter, while the nighttime higher energy periods with motor disinhibition are attenuated. Conversely, in the spring/summer higher energy states with accompanying motor disinhibition and elated or irritable mood states intensify in the afternoon, are of longer duration, and reach their peak in the late evening and night.

2. Poor modulation of drives (aggressive, sexual, appetitive, acquisitive) associated with excessive anger/fight-based behaviors (critical, sarcastic, demanding, oppositional, overbearing, "bossy," easily enraged, prone to violent outbursts), and/or self-directed aggression (head-banging, skin-picking, cutting, suicide attempts), or flight-based behaviors (separation anxiety, clinginess, panic, phobia); as well as premature and intense sexual feelings and behaviors (precocious curiosity about sex and early expression of sexual impulses, as well as inappropriate public displays); appetite dysregulation (binge eating, purging, and anorexia); and poor control over acquisitive impulses (buying excessively and hoarding).

3. Sleep/wake cycle disturbances, including initial insomnia, middle insomnia, early morning awakening, and sleep arousals, as manifest by night terrors and nightmares (often containing images of gore and mutilation, as well as themes of pursuit and abandonment), sleepwalking, confusional arousals, bruxism (teeth grinding), and enuresis (bedwetting), as well as a tendency toward periodic lengthening or shortening of sleep duration, often dependent on circannual changes in light/dark and temperature cycles, as well as the availability of regular social zeitgebers (time givers).

4. A low threshold for frustration in situations that require sustained attention, interest, and effort is manifest by difficulties with postponement of immediate gratification, such as waiting one's turn, or denial of expressed needs, changes in planned activities, or making required transitions from one context to another. This deficit, combined with poorly regulated attentional focus, often results in maladaptive responses, such as seeming not to listen, interrupting or intruding on others, and disruptive, oppositional/defiant, and provocative behaviors, or—in the extreme—temper tantrums and aggressive rage attacks, often followed by sullen withdrawal and expressions of remorse. Episodes of anger dyscontrol, temper tantrums, rages—usually of more

than half an hour in duration—may occur spontaneously, but are most often precipitated by limit-setting attempts by parents or other authority figures, and are commonly associated with the use of profane language and/or the expression of physical violence.

5. Poor self-esteem regulation is manifest by extreme rejection sensitivity, associated with feelings of insecurity, worthlessness, humiliation, and shame, or alternatively, the individual is overly optimistic, arrogant, defiant, with bravado and grandiose ideas of self. Rapid and intense idealizations and devalutions of self and others are associated features.

6. Deficits in the capacity to habituate when exposed to novel, repetitive, or monotonous sensory stimulation. A tendency to overreact to stressful emotional stimuli and to become overaroused, anxious, or fearful in response to transitions in context, separation/loss/ rejection, as well as anticipated separation/loss or rejection.

7. A tendency toward increased cycling, increased aggression/oppositionality, and/or psychotic symptoms when exposed to antidepressants, stimulants, corticosteroid derivatives, and caffeine.

8. Executive function deficits as manifest by difficulty shifting cognitive set, planning ahead, strategic planning (unrealistic estimates of energy resources and time requirements for the accomplishment of tasks), as well as difficulties maintaining focused attention. Working memory and word retrieval deficits are also common. This executive dysfunction is often associated with problems making transitions from one context to another, distractibility, excessive daydreaming, poor organizational skills, and performance deficits in school, particularly in the organization of written expression (see Chapter 11).

9. Poor modulation of motor outflow and motor movement (dyspraxias, dysgraphia, pressured speech, fidgetiness, finger-tapping, and tics).

10. Commonly comorbid with other *DSM-IV* diagnoses including: enuresis, night terrors, separation anxiety, panic and phobic disorders, attention-deficit disorder (ADHD), obsessive-compulsive disorder (OCD), oppositional defiant disorder (ODD), conduct disorder (CD), Tourette's syndrome, Asperger's syndrome, nonverbal learning disabilities, and substance abuse.

11. A family history of recurrent mood disorder and/or alcoholism, as well as other bipolar spectrum disorders. When full syndromal

onset occurs before the age of nine, a history of bilineal familial transmission is commonly observed—it appears to be coming down both the mother's and father's sides.

Could a common frame of reference encompass these seemingly disparate symptoms—exaggerated startle and stress responses, separation distress, sleep/wake disturbances, heightened and inhibited sensory states, elation/irritability and depression, high- and low-energy states, and poor control of impulses, particularly seen in the tendency for aggressive rages? Can biological differences attributable to a genetic predisposition and environmental interactions explain this unusual combination of symptoms and behaviors?

To answer these questions, we need to understand the architecture of the brain and the processes by which it communicates with the body, and the world around it.

INSIDE THE BRAIN: THE LIMBIC-DIENCEPHALON

The human brain is the most complex structure on earth. Its three and a half pounds of gray and white matter compressed into a structure no larger than a grapefruit sits above our bony spines. Packed into this space are perhaps 100 billion brain cells. Each of these cells may make thousands of connections with adjoining or distant cells. There are likely to be more than 100 trillion possible interconnections. A final measure of the brain's complexity is its dynamic nature: It changes constantly and undergoes continuous modification in response to environmental stimuli.

A major task of the nervous system is to maintain the regularity of the internal environment—homeostasis—and to integrate and modulate incoming information from our senses. Although virtually the whole brain is involved in maintaining homeostasis, neurons that control the internal environment are concentrated in the hypothalamus, a set of nuclei located in a small area in the center of the brain called the diencephalon. The hypothalamus interacts with the limbic cortex—the emotional brain—and the cerebral neocortex—the thinking brain—via hormonal, neuropeptide, and neurotransmitter systems. The hypothalamus and closely linked structures in the limbic system keep the internal environment constant by regulating four related functions: hormonal secretions, the autonomic nervous system, the emotions and drives, and body temperature (see Figure 8.1).

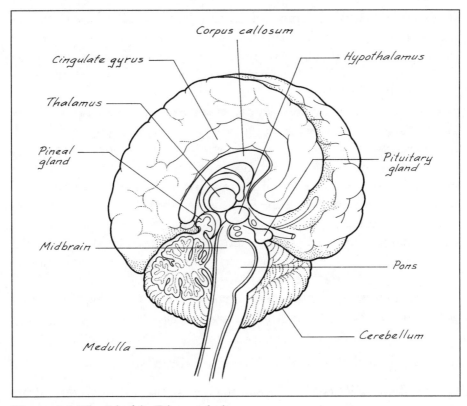

Figure 8.1 The Limbic-Diencephalon

Autonomic Nervous System

The autonomic nervous system automatically controls glands and structures such as the lungs, heart, blood vessels, and pupils of the eyes. Linked with the brain's hypothalamus and spinal cord (which carries information from our senses), this system is influenced by the central nervous system but is responsible for activities over which we have no conscious control. In fact, the autonomic nervous system harks back to our reptilian ancestors.

The autonomic nervous system consists of two subsystems—the parasympathetic and sympathetic systems—that act more or less in opposition to balance each other. The sympathetic-system nerves work as a unit and deal particularly with the body's reaction to emergency. In times of physical danger or stress, they cause sweating, increase blood pressure, and mobilize the organism for fight or flight. The lack of a properly functioning sympathetic nervous system becomes evident under circumstances of stress. Body temperature cannot be regulated when environmental temperature varies; the concentration of blood glucose does not rise in response to urgent need; instinctive reactions to fright and danger are lost; and a host of other serious deficiencies occur in the protective forces of the body.

In direct contrast to the sympathetic nervous system, the parasympathetic system puts a brake on the heart rate, contracts pupils, and feeds blood away from brain and muscles to the intestines. Normally, these two opposing systems maintain a balance in the body. Under stress, the sympathetic system dominates; during relaxation, the parasympathetic system takes over (see Figure 8.2).

Different patterns of activity of the autonomic nervous system can produce different emotional states. Acting through different parts of the limbic-hypothalamic system, the autonomic nervous system elicits different types of emotional behaviors, such as the stress, startle, and rage responses. Importantly, all of these responses are clearly magnified and/or poorly modulated in children with bipolar disorders.

The Brain and the Limbic-Diencephalic System

Over millions of years of evolution, the human brain has developed from the bottom up, with higher centers developing as elaborations of more primitive parts. Near the center of the brain is the area on which most mood disorder researchers focus—the limbic-diencephalic system. This is composed of the limbic system, the hypothalamus, and the brain stem. In addition to its involvement in emotion, memory, and motivated behavior, the limbic system influences all parts of the body's endocrine system by controlling the release of hypothalamic hormones that regulate behavioral reactions to environmental events.

Limbic System
The term "limbic" was originally an anatomical designation given by Pierre Paul Broca in 1876 to a ring of brain tissue containing a group of structures closely connected to the hypothalamus. These structures contain the hippocampus, the amygdala, and the septum. They form a border (limbus) around a ventricle, or fluid-filled cavity, in the center of the brain that bathes many of the structures of the limbic system with chemical messengers from the adjacent hypothalamus. The hippocampus and the amygdala are the two key parts of the primitive brain that, during

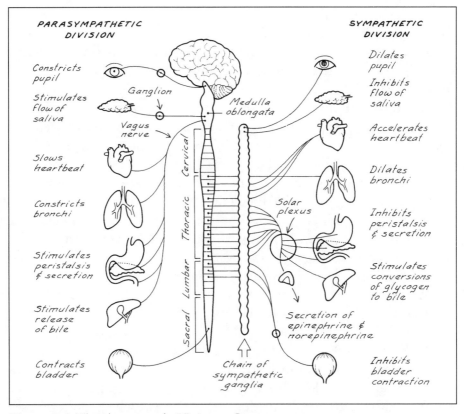

Figure 8.2 The Autonomic Nervous System
The sympathetic and parasympathetic divisions of the autonomic nervous system and the organs and glands that are stimulated or inhibited by their mutually opposing effects.

evolution, gave rise to the cortex and then the neocortex (the thinking brain).

The brain, excluding the brain stem, could be viewed as two concentric shells surrounding this central ventricle. The inner shell, or limbic lobe, contains the amygdala, hippocampus, and septum as well as other important regions that receive, integrate, and interpret information from the senses and regulate emotion and modulate its expression. The structures of the limbic system are connected by a complex series of circuits that employ neurotransmitters and neuropeptides as information messengers and respond to hormonal, temperature, and other sensory influences. Within the network of limbic circuitry, internal as well as external sensory states and the imprint of experience is superimposed and remembered.

From Sensation to Feeling

The limbic system (see Figure 8.3) appears to act as a central information processing system, channeling the sensory input, regulating the motor output pathways of the brain, and imbuing the processes with emotional meaning. The structures within the limbic system do not receive any sensory input directly; rather they interact and exchange information with the neocortex, the hypothalamus, and the autonomic nervous system. As the mediator, so to speak, of human feelings, the limbic system receives, regulates, and assembles highly organized information derived from sensations, momentary events, memories of events, and emotions associated with those events. The limbic forebrain acts as a filter for the sensory receiving areas of the brain prior to the assignment of emotional meaning to an event or experience. Additionally, through its reciprocal relationship with the hypothalamus, it governs sexual desire and hunger and thirst as well as the response to fear and the self-protective mechanism of fight or flight. It is no wonder that researchers in the field of bipolar disorder focus on this region of the brain.

Startle Response—An Overresponsive Early Warning System

When presented with a series of bright lights, babies first startle, then gradually respond less and less. The increase in heart and respiratory rates seen after the initial startle gradually diminish. "Habituation" is the term used to describe this protective response of closing down the nervous system.

Many bipolar children have a marked tendency to experience more intense startle responses from a very early age.

The startle reflex evolved to protect animals from blows or predatory attacks by quickly stiffening the limbs, body, and neck muscles before the decision to flee or fight. So it is directly linked to the biological "equipment" that generates the stress, or fight-or-flight, response.

We now know that these pathways involve the flow of information from sensory neurons in the body traveling via neurochemical pathways to the cerebral cortex and amygdala, a structure that resides within the temporal lobes of the limbic system and is directly connected to the hippocampus.

The Amygdala

The amygdala is the brain structure that commandeers rational response and leads to the expression of powerful and unmodulated emotion in full-scale rage attacks.

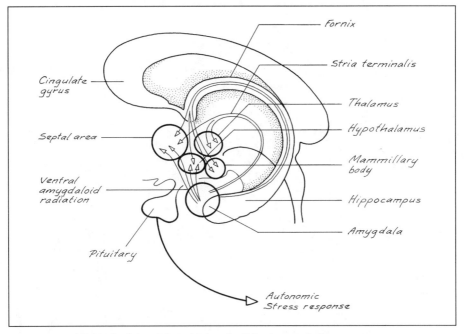

Figure 8.3 The Limbic-Hypothalamic-Pituitary Axis
An overview of some of the connections between the limbic system, hypothalamus, and autonomic nervous system. A proposed neural circuit underlying emotional expression starts with the mammillary body of the hypothalamus as the site of output for expression of the emotions through its projections to the midbrain (not shown). The cingulate gyrus that projects to the hippocampus is considered to be the receptive field for emotional information in the cortex. The hippocampus combines this and other inputs and organizes the information to be transmitted to the mammillary bodies in the hypothalamus, thus completing the circuit.

In the brain's architecture, the almond-shape amygdala is poised like an emotional sentinel or alarm center and is involved in fear responses and in initiating the first stages of the assembly of emotional memories (see Figure 8.4). The amygdala receives signals that are of potential danger: (1) Signals from the eyes and ears travel first to the sensory thalamus (2), which transmits partial information about the stimulus to the amygdala (3), allowing a more rapid response well before centers in the visual cortex, or thinking brain (4), have fully assessed the complete nature of the signal. A primitive emotion such as rage takes this route to the amygdala, causing a response that is totally raw and unvarnished. Most of the signal, however, is delivered to the visual cortex, where it is analyzed and

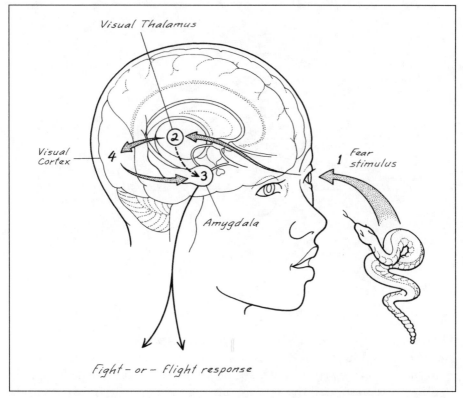

Figure 8.4 Neuronal Pathways of the Fight-or-Flight Response

assessed for meaning and appropriate response. If this more measured response of the signal confirms that it indeed poses a threat, the fight-or-
flight response is triggered in the amygdala.

The amygdala is not the bad guy of the brain. If ears register a growl
and eyes perceive an animal that looks like a lion, the amygdala provides
a rapid and perhaps lifesaving response.

Studies in humans, using new functional magnetic resonance neuroimaging techniques that allow brief time-elapsed observations of the
brain, have shown that the amygdala is activated in response to the sight
of frightening faces. Other reports describe individuals with complete destruction of the amygdala who cannot form accurate social judgments
based on facial expression.

Incomplete or confusing stimuli from the sense organs signal the
amygdala to scan the environment for danger. Bipolar children and those
with learning and attentional deficits have significant problems with the
integration of sensory information. Such disturbances may cause bipolar

children to misinterpret a casual touch as a threatening gesture or to over-react to normal social verbal cues. These children can become hypervigilant and show paranoid tendencies as well as express severe and prolonged defensive reactions. For instance, they can become oppositional or aggressive, or they can withdraw. These overreactions could derive, in part, from the isolated activity of the amygdala, cut off from the modulating influences and accumulated wisdom of the higher cortical centers, through which attention and motor behavior are coordinated. Or perhaps some sensory-perceptual disturbance provides a confusing signal to the brain, or both.

The Hippocampus

The hippocampus looks like a wishbone that fits snugly against the inner wall of the neocortex. It is the gateway from the neocortex to the rest of the limbic system, and it plays a central role in processing and distributing information from the cortex to other parts of the limbic system. In effect, the neocortex and the sensory nervous system feed information to the hippocampus, and the hippocampus then returns the processed information back to the neocortex. Somehow, within this loop of nervous tissue, sensory information is analyzed and brought together to register an event, imbue it with emotional meaning, and store it in memory. But just how is sensory information from the environment registered in the brain?

The Hippocampal Theta Rhythm: A Signal of the Processing of Sensory Information

In 1953 John Green and Arnaldo Arduini at the University of California at Los Angeles placed electrodes in the hippocampus and neocortex of rabbits, trying to record the electrical activity of both structures simultaneously. They found that brain waves oscillating at about four to seven times per second, called theta waves, were the most prominent electrical signal recorded from the hippocampus.

Neuroscientist Dr. Jonathan Winson of New York University has proposed that the theta rhythm in lower animals is a signal of the neuronal processing of sensory information that may have evolved originally to coordinate all sensory input with cycles of scanning and exploration of the environment. Such focused attentional responses are likely to have evolved in direct relationship with efforts to rapidly distinguish between predator or prey and therefore represent important survival behaviors that are closely linked to fight-or-flight behaviors.

Alternations in theta rhythm might act like a gating mechanism, switching the path of information flow through the hippocampus during different states of "fearful" arousal stimulated by the amygdala. A "state" refers to the degree of attentiveness, the variation in mood or motor responsiveness. So, the theta rhythm could be seen as a reflection of an important brain mechanism that enhances or withdraws attention from external or internal stimuli. It may operate as a selective filter that either prolongs our attentional focus or habituates to a signal from the environment.

When brain functions are balanced, people can make smooth transitions from one state to another. They are able to switch gears from inattention to attention, from fear to receptivity, from drowsiness to alertness, from relaxation to readiness to action. A modulation process balances the flow of sensory information coming into the central nervous system. Poorly modulated arousal systems would predispose to emotional imbalance and distractibility of attention. Bipolar children seem to experience almost any transition that requires shifting the focus of attention or giving up stimuli that they are focusing on as threatening and unmanageable.

Sometimes the brain of the bipolar child appears to register sensory experiences too intensely; at other times, events are registered barely at all, with wide variations. When overaroused by sensations (internal or external), the child reacts as if the sensations are irritating, annoying, or even threatening. Thus, the child may be extremely distractible because he or she is attending to too many stimuli and is unable to discriminate between those that are useful and those that are irrelevant. Such a deficit in sensory equilibrium could contribute to the extreme expression of the two poles of the stress response—fight-oppose or flight-avoid. This disequilibrium could result in behaviors that are negative, defiant, oppositional, aggressive, or alternatively fearful, anxious, or cautious—socially maladaptive behaviors commonly seen in early-onset bipolar disorder.

Bursts of Rage and the Theta Rhythm

Irrational rage attacks are the most disturbing behavior of children with bipolar disorder, and certainly the one that most disrupts family life and sours relationships. Psychological explanations clearly do not do justice to these overwhelming assaults on the ordinary boundaries of self-control. The amygdala may be one area of the limbic system involved in the expression of unmodified emotion; the septum is another.

For many years researchers have known that electrical stimulation or surgical destruction of the septum (the source of the hippocampal theta rhythm) produces profound effects on the expression of emotional behaviors. The term "septal rage" has been coined to describe the marked hyperemotionality and hyperactivity seen in animals after lesions have been made in this important area of the limbic system. Distractibility, hyperalertness to approaching movement, explosive startle reactions to auditory and tactile stimulation, and vicious attacks coupled with loud vocalizations are among the many behavioral aberrations associated with septal rage in primates.

In many ways the intense emotionality and reactivity to sensory stimulation that seem to provoke the septal-rage syndrome are indistinguishable from the long-lasting rage attacks so commonly reported in children with bipolar disorder.

Neurotransmitter and neuropeptide pathways that influence the capacity to inhibit theta rhythm in animals may be directly related to dampening or enhancing the effect or intensity of sensory stimuli. Thereby they may affect the degree of behavioral responsiveness in situations of high alertness and general emotional arousal.

CIRCUIT OF EMOTION

The interconnections among the various limbic centers, the hypothalamus, and the neocortex led neuroanatomist James Papez to propose in 1937 that this anatomical circuit is the neuronal substrate of emotion. He claimed that these structures formed a circuit that permitted emotion to arise through neuronal activity in the limbic system and noted that the lesions of the rabies virus principally attack the hippocampus. The intense behavioral and emotional symptoms that occur in the early states of the disease—insomnia, irritability, and restlessness—typically usher in a stage of excitement and profound mood lability as well as excruciating sensitivity to all forms of stimuli, such as light and sound. All of these rabies-related behavioral, sensory, and mood changes are similar to the signs and symptoms experienced by patients with bipolar disorder.

When adults with bipolar disorder describe the heightened sensory awareness that often accompanies hypomania and mania, they describe this awareness as initially pleasurable; however, as the mania escalates, people lose the capacity to halt the incessant barrage of sensory stimulation or to modulate the sensory overload, and the mood turns irritable as mental faculties are overwhelmed.

With the hippocampus no longer able to filter sensory experiences, the world is extremely overstimulating and threatening. Individuals in this state experience intense panic and paranoia and often end-of-the-world annihilation delusions. The famous and often-reproduced woodcut *The Scream,* by the Norwegian artist Edvard Munch, who himself suffered from manic-depressive illness, perhaps best captures this state of unending overstimulation.

Panic, Dread, and a Sense of Impending Doom

Patients in the throes of a panic attack experience a sense of impending doom—each moment is filled with dread and a sense of imminent danger from an unseen, imagined source. Physical symptoms, such as a racing heart, sweating, and short, uneven, and rapid breathing that accompany this fearful state are driven by the autonomic nervous system, presumably activated by limbic sources. A disturbance in the neuronal activity of the limbic system could produce difficulties in registering emotional meaning and cause children to be overalert to stimuli. This disturbance might lead children to display extremes of attentional focus (hypervigilance), emotional arousal, and an overactive startle response. Such children might overreact to environmental stressors and are more likely to experience anxiety and have a tendency to panic. Interestingly, recent population studies have found that over 30 percent of adult patients with bipolar disorder have recurrent episodes of panic attacks. In our survey, high rates of panic symptoms were also observed in children diagnosed with bipolar disorder.

Eli Robbins and his colleagues at Washington University in St. Louis used positron emission tomography (PET)—a scanning procedure that allows visualization of cerebral blood flow and metabolic changes in the brain—on patients with panic disorder. These researchers discovered a circumscribed abnormality in the right parahippocampal gyrus of the limbic system, a region of the hippocampus that lies near the amygdala. In these patients, blood flow to this area is abnormally higher than that in the corresponding area in the left hemisphere.

Also using PET, Dr. Wayne Drevets and colleagues at the University of Pittsburgh School of Medicine recently reported finding abnormalities in patients diagnosed with bipolar disorder who had positive family histories for the disorder. These researchers localized an area of abnormally decreased activity in the prefrontal cortex. Other studies have implicated this area in autonomic responses to stressful and emotionally provocative stimuli. The prefrontal cortex seems to respond when a person is fearful or enraged, and it stifles or controls the feeling in order to deal more effectively with the situation at hand. This area of the neocortex receives the largest sensory projection from the thalamus, possibly for taking in and making sense of perceptions and planning responses.

Hypothalamus

A whole constellation of nuclei participate in the expression of emotion. The hypothalamus works with the limbic system in the genesis of emotion, and together they are involved in the control of hormone secretion and the regulation of the autonomic nervous system. Functionally, this interaction allows coordination between emotional and motivational states and the regulation of visceral functions such as blood pressure, heart rate, body temperature, and size of the eye's pupil.

Many of the clinical features of depression and mania as well as the physiological findings, suggest some dysfunction in the limbic-hypothalamic circuit. One consistently replicated finding is that the interval between sleep onset and the beginning of the first period of rapid-eye movement sleep (REM) is shortened. This shortening of the first REM period is called "shortened REM latency." Another finding, particularly true of bipolar patients who have seasonal cycles, is a seasonal disturbance in body temperature regulation—a difficulty dissipating a heat load in the summer months. Preliminary findings from our own pilot study suggest that childhood-onset bipolar patients run persistently low body temperatures ranging from 96.5° to 97.4°F.

REM sleep and body temperature regulation are closely related. Mammals become essentially cold-blooded during REM sleep, when the primary heat loss mechanisms are practically unresponsive to changes in the ambient temperature. The onset of sleep is usually preceded by a dramatic descent in body temperature. During the first part of sleep the temperature continues to fall, and this is associated with increased heat loss, a relatively high percentage of stages 3 and 4 sleep, and a high percentage of REM sleep. Heat retention, through decreased sweating and blood vessel constriction, appears to be closely linked to REM sleep. These thermoregulatory changes, governed, in part, by warm-sensitive and cold-sensitive nerve cells in the hypothalamus, together with the close temporal relationship of REM onset to the body temperature minimum suggest that the circadian rhythm of REM propensity is one of the major oscillating systems involved in body temperature regulation. Therefore, persistently low body temperature that appears to occur in patients with childhood-onset bipolar disorder may be related to some disturbance in thermoregulation.

The Hypothalamic-Pituitary-Adrenal Axis: Stress and Defense Responses

The four-gram, walnut-size hypothalamus is arguably the most important structure of the limbic system. This "brain" within the brain regulates a host of human processes, including appetite, thirst, sleep, sexual desire, energy metabolism, and body temperature, as well as the timing of many other basic behavioral functions on an hour-by-hour or daily basis. The hypothalamus regulates the master gland of the brain—the pituitary— and the pineal gland, a major part of the daily and seasonal timing system of the brain. The pituitary releases adrenocorticotropic hormone (ACTH), which activates the adrenal gland to release cortisol, setting off the so-called stress response. The pineal gland receives light/dark signals from the environment through another hypothalamic nucleus with the tongue-twisting name suprachiasmatic—the master clock of the nervous system.

The Stress Response/The Defense Response

Stress prompts a series of marked physiological changes. For humans, many times stress results from a change in meaning of a given experience or changes in sensory responses to the environment. As we have seen, the attachment of emotional meaning to remembered events is mediated through the interaction of limbic system and neocortex. A response is then transmitted via limbic connections to the hypothalamus, where it is evaluated in the cortex and then transmitted through the sympathetic nervous system to coordinate the fight-or-flight response.

The release of adrenal glucocorticoids represents the end result of the activation of the hypothalamic-pituitary-adrenal (HPA-limbic) axis. Under most circumstances, this response occurs as a result of the release of specific neuropeptides from specialized neurons in the hypothalamus. In the face of danger, this short-lived reaction helps individuals survive. However, if the stress response is regularly tripped for the wrong reasons, or alternatively, if it cannot be turned off, it can have the opposite effect.

Excessive stress can also cause developmental abnormalities, unhealthy weight gain, heart disease, hypertension, diabetes, depression, and immune suppression.

What Activates the Stress Response?

The major stimulators of arousal and stress appear to be pain, novelty, uncertainty, and conflict. The response to novelty, for example, requires a comparison between patterns and features of the particular stimulus and the remembered characteristics of the stimulus recorded in long-term memory. The greater the difference or dissonance between the pattern evoked by the immediate stimulus and the prior experience, the greater the degree of the adrenocortical stress response.

When adrenal steroids such as cortisol are released into the circulatory system, they reach the brain and influence central nervous system functions by attaching to glucocorticoid receptors—the receptors for cortisol—located in specialized regions in the brain. An intricate feedback loop regulates the availability of these receptors in the dentate gyrus of the hippocampus. Changes in receptor number can alter the degree to which a hormonal signal is "heard" by the cell and how rapidly the stress response can be stopped.

Laboratory studies have shown that the reduction of glucocorticoid receptors in the dentate gyrus, due to exposure to stress or to persistently high blood levels of glucocorticoids, is associated with a reduced capacity to shut off the adrenal stress response. For example, rats that are subjected to stress produced by daily handling shortly after birth develop lifelong changes in the number of hippocampal glucocorticoid receptors and exhibit lower resting cortisol levels and greater sensitivity to cortisol in comparison to unstressed control animals.

Since glucocorticoid receptors regulate gene expression, it is likely that stressors experienced early in life can produce long-lasting effects on the HPA-hippocampal axis. Even transient stress may affect the nerve cells containing glucocorticoid receptors at the DNA level, resulting in changes that strongly influence nerve excitability and perhaps individual capacity to regulate the response to stress. In effect, early experience in combination with genetic predisposition has been shown to set the sensitivity of an individual's stress response.

Individuals with bipolar disorder seem to carry genetic vulnerabilities and sensitivities that predispose them to a low threshold of response to stressful events. But animal studies also have shown that an active nurturing environment can buffer the effects of this vulnerability.

Social Factors That Determine the Intensity of the Stress Response
Although all infants respond to separation with increases in circulating levels of cortisol, the magnitude of these changes largely depends on the degree of social support available during the separation period. The most dramatic elevations occur when infants are completely isolated in a novel environment during separation. By contrast, separated infants who remain in familiar surroundings with other mothers and their infants show minimal signs of distress and minimal increases in adrenocortical activity.

In an elegantly designed series of experiments, Dr. Seymour Levine and colleagues at the Stanford University School of Medicine in Palo Alto, California, chose a naturalistic fearful stimulus—visual exposure to a live caged snake—to test the hypothesis that the presence of familiar social companions buffer stress-induced elevations in cortisol. When exposed, individually or in pairs, to a live boa constrictor contained in a box that prevented direct physical contact, monkeys showed increased levels of vigilance, agitation, and avoidance of the snake, along with high stress-activated cortisol levels when tested individually as well as in pairs. However, when monkeys were exposed to the fearful stimulus in a group, an increase in adrenocortical activity did not occur.

These studies make it abundantly clear that the same stimuli do not act in identical ways and that social relationships can modify fearful situations that activate the stress response. Bipolar children who react fearfully to situations can buffer the greater degree of stress they will likely experience if not isolated and withdrawn from figures of social support.

In addition to heritable vulnerabilities, an individual's susceptibility to undue stress seems to reflect, in part, the effects of early life experiences. Michael Meaney and his colleagues at the Douglas Hospital Research Center in Montreal examined levels of the stress hormone corticotropin-releasing factor (CRF) in infant rats. They found that when mother rats lick their offspring often, the pups produce less CRF. According to these studies, the amount of maternal licking during the first ten days of life is highly correlated with the production of CRF in the hypothalamus of the brain of the adult offspring. In addition, compared with isolated or orphaned pups, licked rats develop more glucocorticoid receptors in the hippocampus. These receptors, when activated, inhibit the production of CRF in the hypothalamus and thus dampen the stress response. Licked rats also produce more receptors for the CRF-inhibiting neurotransmitter GABA in both the amygdala and locus coeruleus, brain regions associated with fear, vigilance, and response to novel environmental stimuli.

Corticotropin-Releasing Hormone Potentiates the Startle Response

Corticotropin-releasing hormone (CRF) is a neuropeptide that participates in the generation of the stress response. Through its actions at the level of the HPA-limbic axis, CRF also plays a key role in the control of neuronal activity in the central nucleus of the amygdala. CRF fibers that pass from the central nucleus of the amygdala directly connect with nerve cells in the forebrain and affect a wide population of brain cells. These same CRF fibers also reach out to norepinephrine-containing nerve cells in the brain stem that regulate emotional arousal and to those that influence autonomic nervous system activity.

This dual regulation pathway calibrates and integrates hormonal response and neurotransmitter release, bringing together the combined emotional and sensory information processed within the limbic system and the vital response of the hypothalamus. Therefore, CRF plays an important role in fear-related processes, notably in the enhancement and inhibition of the startle and stress responses.

INTERCELLULAR COMMUNICATION

In higher animals, the two major pathways of intercellular communication are the endocrine system (the glandular system of the body) and the nervous system. In the endocrine system, specialized cells secrete hormones that are carried in the bloodstream and through the cerebrospinal fluid via an elegant system of connecting chambers to distant parts of the body and influence the activity of specifically responsive target cells.

Hormonal Messages

Neurotransmitters trigger the activity of the hormone neurosecretory cells that reside in the hypothalamus, adrenal, thyroid, and pineal glands. Because of their capacity to translate neuronal activity into hormonal output, they have been called transducer cells.

Most hormones exert their effects in two stages. Initially, the hormone receptor promotes the transcription of a small number of genes. This effect usually occurs within thirty minutes and is known as a primary hormonal response. However, since many of the genes that are transcribed during this initial phase are themselves capable of inducing transcription, these newly synthesized proteins activate additional genes in a delayed or secondary response. A single hormone, therefore, can initiate a complex pattern of gene expression.

Neurons

The other major pathways of intercellular communication in the nervous system are composed of interconnecting cells called neurons. A neuron, the basic cell of the nervous system, consists of a cell body, a long, thin tube jutting from the cell body (the axon), and a set of shorter fibers (dendrites) that branch and reach out to receive impulses from other nerve cells. A nerve impulse travels electrically down the axon until it cannot continue because of a tiny gap—the synaptic cleft—that separates it from other cells. Little sacs or vesicles at the end of the axon spill out chemical transmitter molecules that ferry the impulse across the gap and attach to the cell membrane on the other side (see Figure 8.5).

Each of these neurotransmitters has a certain shape and seeks out a molecule, or receptor, on the adjacent cell membrane into which it fits—like a key and its complementary keyhole. In these cells, the back-and-forth movement of ions, such as calcium, sodium, potassium, and chloride, through the cell membrane is responsible for their excitability and also endows them with rhythmic electrical properties. Chemical and electrical contacts between these neurons permit them to fire in unison as a network. The firing rates of these "pacemaker" nuclei signal light/dark transitions, temperature variations in the environment and within the body, and shape attention. They also provide appropriate timing in motor coordination, adjust levels of arousal throughout the sleep/wake cycle, and even modulate the perception of pain. Is it possible that some dysregulation of pacemaker function exists in bipolar disorder?

Neurotransmitter Signaling Systems

The monoamines, which include norepinephrine, serotonin, and dopamine, are a special class of neurotransmitters. Each of these neurotransmitter systems consists of a small number of neurons that originate in the

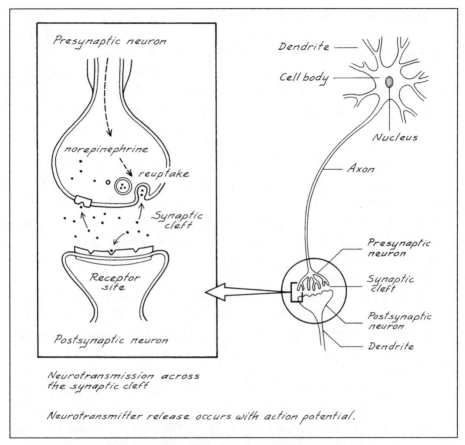

Figure 8.5 Neurotransmitter Release at the Synaptic Cleft
The presynaptic and postsynaptic neurons that release and receive the neuro-transmitter norepinephrine across the synaptic cleft. Norepinephrine is released from the presynaptic neuron and attaches to receptors in the membrane of post-synaptic neurons. It is then taken back up into the presynaptic neuron by a process called reuptake.

brain stem and connect to many regions of the brain, each with its own set of targets. They all prominently connect to the limbic system.

Norepinephrine System
Norepinephrine-containing cells in the brain stem originate in a small cluster of cells called the locus coeruleus. The norepinephrine system may serve to bring an individual to an alert state in order to prepare the brain to deal effectively with a novel environmental situation. The studies of Drs. Floyd Bloom and Gary Ashton-Jones and colleagues at the Salk In-

stitute in La Jolla, California, suggest that sensory neurons in the neocortex may decrease their random firing and respond more strongly to outside sensory stimuli due to increased input from norepinephrine neurons during the alert state. Therefore, norepinephrine firing rates in the locus coeruleus provide an appropriate tuning or modulation of the sensory systems as an individual awakes from sleep or is otherwise aroused into an alert state, enabling the person to mount a response to some novel environmental challenge.

The firing rate of these neurons is variable across the sleep/wake cycle and plays a critical role in regulating the transitions between REM and non-REM sleep stages. Almost totally silent during REM sleep, these neurons fire slowly during slow-wave sleep, and fire at their maximum rate (four to five times per second) during periods of alertness.

While the locus coeruleus sends its nerve terminals widely throughout the brain, only a few brain regions connect to it; the bulk of connecting fibers arise from two other brain stem nuclei. One projection arising from the brain center that uses the neurotransmitter acetylcholine—the giant tegmental cell nucleus—provides a potent inhibitory influence that acts on norepinephrine receptors in the locus coeruleus. The firing rates of these two pacemakers alternate from rapid crackling volleys to complete silence throughout the sleep cycle, mirroring the transitions from REM to non-REM sleep.

Alterations in the firing rate of the locus coeruleus neurons are responsible for activation of aspects of the stress response as well, and are thought to play a role in anxiety and panic states. Distractibility and the disruption of attentional focus, commonly experienced symptoms of bipolar disorder and ADHD, may be related to disturbances in this system that affect the ability to sustain attention and mental effort. Stimulant drugs that enhance attentional focus, such as Ritalin, all increase norepinephrine release. Drugs that increase central norepinephrine transmission, such as tricyclic antidepressants, as well as drugs that enhance dopamine transmission, such as stimulants, have been found to induce hypomania or mania and increase the frequency of cycling.

The neurons that make up the locus coeruleus contain several different neuropeptide receptors, such as neuropeptide Y (NPY), CRF, and the μ opiate receptor, activated by morphine and the naturally occurring opiates. All of these neuropeptides share a common regulatory function with the alpha-2 norepinephrine receptors: They activate a second messenger that resides within the cell, cyclic adenosine monophosphate (cAMP).

This second messenger, cAMP, plays a critical role in cell signaling processes that determine the firing rate of locus coeruleus neurons; therefore, its level of activity directly influences behavioral alerting responses and sleep/wake transitions between REM and non-REM stages.

Dopamine Neurotransmitter System

Dopamine is the principal neurotransmitter responsible for physical movement, reward-motivated behaviors, and body temperature regulation. There are three principal dopamine-producing systems in the brain, and at least two of them are likely to be involved with mood disorders— the nucleus accumbens and the arcuate nucleus. The nucleus accumbens is located at the interface of limbic projections from the amygdala and the hippocampus. It sends fibers to dopamine neurons in midbrain centers that activate motor behavior, and it is well situated to form the circuitry that mediates the behavioral and mood-activating properties of several stimulant drugs, such as dexedrine and Ritalin, known to enhance both dopamine and norepinephrine transmission.

Dopamine-releasing cells in the arcuate nucleus, like similar cells in the locus coeruleus, contain the receptors of neuropeptides such as NPY and μu opiates—the brain's naturally occurring morphine. These receptors interact with the cAMP second messenger signaling system to prolong and/or enhance the effects of dopamine. Activation of these circuits by positive-reinforcing environmental stimuli may influence mood, appetite, and other reward-motivated behaviors. Indeed, a wealth of research on animals leaves little question that the dopaminergic system mediates some of the rewarding properties of stimulants (amphetamines), opiate drugs (morphine and heroin), and cocaine and marijuana. Antidepressant drugs of all classes appear to enhance the function of this reward system.

Antipsychotic drugs that block dopamine receptors and inhibit adenylate cyclase (the enzyme that activates the second messenger cAMP) in the limbic system are extremely effective treatments for the core symptoms of mania.

Abnormal variations in the activity of the dopamine system may affect self-esteem; may contribute to abnormal mood states, such as elation and melancholia; and may result in marked variations in activity/hyperactivity and pressured speech seen in mania and hypomania.

Serotonergic Neurotransmitter System

The serotonergic system consists of a diverse group of neurons whose cell bodies are located in the raphe nuclei and some regions of the reticular-activating system—the brain's arousal system. Its terminals fan out to virtually all regions of the central nervous system. Antidepressant drugs such as Prozac, Zoloft, and Paxil act to enhance serotonin availability in the brain.

The midbrain raphe nucleus provides a dense input of serotonin-containing terminals to the suprachiasmatic nucleus, the master clock of the circadian system. Disruption of raphe activity may interfere with the adaptive changes in circadian rhythms generated by the suprachiasmatic nucleus. Surgical lesions of the raphe nucleus in animals have been found to disrupt rhythmicity in running activity and to result in the loss of the circadian cortisol rhythm. Chronic treatment with the antidepressant imipramine (Tofranil) was found to produce a significant increase in the sensitivity of nerve cells in the suprachiasmatic nucleus. Such an effect could be related to the high frequency of antidepressant-induced switching that has been reported in bipolar disorder.

Sleep disorders have been commonly described in children with bipolar disorders. The normal slow-wave sleep of stage 4 depends on serotonin function. Night terrors and sleepwalking, both commonly observed early symptoms in bipolar children, also occur during stage 4 sleep. Adults with depressive disorders have been found to have persistent disturbances in stage 4 slow-wave sleep even after clinical symptoms of depression have subsided. There are reports of a subgroup of patients with bipolar disorder who have persistently low levels of the major breakdown product of serotonin in their cerebrospinal fluid, even after recovery.

Blood and cerebrospinal fluid levels of serotonin and its metabolites have been found to vary seasonally in an inverse relationship with the pineal hormone melatonin. A number of investigators have reported clear seasonal variations with peaks in April and September. Interestingly, there is a robust correlation between the monthly occurrence of homicides and violent suicides and the observed seasonal rhythms of serotonin.

G-Proteins and Second Messengers

A class of membrane-based proteins known as G-proteins is among the first to respond when a neuronal cell receives a neurotransmitter signal. They are called G-proteins because, in their active state, the protein grasps a cell molecule known as guanosine triphosphate (GTP). In this GTP-bound form, the G-protein activates the next step in a chain of events that leads eventually to a cellular response. Often the signal activates an enzyme like cAMP in such a way that, by adding a phosphorus atom, it can change the enzyme's activity level or allow a protein to bind to the cell's DNA and thereby have a direct effect on the kinds or amounts of proteins the cell manufactures.

So far we have described how certain neurotransmitters, by binding to a specific receptor, stimulate the production of enzymes such as cAMP within the cell that receives the neurotransmitter signal. The question remains: How does an activation of this pathway translate the neurotransmitter's message into some physiological action?

The phosphoinositides, a group of phospholipid molecules that lend structure to the cell membrane, appear to play a central role in signal transmission for a wide variety of neurotransmitters and hormones. When cells are stimulated, a phospholipid called phosphatidylinositol-bis-phosphate (PIP2), is broken down into two compounds: diacyelglycerol (DAG) and inositol triphosphate (IP3), both of which act as "second messengers" capable of igniting great changes within the cell. IP3 provokes the release of calcium from tiny storage pockets in the cytoplasm; the calcium then begins to trigger a number of enzymes. At the same time, DAG sparks the enzyme protein kinase C, which excites yet another string of cellular enzymes. Eventually all this activity reaches the nucleus of the cell.

Both lithium and omega-3 fish oils may exert their therapeutic effect in this crucial part of the signal transduction pathway. As we mentioned, this cycle is a second messenger system that relays and amplifies signals from the neurotransmitters, hormones, and other molecules. Lithium and omega-3 fish oils apparently inhibit or throttle down the activity of this pathway. Dr. Michael Berridge of the Baraban Institute in Cambridge, England, was the first to propose that lithium's antimanic and antidepressant effects worked on this cellular pathway. Subsequently, James Allison and William Sherman at the Washington University School of Medicine in St. Louis found that lithium ions inhibit the enzyme that removes the final phosphate group in this degradation pathway. Paul Worley and Jay Baraban from Johns Hopkins have shown that when cells in a slice of the brain taken from the hippocampus are treated with low levels of lithium, their response to neurotransmitters that cause either excitation or inhibition is dampened. Other investigators have suggested that the target of lithium's effect on cells may be via cyclic nucleotide metabolism. For example, in animals it has been reported that therapeutic concentrations of lithium inhibit the ordinary stimulation of adenylate cyclase, an enzyme that induces cAMP. Sophia Avissar and colleagues of Ben Gurion University in Beer Sheva, Israel, have found that lithium blocks GTP binding induced by the neurotransmitter acetylcholine. Since this effect is a measure of the degree of activation of the important G-proteins, these investigators and others hypothesize that lithium reduces cAMP responsiveness via its inhibition of a G-protein that is known to regulate adenylate cyclase.

It has become more and more appreciated that the long-term treatment of complex neuropsychiatric disorders like bipolar disorder involves the strategic regulation of signaling pathways in the brain and alterations in the expression of specific genes in critical neuronal circuits. Studies over the last decade have sought to identify specific changes in gene expression as a potential source of lithium's therapeutic effect. Indeed, in cell and animal studies, the expression of different genes has been found to be markedly altered by both short-term and chronic lithium administration.

One of the first studies to demonstrate the short-term effects of lithium salts on gene expression was reported in 1991 by Drs. Elyse Weiner, Vasundhara Kalasapudi, Demitri Papolos, and Herbert Lachman of the Program in Behavioral Genetics at the Albert Einstein College of Medicine. These researchers observed that lithium has a dramatic augmenting effect on expression of the immediate early gene activator, *fos*, in animal brain. *Fos* induction, mediated by a muscarinic receptor that activates the enzyme protein kinase C, was found to be exquisitely sensitive to the effect of lithium.

Excessive cell stimulation by gene activators can trigger a prolonged wave of immediate early gene transcription that can lead to degeneration and nerve cell demise. Prolonged immediate early gene transcription serves as a marker of traumatic brain injury and may play a role in neurodegeneration. Degeneration and neuronal death—apoptosis—is the fundamental process responsible for the clinical manifestations of many different neurological disorders of aging, incuding Alzheimer's disease, Parkinson's disease, and stroke.

There is now considerable evidence from brain imaging and postmortem studies that also demonstrates that significant reductions in the number of neurons in specific regions of the brain are associated with mood disorders. Preliminary studies of adolescent and young adult twins suggest a strong correspondence between genetic influence, early-onset depression, and deficits of regional brain volume.

Most recently, chronic lithium treatment has been shown to exert neuroprotective effects against a variety of experimentally induced insults to the brain that lead to neuronal death or apoptosis. Specifically, the work of Dr. Husseini Manji and colleagues from the Cellular and Clinical Neurobiology Program at Wayne State University School of Medicine found that chronic lithium treatment of rats resulted in doubling of the levels of Bcl-2 in the frontal cortex. A neuroprotective role for Bcl-2 has been well established, and expression of high levels of this protein has been found to enhance the survival of cells when exposed to adverse stimuli. These findings raise the intriguing possibility that lithium may exert some of its long-term beneficial effects in the treatment of mood disorders via underappreciated neurotrophic and neuroprotective influences. The robust increase in Bcl-2 levels in the frontal lobe is of particular importance, as emerging evidence is beginning to suggest that deficits in this region of the brain may play a key role in the development of many of the symptoms that are observed in childhood-onset bipolar disorder (see Chapter 11).

NEUROPEPTIDES THAT AFFECT BEHAVIORAL RESPONSE

The effects of neuropeptides such as substance P, NPY, and CRF are fundamental to our understanding of the neurochemical organization of the central nervous system and how it integrates and responds to environmental signals. These chemical messengers all have important influences on the systems that regulate arousal, stress, sleep/wake transitions, appetite, activity, energy production, and the experience of pleasure and pain. The actions of neuropeptides, no matter where they are released, tend to be enduring and to serve a modulating function, controlling neuronal excitability and the effectiveness or stability of neurotransmission.

Many of these neuropeptide-containing neurons innervate structures of the limbic system. The abundance of neuropeptides and their complex pattern within the amygdala, which acts as a focus for a number of peptide pathways and incoming catecholamine pathways, implies that they act to regulate endocrine responses to stressful events and/or to alter emotional responses to fearful stimuli.

Neuropeptides frequently coexist with one another or with monoamine neurotransmitters, such as norepinephrine, dopamine, and serotonin, with as many as three biologically active substances residing within a single neuron. This arrangement greatly increases the possible number of different chemical signals that a neuron can use in communicating with its neighbors.

Substance P

The delicate balance between our experiencing too much or too little pain is largely controlled by substance P, a neuropeptide found virtually wherever primary pain fibers extend. Substance P causes an increased level of excitation at sensory nerve terminals that bring information from the skin and salivary glands and light/dark information from the retina. Recent studies suggest that it also contributes to the degree of stress we experience.

Because substance P is also located in a region of the brain that coordinates the stress response—the amygdala—and because repeated administration of antidepressant drugs causes a decrease of substance P synthesis in the brain, researchers suspected that substance P inhibitors might have psychotherapeutic properties. Indeed, recent trials of various forms of substance P inhibitors have found antidepressant effects in patients with moderate to severe depression.

Many sites within the brain might account for the antidepressant effects of substance P inhibitors. Substance P provides a powerful input from the amygdala to the hypothalamic region that is important for the expression of defensive rage in animals. When researchers injected substance P inhibitors into the hypothalamus of cats, they were able to block the effects of the amygdaloid stimulation that elicits this defensive rage response.

Although the precise mechanism of the antidepressant effects of substance P inhibition is not as yet known, current research suggests that psychological stress causes the release of substance P in the amygdala. Therefore, substance P inhibitors may enhance integration of emotional responses to stress. If this theory is borne out by further research, and substance P inhibitors do not cause an increase in cycle frequency or induce mania, these drugs could become important new treatment options for childhood and adult forms of bipolar disorder.

Neuropeptide Y and Its Effects on Behavior

Over the past decade animal studies have found that NPY has specific effects that are closely linked to behaviors associated with bipolar disorder. NPY has specific effects in the regulation of anxiety, stress, carbohydrate craving, and energy production and on the ability to shift circadian rhythms.

NPY neurons are found in high density in the "master clock" that regulates circadian rhythms, the suprachiasmatic nucleus. The suprachiasmatic nucleus is a receiving station for the flow of information coming from the eyes to the hypothalamus, a nerve pathway that carries information about environmental conditions of light and darkness to the brain.

Several lines of evidence indicate that NPY plays a role in the modulation of the HPA-limbic axis and is a principal part of the signaling system for the chain of activities that allows an individual to respond to stress. In an attempt to understand the long-term effects of NPY on the central nervous system, Dr. A. Inui and colleagues at Kobe University School of Medicine in Japan raised a group of mice that were genetically engineered to produce increased levels of NPY in the brain (about 15 percent above levels in control animals). These mice displayed marked behavioral signs of anxiety and substantial increases in the size of the region in the adrenal gland that produces corticosterone. The anxietylike behaviors of the mice could be reversed by the administration into the brain of a neuropeptide that specifically blocks the action of CRF, suggesting that NPY and CRF may interact to regulate the level of anxiety in response to stress.

CRF and NPY

As we have described previously, corticotropin-releasing factor appears to have activating properties on behavior and to coordinate responses to stress. Direct administration of CRF into the central nervous system produces activation; however, the profile of the behavioral actions of CRF changes dramatically when animals are exposed to a prior stressor. The same dose that produces activation in a familiar environment suppresses exploration in a novel, and presumably stressful, environment. And CRF, in this context, can enhance the reactions of animals subjected to noxious stimuli or averse psychological states.

Thus behavioral activation produced by CRF injected into unstressed animals is transformed into a behaviorally inhibiting effect under stress-ful conditions. Could CRF, through its interaction with neuropeptide Y, and substance P coordinate coping responses to stress that are dependent on other factors, such as degree of arousal or prior levels of fearfulness and anxiety?

Clinically, stress has long been linked to overeating and bingeing on sweets and carbohydrates. This behavior is the most common symptom of appetite dysregulation during the depressive, low-energy periods of bipo-lar disorder. In addition to their actions on the stress response, both NPY and CRF are known to have potent effects on appetite, energy storage, and energy expenditure. After being injected into the hypothalamus, NPY markedly stimulates carbohydrate craving and hormone secretion.

Although bipolar disorder is primarily identified by extreme mood swings, a wide variation in energy levels is also a cardinal feature of the condition. Among the most well-studied actions of CRF in animals is its influence on energy balance. CRF treatment blunts energy storage (energy balance) by simultaneously reducing food intake and augmenting energy expenditure, features commonly reported by individuals experiencing hy-pomanic and manic episodes.

In contrast to the effects of CRF, NPY promotes energy storage through an increase in appetite and reduction in energy expenditure. Cir-culating blood levels of cortisol dramatically affect both systems. An im-balance between CRF and NPY systems produced by disturbances in cortisol levels due to protracted stress responses could be fundamental in the alteration of energy balance observed in bipolar disorder.

CLOCKS THAT TIME US

While the various interconnected brain nuclei and their multiple neuro-transmitter, neuropeptide, and hormonal circuits keep us grounded in three-dimensional space, alerting us and assessing danger, remembering adaptive responses to environmental and social cues, what biological mechanisms anchor us to the passage of time, and how do they influence our behavior? Human-made clocks divide the day into seconds, minutes, and hours. Inside, our bodies keep time quite differently. Cycles may last mere fractions of a second or take hours to complete.

The timing of events within the central nervous system is at least as important as the spatial arrangements of the centers of neuronal activity in the brain. Neurotransmitters, neuropeptides, and hormones must not only lock into their corresponding receptor keyhole, but they must act with appropriate timing—in relation to one other and to periodic events in the environment. Genes with names like Tick Tock or ICER are the gears of the biological clockworks whose role is to coordinate the apparent stable functions of the brain and body that are poised on the paradox of continuous but well-regulated change. Temperature, blood pressure, hormonal secretions, blood sugar, and dozens of other aspects of bodily activity continuously wax and wane according to varying schedules.

Ultradian Clocks

Our inner clocks prefer certain periods for their cycles. Ultradian clocks keep time in units shorter than a day. Our swiftest-running clocks, the ultradian rhythms, do the work of the nervous system. When we are resting, an electroencephalogram shows the brain's electrical rhythms averaging from eight to twelve cycles per second. During the morning, our brain waves cycle at the slow end of this range. They speed up when darkness falls, and cycle most quickly when we are asleep. The ultradian rhythm perhaps most familiar to us is the beating of our own hearts.

For our brains, a day may be marked by sixteen cycles alternating at ninety-minute intervals. Other rhythms may be only milliseconds long, like the cycle in which certain neuronal cells fire, or a few minutes or hours long, like the ninety-minute sleep cycle alternating between REM and non-REM stages.

Quick-cycling rhythms are built into all living systems at the genetic level. Short-cycle ultradian clocks, such as the REM/non-REM sleep cycle, must be remarkably small, perhaps even smaller than a single gene. Subtle disturbances in the clock mechanism or other external factors that perturb the rhythms set by these clocks could very likely contribute to the ultra-ultrarapid cycles of mood, energy, sleep, and activity that characterize early-onset bipolar disorder.

Circadian Clocks

For some hormonal rhythms, the clock may be set to produce cycles of sixty minutes each. A second type of clock measures time in periods about twenty-four hours long. These circadian clocks generate rhythms of REM sleep propensity, body temperature, and daily activity as well as subtler rhythms of when we are most sensitive to pain, how well we estimate the passage of time, or when our bodies are most affected by alcohol.

All human beings have established sleep and activity cycles as well as periods of hunger and satiety, but many other regular cycles take place below the level of conscious awareness, most notably the secretions of the endocrine system—hormones such as CRF, ACTH, cortisol, and melatonin. Interestingly, there are also regular variations in the production of many neurotransmitters, including norepinephrine and serotonin, as well as in the numbers of receptor sites that receive these neurotransmitters.

The various rhythms play an intricate counterpoint, reaching their peaks (acrophases) and troughs (nadirs) at different phases of the circadian day. At given times of the day, month, or year a particular biological or behavioral activity is either necessarily restricted or appropriately undertaken. For example, REM sleep must alternate with non-REM sleep at specific times and in a regular pattern.

Circadian rhythms are described by their period (cycle length) and their phase (relative position in time). If the organization of rhythmicity falters, some rhythms will desynchronize from others. This alteration in the relative coordination of mutually timed events could cause a breakdown in internal temporal order. As a result, oversensitized or desensitized physiological systems that normally prime one another would fail to do so, perhaps leading to many other physiological functions not being switched on or off at the appropriate times.

Circadian Dysregulation or Desynchronization

Alterations in the timing functions of the circadian system have been postulated to play a key role in the causes of bipolar disorder. If you examine the course of bipolar disorder, you find that many people have a pattern of recurrence: The cycles come and go, sometimes at the same time of year.

In childhood-onset bipolar disorder, rapid daily cycles of mood and energy are commonplace. In fact, the majority of children experience an ultra-ultrarapid or ultradian (many cycles within a day) form of cycling, most often characterized by difficulty awakening from sleep in the morning with low energy on arising that then switches at midafternoon or evening to high activity and high levels of energy. These rhythmic disturbances point to the possibility that bipolar disorder is a temporal one in which the timing of biological rhythms is pathologically altered.

A major question posed by researchers is: What deficit in biological systems might lead to a disturbance in circadian or ultradian timing that could account for the rapid shifts of mood and energy states, sleep/wake reversals, and the high rates of ultra-ultrarapid and seasonal cycling patterns that have been observed clinically? Could the same or a similar vulnerability of physiological timing account for the recent finding that the rate of interhemispheric switching is slow in patients with bipolar disorder? Could sensitivity to light and its effects on melatonin release from the pineal gland, alterations in the circadian body temperature rhythms, and the shortened REM latency found in bipolar patients also be related to the same dysfunction of biological timing?

A "Sticky" Hemispheric Switch

Drs. John Pettigrew and Steven Miller from the Vision Touch and Hearing Research Center at the University of Queensland in Brisbane, Australia, have reported intriguing new findings in a group of bipolar patients who were studied while in normal mood states. To study the interhemispheric switching process in these subjects, they examined a high-level attentional process known as binocular rivalry: that is, the alternating perceptual states that arise when viewing different images presented separately to each eye.

Because the cerebral hemispheres can function independently of each other during perceptual and attentional tasks, Pettigrew and Miller hypothesized that the resolution of the conflicting visual stimuli in binocular rivalry might occur by alternating hemispheric activation and that competition for awareness during binocular rivalry occurs between rather than within hemispheres. They have reported preliminary evidence that two unilateral hemisphere-stimulating techniques, caloric vestibular stimulation and transcranial magnetic stimulation, can alter the rate of interhemispheric switching. Interestingly, both techniques have been found to reverse depressive and manic periods in bipolar patients. In their study bipolar patients showed a dramatically slower rate of perceptual switches between left and right hemispheres when presented with a task that measures binocular rivalry.

Other recent studies have reported that perceptual transitions experienced during binocular rivalry involve both the visual and prefrontal cortex. These findings were obtained by measuring brain activity with functional magnetic resonance imaging (FMRI) in humans. In fact, a wide variety of evidence supports hemispheric asymmetries of mood. Imaging studies suggest that there is a greater relative right prefrontal activation in depression. Activation asymmetries favoring the left hemisphere have been reported in mania. In keeping with these activation asymmetries, transcranial magnetic stimulation administered to the left cerebral hemisphere of the prefrontal cortex has been found therapeutic for depression.

The pacemaker for binocular rivalry targets regions at high stages of visual processing in the temporal-parietal cortex. An interhemispheric switch for cognitive style and mood would likely engage both frontal and limbic regions of the brain and have a rhythm similar to that of the ultradian rhythms of cerebral dominance. To explain this, Pettigrew and Miller have suggested that a slowing of the pacemaker for the temporal-parietal cortex also might be accompanied by a proportionate slowing of a pacemaker that governs interhemispheric switching in other regions of the brain, such as the prefrontal cortex, that govern emotional response.

Since pacemakers with different rates have been found coupled genetically in some organisms, a genetic mutation that affected the timing rates of one or more of these pacemakers might account for many of the cognitive and behavioral features of bipolar disorder. But specifically which pacemakers and what functions are disturbed? Could some perturbation in biological timing functions result in the attentional problems and the sleep disturbances as well as the ultra-ultrarapid mood and energy swings so common in childhood-onset bipolar disorder?

Ultradian Cycles of REM–Non-REM Sleep and Waking Performance

Research indicates that the quality of the performance of some mental tasks, such as alertness, varies in cycles whose period is approximately ninety minutes, remarkably like the period of the REM–non-REM sleep cycle. This matches the adult daily sleep/wakefulness cycle, which, as we have seen, develops from briefer sleep/wake cycles evident in infants. As the adult sleep cycle evolves, the basic period progressively lengthens from fifty to sixty minutes to eighty to one hundred minutes. One of the earliest sleep researchers, Dr. Nathaniel Kleitman of the University of Chicago, predicted that the human basic rest-activity rhythm (BRAC) developed from a more primitive rhythm in digestive function that was adjusted to an individual's nutritional needs, and that this basic cycle, which appears in sleep as the REM and non-REM cycles, would be manifest during the waking hours in periodic fluctuations in alertness. Indeed, ultradian rhythms have been found in human waking performance and psychophysiological measures attributable to alertness or attention as well as in a number of ingestive, digestive, and excretory functions.

Circadian rhythms also are known to shape human performance efficiency as well as in physiological processes such as body temperature, rest activity, and sensitivity to light. These latter rhythms can modify the performance of mental functions. Other research has found that ninety-minute alternations in the relative efficiency of verbal (left hemisphere) and spatial (right hemisphere) matching tasks are 180 degrees out of phase, lending support to the notion of alternating rhythms of cerebral dominance. Taken together, research suggests that some aspects of the basic rest/activity rhythm are associated with reciprocal alternations in the activation of the two cerebral hemispheres.

Subjective Alertness, Mental Performance, and Body Temperature Rhythms

Until the mid-1970s, it was believed that there was a strong parallel between the circadian body temperature rhythm and "all" performance rhythms. Then Dr. S. Folkard's groundbreaking studies of time-of-day effects on complex memory tasks, such as verbal reasoning, revealed that there was no single performance rhythm but many, and that while a parallel with body temperature did exist, it was not uniform.

We now know that the capacity to perform different mental tasks is associated with different time-of-day functions, adjusting at different rates to a change in schedule and under the unified control of several biological clocks acting cooperatively. A model that is used to explain the differences in the rate of adjustment assumes that any given circadian rhythm is jointly controlled by two biological pacemakers.

Studies by Timothy Monk and colleagues at the Western Psychiatric Institute and Clinic of the University of Pittsburgh School of Medicine have led to the understanding that temperature rhythm alone does not control subjective alertness and the capacity to perform various cognitive tasks, although it is indeed an important determinant. Rather a cooperative relationship exists between inputs from at least two pacemakers, one that regulates body temperature and another the cycle of sleep and wakefulness.

Suprachiasmatic Nucleus—The Master Clock

In mammals, the response to the light/dark cycle has an important biological function in sleep, activity, twenty-four-hour body temperature rhythm, and reproductive and perhaps social behaviors. Research studies have found that light exerts a dual influence on sleep and activity and other basic biologic rhythms. The twenty-four-hour light/dark cycle acts as a synchronizer for the circadian rest/activity and sleep/wake, temperature, and melatonin rhythms, determining their period and relationship.

Although many sleep abnormalities occur in mood disorders, the most consistent and specific appears to be an abnormal distribution of REM during sleep. The first REM period occurs relatively soon after sleep onset, has a long duration, and often is of a high density. At least two biological clocks govern the regular transitions from waking to sleep and, within sleep, between the stages of active REM and deep non-REM sleep. The suprachiasmatic nucleus sets the rhythm of so-called sleep propensity—the periods within the twenty-four-hour day when we are most likely to be able to fall into dream sleep. In humans, this is usually after lunch at midday and at around 11:00 to 11:30 P.M. These periods also occur at the same time that the twenty-four-hour body temperature rhythm begins to dip. At night, when body temperature reaches its lowest point of the day, the firing of norepinephrine-containing cells in the locus coeruleus all but ceases, and the fast-activity desynchronized brain waves of REM sleep turn on. At the same time, complete muscular paralysis occurs and the body's primary heat loss and heat retention mechanisms almost completely lose their capacity to respond to changes in environmental temperature. All these functions are influenced by a third rhythmic clock in the midbrain, also synchronized to the REM–non-REM cycle, that uses acetylcholine as its chemical messenger (see Figure 8.6).

REM–non-REM cycles alternate throughout the night, their duration strongly controlled by the difference in firing rates between the norepinephrine-producing midbrain locus coeruleus and the acetylcholine-producing giant tegmental cell nucleus (GTN). As with the autonomic nervous system—which receives, transmits, and integrates sensory information—the central nervous system uses a similar dual pattern of cooperation and opposition between norepinephrine and acetylcholine. The locus coeruleus is engaged in a nightly dance with the GTN, a competitive back-and-forth seesaw for dominance that produces the periodic alternations between REM and non-REM sleep states. During the sleep cycle the activity patterns of the norepinephrine and acetylcholine pacemakers are of similar frequency and amplitude, yet together they must be able to synchronize—one starting when the other leaves off—coupling and uncoupling multiple times throughout the night. Whether the transitions of consciousness that take place between REM and non-REM sleep are smooth or choppy depends on a well-oiled switch.

Non-REM sleep is thought to be controlled by the temperature-sensitive cells located in a biological clock in the preoptic/anterior nucleus of the hypothalamus that resides in close proximity to the suprachiasmatic nucleus, where circadian signals and homeostatic processes that regulate body temperature may be integrated. Dr. Pier Luigi Parmaggiani and his colleagues of the University of Bologna Medical School in Bologna, Italy, were the first to demonstrate that changes in the temperature sensitivity of these neurons was the basis for non-REM/REM transitions and could also be a primary component of the process for stabilization of arousal functions after transitions from wakefulness to non-REM sleep. The sleep arousals most commonly seen in childhood-onset bipolar disorder, including night terrors, sleep awakenings, bedwetting, sleepwalking, and abnormal movements (restless leg syndrome), are all examples of non-REM instability.

Does some timing disturbance affect the function of just one pacemaker, or could some disturbance in the rivalry for dominance between REM and non-REM sleep/wake cycles—what we might call a REM-dominant arousal state with non-REM instability—be due to a disturbance in timing regulation between two or more biological clocks? This same question must be asked about the finding of Drs. Pettigrew and Miller that binocular rivalry between left and right hemispheres is disturbed in patients with bipolar disorder. Is the slower alternation rates in interhemispheric switching they found in their study related to some common underlying biological disturbance that produces shortened REM latency and increases in REM sleep periods in patients with depression and perhaps even to the tendency to ultradian and seasonal cycling patterns?

Seasonal Episodes of Depression and Mania

Since ancient times, remarkably regular seasonal recurrences of mania and depression have been an intriguing but unexplained phenomenon. Most contemporary studies have shown that spring and fall are peak times for depression. Hospital admissions for mania undergo seasonal variations as well. Several studies have reported that manic and depressive episodes increase with the difference between maximum and minimum daily temperatures. A high correlation also has been reported between monthly admission rates for mania in Great Britain and seasonal changes in mean monthly day length, daily hours of sunshine, and daily temperature that correspond to the vernal and autumnal equinox.

In one of the largest contemporary studies to examine this seasonal periodicity of episodes, Dr. Gianni Faedda and colleagues recruited a group of 175 patients in Caligari, Italy. In these patients, periods of depression followed one of two patterns: They suffered either fall-winter depression with or without spring-summer mania or hypomania, or spring-summer depression with or without fall-winter mania or hypomania. The two patterns occurred with almost equal frequency.

Figure 8.6 The Clocks That Time Us
Many bodily and behavioral functions have circadian or ultradian rhythms that are entrained by the daily light/dark cycle that acts through the visual pathway to the suprachiasmatic nucleus (SCN). The SCN is the central pacemaker of the clockworks, composed of multiple circadian and ultradian clocks with different intrinsic rhythms, each with properties that contribute to the modulation of important behavioral and physiological rhythms. These biological clocks communicate with each other at set times of the day—times established by the periodic variations in light and temperature that take place over the course of the days and months of the year, as well as through internal clocks that determine the body temperature minimum, a nightly signal that sets into motion the eighty- to one-hundred-minute alternations in REM and non-REM sleep periods. REM onset occurs when the body temperature reaches its twenty-four-hour minimum, a function at least partially regulated through the interaction of the SCN with the pineal gland. Daily and seasonal rhythms in serotonin (5HT) availability determine the rate of melatonin production and secretion from the pineal gland. The raphe nucleus (dorsal) pacemaker influences both the dawn and dusk changes in SCN activity and the REM and non-REM sleep episodes. The cyclic relation between these sleep stages involves the interaction between the nucleus gigantocellularis (GTN), the locus coeruleus, and raphe nucleus (dorsal).

The Clocks That Time Us

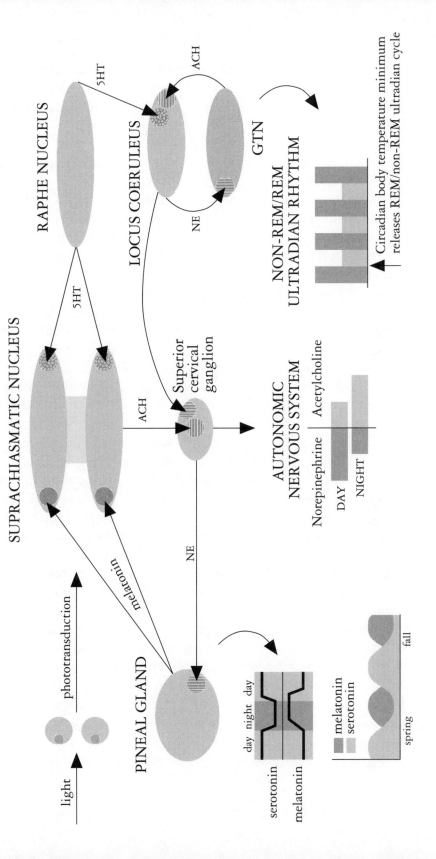

The idea that depression and mania can result from abnormalities of photoperiodic regulation draws further support from the known therapeutic effects of bright light treatment in seasonally cycling bipolar patients as well as from the studies of Dr. Alfred Lewy of the University of Oregon, in Portland. Lewy found that, compared to nonbipolar subjects, bipolar patients exhibited an abnormality in their capacity to suppress melatonin when exposed to bright light.

In a study of bipolar patients with seasonal episodes, Dr. P. A. Arbisi and colleagues of the Department of Psychology at the University of Minnesota in Minneapolis found that while depressed during the winter months, subjects had significantly impaired capacity to dissipate body heat after exercise.

Two primary environmental signals, the light/dark and temperature cycles, have daily and annual variations whose magnitude depends on the northern and southern latitudes. An annual sunshine record displayed in Figure 8.7 shows the periods of the year that correspond to the highest frequency of depression, hypomania, and mania. Strikingly, they occur at the times of the vernal and autumnal equinoxes—the times of the highest rates of change in dark to light or light to dark transitions. Recent studies have similarly found that these time intervals also correspond to the peaks of suicide and homicide in various parts of the world.

The suprachiasmatic nucleus and pineal gland form the biological timing device that measures the daily duration of darkness and light. By transmitting on-off signals at dawn and dusk, the suprachiasmatic nucleus and pineal gland mutually cooperate and oppose each other, much the same way the REM–non-REM pacemakers do, but at a slower pace, on a daily rather than an eighty- to one-hundred-minute time schedule.

The suprachiasmatic nucleus interacts with the environment via a direct connection to the retina and translates changing light intensity into information while regulating the circadian rhythms of body temperature, REM sleep propensity, and cortisol. The pineal hormone melatonin elicits two effects when applied directly to the suprachiasmatic nucleus: It causes immediate inhibition of pacemaker firing rates and, depending on the time of day, can advance or delay circadian rhythms. A timing glitch in this system might be more likely to be unmasked during periods of seasonal change when dramatic light/dark and temperature variations occur.

———

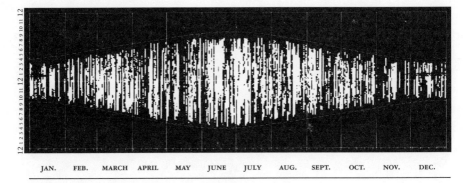

Figure 8.7 The Annual Light/Dark Cycle
The variation in the intensity and amount of light in the Northern Hemisphere recorded each day and divided into twelve monthly intervals. The periods of time inclusive of the vernal and autumnal equinoxes and demarcated between late March through mid-April and mid-September to mid-October represent the peak periods of episodes of mania and depression during the year.

While it probably will be a number of years before the underlying biological basis of bipolar disorder is fully understood, the brain pathways contributing to many of the symptoms and behaviors are becoming more clearly delineated. Major contributions from molecular genetics and neuroimaging studies are adding daily to our fund of knowledge and should, in the near future, help us unlock the mystery of this illness. It is encouraging to think that much of the information presented in this chapter was unknown even ten years ago. From this perspective, there is every reason to hope that the next decade will bring an exponential increase in our understanding of the illness—and perhaps similar advances in its treatment.

PART III

Living and Coping with Bipolar Disorder

The Impact
on the Family

Just the simple word "family" conjures up more associations than probably any other word in the human language. On one level it represents an idealized state—a place where you are loved and supported, the *Father Knows Best* place where every daughter is "Kitten," where brother Bud works hard raking the leaves and shoveling the snow, and where mother Margaret somehow makes the mashed potatoes come out fluffy every time. And while there may be minor mishaps, everything gets worked out and seems warm and funny and complete.

The 1998 movie *Pleasantville* examined just such a world and found out that it all looked great as long as no emotions were expressed, no sexual thoughts ever passed through anyone's mind, and there were no bathrooms *anywhere*. (Nor was anyone ever seen looking for one.) There was no world outside of Pleasantville, and no one owned umbrellas because it never rained in Pleasantville.

And you can bet *no one* had bipolar disorder in Pleasantville.

Today's parents were brought up in this kind of fantasy idea of family life—no matter what their family life was actually like (and it may have been a frightening and dire world touched by the long reach of manic-depressive illness and alcoholism from generations before). But the all-powerful media image is what we carry around with us, despite any reality to the contrary.

So, in the TV series *Father Knows Best,* Bud never called his father a "fucking asshole" and threatened to kill him while he slept. He also never punched holes in the drywall. "Kitten" was never told to run to her room and lock the door because she might be hurt by Bud during a rage that could go on for three hours because his parents said he couldn't watch television. When Margaret was ready to serve those mashed potatoes, she had no trouble getting Bud to join the family. She also answered the phone with the most charming and upbeat voice, never afraid it might be the school calling to say that Bud was out of control again or that it might be a parent calling to complain that Bud had hit or frightened his child.

Family life in a household dealing with a bipolar child is about as unpleasantville as it comes. It is a virtual stew of emotions like guilt, powerlessness, denial, anger, anxiety, fear, uncertainty, confusion, blame, and shame. These are all very ugly words that make us flinch, arousing feelings that most of us would do anything to avoid, but all are feelings that a family with a bipolar child has to endure for months and years at a time.

The fact that most people don't see what goes on inside the home and have no idea what the family is dealing with makes it all the more terrible. All these awful emotions consume a family—chew it up—and no one understands or empathizes. The struggles for survival from one day to the next are invisible to almost everyone but another family dealing with a bipolar child.

This chapter is about reducing that invisibility, taking a good look at what is happening to a family, and talking about some ways of coping and steering the family onto higher ground—someplace not perfect but livable; where energy can be conserved and spent more wisely; where solutions can be found that allow all people within the family to grow and develop their potential; and a place where other emotions are allowed besides guilt and fear. Umbrellas still will be needed, but the weather report does not have to post hurricane warnings every day. The storms can be downgraded and life can go on.

But before any stage of mastery and acceptance is achieved, a host of overwhelming feelings are going to be part of the family's experience.

DEALING WITH DAY-TO-DAY EMOTIONS

Denial and Fear

Long before a diagnosis is made, parents have a nagging sense that something is not right with their child. He doesn't sleep like the books say a baby should; his reactions seem too extreme; he seems always on the go with a purposeful look on his face, but a shambles is left in his wake as he goes off to do yet something else. Parents in other families seem to enjoy their children more.

Some parents attempt to understand these temperaments and behaviors by telling themselves: "He's extremely bright"; "She's so sensitive and artistic"; "These traits are going to make him a very successful adult someday if we can only survive his childhood"; "It's just a phase—he'll grow out of it."

There are stages of recognition, adjustment, and adaptation to an illness, and each family travels through the stages in its own time and its own fashion. When the symptoms are mild and interspersed with periods of good functioning, it is not difficult to attribute them to events such as a death in the family, a divorce, or a temperament that is more sensitive and more easily upset or agitated.

Sooner or later, though, as the symptoms become more severe and disruptive, and as the external world begins bearing down on the parents for having no control over the child, the parents are going to begin looking for professional advice (or they are going to be directed toward professional advice by the preschool teacher or school psychologist).

While most parents who answered our survey said that it was a relief to finally find a name for what was happening inside their child, many reported absolute shock as well as the stranglehold of fear about their child's future. Questions such as: Will she live a normal life? Will she get married and be able to take care of children? Will she be able to live separate from us and be a contributing member of society? loom large and can paralyze a family.

Parents must try not to sap the little energy they have by imagining a future that probably will never be as dire as their fantasies. If parents can concentrate on finding solutions and build from feelings of competency today, tomorrow will sort itself out more easily.

As Helen Featherstone writes in *A Difference in the Family:*

Fears ease as experience discredits fantasy, as mothers and fathers learn that the actual problems of raising their child differ from the ones they imagined. Similarly, small victories over private demons reassure parents about their own ability to raise their child.

As time passes, both parents gain a measure of control, even though important parts of their child's future remain beyond their reach. They know a good deal more about their child's disabilities than they did at first; they no longer wait, bound and gagged, for the ax to fall. If they worry about school placement they can talk to the teacher. In a medical crisis they know which doctor to call. They have learned to navigate in the sea of experts and services.

SHAME

Learning how to steer through the enormously choppy waters of early-onset bipolar disorder is no easy task. Parents are expected to deal with an illness that not only do doctors know little about but one that the doctors are wary about diagnosing in the first place. Parents are set adrift inside a house that has become a war zone, dealing with feelings that alternate from extreme anger at the child to the most unbelievable yearning to help that child, from rage at the outside world for failing to understand what is happening to them to exhaustion in trying to deal with the child. And tucked into that welter of truly terrible feelings is shame—shame that one is unable to control his or her own child, and shame at what one begins to put up with and how abnormal one's life has become. One mother explained what her daily life was like:

> Connor would fly into a rage and start hitting and punching me. He had this wild look in his eyes and I couldn't reach him. I was literally straddling him, holding him down. He would then scream: "Help! Help! She's killing me, she's killing me" at the top of his voice. Then he said: "I can't breathe. It's over, Mom, it's over." And I let go and suddenly the head turns, I see the switch in his eyes, and boom!—the arm is there punching me. And this can go on for two to three hours.

Then she lowered her voice and you could feel her embarrassment even over the phone line:

> I'm ashamed to say that the last forty-five minutes I turned my back on him and let him beat on me as I stood at the kitchen sink, crying and feeling so alone in the world.
>
> At the end of the major rages, the tears come from Connor. He puts his arms around me and says: "Mommy, Mommy, you said the medication would work. I might as well be dead."

It takes many parents years to be able to tell a story like that. Often they can't tell anyone in the outside world until the child has long been stabilized and the violent rages cease. Like battered wives, they present a brighter face to the world and refuse to have outsiders picture their child or them this way.

STRESS OF UNPREDICTABILITY

No childhood disability is easy for parents to deal with, but when one's child is bipolar, one never knows when a violent rage will ignite. Parents describe themselves as always walking on eggshells. One mother said she never knows whether she's going to be awakened with a kiss or a fist in her eye.

Another mother described it this way:

> It keeps everyone on edge, on alert. He is so unpredictable that you can never slip into complacency for fear of ambush. We can't go out to dinner without wondering what disaster might be afoot at home. Once he locked a baby-sitter into the third-floor stairwell.

Things can be moving along at a nice pace, when something comes up and the child revs from zero to eighty in a split second. Not only is being on the scene a nightmare, but one father told us he couldn't even escape the stress from a distance:

> I began to long for business trips. Any chance to be away and have *some* idea of how a day would unfold seemed like an oasis of sanity for me. I'm ashamed to say this, but I would dread making the call home at night to check on everyone. First I would have a few drinks, and then I would place the call with knots in my stomach as I waited for my wife to pick up the phone and give me the report. I felt awful that my wife was left with all of this (and we didn't even know what "this" was then), and then I felt more guilt and shame.

EVERYONE'S A JUDGE AND A JURY

Life inside the home is bad enough, but a trip to the grocery store could unravel the most stable human being, because, sooner or later, the child is going to get tired or ask for a piece of candy, and if the answer forthcoming is "no," a meltdown is likely to occur on the checkout line. And this opens up the opportunity for strangers to offer their parenting advice and comment on the parent's and the child's lack of control.

American society is not tolerant of children in general. Children are not welcome at most restaurants; they're not supposed to make a ruckus. A visit to Italy or Israel would provide a contrast: Children are a part of every event, and the community expects to see them as well as hear them. But in this country, a parent is likely to hear: "Are you going to let her talk to you like that? If one of my kids ever said that to me she'd rue the day," or (and this is the most popular) "Give him to me for a week and he'll be an entirely different child." (We venture to guess that this man would be an entirely different man.)

Parents have some choices: They can ignore the comments, or they can choose to give a simple explanation, such as: "He has a neurological brain disorder that causes him to have something like a behavioral seizure. It's called early-onset bipolar disorder." Either way, the parent is going to feel criticized, humiliated, infantalized, incompetent, and extremely angry and stressed. One mother girds herself and takes control of such situations without even speaking. She hands the advice-giver a card while her son is on the floor kicking and screaming. On it is printed:

Thank you for your advice and concern. My son is suffering with early-onset bipolar disorder, a neurological brain disorder which causes him to feel very irritable and anxious and culminates in tantrums and rages such as you are now witnessing. Screaming and threatening inflame the situation and are damaging to this child.

Because it is obvious that you are concerned about this kind of behavior, may I suggest that you contact the National Alliance for the Mentally Ill at 1-800-950-NAMI to learn more about this devastating illness of childhood and—if you can—please make a donation to support research so that no child should *ever* have to contend with this level of emotions in a little body and a developing brain. Thank you.

This mother tells us that she doesn't always feel the need to hand the card out, but just having it handy creates a sort of armor and empowerment when her anger at someone's intrusiveness and judgmental attitude threatens to derail her or makes her feel helpless and ashamed. She also said that when she does hand it out, she is doing something to raise awareness and to protect the next parent that the "helpful" person in the street may upset.

If trips to the grocery store and nights out to movies or special events or restaurants present multiple opportunities for a meltdown, the family is going to begin to withdraw so as not to stress the child or expose themselves to public attention and possible ridicule. Family forays outside the home will become few and far between. So many parents wrote and told us how guilty they feel that they can't provide a "normal" family life for their other children. One father wrote: "Everything depends on how Anna is feeling that day. We go or don't go depending on her mood. And if we do go, we are on tenterhooks until we get behind closed doors once again. It rips us apart to be viewed as incompetent and incapable in the public eye. I feel so sorry for my other children who are being cheated by Anna's illness."

Thus, the family becomes an island unto itself. Even relatives can add to the stress by being very critical. While we were writing this chapter, we spoke with a woman who described her Thanksgiving day. Her daughter had been put on an antidepressant without the protection of a mood stabilizer, and she was irritable and becoming hypomanic. Before dinner, and while playing with another child, she lost control and hit him in the head with a toy car, in front of a shocked extended family assembled for the holiday. Everyone seemed to blame the mother, who spent the day after Thanksgiving in bed, depressed and terribly demoralized. She suspects that invitations will not be forthcoming, and even if they are, that she and her husband will stop accepting.

Even when people don't offer up criticism and advice, parents of a child with a problem of this magnitude find themselves pulling away from even well-meaning people who may be trying hard to understand. In the normal exchange of conversation most parents find it agonizing to hear about their friends' healthy children and want desperately to shut themselves off from the envy and anger that they feel. Their friends are going to soccer games; *they* are going to psychiatrists. Their friends are visiting Ivy League schools; *they* are visiting children in inpatient units. Rather than feel this degree of pain, the families with a bipolar child avoid the social situations. Sadly, they become all the more withdrawn from social networks.

THE GRIEVING PROCESS

It's impossible for parents not to train their eyes on the prize—bringing a baby home and daydreaming about family outings and holidays, baseball games, visiting college campuses. And sexist as it may sound, there are few mothers who don't anticipate the day when they can finger the lace on wedding dresses as they and their daughters plan that trip down the aisle. Farther into the future is the dream of grandchildren.

Bipolar disorder uproots all these hopes and expectations, as suddenly and violently as an earthquake. It shakes a family to its core; now parents suffer the anguish of watching their child in pain and fear for the quality of his or her future. Hopes and expectations may have to be modified and mourned. One mother whose daughter has the illness and who works with other families in crisis had this to say:

> There was a long time when I couldn't and wouldn't alter my expectations. I kept trying to make her more "normal"; I kept pushing her to be just the way I thought every little girl should be. I would not give up.
>
> Eventually I learned that I was the one who had to change. She wasn't able to just then, and it would take a much longer time for her to reach the goals that I was so desperate for her to achieve.
>
> I finally became more realistic and my priorities changed. The more I learned, the more I came to accept *this* child, the more I loved *this* child. I didn't give up hope, but I wasn't in a dream world either. But there's definitely a grieving process where you have to deal with the sense of loss. It's not that it can't be revitalized every time a friend's child graduates, it's just that we're at a different stage now and can feel the pain, rebalance, and go on.

RECASTING THE PARENTING ROLE

Parents with a bipolar child have to give up on the idea of "typical" parenting skills. All the old bromides—consistency and authority, the parents must be in control so the child feels safe, and so on—don't carry the day inside this family (or at least they don't until the child is stabilized). Any assertion of authority is viewed by the child as the parent dominating him or her, a domination to be resisted at any cost. Something goes off in the child's brain, and a rage gathers. A simple "no" triggers a nuclear explosion. When the exasperated mother of a seven-year-old boy asked her son why he could *never* do anything she asked, he looked at her and said quite baldly: "Oh, I can't do that, that would mean you are in control of my life. I rule the world; what I say goes."

What would motivate this child to feel this way? This mother felt his statement came from a "great sense of grandiosity and perfectionism." Maybe it comes from a sense of defectiveness, and when an adult tries to subordinate the child to his or her will, it elicits feelings that are so bad or uncomfortable that they are not to be tolerated. Perhaps, as we suggested in Chapter 8, the anxiety level of these children is so high that they have to dig in their heels to feel a sense of control. No one really knows, but the Parenting 101 adage that discipline comes from the root "disciple" will seem almost funny after attempting to deal with a bipolar child. They are to be the parents' equals if not the parents' superiors.

So, the parent must step out of time and place and become the parent *this* child needs, not the parent that society (and the parent's ego) dictates. It requires an almost superhuman love, where the parent's expectations are set aside and the needs of the child are met first. A father wouldn't insist that a blind child play basketball because all the other sixth-grade kids are doing it; nor would he sign up his wheelchair-bound child for the football tryouts just because the other ninth-graders are doing it. Parents have to modify their ideas of parenting skills and be very, very brave.

Unfortunately, no one is going to give the mother or the father "Parent of the Year" award. Instead, parents will meet with criticism, dire warnings that they're spoiling the child, or even that they're "frightening the child" by not bending him or her to their will.

It all sounds good. It just doesn't work with a child who's struggling with bipolar disorder. In the next section, we'll talk about some techniques that may work and help to calm some of the disruptions to family life.

DEALING WITH DAY-TO-DAY BEHAVIORS

Raging

For a very long time parenting strategies revolved around adages such as "Spare the rod, spoil the child" and "Children are meant to be seen and not heard." While in some ways we are a more child-centered society, and parents tend not to be as autocratic as they were a few generations ago, most parents feel that to be a parent is to "be the boss," to have control, and to provide exact rules for the safety of the children and the smooth running of a household. After all, they are the adults, they understand consequences, and they know that they have to civilize children and prepare them to coexist in society. Easier said than done with a child who is oppositional and prone to violent outbursts where the parent can be injured both emotionally and physically—no matter how big and strong the parent is.

In order for a parent to begin to come to terms with oppositional and out-of-control behavior, he or she has to have an inkling of what is happening within the child and realize that what may work with a well child will rarely work with a bipolar child.

Why? Well, to begin with, these children don't start the day planning on screaming obscene phrases at parents or threatening them with forks and knives. They don't think to themselves: Today I'm going to trash my room, kick in a few walls, and break all of Mom's porcelain figures that seem to mean so much to her. Instead, they get caught up in a world that seems to demand things from them that they are not equipped to deal with: shifts from their own agendas to their parents' and teachers' demands and the quick changes that take place during the school day. Often these children are unable to make these shifts or comply with these requests. And to make matters worse, often these children are very smart and sensitive to the fact that other people can "go with the flow," so they feel doubly bad about themselves.

Sooner or later, it all comes to a head with the phenomenon known, and feared, by parents as raging. Raging that can go on for hours at a time. It is rarely seen by the teachers and professionals but is reserved for the safe domain of home and family—most especially for the mother.

What causes these almost seizurelike rages, which seem to be most often triggered by the word "no"? The evidence points to neurochemical factors: With the right mood stabilizer or the right combination of mood stabilizers and medications like Risperdal and Zypreza, these outbursts are often eliminated or become less frequent and intense.

But until the stabilization does happen, parents are going to have to deal with wild tantrums and tough times. And as most parents have found out, behavior management techniques do not work with these children: No amount of star-or-sticker charts or time-outs, and no threats of grounding or unplugged TVs and Nintendo sets is going to make a whit of difference. These children are not moved by threats, explanations, or even bribes for very long.

As psychologist Ross Greene explains in his book *The Explosive Child:*

> Consequences can be effective if a child *is in a state of mind to appreciate their meaning* [emphasis added], but they don't work nearly as well if a child is not able to maintain such a state of mind. . . .
>
> What I've learned over the years is that some children become so overwhelmed so quickly by their frustration that their capacity to maintain coherence in the midst of frustration is severely compromised. I've seen that these children are also compromised in their ability to gain access to information they've stored from previous experiences and think things through so as to formulate a well-organized, reasoned response to frustrating situations.

One mother came to recognize the magnitude of the problem and began to think of her child as having a spasm in the emotional part of his brain. He seemed to be in an altered state of consciousness, and she began to realize that her anger and desire to assert her will over his was like pouring fuel on a fire. She wrote about her new awareness of what was happening and how she could best help her son through the rage:

> It is difficult to talk to him and get responses when he is out of control. He gets panicky when I try to restrain him. I am learning, though. At first I would get furious. I don't do that anymore since it is counterproductive and unkind, considering he seems to have little if any control of himself at those times. I've learned to listen to him very closely . . . and he often says "I'm scared." I now try to help him through these incidents. He is conscious, but just barely. I try to stay calm, I try to speak softly and in simple sentences. I avoid too much eye contact. I try to avoid patronizing or authoritarian statements. I don't threaten or shout. I try to help him feel control again. I remain very flexible though alert for my own safety.

Another woman said, "Humor is best. I can sometimes defuse very volatile situations by making jokes. Reasoning with the child is useless. So is force. I make every attempt to stay very calm."

Personal Safety for the Family

Some children in a rage break only their own toys and possessions. Others, however, can do great damage to a house and cause personal injury to their parents or siblings. It serves no one to allow this to go on, but very often it is beyond the control of a parent. We know of fathers who are six feet tall who have had to stay home to protect their petite wives from the violence of thirteen-year-olds. Sometimes a raging child throws objects so forcefully as to cause mild concussions to a family member unlucky enough to be targeted. To put it bluntly, many parents are being abused in their own homes. Many have had to protect themselves by working out emergency strategies to cope with assaultive behavior.

One mother from Michigan told us that she has an automatic dial to her parents' home, and her mother and father come running when her seven-year-old goes into a rage. They quickly roll him in a blanket and restrain him. They even had to construct a "quiet room" where he could cool down so as not to destroy the house or hurt his younger sister.

This woman was lucky because she had supportive parents close at hand who would do anything to help her, and her son was finally stabilized on medications and able to better control his emotions. But many mothers live far from family and are alone with children who suddenly explode. Most parents are loath to call the police to report the assaults of a six-year-old and alert the neighbors to a situation that will appear extremely shocking; many try to tough it out by themselves. Parents from all over the country have told us that they hide all knives and sharp objects and even baseball bats.

While some children get even more panicky if restrained, a therapeutic hold or restraint can help other children gain control and calm down. The parent should get behind the child, take him or her on a bed or floor with the parent's back against the headboard or wall. The parent should then put his or her legs over the child's, wrap the child's hands around the child's middle, and then hold his or her arms over the child's hands. All the time the parent should be saying in a calm, soft voice: "I'm going to hold you until the tantrum is over. I will not let you hurt yourself, or me, or destroy things. I will hold you until this is over and you are safe."

If the child is too big and strong to do this, and a spouse, friend, or emergency team cannot be summoned to the house in three minutes or so, a parent will have to consider bringing the police into the situation—

especially if the out-of-control son or daughter is older and much stronger and much more capable of doing horrific damage.

One woman who has had to call the police described her very wise plan:

> It is difficult to explain your child's situation and what you want done in the heat of a crisis. If violent acts are a possibility, it would make good sense to be proactive and make a plan when all is calm. Call it a "Family Crisis Emergency Plan" and include the child/adolescent, psychiatrist or therapist in making the plan.
>
> I suggest an advance visit to the police station and talk with the social worker, who could then brief the local officers on how to handle a raging child or adolescent if they are called to assist. List on the plan how restraints will be used if necessary, and where the adolescent will be taken (not to jail). The plan should list the phone numbers of the doctor, private therapist, family members, and anyone else who should be notified.

Given the severe consequences of these rages, it's a good idea to isolate what situations or comments trigger the bipolar child and attempt to de-escalate the child before things reach the point of no return. In *The Explosive Child,* Dr. Greene suggests that a parent think in terms of three prioritized baskets: Basket A contains only things a parent should insist upon—safety issues, for instance. Basket B holds items that are negotiable, and Basket C holds all the items that are not worth fighting about given that they could detonate an explosion. Examples of Basket C items might be insisting the child sit at the dinner table and eat with the family, and eat the wholesome dinner the parent has prepared, *not* the pizza the child is screaming for. Give her the pizza, says Dr. Greene.

While the entire family sitting around the dinner table is a pleasant image, a child who tantrums for three hours and throws food all over the kitchen as a result of a parent's strong "request" isn't. Such fantasies have to be let go of for a while.

Many parents have tried these strategies and fashioned others of their own, and have told us that they work. One mother said:

> I used to spend hours trying to get our older daughter to sit in her seat. Then I got more realistic. So when my husband and younger

daughter and I sit down to dinner, I wish she could join us, but if she can't, we three don't have to end up inside a tornado in the kitchen. And as she grows older and gets more stable, we've enjoyed more of a family life.

Another mother observed that whenever her son flew into a rage, he would run out the door. She understood that he needed a quiet place where he could be alone and calm down, and she designated three places on the property where he might go. She told him that she would give him twenty minutes and then come looking for him, and if he wasn't in one of those three places, she would call the police. Thus she understood and respected his way of dealing with his anger, but she placed safety limits around him.

It's obvious that dealing with a bipolar child requires superhuman strength and stamina and intelligently worked-out solutions. Parents will have to find the strategies that work best with the fit of their temperament and style and the child's temperament and needs. It's safe to bet, however, that the child won't be the one to change first. The parents, who are infinitely more flexible, will have to exercise that flexibility for quite a while. But there is every reason to believe that reasonableness will come back into the relationship once the child is medically treated and becomes stable.

When Child Protective Services Visits

It's one thing to sustain the remarks of family members and the stares of people in the grocery stores, it's another to fear the knock at the door of Child Protective Services. For anytime a child screams at the top of his or her lungs (for long periods of time) the thought of abuse will cross a neighbor's mind long before he or she thinks: I wonder if that child is bipolar.

Chances are that a parent of a bipolar child will entertain a visit or two before the child becomes stable. One mother wrote about her first visit with a sense of humor purchased only with the passage of time:

When they showed up at my house, the air-conditioning was broken and my basement had flooded the day before. My house looked like a war zone and all three of the kids were running around in their underwear (I was relieved they weren't nekkid).

After talking with my husband and me, and the kids, and looking into my medicine box (so we could spell out all the medications) they were satisfied that I was doing the best job I could—and actually a very good job considering the circumstances. They closed the case altogether about six weeks later.

She went on to advise other parents: "Keep your chin up . . . and try to keep the house straightened (usually they make a follow-up visit).

We spoke with this mother over the telephone and asked her if she didn't feel angry at and humiliated by CPS and the neighbor who had called them. She replied, "In my opinion, they all cared enough about the welfare of my child to investigate it. It was kind of a relief because once I knew them and they knew me, I wasn't stressed about it anymore. I explained things to my neighbor in detail and now she is a part of the team and is a great help and support to me. I respect her caring. What kind of neighbor could hear this and do nothing?"

Another mother we spoke to said that she keeps a binder of all the medications and charting she does and IEP materials for school, so it's easy to educate CPS when they come to investigate. The binder shows her to be an attentive mother dealing with an impossible situation and she feels a sense of control.

Still, this wasn't quite what anyone pictured as she opened the gifts at the baby shower, and it takes time to get over your parenting being questioned by the state. Taking the time to get to know your neighbors and educating them about the illness and the child's behaviors may preempt this kind of upsetting visit and may net a supportive friend as well.

Dealing with Suicidal Behavior

The emotional roller coaster that parents and siblings must ride is bad enough. But by far the most harrowing emotion is the fear that the child may kill him- or herself. Parents have said to us over and over: "Do you have any idea what it's like to hear our seven-year-old say, 'I'm a stupid dummy, everyone hates me and I may as well be dead'?"

Clinical reports show that children as young as five and six years old have made suicide attempts. Psychiatrist Cynthia Pfeffer of Cornell University Medical College has reported that her studies of children reveal that approximately 75 percent of children who are psychiatrically hospitalized are suicidal, while about 33 percent of those treated outside the hospital are suicidal.

The burgeoning statistics on adolescent suicides are deeply disturbing. It is estimated that five thousand teenagers kill themselves in this country every year. Suicide is the third leading cause of death in adolescence. In *His Bright Light,* author Danielle Steel wrote about her bipolar son's first suicide attempt:

> I considered what had happened an aberration, because he had been off lithium at the time. I knew that once back on, it was unlikely to happen again. But what I underestimated entirely, or had never been told, was how lethal his disease was. In my view, it was something that could make him unhappy all his life, but not something that could kill him. I missed that message completely.

This is not an easy message for a mother or father to absorb. It is almost impossible to second-guess what's going on inside a teenager's mind. Suicidal intentions are often expressed in subtle and ambiguous ways, and most families are not prepared to judge the seriousness of a threat.

If relatives even suspect that the child is thinking about suicide, they should call the treating psychiatrist immediately and alert him or her to that fact. Depending on a variety of factors, hospitalization may be required. Suicide is often an impulsive act: A child can be having a glass of milk in the kitchen one minute and leap from a bedroom window the next. It happens that fast; it happens that unexpectedly. The notion that people who threaten suicide never actually go through with it is a dangerous myth.

Warning Signs
A child does not have to exhibit all or even many of these signs, and yet he or she may be actively suicidal. These are the common warning signs of suicidal intention:

- Depressed mood
- History of a previous attempt
- Decline in school performance
- Increased social withdrawal
- Loss of interest and pleasure in easily enjoyable activities
- Changes in appearance—for instance, no longer caring about one's hair or clothing
- Preoccupation with themes of death—the youngster may begin to read books with themes of death and dying

- Increased irritability and behavior problems
- Giving away important possessions
- Use of drugs and alcohol
- Changes in sleep and/or appetite patterns
- History of abuse and neglect
- History of a sense of failure
- Verbal expression about self-destruction—for instance, a youngster who actually says "I wish I were dead"
- No concern about making plans for the future

Triggers

A bipolar adolescent or child may show a number of these signs at many times during the year, but one who is potentially suicidal may make an attempt after a variety of events. These may include the breakup of a romantic relationship, disciplinary problems with parents, difficulty with schoolwork, or an injury to self-esteem, such as a failure to win an important award or position.

The most dangerous situation where suicidal impulses may be acted upon, however, is if the child is in a mixed state—he or she is experiencing a combination of the terrible feelings of depression with the frenzied agitation and energy of mania. While mixed states can occur naturally, very often they are induced by the use of antidepressant therapy in a bipolar individual. Antidepressant medications can increase the frequency of cycling and therefore produce protracted periods of mixed states.

When a child switches from one state to the other, he or she is experiencing symptoms from both poles of the condition. For example, the child may be very active and energized, and yet her mood may drop precipitously into a state of depression, accompanied by feelings of hopelessness, helplessness, and rage. If, during this time, suicidal thoughts surface, as they frequently do, the energy to act on those suicidal thoughts is available.

Since it is well known that suicides in bipolar patients most frequently occur during mixed states, parents can help prevent this state from occurring by ensuring that the child is not placed on antidepressants without mood stabilizers. They should watch closely for any of the signs of mania or hypomania occurring simultaneously or depressive and manic symptoms alternating very rapidly back and forth. One young woman described this unbearable state as her mind being flooded with unstoppable frenetic energy and yet feeling physically immobilized.

A father whose daughter started to express suicidal thinking at the age of ten advised other parents on the BPParents listserv how he and his wife dealt with the problem:

> I think the basic rule of thumb is to take every sign seriously. First we let the psychiatrist and therapist know. We also immediately danger-proofed the house: We got rid of plastic cleaner bags; we put scissors, knives, and razors as far out of reach as possible. We locked up every bottle of aspirin and all pills in a tackle box with a combination lock. Our daughter commented to us, even while having these suicidal thoughts, that "Now I feel safer."
>
> We also learned how important it was for us to stay calm and look calm. She must be scared to death to have these feelings, and it's reassuring to her that we're calm, in control, and will protect her.

Another mother wrote:

> I didn't leave her alone and we spent a lot of time together doing quiet things like reading stories. I let her talk about her feelings, but kept her as distracted (doing calm things) as possible.

We cannot emphasize how important it is that all guns be removed from the property and that the child not be allowed to spend any time over at a relative's or friend's house where there might be access to guns or other weapons. This is a time where only complete disclosure may protect the safety of a child who may be dealing with suicidal impulses.

One mother told us that the doctor had talked with her suicidal nine-year-old son and told him some very helpful and reassuring things. She reported what the doctor said and how her son responded:

> He said that suicidal thoughts were a symptom of depression just like coughing and sneezing are symptoms of a cold. When the depression begins to subside, so will the suicidal thoughts, just like a cough goes away when you get over a cold. My son really latched on to this, it made him not feel so guilty and responsible for the terrible thoughts, and he made a pact not to try to hurt himself anymore.

Very often parents and teachers avoid introducing the subject of suicide because they are afraid it might "plant ideas." "To the contrary," says child psychiatrist Rosalie Greenberg, "asking a young person about self-destructive wishes can help make him or her feel more understood and less trapped. Ignoring suicidal thoughts or behavior is a way of making suicide more likely to happen."

Brothers and Sisters

In the middle of all this often stands a brother or sister—little people who have no way to fathom what is going on, and no way to cope with the chaos in the household. The order of life and the hierarchy of a household seem suddenly out of whack. The other children see their mother and father—the authorities in their lives—tense and acting unauthoritatively in front of their sibling. The dog is being wagged by the terrible tail of a sickness they can't see, and the well siblings suffer significant losses. The first loss is that of their brother or sister.

While the sibling bond was long considered secondary—an adjunct to the parent-child relationship—recent research suggests that siblings can have as great an influence on each other as their parents, and sometimes an even greater one. As author Victoria Secunda writes in *When Madness Comes Home:*

> Siblings are each other's first and most enduring partners in life. For one thing, they are of the same generation. They are partners in *time,* with an infinite future of mutual influence ahead of them. For another, they are partners in *development,* closer to one another in evolutionary steps than to the senior generation.
>
> Siblings are also partners in *distribution,* vying for the same parental "goods"—who has the bigger allowance, later curfew, larger piece of the pie. And they are partners in *intimacy,* for the relationship is a dress rehearsal for friendships and romantic ties later on. Siblings often share their rooms, their toys, and their innermost secrets, the ones they wouldn't think of telling a grown-up.

But, she says, it's *because* of this identification that an illness of a sibling can be so damaging to a brother or sister. The partnership just spoken of is turned on its head when bipolar disorder affects one of the children. A host of traumatizing experiences can overwhelm the well siblings. Their privacy may be invaded, their toys and possessions destroyed or commandeered; they may suffer physical injury or even sexual molestation.

Many younger siblings become the target of the anger of an older ill brother or sister if they annoy or irritate him or her (an easy thing to do when someone is in a chronically irritable mood state). Mothers have confided to us that they watch their children like hawks because well siblings have been choked, had their ribs cracked, been hit in the head with rocks, and have been told that they would have their ears sliced off. When the ill child is raging, siblings have been told to lock themselves in their rooms or in the family car.

The well sibling will look desperately to the mother and father to provide protection against a brother or sister who may be threatening or abusive. What the well sibling probably will see are two exhausted, grief-struck, and confused people, busy running to doctors' appointments, beginning to pull away from social networks as they become bankrupted of energy and joy by an illness they don't understand.

Not only do well siblings often feel unsafe, but they become consumed with resentment and jealousy because so much of the parents' attention and energy goes toward worrying over and solving the problems of the ill child and not to taking the well children's traumatization and fears seriously. They will feel angry that the ill child has so disrupted family life and quashed all the good times that families should share. Well siblings also can become socially isolated. The turmoil and uncertainty that overtake the household often prevents children from inviting friends home. They are embarrassed by their sibling and begin to worry that others will think that they have a "touch of it" also.

It is common for the well siblings to feel emotionally disenfranchised—that they are not allowed to express natural feelings of anger and fear. As Victoria Secunda writes:

> They learn to suppress their own intense feelings, particularly of anger, which might be construed by the parents as a sign that these children, too, are going to pieces. Siblings often learn that *any* outbursts will be met with parental disapproval. To protect their parents, and to reassure themselves that they are not next to become ill, they may feel they have to act "weller than well." They can no longer be themselves.

Even in the best of situations, where the siblings love and appreciate one another, the well siblings will be bitter about the limit-setting that their parents enforce for *them*—and the seemingly disparate anything-goes attitude the parents adopt in response to the outrageous things their ill sibling does and says. Parents will hear loud refrains such as: "How come he gets away with everything?"; "Why doesn't she have to abide by the rules of the household?"; "Why do you let him use that foul language and tell me that I can't?"

Indeed, it's quite a feat for parents to be two-tiered disciplinarians, and parents may hold themselves to some impossible standard and suffer even more guilt. But parents have to remember that no parent—*anywhere*—gives attention that is microscopically equal to each of his or her children.

Parents should sit down with the well siblings and explain frankly some of what the ill child is experiencing. They can validate the well children's right to be angry and confused, the well children may have a different interpretation of what is going on around them. Parents can say something like:

> You know that Ryan has unique problems, and for some reason, he experiences any limit-setting in a catastrophic way. If we tell you "no" you are able to hear us. But, unfortunately, Ryan cannot, and we feel that it is better for the family to eat dinner, do homework, watch a movie, or play a board game without a three-hour rage going on in the background. When that happens, nothing good can happen in this house.
>
> The doctors are not even sure what is going on in Ryan's brain, and we are trying very hard to come up with some solutions that will keep everyone safe, while we and the doctors try to find out some answers and get Ryan more stable. But it's perfectly understandable that you feel angry and shortchanged, and we feel very bad about that.
>
> However, you didn't cause this, you are not responsible for fixing it, and we will not let him hurt you. We will protect you.

The parents should encourage the siblings to ask questions and to register their fears and complaints. Sometimes it helps simply to be *heard*. It should not be assumed, however, that a lack of questions or curiosity implies that the children are not in turmoil. In fact, silence may be a clue as to how upset a child really is, and the parents may have to provide some prompting to get the conversation going.

We spoke with Dana, a thirteen-year-old girl whose older sister, Monica, had early-onset bipolar disorder and who had been in grave shape throughout Dana's early childhood. Dana remembers visiting Monica in the hospital, and to this day speaks with pain about seeing the "ugly, horrible, little room with bars on the window that they put Monica in." She said she wanted to see Monica, but when we told her about Dr. Victor Fornari's advice in Chapter 13 of this book that siblings should see each other in a visiting room, not on the unit, she agreed that that would have been a much less traumatic memory for her. She also said: "I liked that my parents told me everything that was going on, but I wish I didn't know so many of the details because they were very disturbing to me. I couldn't bear hearing about Monica in restraints or having shock treatments. I would tell other parents to discuss things with their kids, but give a slightly softer and reassuring picture of things. Too much reality was hard for me to take." Dana concluded by telling us: "I think the best thing my parents did was try to give me extra attention; they tried to do special things with me, and they put me in therapy where I could really confide all my feelings in someone who could understand and not have her heart break as she listened to me. I will always be grateful to my parents for recognizing my need to be in therapy. It meant everything to me."

WHEN MORE THAN ONE FAMILY MEMBER HAS BIPOLAR DISORDER

Studies have shown that the earlier the onset of bipolar illness, the more likely first-degree relatives (parents, grandparents, and siblings) are to have the illness. In many cases, the diagnosis of a child will reveal a formerly undiagnosed condition in one of the parents. Also, it is common that when a parent understands the presentation of symptoms in one child, he or she is quicker to recognize the early symptoms in a younger child (if they are present), or to reframe some of the behaviors in an older child that have been explained away by "a particularly rough adolescence."

Before we talk about the complexities of a family with more than one ill child, we'd like to focus in on the family where both a parent and child have the disorder. We interviewed a mother who was formally diagnosed several years before her first child (a son) began to show the symptoms and behaviors of early-onset bipolar disorder. She spoke of the myriad feelings they both had about sharing the same diagnosis.

Certainly, as a bp parent, I have a tremendous compassion and understanding and patience for "acting out." While my husband has

educated himself about the illness, he can't possibly truly understand the sometimes subtle differences between chosen behavior and
when rage and heartbreak take over Greg's body and soul. I *know*
that horrible feeling. I know what a relief it feels like to destroy,
hurt, and self-mutilate in order to purge yourself of the monster
within.

But maybe I identify too much with him—projecting my fears
onto him. Maybe if I weren't bp, I could be firmer, establish boundaries . . . maybe being so forgiving hasn't been in his best recovery
interest.

However, being a bp parent has, in a way, forced me to take real
responsibility for illness management. No longer can I act out. I
must model successfully life and coping strategies. But then, sometimes, my husband holds me up as a standard. For example, he'll say,
"You're managing, why can't he?"

Greg is now fourteen years old and finally becoming stable after years
of a distressingly jagged course. She speaks with such sadness about his
early adolescence:

As Greg pushed further into adolescent behaviors and his bp behaviors became worse, layered with bitterness and hurt, even I have noticed that I have to distance myself from him. Before he stabilized
he would spend all day raging, cursing, whining, complaining,
picking fights, talking nonstop, basically exhausting everybody.
Then, just when I close my sweetly medicated eyes and float off to
sleep, I'll hear him sobbing in bed. I'll go to him and talk softly to
him, but part of me yearns for the simpler times of rage and outbursts of his younger years—cycles that could play out and end in
cuddles and hugs. As he gets older and naturally separates himself
from me, he is bound to me by his illness. He hurts me but also
needs me.

Later on, as we continued this email discussion, she wrote back in a
lighter tone:

Just had a few thoughts about being "bp squared":
1. Humor. Because we are both bipolar, we can share "inside" jokes.
   For example, this morning there was an ad in the paper for the

HBO show *Six Feet Under,* and I said: "Greg, isn't one of the people on the show bipolar?" "Yeah," he said. And I said, "You know, we are so hot in Hollywood right now. There's Sally Field on *ER,* that guy on *Once and Again,* Karen on *Will and Grace,* Robert Downy, Jr., . . . Tony Soprano's on lithium . . . it's just 'the thing' right now."

2. Medicating in company as a lifestyle.
3. He knows he holds a very special and unique spot in my heart because we are so alike.
4. "Normal" in our household is a very open and inclusive arrangement.
5. Greg gets the opportunity to nurture and give from his own life experience and therefore has moments of showing me the bright side too. He is not the only "patient" in the house and knows there is someone he can talk to about things only a therapist might understand. He knows I'm not going to judge him or say: "That's crazy."
6. We can learn from each other.

If this family is "bp squared," let us introduce you to a mother in Oregon who has what she refers to as a "bp-saturated family." Not only has her husband been diagnosed as having bipolar disorder, but her eleven-year-old daughter and her six-year-old son also have the illness. Her third child, a five-year-old, seems unaffected. She said:

My biggest frustration has always been trying to balance keeping a bipolar adult stable and giving my bipolar children the environment that they need in order to be stable. They often seem to have such opposite needs, and it is a juggling act trying to give one what he or she needs without triggering the others' issues. I very often point out to my husband that the "have nots" are outnumbered by the "haves."

She goes on to explain what happens when one family member loses control. She has dubbed it "the bipolar bounce":

My son will run around all hyper and become annoying, which triggers a tantrum in my daughter. She then blasts her stereo so she doesn't have to listen to him. This triggers my husband, who begins to get annoyed and raises his voice so that everyone will stop. His upset unsettles me and makes the kids more anxious. . . .

My strategy when dealing with the bipolar bounce is to do all in my power to keep everyone separated. My eleven-year-old, Lauren, has a TV in her room with a VCR and I offer a trip to Blockbuster to motivate her to stay in her room without feeling she is being punished. I couldn't let them all in the car with me as the car is one of the worst places when both kids are acting up. So I even bribe her to stay home with her dad with an extra rental of her choice. . . .

Two down. I then took my bipolar son and my youngest to Blockbuster. Blockbuster was tricky, but managed okay with just Sam and Cally. Had to pay the eighteen-dollar fine at Bbuster from our late returns of our last rentals (typical around here). However, still the best investment I know how to keep my bp kids separate when both cycling. This only works since we added a second VCR to the house. . . .

Sam was a handful all day, but managed to hold things together till about 6:00 P.M. I count down the hours of the day till 7:00 P.M. and I can give him his evening clonidine. Six P.M., dinner—ended up feeding everybody in a different part of the house. Not fun for me, but more fun than the alternative of sitting around the table feeling like Captain Bligh waiting for the mutiny. While having to be overinvolved with Sam, Cally colored all over the walls of her room with a black crayon. . . .

Just as I finally get Sam and Lauren and Cally asleep, my husband decides he wants to start working again. He has ended up spending the day isolated, feeling alone, wishing he and I could have time together and time to do some of the projects we need to get done. These are hard feelings for any adult, but harder for a bp adult who either internalizes it into a depression or externalizes it into a manic need to get the heck out of here and do something FUN!! . . .

I sleep from 11:00 P.M. until 3:00 A.M., when Cally gets up for a drink. Go back to bed with her till 5:30, when Sam wakes up, hyper and ready for a new day. I stay in his room with him in these early hours, trying to get him to quietly play Legos, Lincoln Logs, something—so he doesn't wake up the others. He wakes in an okay mood, but suddenly starts using the Lincoln Logs as swords and shouting and making fighting sounds. As I put them away and leave his room for a minute to check on the status of the others, he takes out a pair of children's scissors from his desk and cuts up all his pajamas from his drawer. . . .

So begins another day. . . .

This mother then told us:

The most important piece to put in place when raising two bp kids, or a bp child and spouse, or bp children and spouse—whatever you might want to call a multiple-affected bp household—is to build a support system for your family.

Building a support system:

1. It doesn't just happen. You have to create it.
2. Identify those people around your family that are in a position to be helpful to you or your kids. This might be family, teachers, administrators, neighbors, coaches, members of your church or synagogue, friends, doctors, other professionals such as a lawyer, dentist—whomever.
3. Once identified, educate. Be proactive. Let these people know about COBPD. Give them some basic information pertaining to your child and familial situation. If you stick your head in the sand and think people won't notice something is "different" with your child or "wrong" with your family, you are inviting trouble, and you are missing an opportunity to help your child and strengthen your family. Of course it is important to use discretion and always protect the privacy of the bp kids/adult. Be certain you have identified those people who are in a position to help your family. I am not suggesting you broadcast to everyone that your children have a psychiatric illness. Be selective about the people who are in a position to be helpful and that you think are trustworthy.
4. Don't shelter these identified people. Let them see some of the rages. On several occasions when my child was raging in the car, I secretly dialed my parents' phone number from my cell phone and let them hear what I was dealing with. Once I even dialed our psychiatrist's office number after hours and the shouting, raging, screaming, "wanting to be dead" outburst she was having was left as a message on his answering machine. (This particular rage was over being told she couldn't have a hot dog as we left the

skating rink because we were on our way home to eat dinner—
and she was ten years old at the time!) If you try to shelter your
child's behavior from everyone, they will not believe you when
you describe the fits of rage.

5. Use the cybercommunity as a support. Learn from others' experiences, medicine trials, mistakes, victories. Use the Internet to
stay as informed about COBPD as possible. This is important as
you advocate for your child and continue to educate those around
your child about his/her behavior.

Having a good support system is the only way I have survived,
and the only way my children, both bp and not, have survived each
other thus far. I know that in a crisis, there are at least four or five
people I could call to come and help. This crisis might require separating my non-bp child from her siblings. It might require separating my two bp children from each other. It might require
separating all the kids from their bp dad. Whatever the cause of the
stressful situation, there will always be times when the best way to
prevent one bp member from triggering another bp member is to
separate them. Usually it is my wonderful parents who come to the
rescue.

Both families who shared their stories spoke of the transformation that
occurred when medical stability became the norm, and of the value of
therapy—both individual and family. Each family does seem to work
things out in its own way, its own time, and its own style. We are in awe,
however, of the battles these families must wage and manage with
minute-to-minute timing, and how they have developed intelligently
worked-out coping strategies. This may not be *Father Knows Best;* it's simply love of the highest order.

MARITAL RELATIONSHIP

The empathic reader may feel for the parents of children with early-onset
bipolar disorder or recognize aspects in his or her own family life. These
parents carry a terrible burden. They trained at no special school, they
have no experience to guide them, yet they are forced to deal with an illness that they *and* the professionals know little about. If the emotions of
the situation don't paralyze them, then dealing with the schools, hospi-

talizations, and cost of psychiatric treatments may. No matter what the parents do or don't do, say or don't say, it is likely they will feel they're doing it wrong, saying it wrong, and that the greater world and the rest of their family are holding them accountable.

Marriages are placed under heavy strain. The sheer exhaustion of trying to deal with all this leaves a husband and wife with little energy for evenings out. They may begin to realize that every conversation centers around the problems of their ill child and that they don't have the energy or wherewithal to demand and reserve time for themselves and to develop a plan for their own needs and pleasures in life. Yet if they don't, they'll have less energy. One woman wrote, "Your marriage can just disappear, as you become 'roommates' surviving a crisis together."

Indeed, without strong support, these marriages are at extremely high risk. Any chronic illness in a child places a terrible stress on a couple, but a couple with one (or more) bipolar children usually means that the mother or father has the illness him- or herself or grew up with the often-devastating consequences of it in the family of origin and may feel unable to deal with it again.

Denial abounds, especially, it seems, on the part of the fathers, who may feel the need to minimize the severity of the problem. This places most of the burden on the mother, who may resent the hand she's been dealt and feel an enormous amount of anger as her partner stays above the fray. He's at work; she's in the trenches.

Many mothers have told us that they give up career dreams and satisfactions so they can keep their child safe and that they spend most of their time running to doctors' appointments and dealing with schools. They feel that they are on the front lines alone all day, only to have their husbands walk in at night and offhandedly remark that the house is a mess. (One woman who had been dealing with a hypomanic child, trying to appease her so that raging wouldn't begin and the medications could kick in, responded to her husband: "Yes, I ate bon-bons all day and watched *Oprah* and then I took a nap. It was a totally relaxing day.")

Often the parents don't see eye to eye on the desperate need for treatment. If a mother knows in her heart that something is definitely wrong and her spouse's response is "You baby him, that's half the problem," then she will feel all the more isolated, alone, and accused.

A mother or father can be in denial and say things like: "All she needs is love" or "There's nothing wrong with her, she's just got strong feelings." While appearing to be at odds with each other, however, the spouse who makes the filled-with-denial but positive and hopeful statements actually may be acting out the silent wishes of the others to allay the terrible fears that haunt them both.

We also know women who try to protect their spouse from seeing the full extent of the problem. One doctor told the mother of a young girl whose father thought she was just dramatic and spoiled to step back and stop intervening to spare her husband the brunt of the girl's behavior, and to let him witness one of the meltdowns. She wrote:

> So I did. One day she exploded in a rage when he needed to take a shower first to make the train to work (and her school didn't start for another hour). She went flying into her bedroom screaming, "Then I'm going to turn on the cold water full blast in here and burn him!" The screaming and crying went on and on and she trashed her room. That night he said to me, "I think you're right." It took a month but I'm glad we waited until he was in agreement on the need for treatment.

Not all couples will be so logical. The stresses are so great that people without a mood disorder can crack and say or do abusive things. When one (or both) of the parents manifests the illness or carries genes for alcoholism or bipolar disorder, the situation becomes even more dicey. Grief and anger and confusion and grudges can build up to incendiary levels, and few people act maturely or kindly under this constant barrage of the ill child, the constant demands of the other children, and the demands from each other. If these marriages do not get support, they can be doomed as the couple are driven further and further apart, filled with disappointment, bitterness, and resentment. The marriage can become a kind of hell itself.

It is imperative that couples seek help from outside supports. Couples therapy is a safe place where both can air their feelings and attempt to come up with better coping skills. Plans for buffering them both can be made in this arena. A couple can begin to let go of some of the rancor and begin to pull together.

In order to pace themselves so that they can be a couple and be more effective parents, parents need respite—short-term specialized child care, the gift of time. They can't go this alone.

Where would they find a break from all the tension that they endure nonstop—twenty-four hours a day—and the debilitating stress that can affect their own mental and physical health? A call to the local department of mental health (children's services) may provide funds and a list of trained providers. Sometimes a local university with a psychology department can recommend an interested and energetic student who could do some respite care on weekends or afternoons.

The following organization offers programs and services for children with disabilities and their families:

- ARCH National Resource Center for Crisis Nurseries and Respite Care Services. This center provides fact sheets and general resource sheets (including state contact sheets) about respite care. ARCH also operates the National Respite Locator Service whose mission is to help parents locate respite care services in their area. They can be reached at 1-800-773-5433 and www.respitelocator.com.

A husband and a wife need to learn to take care of themselves and each other, or they will never be able to deal effectively with their children and the unbelievably difficult and complex situations this illness will foist upon them. Before it takes a village to raise a child, it takes a couple pulling in the same direction, seeing the illness for what it is (not what one wishes it to be), mourning what has happened to the family together, and working toward better solutions for everyone.

One mother said it well when she wrote: "Each time we fly anywhere, I listen as the flight attendant tells us to put on our oxygen masks first and then place them on our children. This was a hard life lesson for me to learn, but I've finally got it now. Putting on your 'oxygen mask' first enables you to properly adjust your children's."

School: A Child's World Beyond Home

Children spend half their waking hours in school, a place that demands concentration and alertness, proper behavior, group and individual effort, and an ability to consolidate information quickly, to build on this information, and to reproduce it on pop quizzes, exams, and term projects. It is a fast-paced day with many transitions, much stimulation, and a host of complicated social interactions with peers.

Now take a child with bipolar disorder, who may have difficulty making transitions, or who may have comorbid syndromes that make him or her distractible, inattentive, anxious, or so perfectionist that he or she must complete everything to such an exacting standard that very little progress can be made. This child may be sleepy from medications or may have cognitive difficulties as a result of them. This child may be trying desperately to interpret social cues, may be feeling very bad about him- or herself, and possibly may be building up a head of explosive frustration. Additionally, as we will discuss in Chapter 11, these children commonly have associated learning disabilities and executive function deficits which further complicate their acquisition of knowledge and adjustment to academic demands.

Add to this a child whose illness is waxing and waning, whose energy levels are often reduced or significantly increased, and whose thought and behavior and "availability for education" is variable depending on the season and the severity of the cycling pattern, and it's not hard to see that many children with bipolar disorder need to be cut some slack in school—they need special accommodations.

When it comes to getting the school to make accommodations or to find a better placement for the child, no parent is in the Oliver Twist position of saying, "Please, sir, I want some more." The parent needs no begging bowl, hoping against hope that someone will dish out the very thing requested. Thanks to sweeping legislation passed by Congress, the law is behind the parents. They are guaranteed the right to have every say in how their child is educated.

If a parent can become acquainted with educational law and understand what kind of modifications a child needs to be successful in school, the parent has—at last—entered a level playing field.

The Law

The Fourteenth Amendment of the Constitution of the United States provides that no state shall "deny to any person within its jurisdiction the equal protection of the laws." If a state provides free public education (and they all do) then that free public education must be available to all of America's children.

When we think of the phrase *Brown v. Board of Education,* we think of Kansas, Thurgood Marshall, and integration in schools. But this landmark case is cited not only for its racial finding but also for the proposition that the right to an equal education is a fundamental human right—no matter what a person's color, no matter what a person's disability.

And from this root source came the Rehabilitation Act of 1973, which made discrimination against individuals with disabilities unlawful in three areas: employment by the executive branch of the federal government, employment by most federal government contractors, and *activities which are funded by federal subsidies and grants.* Section 504 mandates that *individuals with impairments that substantially limit a major life activity, such as learning, are entitled to academic adjustments and auxiliary aids and services, so that courses, examinations, and services will be accessible to them.*

Two years later, in 1975, Congress enacted a statute titled the Education for all Handicapped Children Act, which is now referred to as the Individuals with Disabilities Education Act (IDEA). Reauthorized in 1997, IDEA provides funds to elementary and secondary schools for public education. Under IDEA, schools are responsible for identifying and evaluating students with disabilities who require special education and services and following through and providing them with a blueprint called an Individualized Education Program—the IEP we will talk so much about throughout this chapter.

But IDEA also stipulates that these services are to be provided in the least restrictive environment (LRE) appropriate to the child's needs and that the child should be integrated with other children, with and without disabilities, and still receive special services. Parents will hear this referred to as "inclusion."

A Closer Look at IDEA

Because IDEA provides money to schools to educate children with disabilities, the term "disability" must be defined. Although we have italicized the disabilities that are used most often to describe bipolar children, the statute reads like this:

(3) CHILD WITH DISABILITY—
(A) IN GENERAL—The term "child with a disability" means a child—
(i) with mental retardation, hearing impairments (including hard of hearing and deafness), speech or language impairments, visual impairments, deaf-blind, *serious emotional disturbance* (hereinafter referred to as "emotional disturbance"), orthopedic impairments, autism, traumatic brain injury, *other health impairments,* specific learning disabilities; and multiple handicaps and (ii) who, by reason thereof, needs special education and related services.

If a child's impairment is moderate, he or she may not qualify under IDEA, only under a Section 504 plan. This plan does not require formal evaluation of the disability, and it covers accommodations that can be implemented at the school building level and does not typically call in resources. A child who is undergoing the evaluation and IEP process probably should receive services under the Section 504 until the IEP is designed and implemented.

The Question of Classification

Thirteen classifications entitle a child to full services and accommodations throughout the school day, but as we pointed out, the ones most likely to be applied to a bipolar child are "other health impaired" (OHI), "specific learning disability," or "serious emotionally disturbed" (SED), more often referred to as "emotionally disturbed" (ED).

Most parents should shoot for a classification of OHI, because it specifies that a child should have special education when "the condition is a chronic or acute health problem that results in limited alertness, which adversely affects educational performance." That fits. However, in some states, in order to receive extensive accommodations, such as a private therapeutic day school or residential schooling (therapeutic boarding school), the "emotionally disturbed" label might be required.

Emotionally disturbed is defined by the law as:

A. An inability to learn which cannot be explained by intellectual, sensory or health factors; or
B. An inability to build or maintain satisfactory interpersonal relationships with peers or teachers; or
C. Inappropriate types of behaviors or feelings under normal circumstances; or
D. A general pervasive mood of unhappiness or depression; or
E. A tendency to develop physical symptoms or fears associated with personal or school problems; or
F. Schizophrenia.

Hearing a child spoken of as "emotionally disturbed," which seems to suggest poor parenting, familial problems, or a vague negative judgment of the child himself rather than a medical illness, is guaranteed to raise the hackles of most parents, but the definition really doesn't suggest any of that. If the label is used, however, a parent should take special care to make sure this doesn't group the child with students with more delinquent behaviors. A friend of ours whose daughter's IEP bears the labels bipolar and "emotionally disturbed" said:

I think the word "disturbed" disturbs me. But Webster's says the meaning is "showing symptoms of mental or emotional illness." That about sums it up! I have personally not got caught up in the wording as long as I am able to receive the best benefits I can for my daughter (I got her into a therapeutic day school), and as long as I can keep her there, and she remains happy (for once in her school life), I will let them use what words are needed.

One woman whose child had had some trouble with aggression in school said:

The only reason I keep him under the ED label and do not fight for the OHI label is because an attorney said that if James ever has trouble in school of a physical nature, fighting, throwing things, etc., he is less likely to get into serious trouble if his illness was the cause and he is under ED. I am just taking precautions.

Another mother wrote:

We started our daughter as OHI, then accepted SED after her hospitalization so they would pay for the therapeutic day school after discharge from the hospital. I don't see any difference in services. This is the key question to find out in advance.

Every state has slightly different rules and ways of classifying students, so it may be best to talk to an educational consultant before you set out on this journey.

Educational Consultants

Because the whole IEP process is complicated—especially for parents dealing with it for the first time—it is often a good idea to find an educational consultant who can assist from the ground up. Some consultants help draft all necessary correspondence, starting with the request for the evaluation, and then help draft the IEP and attend the IEP meetings. They can empower a parent and assist him or her in obtaining the necessary services. Down the line they can help measure the implementation and progress of the IEP and, if necessary, help refer the child to a therapeutic day school and show the parent how to make that kind of move happen. If the school does not provide the education that is appropriate for the student, the services of an educational attorney will be needed. The way to find an educational consultant is to network with people who have used one or speak to the social worker or teacher at the child psy-chiatric unit of a major teaching hospital in the area. The Independent Educational Consultants Association has a list of reputable consultants in all areas of the country. Go to http://www.iecaonline.com or call 703-591-4860 to obtain names and phone numbers. Parents can start there and begin making phone calls and asking questions. Another idea is to call the National Alliance for the Mentally Ill group in your area and ask for a referral (see Resources on page 420).

Some agencies that deal with the protection of children offer educa-tional consulting for free. Some consultants charge, and some are paid for by state or federal funding. A few parents have told us that consultants paid by the government agencies may (and we said "may") not push as hard as a consultant with no obligation to the government, but this is, of course, very individual.

The qualification that any consultant must have is that he or she must understand bipolar disorder and its impact on learning so that he or she can help draft the best IEP that truly meets the needs of the child and that can provide the child with all the services in acute as well as non-acute situations.

EDUCATIONAL ATTORNEYS

The best way to find an educational attorney is to network with other par-ents who've worked with one and been pleased with the relationship and the outcome of his or her work on behalf of their child. Another way to get a recommendation is to talk to a trusted neuropsychologist. He or she may have testified in a case and be familiar with an outstanding attorney. The attorney must be very knowledgeable about bipolar disorder also or be willing to talk with the treating psychiatrist and find out how the ill-ness is impacting the child's "availability for education."

Some lawyers require a retainer and, if the case drags on, the fees may become quite high. If the court finds for the parents, the attorney's fees are paid by the school system. (Parents who have paid the lawyer up front will be reimbursed.) If the school system prevails, however, the responsi-bility for the legal fees rests on the parents.

Sometimes the cost of representation is out of the reach of parents, but there are free legal services and law clinics throughout the country. The American Bar Association provides a listing of Legal Services and Pro

Bono Programs in each state. Call the ABA at 312-988-5000, or sign on to its web page at http://www.abanet.org to see a list for each state.

Another idea is to check the local phone book under "Community Services" and/or "Legal Services," or call a local agency that deals with children and family issues. Attorneys' fees will be discussed on page 307.

INDIVIDUALIZED EDUCATION PROGRAM (IEP)

How Does a Parent Initiate an IEP?

A child cannot receive services until a full evaluation is completed. A parent should request the evaluation in writing but should first talk to the special education director and guidance counselor and ask how their system initiates the process. Most school districts ask parents to sign consent forms that make their child a "focus of concern." Once the process begins, the child is observed in the classroom, and a number of standardized tests that pinpoint IQ, specific academic strengths or weaknesses, and language and communication abilities are administered. Psychological assessment tests are administered as well.

All the testing can be done by the school system and costs parents nothing, but parents should bring their own independent assessments to bear on the procedure. If the independent assessment discovers problems that are closer to the parents' contentions than the school's, the school may have to pay for the independent assessment, but it may take a due process hearing to recover these costs. (Parents should remember that if a doctor feels these tests are "medically necessary," the insurance company may pick up a large percentage of the costs. Check with the insurance company first.)

We asked educational attorney Elizabeth Jester in Washington, D.C., whether a parent should make the effort and spend the money to have an independent assessment done. She said:

> I strongly recommend it. Schools should certainly do more than a screening, but sometimes the testing is not in-depth, and if you go the independent route you can choose a very experienced tester who hopefully understands the panoply of symptoms and difficulties a child with bipolar disorder can suffer, and who will write a *very* specific report. Since the IEP is the critical document from which all

services and progress benchmarks flow, the quality and comprehensiveness of the baseline assessments cannot be underestimated.

Who Attends the IEP Meeting?

The maximum amount of time allowed to pass between the parents' request and/or agreement to conduct the evaluation to the IEP development differs from state to state, but most regulations cite a time line somewhere between fifty and 120 days. This is why a parent should begin this process as early as possible so that the school year does not slip by without modifications in the child's program.

Once the evaluation is completed, parents are contacted and a mutually acceptable time and place are set for the IEP meeting.

The following people are usually a part of the IEP development team:

- Parents
- Child's teacher or teachers
- District representative who is able to provide or supervise the provision of special education
- Special education teacher
- Guidance counselor
- School psychologist who conducted the testing
- Service providers

One or two parents will sit at a table with four, five, or six school professionals, which may be extremely intimidating. Therefore, parents should feel free to bring an advocate—the independent tester, the child's therapist, psychiatrist, educational consultant, and so on—if they feel it would present a more complete picture of the child, bipolar disorder, and its effects on learning and classroom behavior.

How Should a Parent Prepare for the IEP?

Recommendation 1: Be Prepared to Educate
If parents decide to disclose the bipolar diagnosis (and the general consensus is that parents should be open and aboveboard about it), they need to understand that few people realize that bipolar disorder can exist in childhood and that it can look identical to or be comorbid with attention-deficit disorder with hyperactivity and/or extreme anxiety, obsessive-

compulsive disorder, and Tourette's syndrome. *So, it's up to the parent or the parent's professionals to educate the staff and ensure that everyone understands the condition and its effects on the child and the learning process, and what the child needs to be successful in school.*

One woman wrote of her efforts to do this education in preparation of her list of modifications in her son's program. She said:

> I spent all weekend preparing a list of recommendations for his IEP. They were all-encompassing, covering every angle. I typed a brief description of bipolar disorder with mixed states so that the teachers who didn't know what it was could read it. I attached a few documents detailing different information about bipolar disorder, including Dr. Charles Popper's list of the differences between ADHD and bipolar disorder [see pages 38–40]. I wrote up a contingency plan for the occurrence of another manic episode. I also wrote a list of coping strategies for the teachers to deal with him in class. At the beginning of the packet, I took the time to list my concerns for my son and the reason why I called the meeting. I did a lot of work. I felt so empowered (and proud).
>
> I walked in there with these big packets, and I passed them out and we went through them. My list of modifications was major and they agreed to adopt all of my suggestions and modifications pretty much without question, and they are willing to test him further to help him.

People tend to be more helpful when they understand what they're dealing with, so preparing and educating the school personnel (graciously and sincerely) can move the process along because everyone is approaching it with the same fund of knowledge. (Elizabeth Jester, the educational attorney, suggests that a parent send the information about bipolar disorder to the planning team a week or so before the meeting, so the educators can read the materials, think about them, and view the child and the IEP modification requests through very different—and, it is hoped, more sympathetic—eyes.)

Recommendation 2: Prepare a Binder
Another idea that proves a parent's credibility and braces his or her advocacy abilities is to *prepare a three-ring binder for the IEP.* It should have a large pocket on the outside into which a picture of the child can be

slipped, along with his or her name. The picture helps humanize your child and reminds all involved that they are talking about a little human being and not just a problem. Also, if the child's artwork or writing are particularly wonderful, it is nice to show some of the child's strengths before launching into the catalog of weaknesses.

The spine of the binder should carry the name of the child and the year and grade the child is in. Use dividers and organize the following sections:

1. Important contacts and telephone numbers with any pertinent notes.
2. All correspondence with the district and school system in chronological order.
3. School (and any independent) assessments.
4. Medical records.
5. The child's report cards, progress notes, and discipline records.
6. Examples of the child's work (to show which areas need remediation).
7. Any former Section 504 plans or IEPs.
8. List of questions that need answering during the IEP.
9. List of modifications and parent's expectations of this IEP.
10. Long-term goals and short-term objectives.
11. Information on parent's legal rights and due process.
12. Any relevant articles or information.

Thus organized, a parent can locate any relevant piece of information quickly and efficiently (and impressively).

A parent's clothing style, and even the briefcase he or she carries the binder and assorted materials in, adds or detracts from his or her credibility. A professional, polished, businesslike appearance not only adds to the appearance of competency and seriousness but makes the parent feel more competent and powerful in what is often an uncomfortable situation.

Recommendation 3: Rehearse the Meeting
It is also an excellent idea to practice how the meeting will be started and how you will get across the points you want to make, even if there are objections. If both parents are attending, they should rehearse who will

bring up what points and when in the presentation, and who will address possible objections. Parents should also decide which one is going to take meticulous notes of the meeting or operate the tape recorder.

Starting the Meeting

Before a parent starts the meeting, he or she should take a deep breath and remember something Barbara Coyne Cutler writes in her excellent book *You, Your Child, and "Special" Education:*

> The full implementation of the law depends on parents. Rights are not favors. They are not gifts from administrators or teachers; they are not windfalls. . . .
>
> People who withhold services and treatments from your child or who deny you the opportunity to get involved in shaping his or her program are themselves breaking the law. School systems are now obliged to take the rights of children very seriously.

Parents should do their best not to appear defensive. They can begin the meeting by introducing the advocates or professionals attending. A phrase such as: "We've brought ____, Sarah's ____ who has been helping us prepare for this IEP and would like to explain a bit about bipolar disorder and its impact on Sarah's performance in school."

Then the school professionals will discuss the results of the testing, where they've pinpointed weaknesses, and make suggestions for modifications in the academic program and daily schedule.

Because no one understands this child and this illness like the parent or parents sitting at the table, it's important to have a list of modifications ready to spell out.

Sarah's mother sent us her list of modifications as well as the strategies she advised the school to employ to help her daughter learn, and she has given us permission to include them here:

1. Because of her bipolar disorder Sarah is easily distracted and needs access to a low-distraction environment.
   a. Provide a classroom seating away from distractions. There should be a private study place (such as a study carrel) and a place to work one-on-one with a fellow student.

b. Provide a safe place outside the classroom that is available upon request.

c. Have her sit in the front row of desks in the classroom, near the teacher.

2. Because of her bipolar disorder she has abrupt mood swings, depression, hyperactivity, and she can be impulsive.

a. Avoid arguments.

b. Set firm boundaries with consequences she understands.

c. Schedule frequent breaks that involve physical activity such as running an errand or getting a drink.

d. Develop a private two-way signal system with teachers and Sarah so that Sarah can make them aware of her level of emotional intensity. By giving a "thumbs-up" she can imply that she's really fine; by spreading out all five fingers she can signal that her intensity level is high. If the intensity level is high, help Sarah decide on an intervention, such as moving to her private area or leaving the classroom. (I also said that if she leaves the classroom, the teacher should tell her she will be calling her destination to make sure she got there. This is to avoid Sarah wandering the hallways for fun.)

3. Sarah has off-task behaviors.

a. Try to redirect her behavior.

b. Ask her if she feels she needs a break in her alternative seating area.

c. Give her a preferred task to do as a substitute. Have her do makeup work later if needed with the thought that she may already know the material and the off-task behaviors may be due to boredom.

d. Offer choices such as going to her quiet area outside the classroom or down to the special ed or resource room.

e. Schedule time to meet with psychologist to learn self-awareness and self-calming techniques.

f. Always give her one minute to process when asked to make decisions.

4. Sarah is very anxious and has fear of failure.

a. No timed tests.

b. Substitute some written tests with oral tests.

c. Decrease assignments.

e. Assign little or no homework. (See discussion below.)

5. Sarah has difficulty with transitions, obsessive behavior, perfectionism—especially about work completion and quality.

a. Reduce writing by using a computer. This decreases perfectionism by eliminating a lot of writing (which for Sarah must look perfect) and helps with endurance during intense work.

b. Allow her to finish tasks before moving on. (This is extremely frustrating to her.)

c. Give warnings and prompts to the next activity.

d. Teach her to use visualization techniques to carry away obsessive thoughts and worries.

6. Sarah has periods of low endurance and difficulty with concentration and memory problems due to medications.

a. Schedule frequent breaks.

b. Give extra time for getting work done and for tests.

c. Decrease workload, such as assigning fewer problems on each page.

d. Eliminate work for concepts she already knows.

e. Assign little or no homework.

7. Sarah is a visual spatial learner. She needs time to visualize verbal input.

a. Pause during verbal presentations to give her more time to visualize what is being said.

b. Use manipulatives, visual material, videos, models, and computers.

c. Give her the big picture—help her see how the parts relate to the whole.

d. Let her observe, if she wants, before trying tasks.

e. Encourage creativity in all areas.

8. Sarah is disorganized and does not keep track of assignments.

a. Give her a planner book and teach her how to use it.

b. Email or fax parents list of assignments and news of upcoming projects or tests.

9. Sarah has difficulty maintaining friendships and resolving conflicts with peers.

a. Provide social skills classes in using appropriate behaviors with peers.

b. Provide one-to-one time for discussing specific problems and solutions.

10. Sarah experiences peer resentment toward her due to her special treatment.

    a. Explain to classmates that people learn in different ways, and this is what Sarah needs to help her learn.

    b. Have school consider a disability awareness unit about "silent" disabilities like Sarah's.

11. Sarah has frequent somatic symptoms resulting in numerous visits to the nurse.

    a. Nurse should eliminate temperature taking unless she shows obvious signs of fever. Let her rest for fifteen minutes with an ice pack on her forehead and behind neck. Send her back to class after this cool down.

Some other ideas for modifications that may help a child are:

- Setting up a tape recorder for the student to help with writing difficulties.
- Setting up a portable computer or Augmented Writing Device (AWD) and helping the child with keyboarding. The machine is visual, provides instant memory prompts, and the keyboard overcomes visual-motor writing problems and perfectionism regarding handwriting.
- Permitting the student to use a calculator.
- Providing enriched programs for areas of giftedness.
- Adapting physical education (many exuberant and active children in a gym can be very overstimulating for a child with bipolar disorder). A small group with a different kind of focus may be good for the child.
- Setting up a class in social skills.
- Assigning a person (a guidance counselor or special ed teacher) to go to at end of day for fifteen minutes to talk over the day, to review and debrief, so the child doesn't come home and dump all the stress on the family, thus causing more stress as everyone gets angry.
- Assigning a teacher who is flexible, emotionally sensitive, recognizes the child's uniqueness, and can give him or her a lot of positive feedback, a teacher with a calm demeanor, who can provide clear structure but maintain flexibility and is well suited to working with this population of students. A careful matching of stu-

dent to teacher is a helpful strategy that requires the support of school administrators.

- Assigning an aide who can provide one-on-one assistance and keep the child on task and comfortable with transitions.

Constructing the IEP

The Individualized Education Plan, constructed by the school team, is a written statement of the goals, objectives, and services that will be delivered to assist a child with special educational needs. A well-written IEP will proceed from a listing of a general goal to very specific measurable objectives accompanied by a timetable in which those objectives will be met. Federal law dictates that it include six required parts:

1. A statement of the child's present level of performance.
2. A statement of the goals and objectives.
3. A statement of special education services to be provided.
4. A statement of the extent to which the child will participate in regular education.
5. The date the special educational services are to begin and the expected ending date.
6. The criteria for determining if the objectives are being met.

The IEP goals should be written in the order of priority—the most important goal is first, the second most important is next, and so on. The language should never be vague.

The following questions should be answered:

- What service is to be provided?
- Who will provide the service, the specialist, the teacher, the aide?
- What teaching methods will be used?
- Where will the services be provided, the regular classroom, the resource room, in a special education class? With a small group? Will it be one-on-one?
- How often will the services be provided? How many days per week?
- Will the sessions be thirty, forty-five, or sixty minutes in length?
- Are the services to be delivered to the child alone or to a small group? What is the cap on that group? (You want to see no more than

four or five.) When will the services start? Immediately? Or within thirty days to allow time for the hiring of a qualified specialist?

A Model IEP for a Child with Bipolar Disorder

Unfortunately, bipolar disorder is an illness with wide variations in energy, mood, and motivation, and it tends to be seasonal. This means that academic progress with modifications can work wonderfully for a while, but a child may experience breakthrough episodes at different times of the year, despite proper medication. There may be times when depression predominates and the child can barely get to school or produce close to his or her ability; other times, the child may become activated and hypomanic and more difficult to handle in the classroom. Some children will experience a rocky road when new medication trials are initiated; some children may even require hospitalization during the school year and miss weeks and weeks of learning.

Therefore, we asked educational consultant Suzanne Faustini, L.S.W., the director of the Ohio Protection and Advocacy Association in Cleveland, to write an IEP that might provide guidelines for educating a child with bipolar disorder. She explained that an IEP starts with a baseline assessment. It describes the child's level and the problems the child is having. This baseline information is followed by a listing of goals and then by a number of objectives designed to help incrementally reach those goals within a one-year period.

Faustini drafted the following hypothetical IEP but cautioned us to explain that every student is different and will require different levels of intensity and involvement in his or her IEP plan. This hypothetical IEP is for a more severe problem and was developed to give parents and educators an idea of some of the possibilities.

HYPOTHETICAL BASELINE INFORMATION AND
DRAFT IEP FOR A BIPOLAR STUDENT

Elan is a personable individual who shows good attention and task orientation for very short periods of time. Elan has been diagnosed with bipolar disorder. His emotional and academic availability is variable and quite unpredictable. Physical complaints are often present both in and out of school. Presently Elan has a difficult time getting up in the morning, and he is often late or does not come to school at all. He can appear tired, bored, irritable, and explosive and has poor judgment and decision-making skills. Other times Elan can act extremely energetic (needs to move), he can be talkative and distractible. He can be extremely impulsive.

Elan has difficulty expressing his feelings and frustrations, and he often has negative and hopeless thoughts. When unable to do something others might consider simple, he feels a sense of failure. He does not have good problem-solving skills or stress management techniques. He often resorts to self-inflicted wounds and talks of suicide.

Elan's concentration and ability to attend and focus can be extremely impaired because of his limited alertness and attendance difficulties. His lack of interpersonal skills causes peer difficulties and limits his ability to establish healthy relationships with his peers and adults.

At other times—usually when he has high energy levels (he is becoming more manic)—he feels his understanding is superior to that of his classmates and that this negates his need to complete assignments. During these times, he can be disrespectful to adults, oppositional, and provoking to his peers.

Currently Elan is very compliant about taking his medications, and he has the desire to do what it takes to manage his disorder.

Consistent positive understanding and intervention is necessary for improving his self-esteem and allowing him to be accepted through his good and bad times. Staying calm and speaking to him in a reassuring tone is a must.

Elan is in need of a smaller, very structured setting that would be sensitive to his psychosocial needs. He presently does not do well with change or too much environmental stimulation. Counseling and support services such as a safe place and/or a person to go to when he feels overwhelmed or is having negative thoughts is necessary. A support group with like peers would be ideal if available. Flexibility in this plan is a must.

Goal #1: Elan will learn and apply strategies to independently divert bad thoughts.

Objectives:

A. Elan will go to the school counselor/psychologist twice a week (more frequently as needed).

B. Elan will explore negative thoughts with counselor and develop strategies for diverting them independently.

C. Elan will tell an appropriate adult when he has negative feelings he cannot manage.

D. Elan will use a variety of strategies learned and document results in a journal at least two times weekly.

Goal #2: Elan will develop other techniques to relieve anxiety rather than resort to harmful behaviors.

Objectives:

A. When faced with a stressful situation, Elan will explore options with counselor.

B. Elan will address anxiety-causing topics, which may be suggested by staff, in a journal at least one time per week.

C. Elan will talk to an adult when feeling explosive or is becoming out of control. He will remove himself to a safe place/person before harming self or others.

D. Elan will identify triggers that contribute to harmful behaviors and problem solve alternatives with counselor.

Goal #3: Elan will increase his time on task with only one redirective from 2–3 minutes to 10–15 minutes.

Objectives:

A. Elan will comply with all redirection, such as nonverbal cues, the first time.

B. Elan will increase the number of daily assignments he completes within a specified amount of time, determined by the teacher and his ability for that day.

C. Elan will stay focused for 10–15 minutes—or longer—on any given subject.

D. Elan will utilize problem-solving strategies when needing a break to refresh and refocus.

Goal #4: Elan will increase his communication skills in a variety of settings.

Objectives:

A. Elan will seek assistance in problem solving from appropriate adults.

B. Elan will practice using communication skills at least one time per week with staff and in his journal.

C. Elan will ask an adult when he needs to move around and/or go to a safe place.

D. Elan will tell an adult when he feels he may be getting out of control.

E. Elan will converse positively with a peer three times a week. He will note any positive changes he notices as a result of these interactions.

Goal #5: Elan will achieve grade-level work with a success ratio of four out of five assignments completed in all classes.

Objectives:

A. When given an assignment, Elan will complete four out of five of them accurately, legibly, and on time.

B. Elan will ask for extended time, modified work, etc., when he feels overwhelmed. (Parent will have to do this initially.)

C. Elan will accept redirection cues from the teacher when off task.

D. Elan will use a homework notebook daily to record all assignments. Teachers will check for accuracy and sign. Parent will sign to verify homework is completed.

MODIFICATIONS NECESSARY AT THIS TIME

Assignments will be broken down into manageable parts with clear and simple directions, given one at a time.

Preparation for transitions.

Ensure clarity of understanding and alertness.

Allow most difficult subjects to be taken in the afternoon when he is most alert.

Extra time on tests, class work, and homework.

Allowances made for unpredictable mood swings and skill functioning.

All staff involved with Elan will be provided with training on bipolar disorder.

Awareness of potential victimization from other students.

In extreme cases where Elan gets out of control and may do something impulsive or dangerous, a crisis-intervention plan will be implemented.

Positive praise and redirection.

Report any suicidal comments to counselor/psychologist immediately.

If there are ever times when Elan's mood disorder makes it impossible for him to attend school for an extended period of time, home instruction will be provided to assist him in keeping up with his academics.

An aide will be placed within Elan's classroom to ensure his well-being.

The aide will assist the teacher with all the students who need it also.

Since Elan does not do well with unstructured times, such as lunch and recess, the aide will accompany him as a buddy during those times, without drawing undue attention to him.

BEHAVIOR PLAN

Goal #6: Elan will decrease explosive outbursts.

Objectives:

A. Elan will seek adult assistance before lashing out with aggressive behaviors.

B. Elan will remove himself and seek time out and/or safe place when feeling explosive.

C. Elan will learn and apply strategies for anger control.

D. Elan will postpone making important decisions during a depressive state.

E. Elan will recognize possible early signs of an impending manic or depressive cycle and talk about them to his psychiatrist.

F. Elan will earn points for all of the above. Points can be accumulated toward a day without homework or something special that will motivate this child.

FUNCTIONAL BEHAVIORAL ASSESSMENTS AND BEHAVIOR INTERVENTION PLANS

As we mentioned earlier, many children with bipolar disorder don't act out in school, but save their frustration and upset for home and mother.

However, some children can't control their actions in either locale and the school may try to discipline, suspend, or expel the child due to unruly behaviors without understanding that many of the behaviors are a result of the bipolar disorder. Parents should ask that the school district conduct a Functional Behavioral Analysis (an FBA) and based on that, a Behavior Intervention Plan (a BIP) be written into the IEP.

Actually, the law will demand that this be done eventually as it is concerned that too many days of suspensions deprive a child of a free and appropriate education (FAPE). Thus it requires that a Behavior Intervention Plan be put into place before an eleventh day of suspension is decided upon (we would hope that a BIP would be written into an IEP long before that).

The purpose of the Functional Behavioral Analysis is to determine which triggers are setting off unacceptable behavior. Only if a team can speculate about or hypothesize the function the behavior has for the child will the team be able to intervene to manipulate the environment to ease the conditions resulting in that undesirable behavior and/or help the child make a better choice. Here the parent and doctor can make many suggestions. Below are some example scenarios commonly seen with bipolar children and adolescents:

Example A:
Antecedent: Student doesn't seem to be able to stand in line. The student has sensory integration issues and is probably feeling claustrophobic, trapped, etc.
Behavior: Student kicks, pushes, and swears.
BIP: Allow the student to be last in line so she can create the space around her that she needs to feel comfortable and not irritated.

Example B:
Classroom Problem: Whenever the child is playing during unstructured play time he starts shouting at the other children that they aren't playing the game right, and that they are cheating. The other children raise their voices, and within a few minutes everyone playing with this one child is agitated, and angry.
Antecedent: The child does not have appropriate social skills, and needs to control the situation, and the other children.
BIP: The child needs social skills instruction that should be provided

by the school through the school social worker. Because the child does not play appropriately in an unstructured situation, the teacher could keep this child busy with some other activities after he has finished his work. If there is an aide in the classroom, or if this child has an aide, then the aide can keep her eye on the social interaction in the group, and remove the child before he escalates and is yelling at his peers.

Many children with bipolar disorder have comorbid learning disabilities that complicate their hours in school and make then feel constantly frustrated, angry, and humiliated. They often simply shut down and "leave the playing field."

Example C:

Classroom Problem/Behavior: The child refuses to do his schoolwork and just sits at his desk doing nothing. He does not ask for help, and even when shown what to do, continues to sit there.

Antecedent: Some of the classroom assignments confuse the child and he doesn't know how to do the work. He feels embarrassed and frustrated. He often feels that he doesn't understand what he is supposed to do and feels that he isn't very smart. He doesn't know how to handle these feelings and he shuts down.

BIP: 1. Since the child may have sequencing difficulties, he may not be able to understand oral instructions that have two or more steps in them. The teacher could stop by the child's desk and make sure he understands the directions by having him say them back to her.

2. If there is a reading problem, again, the child may not be able to read the directions well enough to understand what he needs to do. The intervention would be the same as above with the teacher unobtrusively giving the student the directions at his desk.

3. The child's desk might be in a position in the room where it is hard for him to hear or see the teacher when she is giving directions, and his desk could be moved to the front of the classroom near the teacher's desk.

4. The classwork being given to the child might be too difficult for him because of deficits he has in that area. If there are known LDs, the classroom work must be at the appropriate level for the child to work independently.

5. Sometimes the amount of work on a page is too much for a child. The teacher can cut and paste the work so that there is not as much of it on the page.

Example D:

Antecedent: Adolescent with bipolar disorder is bullied overtly or covertly by other student(s).

Behavior: Student cuts class, does not show up for class, or leaves school grounds completely.

BIP: Because taunting by peers is so difficult for a child with bipolar disorder to handle, he needs a safe place to go to when he feels threatened emotionally and/or physically by other students. This "safe place" can be the counselor's office, a "safe teacher's" room, or the resource room. He needs to be able to go to his "safe place" without fear of penalty or repercussions (that he now faces a detention or suspension) for taking care of his emotional needs in the type of crisis being bullied causes a teen with bipolar disorder.

In addition, the schools across America need to be more aware of the problems bullying cause, and need to implement programs to prevent it from happening. There should be zero tolerance for bullying.

The Behavior Intervention Plan should be reviewed frequently to assess whether or not it is effective and whether a different placement might be needed for the child.

Naturally, for a bipolar child, it all starts with proper mood stabilization, and in many cases, addressing the attendant learning disabilities that may be causing frustration, hopelessness, and perhaps anger when approaching work that uncovers these learning deficits.

The Center for Effective Collaboration and Practice is a national organization that helps students with emotional and behavioral problems succeed at school. The organization has a comprehensive site that discusses the philosophies of a Functional Behavioral Assessment and demonstrates how a team collects the data and writes the Behavior Intervention Plans. You can find them on the Internet at http://www.cecp.air.org/fba/problembehavior/main.htm.

Other Sections on the IEP Form

After the baseline level and the goal and objectives are notated in the IEP, the IEP team notates how progress is to be measured. Some students will be tested periodically, or the teachers and counselor will fill out a standardized checklist, or progress will be charted every few days or on a weekly basis. (These measurement instruments are placed in the "Criteria" section on the IEP form.) Finally, a percentage goal is assigned which attempts to determine what percentage of mastery is realistic: 75 percent? 80 percent? 100 percent?

The goals are looked at every nine weeks or so. If progress is not being made, an IEP can be reconvened at any time to make adjustments or to put other modifications in place. It is important to remember that an IEP is an organic document that can be modified at any time. Parents who wish to reconvene the IEP planning team should put the request in writing.

Parents should keep in mind that the IEP must be constructed in just such a specific manner, because if the time ever comes when they must prove that a small therapeutic school is better for their child, they're going to have to produce evidence that the child's needs cannot be met in the large public school environment, and everything will start with the IEP.

Self-contained Classroom Versus Scheduled Time in a Resource Room

The least restrictive environment is a regular classroom, with time scheduled in the resource room or school psychologist's office for remediation or therapy. But some schools have self-contained classrooms that have smaller numbers of students and less hustle and bustle, and it may be a more appropriate learning environment for a child having trouble with distractibility and overstimulation. Everything will depend on the grouping of students in that self-contained classroom and what each student's challenges may be. If a child with bipolar disorder is gifted in certain areas, the student should be placed in the high math or high science classes with the rest of the gifted students in the school, if possible, or have one-on-one tutoring.

What Are the Possible Derailments on the Way to a Proper IEP?

It is hoped that everyone at the meeting is working in tandem and a proper IEP is under construction for the student; but comments or objections may arise that could derail the process and obstruct the parents' goals for the IEP. If a parent hears any phrases that sound like: "We don't have this kind of money"; "We don't have this kind of specialist or staffing"; or "We have many students here. Your child is not our only concern"; the parent can respond calmly that "the law states that our child is entitled to a Free and Appropriate Public Education (FAPE), and a placement must be offered that allows our child's educational needs to be met and that can make our child 'available for education.' "

To put it another way: Legally, no school system can say any of those statements and be in compliance with the law. If they have to pull in private staffing to meet the child's needs, then that is what they'll have to do.

Teachers should recognize that these laws also can empower them and that they have every right to request additional in-service training, help within the classroom to manage that special ed child (an aide, a teacher who comes in part of the day to help, volunteer adults, a college intern, a psychology or social worker intern, or even a high school student assigned to help the student). No teacher should be asked to deal with all these modifications without complete training and adequate support services.

The Meeting's End

At the end of the meeting, the parents may be asked to sign the IEP. No IEP should ever be signed on the spot but should be taken home and mulled over when the parents are a bit less spent and exhausted. If a day later there are some questions that need clarifying, the parent should call the special education director and discuss any changes. Only after clarification or correction should an IEP be signed saying that the parents accept the IEP plan.

If the plan has been well constructed and the school personnel have worked hard to promote success for the child, a phone call to the special education director and a note of thanks to each participant would be a very appreciated finale to the IEP process. Parents who have a positive response should bear in mind how much effort everyone is putting into this child and his or her problems. Much of the information about bipolar disorder is certain to be new to the school personnel, and they will be unsure as to what modifications will work (or will be less successful), and uncertainty can exist for them as well as the parents.

What If the IEP Is Unacceptable?

In the cold glare of morning, with no warmth shared around a table, parents may find themselves looking at an IEP that is not specific, that may be indifferent to some of their concerns and asked-for modifications, and that simply may not be right. It's so tempting to let it pass, hope for the best, and look like a "reasonable and nondemanding" parent.

Let that thought pass on by. The parent is the only one who can ensure that a child is more comfortable in school and thus gets a better education.

In most cases, the school will make the requested changes. Just calling the director of special education and announcing an intention to reject the IEP may result in the services requested. Sometimes, however, the school digs in its heels and thinks parents will go away. In such cases parents have three choices: They can call another meeting and go over their objections; they can go to mediation and hope to resolve the differences; or they can pursue their right to due process—they go to court. If parents decide to go to mediation or due process, they should hire an educational attorney to represent them.

It may be that the IEP is a beautifully written document, but a parent begins to notice that the promised services are not happening or that they happen in a very scattershot manner. This is a violation of a contract and the more documentation a parent has, the better the case for holding a due process hearing.

For instance, everything that is supposed to be happening according to the IEP and does not should be noted in a personal log and a letter should be sent to the director of special education about the omission. If a phone conversation was held between a parent and someone at school, a letter should be written that says: "This is to follow up in writing what we discussed on the telephone today . . . "

A parent cannot assume the IEP is being followed (often the special ed department has the best of intentions but the academic and other teachers outside that department are too busy to even look at the document and comply with its dictates). A personal log with all correspondence will graphically point out any lack of services or aids that will prove that the school is out of compliance with the IEP. Hearing officers do not like to see that a school is out of compliance with the IEP, so log faithfully.

Before things go to due process, parents should investigate calling their state's protection and advocacy group. This is a nationwide network that, among other things, devotes considerable resources to ensuring full access to inclusive educational programs. A phone call or letter from the Protection and Advocacy group requesting accommodations (or that accommodations be complied with) or the presence of one of their personnel at an IEP meeting almost always results in a parent getting what is needed for his or her child.

To find the P & A in your state, call the National Association of Protection and Advocacy Inc. at 202-408-9514; or look on the web at www.protectionandadvocacy.com and click on "P & A's/CAPS."

Mediation

Mediation is an informal procedure that brings the parents and the school personnel together with a trained, impartial party—the mediator—in order to reach a solution to the problem. The mediator's role is to facilitate communication, keep some order in the room, and, it is hoped, persuade the two parties to come to a mutually satisfying agreement about the child's educational program. Before entering mediation, parents should have the assistance of an advocate and/or an educational lawyer.

Due Process Hearing

If a parent is unhappy with any decisions made by the school system about the child's classification, evaluation, program, or placement, IDEA gives him or her the right to challenge the school system's refusal to find a solution that the parent can live with. The choice of going to due process must be carefully thought out, and the underlying motivation should be substantial, however, because it can be expensive if a parent loses (and the school system is not required to pay the parent's lawyer), and it can be emotionally wrenching.

The Attorney's Fees

Parents also need to know that—in many cases—they will have to pay the attorney and expert witness fees *up front* until the case is decided. In other words, they must advance the money and will be repaid if they win the case in court.

In some states there are caps on the fees charged or there are educational attorneys who can do a certain amount of pro bono work and take fees only from the Board of Education if they win the case.

But parents need the best educational attorney they can find, and sometimes that means putting aside the money to pay for the case to proceed. Most educational attorneys do not work on contingency (check http://www.edlaw.net/service/attylist.html for a list of educational attorneys in your state).

Just what are those fees incurred by the parents throughout the due process hearing? We'll use the tristate area of New York City as an example on the high end, but your educational attorney will explain his or her fees so that you and your spouse can decide how far you want—and can afford—to take this.

The average due process hearing runs about ten days. Each day, before the hearing, you will be expected to show up with a check for $2,500 for your attorney's daily fee. One or two expert witnesses will be called and their fees can range from $2,000 to $4,000 for a day of testimony (also paid by the parents up front). After both sides present their case, the hearing officer orders both the parents' and Board of Ed's counsels to prepare and file briefs as well as reply briefs based on the testimony contained in the transcripts. This may take two and a half to three days of a lawyer's time and at $250 an hour, this may cost the parents over $5,000. Thus, a parent is looking at fees that run from $25,000 to $50,000. (Remember, this is the high end, but you have to know the realities of your situation.)

A new law states that a judge must order reimbursement if the parents win the case, and only then will most of the costs be returned to the parents. It's a lot to consider (especially if one or both parents are professionals who charge hourly fees themselves and must factor in the unrecoverable loss of income for all the time spent preparing for the hearing and being present at the multiple days of hearing).

However, if your child needs several years of expensive schooling, and the merits of the case are good, you have to measure advancing $25,000 or $50,000 against the $175,000 or more such schooling would cost.

The other thing parents should understand is that the school system risks the possibility of losing and having to pay not only your attorney fees, but the attorney representing them, their expert witnesses, and the school placement you've requested. Your winning the case could also set a precedent for other parents in the state, so make no mistake about it, the case the Board of Ed presents will be hard fought. In other words, the needs of the child will pale next to the money the school district stands to lose. Therefore, expect that it will be inferred that you and your parenting abilities are a significant source of your child's issues. Your "shortcomings" and virtually every excuse other than the school district's ability to appropriately address the educational needs of the child will be used as an explanation for the child's difficulties in school.

One mother we know was widowed in her thirties and had to work to support her daughter who had a severe case of dyslexia. After exhausting all the opportunities for remediation in her school district, the mother brought a due process hearing to obtain a placement for her daughter in a special school for dyslexic children. During the hearing, her status as a single parent and her travel for work were brought up as a source of her daughter's learning problems.

If a parent does decide to push ahead, he or she writes a letter to the school district's special education director explaining the background of the dispute and requesting a "due process hearing under IDEA." This letter should be sent by registered mail.

A hearing must be scheduled within thirty-five days of the receipt of this letter, and an "impartial hearing officer" will preside over it. If either the parent or the school feels the officer is not impartial, IDEA allows for an objection, and another will be decided on or appointed by the state education department.

If parents challenge a placement or a portion of the IEP, the initial burden is on the school system to prove that the placement or IEP is appropriate. If the school system puts on evidence to support the appropriateness of the program, the parents then go forward and attempt to rebut those assertions. If the school system fails to prove appropriateness of the placement/IEP or the parents successfully rebut the system's assertions, then the burden shifts to the *parents* to prove that what they are seeking is appropriate.

For example, if a school system proposes placing a high-functioning bipolar child in a program populated by low-functioning conduct-disordered children, the school system presumably would not be able to meet its burden of proving that the placement was appropriate. The focus of the hearing then shifts to the parents.

If the parents have an alternative placement, it is not automatically granted. Rather, the parents must then prove that their placement proposal is appropriate—that the program they are proposing for their high-functioning bipolar child is populated by high-functioning children with similar disabilities.

The parents and their lawyer will present "evidence," such as independent testing and evaluations, the child's school records, and testimony from advocates, teachers, and the child's psychiatrist and other therapists.

The entire proceeding will be extremely clinical and businesslike; there will be nothing warm and fuzzy about it. Therefore, it can be a very trying situation for parents. But this is the nature of such a hearing. The focus for the parents should be the end result, not the means to achieve that result.

The hearing officer hears both sides and issues a written decision within ten days of the first request for the due process hearing. As we already mentioned, if the parents prevail, their attorney fees are paid. The school always pays for the hearing officer, the court reporter, the school's attorney, the electronic transcript, and any substitute teachers hired to replace testifying teachers *no matter who prevails in the hearing.* Because it is an expensive proposition for the school system, many will try to resolve the differences before things lead to the due process hearing.

If the hearing officer rules against the parents, they have the right to appeal and have the case heard by a hearing review officer who is not a part of the state's educational agency. If that hearing also rules against the parents, they may bring a civil action suit against the school system in a state or federal court. From there the parents and attorney can bring the appeal right up to the Supreme Court. But we hope this process never goes beyond the early, less expensive, and certainly less time-consuming recourse of mediation. These appeals could take over a parent's life for a very long time. A lawyer and advocate can advise parents when it's time to find another solution or to compromise and use their energies in other ways, or they can say why this test case might be important in the laws of the land. It may set a precedent. Whether a parent has the stamina and stomach or pocketbook for this is extremely individual.

WHEN IS IT TIME TO SEEK OUT A SMALL, THERAPEUTIC DAY SCHOOL?

The time may come, even with a comprehensive IEP in place with full implementation, when it becomes clear that the public school situation is not the appropriate place for a child with bipolar disorder, and he or she might be far better off in a small, therapeutic program. This is a separate school (public or private), usually with a small number of children with a small class size (six to eight children), in a classroom with a trained special education teacher and a trained aide. The children receive academic subjects along with group therapy, individual therapy, and sometimes family therapy, and art and music therapy.

Now the job of the parents is to prove to the school system that an "appropriate" education for their child cannot take place in the larger public school environment: Rather, the appropriate program for the child is one designed to deal with children who have these types of learning impediments and a waxing and waning set of symptoms.

Most public schools start a child in a regular classroom, then add services, then possibly place the child in a self-contained classroom within the public school setting. If the child has been hospitalized or has made a suicide attempt, there will be documentation of a severe problem that probably can't be handled within the public school setting, but parents typically have to fight to secure placement in a therapeutic day school. Start pursuing a placement while the child is in the hospital or step-down to a day hospital (the child spends part of the day at a hospital program) temporarily until a placement can be found.

A meeting is held and everything is laid out on the table. The child will not qualify for a special school unless the IEP is written in such a way that it cannot be implemented in the regular classroom, since the law requires that a child must be educated in the "least restrictive environment" (that meets his or her educational needs). The IEP must specify that the child is to have a small, structured, self-contained classroom taught by a special education teacher. In addition, mental health staff should be on hand to perform one-on-one services and monitoring.

Parents may want to consult an educational consultant for guidance on what schools are state-approved and can be suggested as possibilities. (School districts often do not tell parents all the schools that are possibilities.) Networking with other parents is often the best way to find out which schools are appropriate and have been paid for by district funds in the past. The State Education Department Special Education Division can also give parents a list. The school may not necessarily disclose a complete listing.

Parents should visit each school, but they should understand that, before they can visit, a "formal referral" package consisting of all the child's records must be sent from the referring district. This process can take two weeks or longer if the public school performs this service. Educational attorney Elizabeth Jester told us that she gathers the entire packet (the medical records, the IEPs, hospital records, if any, the psychiatrist's recommendations, the school records, etc.) and sends them to potential schools immediately so that parents can begin looking at the programs.

Parents should note their impressions on paper to help remember what each school has to offer. These will be useful to support—or refute—a placement in that particular school. The following list can be typed up as a form, photocopied, and kept in a binder so that information on all the schools is in one place.

Name of school
Phone number, address, directions to school
Principal, headmaster, or director's name
Cost of annual program
Does program run nine months, ten months, twelve months?

1. Curriculum and Level of Challenge
Describe the type of students (and their families) who attend this school.
> What are their educational labels—OHI (Other Health Impaired)? ED (Emotionally Disturbed)? What are their major difficulties?
> What is the number of students in the school? What is the gender ratio?
> What is the average IQ of students in this program?
> Is there a minimum IQ cut-off for admission?
> Are there enrichment programs for gifted students?
> Is there access to computers?
> What is the curriculum?
> Is classroom graded or ungraded?
> Are classrooms structured by subject, grade, or ability?
> How many students in each class? Ratio of teachers to students? Students' age range?
> Is academic program adjustable according to student's variation in energy level, mood, and motivation?
> Does the child have free time during the day? How is it structured?

2. Teachers and Staff
> How many teachers?
> Certified to teach individual subjects?
> Certified in special education?
> Are their psychiatric nurses or aides?

3. Treatment, Discipline, and Social Development

DISABILITIES/SPECIAL SERVICES

What proportion of the students are on medication?

How are medications administered? Is there a doctor or nurse on staff?

Is there a hospital affiliation?

What is the training and background of the therapeutic staff?

Psychiatrist on staff? Psychologist on staff?

Other mental health professionals?

Are there any rules about not permitting outside prescribing psychiatrists for students who are enrolled in school? Will their psychiatrists willingly consult with child's present doctor?

Is there therapy or counseling? How often and who provides it?

Are there groups? Social skills groups?

Is the family invited to school and involved in a family therapy? Is it mandatory? If yes, it should be noted in the IEP. Once on the IEP, the parents are in a strong position to have the costs they incur in attending the therapy (transportation, lodging, etc.) paid for by the school system.

What is the psychological orientation of the school:

Strictly behavioral?

Psychodynamic?

Cognitive therapy?

Combination or other?

DISCIPLINARY PROBLEMS, POLICIES, AND PROCEDURES

Do they call parents?

If school uses a point system, is it based on taking away points for bad behavior, or earning points and privileges for good behavior?

If the school uses a level system, what are the new privileges and responsibilities that come with each level?

OVERALL PHILOSOPHY

Describe the philosophy of the school and what kind of success rate it's had with students. What colleges do their students go on to attend?

Difficulties in Finding the Right Fit

Unfortunately, often a geographical area has few good placement options. If a school's reputation is good, there is a waiting list to fill limited seats. Some schools are for lower-functioning children (children with mild to severe retardation or other neurological problems), and some schools are mainly for children with behavioral disorders (BD). Parents of children with bipolar disorder need to stress how "vulnerable" their child is, and how impulsive, and that it would be potentially harmful to put the child in a school with mostly behavioral disordered children who may teach them delinquent behaviors.

A parent should not come back and say to the school system: "This is not the best school for my child" because the law states that an "appropriate" education is required, not the "best" education. ("Appropriate" is usually interpreted as "minimally appropriate.") Be prepared to suggest alternatives and support the choices with expert recommendations from the psychiatrist and educational consultant or attorney.

WHEN IS RESIDENTIAL TREATMENT THE RIGHT WAY TO GO?

Sometimes a school that meets the needs of a student just doesn't exist in the area close to home, or the time comes when a child cannot effectively be managed at home. It becomes obvious that a change in environment with a twenty-four-hour peer group and a number of nonparental authority figures may be in the child's best interest. This residential placement is one of the most difficult decisions to make. Parents will suffer guilt, feelings of having failed the child, and grief that they're sending their "baby" away.

Educational attorney Elizabeth Jester always tells the parents she works with: "Nothing is forever. You're not putting your child away, you're enabling the child to get an education and learn skills he or she may not be able to learn inside the family. I've worked with numerous students who, after twelve to eighteen months in a residential school, really get their act together. Away from the close atmosphere of the home environment, they can blossom and mature. And the entire family gets to put itself back together again as well."

Parents should bear in mind that residential schools are not institutions or jails, they more resemble boarding schools, but they have a staff and a program equipped to deal with and especially designed for students having specific problems.

Residential schools cost a whopping amount of money. We've heard fees that range from $56,000 to $125,000 per year. School districts will have to pay for this kind of schooling if they fail to offer the child an appropriate educational placement that meets the child's needs.

A Model School for Children with Bipolar Disorder

There are times when the public school—even with all accommodations on board—will not work, and when there is no option of a therapeutic day school or a residential treatment center. If a child is unstable or school is too much of a stress, a parent may have little choice other than to homeschool that child until stability is gained, or a better educational situation for that child can be located.

Understanding how truly difficult it can be to find the right fit for a student with bipolar disorder (and often comorbid learning disabilities), we were particularly interested in learning of a school in Austin, Texas, that is the first school designed specifically for bipolar/ADHD children. It is a model that doesn't require great sums of money and that could be replicated almost anywhere in this country by a group of dedicated parents. The Austin Harvard School was founded four years ago by Glad and Richard Curlee who had two young children who were onsetting with bipolar disorder and no school situation that was right for them.

The Curlees thought about homeschooling, but since Glad is a licensed marriage and family counselor she decided to start a school because, as she said: "I wanted my children to succeed in life and I wanted others to succeed with mine."

In December of 1996, her school became a 501(C) organization and opened its doors with eleven children (the school is K through 9). "That first year, we thought we were an ADHD school, but the majority of the kids had mood swings and were actually undiagnosed but truly bipolar," Glad told us. Although they initially started with special ed teachers, they found out that the children seemed to learn better with a CD-ROM program called Switched-On Schoolhouse. Glad explained:

> This kind of curriculum focuses them. Each student has a carrel and
> a computer and earphones, and the curriculum is visual, auditory,
> kinesthetic, and allows each child to progress at his or her own speed.

Because the curriculum is rich and comprehensive, our teachers don't
have to spend as much time doing lesson planning and grading and
they can deal with each child's behavioral and emotional issues.

We called Alpha Omega, the producers of Switched-On Schoolhouse in
Phoenix, Arizona, and spoke with Nancy Halle. We asked her to explain
their curriculum. Her discussion and the demo materials she sent us
showed that Switched-On Schoolhouse's curriculum is an advanced,
multimedia-based learning environment. It incorporates video clips,
sound files, animations, computer games, drills, and tests. Nancy said
that they've heard that ADHD kids do well with the program because
they can see it, hear it, and touch it, and it focuses learning. The student
can turn it on and off as attention waxes and wanes, but any work that the
student skips or fails to answer correctly comes up at the end so he or she
can't move on until the lesson is mastered. This way, no child's lack of
learning "slips through the cracks."

This system even grades tests and records them on the student's file and
lets the teacher know how long the student spent on each subject, so the
teacher can see how quickly or slowly the student is grasping that subject. An extensive diagnostic test, which is part of the program, tells the
teacher the child's true level and identifies strengths and weaknesses the
child may have, or where the holes in the child's education are at that particular point in time.

Core subjects for an entire grade level costs under $300. It is, however,
a Christian curriculum and though the religious content is woven spo-
radically through the text, this may be an issue for some parents. (While
only available for public and charter schools, a similar but secular program called Odyssey Ware is published by Pathway Publishers at 1-877-
795-8904; www.pathwaypublishers.com.)

One mother at Austin Harvard explained one of the values of a computer curriculum for bipolar children and how the school uses this program to accommodate her son's illness. She said:

He missed the first two weeks of school due to his illness. When he
came back, they simply rearranged his planner and let him get
started like he hadn't missed anything. That is another advantage of
the computer-based curriculum for these kids: It can be self-paced
and tailored to the needs of the child. The child is not allowed to
slack off, however. The teachers decide where the child is supposed

to be at in the curriculum and that is put into the child's daily planner. The child is expected to keep up with this plan, but it can be
modified according to need.

A Day at Austin Harvard

Austin Harvard has a dress code of sorts—one uniquely suited to children
with bipolar disorder and their sensory issues. Glad decided that since
these children are difficult to get up in the morning and often have difficulty deciding what to wear, she would keep things simple: There is a teal
Austin Harvard collared shirt. For those kids who cannot tolerate collars,
there is a teal Austin Harvard T-shirt. (The kids voted on the color.) They
can wear jeans, shorts, pants, or skirts with the shirts. Because Glad understands that some kids cannot stand "nubbies" on socks, socks are not
required except on days they have gym.

The day begins with a half hour "Devotion," which is a practical lesson about life. It typically is a story with a point about a good choice or
an inappropriate choice. This is an interactive discussion that goes on for
thirty minutes. "This time lets them wake up or calm down," Glad told
us. "At eight-thirty they go to class."

There are two classrooms: the five- to eleven-year-olds are in one classroom; and the twelve- to fifteen-year-olds are in the other. There are two
teachers, Glad, Richard, and the school's principal, Kim Belknap. Parents
come in to help also. When we questioned Glad about the age span of the
kids in the same room, she said: "Many of our children are somewhat immature and they feel comfortable with younger children. Also, the older
children feel competent and help out the younger ones. It fosters a sense
of community."

The children tape record all their lessons and answer questions about
the lessons on paper so they do learn writing skills. Each student is assigned a study partner and the two monitor each other. When they are at
their computers, the kids can only talk if they raise their hands.

If a student finishes all of the work, there is no homework (unless
they've blown off the school day). The only homework is studying for
quizzes and tests. One of the parents at the school wrote us and said: "If
our son applies himself during his workday, homework is basically test
prep. If he chooses to 'blow off' a day, he'll have to work at home. I do
think the school is sensitive to the issues which occur in the late afternoon
when stimulants wear off."

There is a Social Skills class taught two times a week by a licensed professional counselor where various subjects are discussed. When we asked Glad for an example, she answered: "We'll discuss lying. Why do people choose to lie? The children are always being taught that there are inclinations and choices; good choices and bad choices. We also spend a lot of time talking about anger. She expanded on this:

> When we're scared, we often get angry, but when we get angry, we give away our personal power to someone else. We go through a process which helps them identify what they're angry about and what they can do to win. How can they maintain control but still get their point across to the other person? We suggest ideas such as talking calmly or taking a time out for a few minutes and then reapproaching the situation and telling the person how he or she feels. I always tell them I want them to feel appropriate control of themselves in a situation. The children offer solutions to each other and thus they learn the tools themselves.

The kids have science lab, and art, gym at the nearby Y, and every Friday is a field trip relating to the work they're doing. For instance, the seventh-graders in Texas study the history of their state and they make trips to the Alamo, and to the frontier village of Gonzales to watch the reenactment of the Battle of Gonzales—that sort of thing.

Because so many of the children have comorbid learning disabilities, there are methods of remediation customized to each child. Glad explained:

> If the child is dyslexic and needs assistance we often take them through the Stevenson Language Program. We also use the clay techniques explained in the Davis "Gift of Dyslexia" program. Since our curriculum is computer based, this helps our dysgraphic students. We do scribing as needed. We use manipulatives and Semple Math. Writing or taping the math steps for a given concept and allowing the students to review them before they begin their lessons is a great help.

The school's philosophy is that each child has a learning style and the teachers want to help the student discover how he or she learns best. One child may discover that he or she can benefit from the use of a "white noise" machine to block out distractions, while another may learn that he or she actually absorbs verbal instructions best while doodling on paper. But once a child discovers the learning style that works best, he or she will be able to effectively use that knowledge to shape the way he or she approaches future educational pursuits. One mother wrote us: "We have discovered that our son is an auditory learner, but the best part was when he realized it himself last year."

Behavioral Issues

Austin Harvard uses a token system for good behavior and a consequence system for behavior that is not productive. If the student stays on task, has a good recess, participates in devotion, then he or she receive tokens. For every subject that is finished, the student gets ten points. They are each working toward one hundred points a day and if the student earns even fifty, he or she gets to buy something in the school store and gets free time or an extra art class. A chart is kept on the door each day.

If a child begins to feel anxious or overstimulated or begins to feel a rage gathering, he or she has several options. There is a lunchroom the child can go to; there is a punching bag he or she can use to work out some aggression in a safe, private place. Rarely does a child need to go home. "Unless a child needs hospitalization, we keep them in school. Missing school is not preparing them for the real world," said Glad.

If a child's behavior is not up to the standards set, he or she is typically given a consequence. This is more likely than not an assignment where the student has to write sentences over and over again. "They hate to write," Glad said with a laugh, "so they tend not to go there. Sometimes they're assigned push-ups, but they always learn that certain behaviors are acceptable and certain are not."

One mother, whose son is a student at Austin Harvard, wrote us:

> It's the social/emotional child that concerns me. We chose AHS for many reasons, but perhaps the most important would be the *constant* social skills, consistent approach to discipline, attention to "people skills" which will help prepare my fourteen-year-old for the real world. He has (in the past two and a half years) already developed many coping strategies and anger management techniques which give him control. He's being given every opportunity to become a happier, healthier teenager.

The philosophy at Austin Harvard is to work very closely with the parents and the children. The parents report troubles at home to the Curlees instead of hiding them, and—as a team—they attempt to work through the problems. One girl had a rage because she didn't like the sandwiches her mother was preparing for her lunch. They discussed it with Richard Curlee, who acted as a mediator and he got the student to agree to take responsibility and make her own lunch every day. "We don't want to be an RTC," said Richard Curlee, "because after a child returns home from one, the family hasn't developed skills to cope with the child and the illness. If we work with the family, supporting them and dealing with the many issues, it's a twenty-four-hour learning environment and families eventually get to be families."

The medical aspects of the child's illness are well attended to also. As the principal of the school, Kimberly Belknap, explained:

Before each visit to the psychiatrist, we generate a report covering anything that needs to be addressed. Our parents have come to rely on and appreciate the importance of our input. When the doctor is unwilling to receive the input from us, the parents use the report information and act as a go-between. . . . Our reports help the doctors and therapists who are treating the children get a good picture of the child's functioning at school, and help the doctor assess whether the child is stable or not. He or she can then make changes in medication regimens to increase stability or ward off possible breakthrough episodes.

Tuition and Other Practicalities

The tuition at the Austin Harvard School is $5,500 a year. For some of us who just learned that New York City nursery programs cost $15,000 a year, this doesn't seem like a lot of money. Richard Curlee did tell us that each parent is expected to fund-raise $11,000 or pay the difference. They have different kinds of fund-raisers throughout the year and all the parents help out.

The parents must spend eight hours a semester helping out in the classroom, and there is a mandatory meeting one evening a month.

The school is a storefront building set up with a waiting room, two classrooms, a lunchroom that can double as an art room, three offices, and a bathroom. The actual square footage is 2,300 square feet.

Because the school is young yet, and because the school requires that children with bipolar disorder be medicated, it is not accredited (with the exception of the ninth grade). When we asked how students do after Austin Harvard, Glad told us that one of their students just went on to high school in a public school and is doing very well. The school is only four years old, so each year will see more children making the transition and we'll report outcomes at another time.

How Do Students Feel About Austin Harvard?

One mother answered the question "Is your child happy attending Austin Harvard?" with this statement: "He started last year right after the spring break and really struggled with the discipline, but during the summer all he did was talk about going to school again."

A fifteen-year-old student gave us a written account entitled "Why I Want to Go to the Austin Harvard School." In it he explained:

I think they can help me with my frustrations with studying. The teachers also teach you discipline and cooperation with students, they also teach you how to express yourself without hurting anyone. Mr. Curlee, the dean of the school, is very funny but very strict. I like him and respect him very much. I also respect the teachers and the principal, Mrs. Belknap, and the founder of the school Mrs. Curlee.

The nice thing about the school is the teachers teach with computers and audio and visual tools. Instead of writing things down all the time, you get to use a computer and tape recorder.

I expect to learn all kinds of skills at this school—like computer skills, expressing my feelings, learning respect, learning how to help others, learning how to cooperate, learning how to communicate feelings so they can be solved, etc. If I can do these things, I can do anything I want to. I'll just remember the two rules Mr. Curlee explained to me: "I love you and there's nothing you can do about that."

We want to applaud Glad and Richard Curlee for pioneering a way to teach children with bipolar disorder and for having the vision and the dedication to make a difference in the lives of these children and their entire families. It is hard to believe that they accomplish all this with an annual budget of $200,000.

We asked the Curlees if they might consider conducting workshops and showing other motivated parents how they've done all this and they said they would welcome inquiries. Contact Richard Curlee at the website of the school: http://www.austinharvardschool.org.

For more information about the computer program, Switched-On Schoolhouse, visit www.aop.com or call 602-438-2717.

EDUCATION OF THE PARENTS

It will seem obvious—from all of the above—that a parent will have to immerse him- or herself in basic educational law, public education, the educational needs of a child with bipolar disorder, and various programs that may be effective for their child. Just as finding the right doctor, getting the right diagnosis, and getting the child properly medicated are the first steps, the educational piece of the child's life is also critical.

As we close this chapter, we'd like to point out some resources that will make the entire journey through the educational maze a far easier one. For information on state regulations, IDEA, and IEPs, contact the state Department of Education, or log on to the following websites:

Ld online (http://ldonline.org)
Wrights Law (http://www.wrightslaw.com)

For information about therapeutic schools or summer character-building programs, contact:
The National Association of Private Schools for Exceptional Children (NAPSEC)
1522 K Street, NW, Suite 1032
Washington, DC 20005
Phone: 202-408-3338; fax: 202-408-3340; email: napsec@aol.com

Peterson's Private Secondary Schools
(http://www.petersons.com/private/select/pssns.html)

Woodbury Reports Online (http://www.woodbury.com)
www.spectrumcenter.org

Family Light
http://bridgetounderstanding.com

The Neuropsychological Testing of a Bipolar Child

On the front lines of a war, medical personnel learn to triage and deal with the most dire cases first. Parents of a bipolar child also triage naturally and spend all of their energy trying to cope with the child's out-of-control behavior, the other siblings in the home, and the public at large. They run themselves ragged looking for a doctor who can give a name to the problem and who can begin treatment so that the rages cease, the mood is stabilized, and the child and the home life become more peaceful and predictable.

Until that time arrives, however, parents are going to start each day filled with anxiety as they attempt to get the child up and out to school, and try to divine the mood of the child and whether or not he or she can sustain the school day without incident. The behaviors of everyday life, the simple things that other families take for granted, are such all-consuming tasks that rarely on the front burner is the question "I wonder what my child's academic strengths and weaknesses are and how I can get a comprehensive evaluation of them?"

But evidence is emerging that learning disabilities, attentional problems, and deficits in the area known as "executive functions" are a significant associated feature of early-onset bipolar disorder. When we revisited our original study for this book and homed in on the question "Does your child have a learning disability?" One hundred sixteen parents answered that question, 60 of them (52 percent) indicated that their child had an identifiable learning disability. (Few of these children had had comprehensive neuropsychological evaluations that examine the area of executive functions that we will talk so much about in the pages that follow.)

Any deficits that impede the acquisition of knowledge and impact a child's performance in school compound the effects of a mood disorder and erode an already compromised sense of self-esteem. These learning difficulties tax, frustrate, and irritate the child, and it becomes difficult to know which behaviors are a result of irritability caused by shifting moods, and which behaviors are a response and rally to the narcissistic injury caused by the child's feelings of inadequacy as he or she is steadily challenged by greater academic expectations with each advancing school year.

In other words, an underlying neuropsychological deficit or an unrecognized learning disability could independently produce low self-esteem, irritability, and angry outbursts relating not so much to the mood disorder, but to the child's inability to perform academic tasks. In fact, these learning disabilities can continue to exert significant influence long after the mood has been stabilized. That is why we so strongly recommend a complete neuropsychological battery for every child diagnosed with bipolar disorder.

WHAT EXACTLY ARE LEARNING DISABILITIES?

A learning disability is assumed to be present when a child with a normal or high IQ is two years or more behind his or her classmates. Another definition of learning disabilities can be gleaned in public law books. U.S. Public Law 94–142 of the federal register, Section 121A, Volume 5 of 1977, states that learning-disabled individuals are:

> Those who have a disorder in one or more of the basic psychological processes involved in understanding or in using language, spoken or written, which disorder may manifest itself in imperfect ability to listen, think, speak, read, write, spell, or do mathematical calculations.

These are broad and rather noninclusive definitions of learning disabilities which address mostly verbal disabilities and fail to take into account the nonlanguage domains and areas of executive functions. A specific learning disability is a breakdown in one particular task area, whereas executive function deficits cut across many domains and impact all arenas of life—both academic and nonacademic.

Therefore, children with bipolar disorder should be tested with a comprehensive battery of intelligence, academic, neuropsychological, and psychological tests. These tests identify areas of strengths and weaknesses and not only do much to explain the problems to the parents and the teachers—and to the child—but their findings direct remediation efforts. Parents and the school system need this critical evaluation when developing an Individual Education Plan—the IEP which we discussed in the preceding chapter.

Treatment can then focus on a three-pronged approach: stabilizing the mood with medications; addressing the cognitive, organizational, and sensory problems through tutoring, remediation, or occupational therapy; and instituting a psychotherapy to help the child realistically assess his or her talents and areas of vulnerability, and to help the child come to terms with the distressing and disturbing feelings that both the illness and a learning disability may engender.

A neuropsychological evaluation also gives parents and the professionals a baseline so that they can retest periodically and see if medication, remediation, and therapy are having the desired effects.

Who Should Test and How Do You Find This Person?

Children should be tested by a child neuropsychologist. This is a professional who has specific training and supervised experience in the assessment and treatment of patients with brain disorders, and disorders of the central nervous system. Typically, a neuropsychologist has a doctorate in psychology and two years of postdoctoral training within a neurological or neurosurgical setting (one year in a general setting; one in a children's unit). A neuropsychologist is licensed by the state.

The child's psychiatrist should be familiar with good neuropsychologists; the pediatrician can often be of help, or a pediatric neurologist will undoubtably know the best neuropsychologists in the area.

How Much Does Testing Cost?

A comprehensive battery of tests can easily require eight hours of direct consultation, as well as additional hours for reviewing records, data analysis, and the preparation of a written report, and will cost in the range of $2,400 to $3,000. Some insurance companies may reimburse a certain amount of testing fees, but many do not. It's a good idea to call your insurer and see if they do cover it, and whether a precertification is required.

The Battery of Tests

We spoke with Dr. Steven Mattis, clinical professor of neurology at Weil-Cornell University Medical Center in New York City, who has been focusing much of his research attention on the neuropsychological profiles of children with bipolar disorder and is one of the nation's authorities in this area. We asked him to give us a list of a standard battery of tests that might be given to every child with bipolar disorder. While there are over a thousand instruments of assessment utilized, and each neuropsychologist will use those based on his or her training and clinical experience, Dr. Mattis listed the ones he frequently relies upon as the screening battery (naturally, as problems are uncovered, other instruments will be recruited to examine the hypothesized deficit more closely).

We will list the complete battery as a total, and then describe certain measures in detail. A full discussion of each test and each learning disability would require a book of its own, but we will focus on several tests as they seem to reveal something significant about the cognitive and motor difficulties often seen in children with bipolar disorder.

TESTS OF INTELLIGENCE

"First you need a good test of general intellectual ability," says Dr. Mattis. "The Wechsler Intelligence Scales for Children (WISC-III) is the most commonly used and it is the jumping-off point of neuropsychology."

The intelligence test *samples* many of the cognitive skills that are needed to learn in school, thus it is considered a predictor of academic capabilities.

The WISC-III is made up of thirteen subtests: six have a higher verbal loading and are scored as the Verbal IQ; seven are less dependent on language and can be viewed as an indication of the child's nonverbal reasoning, spatial processing skills, attentiveness to details, and visual-motor integration. These seven subtests are scored as the Performance IQ. Thus, three scores are computed: the verbal IQ, the Performance IQ, and the full-scale IQ.

Since many parents receive these WISC-III scores and don't fully understand what the subtests mean, we want to explain what each subtest sets out to measure:

Verbal Subtests
Information: Measures the child's fund of general knowledge and reflects his or her alertness to the everyday world.
Similarities: Measures logical and abstract thinking ability necessary in recognizing essential relationships between objects or ideas.
Arithmetic: Measures arithmetic reasoning and facility with numbers using mental math.
Vocabulary: Measures verbal expression and knowledge of spoken words.
Comprehension: Measures social judgment, practical knowledge, and common-sense reasoning.
Digit Span: The child repeats digits that the examiner reads, forward and backward. Measures concentration and immediate auditory rote-sequential memory, as well as spontaneous organizational ability.

Performance Subtests
Picture Completion: The child looks at pictures with missing details and tells the examiner what parts are missing. Measures visual alertness and detail discrimination.
Coding: Measures visual-motor coordination and short-term visual memory.
Picture Arrangement: This requires a child to put pictures in order so that the story they tell makes sense. Measures visual comprehension, sequential organization in social situations, and planning ability.
Block Design: This test measures the child's ability to look at the whole pattern, then break it into parts, and finally to reconstruct the whole using blocks. Measures visual perception, motor coordination, and manipulative skill.
Object Assembly: The child is given puzzle parts and must complete the puzzle. It measures a child's ability to make a whole out of its parts.
Symbol Search: Measures visual alertness and motor speed under the pressure of a time limit.
Mazes: The child has to find the way out of a maze by using a pencil. Performance is also based on time. Measures graphomotor planning, visual-motor coordination and speed; fine motor coordination and following directions.

As Drs. Steven Mattis and Demitri Papolos began to examine a pilot group of forty diagnosed bipolar children, they noted certain patterns in the WISC-III scoring. The first observation was that unless there was a concomitant language disorder, these children (about 85 percent of them) typically had higher verbal than nonverbal scores.

Drs. Nancy Austin, Demitri Papolos, and Gianni Faedda reported on this IQ testing pattern of bipolar children in a poster presented at the Fourth International Conference on Bipolar Disorder in Pittsburgh, Pennsylvania, in 2001. They compared the WISC-III scores of a group of children diagnosed with bipolar disorder (ages six to twelve) to a matched standardized sample, a learning disabled sample, and an attention-deficit disorder with hyperactivity sample. The children with early-onset bipolar disorder had significantly higher full scale IQ scores and significantly higher verbal IQ scores than the other groups of children.

A Closer Look at Testing Results

One boy's testing on the WISC-III looked like this:

Verbal Tests	Scaled Scores	Performance Tests	Scaled Scores
Information	16	Picture Completion	10
Similarities	17	Coding	13
Arithmetic	15	Picture Arrangement	13
Vocabulary	16	Block Design	10
Comprehension	19	Object Assembly	8
Digit Span	9	Symbol Search	17
		Mazes	13

Scores of 9 to 11 are average; 12 to 13 are high average; 14 to 15 are superior; 16 to 17 are very superior; 18 to 19 are exceptional.

On any individual subtest of WISC-III, the standard score can extend from a minimum of 1 to a maximum of 19. Note the disparity in scores on the test results above. This is referred to as "scatter." This is commonly seen in children with bipolar disorder, but it is seen with ADHD children and others as well. If the central nervous system is intact and motivation is uniform, generally the subtests should be within a 3- to 5-point spread.

In other words, there should be some consistency or similarity. If, as is so often seen with children with bipolar disorder, ADHD, and other disorders, there is significant intertest variability, the tester has to begin asking why.

In the above-mentioned pilot study of forty children diagnosed with early-onset bipolar disorder, Drs. Mattis and Papolos have observed that the majority have low scores on the object assembly and block design in the Performance IQ subtests. Naturally, this must be tested against a group of ADHD children and a control group to see if this pattern differs in a comparison group of age- and sex-matched children. (However, the presence of this pattern doesn't diagnose bipolar disorder, and its absence doesn't rule it out. It is merely an observation that must be tested.)

What Does the IQ Really Mean?

Intelligence test scores are plotted against a normal bell curve. The WISC-III has a mean IQ score of 100 and a standard deviation of 15, so, statistically, 68 percent of people will obtain scores that fall between 85 and 115.

Below are the scores and general population statistics:

130+	Very Superior	About 2 percent of the population
120–129	Superior	About 7 percent of the population
110–119	High Average	About 16 percent of the population
90–109	Average	About 50 percent of the population
80–89	Low Average	About 16 percent of the population
70–79	Borderline	About 7 percent of the population
Below 69	Intellectually Deficient	About 2 percent of the population

Other tests of general intellectual ability may be administered, depending on the age of the child and the tester's preference: the Stanford-Binet, Raven Progressive Matrices, etc. Children older than sixteen are often given the Wechsler Adult Intelligence Scale (WAIS-III). Children between the ages of four and a half and six are often given the Wechsler Preschool and Primary Scale of Intelligence (WPPSI-R).

What Does It Mean If My Child's IQ Drops?

Parents often write to us with great alarm when more recent testing shows a drop in the IQ of their children. They want to know if brain damage is a possibility. Dr. Mattis said that it is extremely rare for a child to actually lose brain cells although a large decrement in scores must be taken seriously. There may be several reasons for this decrease in scores and parents should not panic.

The scores may be lower simply because the child's ability to pay attention may differ with each testing period or the time of day in which he or she is tested, or there may be a difference in testers and their interpretation of the child's responses.

Then again, children dealing with a mood disorder, medication trials, attentional problems, and perhaps multiple learning disabilities may fail to keep pace with their age group and may begin to fall behind in their general fund of knowledge or their capacity to learn new information. They may test less well as their cohort goes on to attain information, unburdened by the above-mentioned factors.

However, Dr. Mattis shared an interesting insight into the bipolar children he has been testing. For every subtest, a child must fail several consecutive items before the subtest is terminated. The examiner then moves on to the next task.

In his entire career, Dr. Mattis has seen only one group of children intentionally give incorrect answers to move the tester along: the children who come to him diagnosed with bipolar disorder. Whether this is a form of control, oppositional behavior, inability to deal with failure so they control the failure, or something we can't yet identify is a question that remains to be answered. It's just a fascinating observation that bears further scrutiny. But this attitude and behavior would also contribute to what is seen as a decrement in the testing scores.

A Suggested Battery of Tests

After the testing of intellectual ability, Dr. Mattis recommends a test of sustained attention. Sustained attention is different from the ability to mobilize attentional processes for brief episodic periods. The Connors Continuous Performance Test and the Tests of Variable Attention (the TOVA) examine attention over a much longer period—fourteen to twenty-two and a half minutes—and one or the other is frequently administered.

Both of these measures of sustained attention are computerized tests that are able to measure discrete aspects of attentional functioning.

Below are other tests that should be included in the battery:

Tests of Academic Achievement

The Woodcock-Johnson Psychoeducational Battery—Revised is a norm-referenced test for ages three to eighty. This battery provides extensive testing of reading, decoding, comprehension, and mathematical calculation and the ability to understand math concepts and apply them. It yields samples of dictation and writing. It measures the child's understanding of content in science, social studies, and the humanities.

The Wide Range Achievement Test-3 (WRAT-3) is a norm-referenced test for use with children five and up. It tests decoding, spelling, and arithmetic.

Two other tests that may be utilized are the Gates-MacGinnite Reading Test and the Gray Oral.

Tests of Language

An evaluation of expressive and receptive language function should also be conducted. Dr. Mattis often includes the Spreen-Benton Token Test as a measure of receptive language; the Boston Naming and the Picture Vocabulary (Peabody) as tests of naming ability and sentence repetition ability. He assesses Buccal-Lingual Praxis when he has a child repeat different phonemes or multisyllabic words.

Tests of Executive Function

In the evaluation of bipolar children, Dr. Mattis places a heavy emphasis on tests of executive and motor function and many of these tests will be described in detail later in this chapter.

Motor Tests of Sequenced Movement

Luria Test of Praxis
Fine Motor Coordination
Purdue Pegboard or the Grooved Pegboard
Hallstead-Reitan Finger Tapping Test

Projectives

Three Wishes
Rorschach Inkblot Test
Thematic Aperception Tests (TAT)

What Are Executive Functions and Why Is Everyone Talking About Them?

As we delve into this huge and complicated subject, let's recall that the frontal lobes of the brain (including the prefrontal cortex, which is a layer of tissue that lies just behind the forehead) are the most forward part of the brain, in front of the motor areas.

The frontal lobes coordinate speech, reasoning, problem solving, strategizing, working memory, attention, self-control, motor sequencing, and other processes central to higher functioning. As Dr. Elkhanon Goldberg writes in his elegant book *The Executive Brain: Frontal Lobes and the Civilized Mind*:

> The frontal lobes perform the most advanced and complex functions in all the brain, the so-called executive functions. They are linked to intentionality, purposefulness, and complex decision making. . . . The frontal lobes are to the brain what a conductor is to an orchestra, a general to an army, the chief executive officer to a corporation. They coordinate and lead other neural structures. Frontal lobes are critical for every successful learning process, for motivation, and attention. . . . True to its "executive" functions, the prefrontal cortex is probably the best-connected part of the brain. The prefrontal cortex is directly interconnected with every distinct functional unit of the brain. It is connected with the posterior association cortex, the highest station of perceptual integration, and also with the premotor cortex, basal ganglia, and the cerebellum, all involved with various aspects of motor control and movements. . . . (It is connected to) the hippocampus and related structures, known to be critical for memory; and with the cingulate cortex, presumed to be critical for emotion and dealing with uncertainty. In addition, this command post connects with the amygdala . . . and the hypothalamus. Last but far from least, it is connected with the brain stem nuclei in charge of activation and arousal.

He concludes with this powerful statement:

> Of all the structures in the brain, only the prefrontal cortex is embedded in such a richly networked pattern of neural pathways. This unique connectivity makes the frontal lobes singularly suited for co-

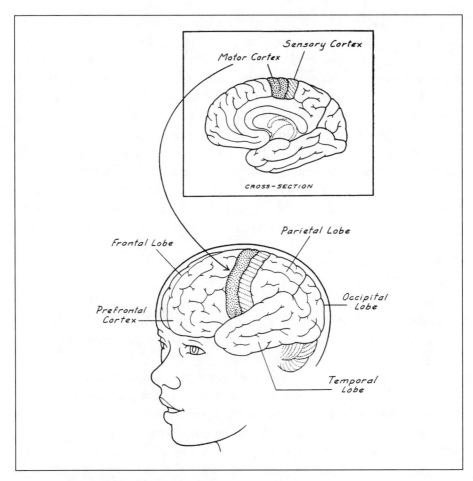

Figure 11.1 The left Hemisphere. Showing the Cortical Lobes, Sensory Cortex, and Motor Cortex

ordinating and integrating the work of all the other brain structures—the conductor of the orchestra. . . . *This extreme connectivity also puts the frontal lobes at particular risk for disease* (italics ours).

Research has shown that children with attention-deficit disorder with hyperactivity, as well as children with Tourette's syndrome, have deficits in the areas of the frontal lobes. It is now suspected that most children with bipolar disorder have problems in the frontal systems, and when the prefrontal lobes don't work correctly, there is a major impact on the ability to pay attention, to devise plans, and to alter them if needed.

The child with this impairment is more prone to reckless and impulsive actions. He or she will seem distractible and disorganized and will often skip from subject to subject, fail to develop a fount of knowledge, and often display a motoric restlessness. This problem or problems in the domain of executive functioning, governed by the frontal lobes, may be why there is such comorbidity between ADHD and bipolar disorder, and Tourette's syndrome and oppositional defiant disorder.

Actually, brain imaging has shown that the frontal lobes may be divided into seventeen or more subregions, each responsible for a slightly different kind of work that the human performs, so a problem anywhere in this area will impact the way a child approaches and performs any task.

Let's delve a little deeper. Whenever a human being approaches a problem or a project, he or she must recruit the following executive functions:

Analyze the problem
Plan and implement the strategy
Anticipate problems
Organize the way the strategy will be accomplished (break it down
    into its components and effectively assign a time segment for each
    substrategy to be accomplished)
Monitor the progress and assess whether the plan is working
Remain flexible and reformulate the plan of attack if the monitoring
    and assessment process shows it not to be working
Reassess the new strategy that has been implemented
Follow the adjusted plan through to the finish

Executive processes have been described as a group of diverse integrative, organizational, and supervisory functions that primarily involve the control and regulation of attention, cognition, and behavior according to the demands of a certain situation and a person's needs, plans, and goals. As one can see, strategizing, organizing, marshaling intention into movement, flexibility (changing set when it is recognized that the original strategy isn't working), and constant monitoring are crucial to the completion of any task. The "executive" must relinquish a strategy that is not working and employ cognitive and motor skills to move onto something else.

Children with bipolar disorder often can't organize and break down the problem and assign time factors to each subunit, they are inflexible when they need to move off track and try something new. They will continue to attempt the same strategy when it is apparent to others that it is not working (they will "perseverate"), they might not be able to put a plan into action or sequence it (exhibiting problems with intentionality or motor sequencing difficulties), and they won't be able to attend and follow through.

Working Memory

Also guided by the frontal lobes, and a significant part of the executive functioning of the prefrontal cortex, is working memory. We are constantly selecting bits of information stored in memory and bringing them to bear on any task we choose to perform and carry out. Short-term memory is remembering a phone number for a few seconds; working memory involves the ability to hold data in short-term memory while manipulating it toward problem solving or sequencing it in a logical order.

Studies conducted using functional magnetic resonance (fMRI) have examined working memory and found that if subjects were shown faces or consonants, they would process them in visual processing areas in a rear part of the brain initially, but as pauses were built into the test and the memory load grew heavier, activity increased in the front area of the brain. A key part of the prefrontal cortex and certain other brain areas stayed active, impressing researchers that these areas were involved in the active maintenance of information in working memory.

Bipolar children also seem to have problems with working memory. This is not surprising since they seem to have some problem in the prefrontal cortex of the brain.

An Explanation of Some of the Tests of Executive Function

Let us list some of the major tests of executive function:

The Wisconsin Card Sort
Tower of London
Tower of Hanoi
Trails A & B
Stroop Color and Word Test.

The Wisconsin Card Sort is a measure of abstract conceptual skills, cognitive flexibility, and the ability to test hypotheses and utilize error feedback. It also measures the ability to relinquish a hypothesis when it is no longer applicable. This test can be done manually with cards, or on a computer.

The child is given a set of stimulus cards that differ according to several different principles. Four of the cards are laid down as target cards and the child must generate a plan to sort or match each card to one of the targets. The examiner will inform the child if his or her response was right or wrong. The child then continues sorting according to the "correct" criterion.

At some point, the criterion shifts and the child must adjust to the new principle and change strategies. This continues over a number of trials.

Patients with lesions of the lateral portion of the prefrontal lobes often perseverate on the first sorting criteria, tend to finish significantly fewer categories, and make more total errors than controls or individuals with other types of brain lesions. Bipolar children tend to get stuck in the use of the previously correct principle as well—they perseverate. They find it hard to "change set" and smoothly assume the new strategy and then change set again as they respond to the feedback that was deemed correct previously but is currently not working. These difficulties and their inflexibility are often revealed by the Wisconsin Card Sort.

The Tower of London requires the child to move colored beads onto pegs with the least number of moves so that they achieve an arrangement (a model) that is in their view.

The Tower of Hanoi uses three pegs also, and the goal is to move all the discs from the left to the right one, moving only one disc at a time and never allowing a larger ring to rest on a smaller one. The number of moves and the time it takes is scored by the tester.

Trails A and B are tests that are timed paper-and-pencil tests. They have a motor component and examine sequencing and set changing abilities. Again, children with deficits in the frontal lobes—such as bipolar children and children with ADHD—may perform poorly on these tests.

Stroop Color and Word Test has various formats, but it is basically a sensitive measure of perceptual interference. Names of colors are written on a sheet in inks that don't match the verbal spelling "blue" or "green," etc. The child is asked to override the visual signal and interpret the literal symbol (the word). In other words, one has to inhibit the response to name the color in order to read the word.

The Stroop tests the ease with which the child can shift his or her perceptual set and conform to changing demands. Children who are impulsive have trouble doing this, as do children who have executive function difficulties.

This test is actually given to older children whose reading skills are fluent and intact (a dyslexic child will happily ignore the words and focus on color only, thus negating the gauge of the test).

EXECUTIVE MOTOR SKILLS

Almost all tasks—by definition—involve not only analysis, planning, monitoring, and adjustment of strategy, but images and ideas must be translated into sequenced motor acts. This activity most likely involves the prefrontal cortex and the motor cortex—the strip that begins the frontal lobes. *Praxis* is a Greek word meaning "doing, action, practice." It is the ability to interact successfully with the physical environment and to plan, organize, and carry out a sequence of unfamiliar actions. When a child persists in a motor activity or has an inflexibility or difficulty in initiating an activity, he or she is said to have a dyspraxia.

The Luria Test of Praxis asks a child to imitate a one-handed task requiring three sequenced hand positions while saying the verbal commands aloud. An inability to perform a sequenced motor act while stating the commands reflects a disassociation within the individual between his own thoughts and actions that is distinctly characteristic of a marked defect in executive processes. Dr. Mattis has observed that most bipolar children will have difficulty performing the Luria Test of Praxis smoothly and without perseveration.

THE PROJECTIVE TESTS

Almost everyone is familiar with the Rorschach Inkblot Tests. Children look at the images and describe what they see. In some ways they are mirrors of the mind.

Other projective tests such as the Thematic Aperception Test—the TAT—shows a child a scenario and asks him or her to make up a story around the picture. What the child produces is often an expression of the child's private world of thoughts, fears, and wishes.

Dr. Mattis also noted differences in the bipolar children's answers or thoughts in the projective tests. "I tend to hear more about blood and guts and people being ripped apart and death; or the children are so affected by unsettling imagery that they report that they see 'nothing,' " he said. (This gory imagery would fit with the night terrors these children suffer and sometimes remember; see our discussion in Chapter 7.)

HELPING THE CHILD WITH SPECIFIC LEARNING DISABILITIES

Children with specific learning disabilities, such as dyslexia or written expression problems, need remediation provided by a teacher or tutor trained in special education techniques. The school may have someone on staff who is highly competent, but this may be the only learning specialist covering four hundred children. If the remediation is handled by the school, we strongly suggest that an independent tester monitor the progress each year. The school will do a triennial review if the child is classified and has an IEP, but three years is too long to wait to find out that the child is not making appropriate progress. Some parents will want to deal with private tutors after school. Again, we suggest independent testing on an annual basis (not an entire neuropsychological evaluation, just tests that probe the disability the child has).

HELPING THE CHILD WITH EXECUTIVE FUNCTION DEFICITS

While methods of remediating dyslexia are well established, helping the child with deficits in the areas of executive functioning is not so prescribed. "This is the child who may need help in many areas of daily living," says New York City neuropsychologist Dana Luck. Children with executive function difficulties are highly dependent on adults to help them structure and organize their environment.

Dr. Luck told us that most often it is the parents who have to provide a highly structured home environment to help the child accomplish certain routines successfully. Each routine—each "package of behavior"— must be broken down and rehearsed independently before a complete set of responsibilities can be fulfilled.

For instance, to complete the morning routine, certain grooming, dressing, and organizational tasks must be addressed. All clothing should be simply organized, all books, music, and sports equipment should be in one place and always in that place. If the child dallies in the bathroom with too many choices of toothpaste and mouthwash, there should be nothing there but the toothbrush and one tube of toothpaste. In other words, streamline all possible distractions.

The child should be given prompts: "In order to go out to the school bus I need . . . my book bag, my coat, my recorder . . ." The prompt before the child leaves school is: "What do I need to do tonight and what do I need in my book bag in order to do it?" At school, a teacher or aide should help the child follow a set of steps to accomplish the prompt.

How Does the Child with Executive Function Difficulties Fare at School?

Not well. These children might always seem disorganized. Homework, notes, workbooks, and planners might make it home some nights and not others; homework that is completed may never make it back to the teacher.

If this student has a major project assigned for three weeks hence, he or she may have trouble remembering to bring everything home in order to plan the project and have difficulty getting organized in one place. Then, he or she can find it difficult to settle on a topic.

These are the children who sometimes can't "see the forest for the trees." If they do choose a topic, they might not be able to break it down, outline the way it will be explored in the paper, and discuss the subunits in an organized, sequenced fashion. (If there are written expression difficulties or graphomotor problems, the task becomes all the more daunting.)

These children also have difficulty with timing and pacing. They underestimate how long each section will take to accomplish, they have trouble "getting going," and they tend to procrastinate and leave everything until the last minute. Parents and teachers may grow exasperated and the child may be viewed as lazy, "not trying hard enough," or stubborn and oppositional.

Actually, because of the problems with executive functioning (and any other learning disabilities they may have) they can't seem to find their way into what often seems a gigantic and undoable task. This has a serious impact on the child's feelings of self-worth. Their self-confidence and self-esteem plummets, and most academic tasks become so unpleasant, engender so much anxiety that they begin to refuse to even try, or give up quickly if they can be coaxed to give it a try. Naturally, this anxiety impacts their level of attention, exacerbates any learning disabilities, and seriously impacts the mood of the child (the very thing the doctors and parents are working so assiduously to keep stable and in the positive range).

When a child finds things so effortful, it takes a toll on him or her. He or she may become irritable, fatigued, hyperactive, and begin to avoid situations that require extended effort or feign disinterest in them. The child may simply "quit the playing field." As Dr. Luck says: "Even for a child who doesn't have a specific learning disability, problems in executive function can significantly impact his or her academic performance and progress and achievement, particularly as the task demands require greater independent functioning."

Dr. Luck also told us:

> In lower grades, the academic work is often organized and separated for the child—for instance, a work sheet will be all addition or all subtraction. Later on, when academic work is more integrated, the child must be monitoring, asking "Which problem is this and what am I supposed to do?" When the child gets to higher level reading where paraphrasing is required and inferential and deductive thinking comes into play, children with executive function difficulties are going to experience more problems. Here these children have difficulty sorting out details or they may get stuck in a detail, and since they often can't prioritize the level of importance of details, they often begin underlining everything in a textbook or fail to get started doing anything. . . . Homework is almost always a hot spot. The child should have a place to work that has pencils and other supplies always available. Then the child must learn that it's normal to spend ten minutes setting everything up to begin the homework. It may help if the parent sets an external timer so that the child becomes aware of pacing and moving along. The tone of the time spent working should be kept "cool." Anger and frustration should be minimized both by the child and the parent.

Dr. Luck suggested some highly useful techniques to help these children. She said that because these children can't separate out main themes from supporting detail, they should be taught to utilize the cues in a textbook such as pictures, captions, and headings.

It is perfectly acceptable to look at the questions at the end of the chapter first so that they are primed as to what is considered important and they can read looking intently for that information and give less weight to some of the other information. They shouldn't underline until they've looked at those discussion questions and all the pictures, captions, and headings. These children need to think macro rather than micro.

If all the work can't be finished (and most nights it won't be), this should be added into the IEP (see Chapter 10). There should be constant communication with the school. The parent should understand how difficult this is for the child and the child should be encouraged and rewarded.

Dr. Luck said that the children need to learn to advocate for themselves. They need to understand how to ask for help, and to accept some responsibility. They should learn how to go to the resource room for help. If they do something with a partner, they shouldn't work with a best friend, but with someone who needs their strengths and has strengths they don't have. If a child recognizes that he or she is lively and dynamic and presents well, he or she should pick a partner who organizes and researches well. Choosing people who complement your strengths and compensate your weaknesses is smart choosing and is something they should continue to do throughout life in work and social situations.

"Always the children should compartmentalize their difficulties," concludes Dr. Luck. "Just because they have difficulty in one area doesn't mean they're not truly strong in another."

In fact, these children often have gifts and see things in novel ways that result in very creative thinking and performance. They are often referred to as "out of the box thinkers." Children with learning disabilities often are keen observers and they notice things others don't. Children with high energy and a motoric restlessness may grow up and be able to work long hours with an intense focus. Many children with dyslexia have strong visual abilities, and many have an enhanced sense of vertical balance and may excel at sports such as riding, skiing, or diving. Parents and teachers need to see the unique talents these children have and build upon them.

If parents can get their children evaluated well before they reach the higher grades in school, and help relieve the potentially snowballing pressures as a result of these sometimes hidden disabilities and deficits, then they won't be blindsided as adolescence enters the picture. They won't think that every problem has a root cause in hormonal cascades or the condition of adolescence itself. Nor will everything be laid at the door of the mood disorder. The parents will have explored and dealt with one of the problems certain to impact profoundly on the child's sense of mastery and self-esteem. Hopefully the child then reaches this critical passageway in life with the academic playing field a bit more level—paved by understanding and remediation.

The tasks of adolescence—complicated by a mood disorder—are challenge enough for any teenager.

Navigating the Shoals of Adolescence

Parents look forward to the teenage years with all the enthusiasm they reserve for an extended stay in Dracula's castle with the crucifixes confiscated from their suitcases. In fact (and just to continue the horror-story metaphor), most parents seem to equate an emerging adolescent with the Frankenstein monster—docile one day, then suddenly zapped with a bolt of electricity (the hormones), and rising quickly to pillage the countryside.

But for parents of bipolar children, such nightmarish forebodings are even worse. Hormonal surges can trigger cycling (or more severe cycling). These adolescents can be impulsive, hypersexual, and indulge in extremely risky behaviors. Grave dangers abound: unwanted pregnancy, sexually transmitted and life-threatening disease, recklessness behind the wheel of a car, and substance abuse. Their outrageous, provocative, and oppositional stunts can land them in the juvenile justice system, and their poor judgment can cause dire consequences out in the world.

Every parent we spoke to voiced terrible fears about such possibilities. All asked: "What will happen to our children in adolescence and the aftermath?" All assume that because the illness began so early and appears so pernicious, the course will go from bad to worse.

But according to investigators who have followed bipolar teenagers over a period of years, these forebodings do not necessarily become fact. To the contrary, there is reason for parents to feel hope.

Dr. Thomas McGlashan followed thirty-five adolescent-onset bipolar patients for fifteen years, and he found that although the adolescent-onset patients displayed more delusions and hallucinations and were more explosive and disorganized than the adult-onset patients, the adolescent patients went on to have an equal or superior outcome to those with the adult-onset form of the disorder.

Dr. McGlashan's study, published in the *American Journal of Psychiatry* in 1988, examined the lives of a group of people in their mid-forties who became symptomatic in the teenage years and compared their outcomes to a group of people in their fifties who became symptomatic as adults. He failed to find significant differences in their marital status, parental status, living situations, length and number of hospitalizations, and amount and severity of symptoms. But where differences did exist—for example, in the frequency of social contacts and amount of work time in the previous year—the adolescent-onset patients were "consistently superior."

Dr. McGlashan himself was surprised by the findings and offered two hypotheses:

First, adolescent-onset mania may be a milder variant that, however, looks more severe because it emerges during a developmentally vulnerable period when defenses are in flux and coping strategies are poorly developed. With the passing of adolescence, however, the disorder becomes less penetrating in its virulence. Second, adolescent-onset mania may not be a milder variant but may emerge at a time when personality structure is flexible enough that the individual can develop ways of coping more effectively with the illness.

Dr. McGlashan speculated that adults who develop the illness may be more set and rigid, temperamentally less flexible and able to adapt to the vagaries of the illness.

More recently Dr. Michael Strober, director of the Adolescent Mood Disorders Clinic at the University of California, Los Angeles, and a leading researcher who has followed bipolar teenagers from the age of thirteen into their late twenties and early thirties, had even more promising data to offer parents. During a phone interview, he said: "There is no basis for assuming automatically that just because the illness is more familial and presents earlier these young people are going to have a chronic relapsing course. In fact, our data suggest a less malignant course than what is reported in the adult literature."

We asked him what he has seen happen to his study group as the youngsters move through adolescence. He replied, "The course is quite variable and difficult to predict. Some kids emerge into a more sort of classically identifiable cycling affective illness. Others continue to have a persistence of extreme, irritable, explosive, and emotionally labile behavior. On the other hand, I have seen kids who have actually quieted down."

Compared to clinicians who have not studied the course of the disorder longitudinally, Dr. Strober is much more sanguine about bipolar adolescents. He said:

It is true that, as children become teenagers, the expression of their psychopathology can become even more problematic for their parents. They can become drug abusing, sexually impulsive. . . . There's always the risk that the illness will be colored by the age in this way, and vice versa.

But, even with the difficulties, there's also a greater capacity for reasoning and restraint in judgment in adolescence. People assume the opposite—that teenagers become unreasonable and even more disruptive, and that does happen. But there's much more malleability with behavior and potential for therapeutic efforts with teenagers than in young children.

Dr. Strober recommends, as we do, that psychopharmacological treatment administered *with* psychotherapy is imperative to treat the illness. He talked of how mood states have influenced the development of personality and interpersonal relationships, and also how the mood states affect intrapsychic development. Not only does a supportive therapeutic therapy address all these issues that are intertwined with the illness, but having a close, trusting relationship with a doctor can help a teenager make better choices for him- or herself.

We then asked Dr. Strober what factors seem to predict a better course of illness and about the results of the ten-year study that he and his group are about to publish. He said:

In our studies, the kids who do best are the kids who have the classic manic-depressive cycles, the kids with pure mania bounded with well periods. The kids with pure manias have the lowest likelihood of relapse. Granted, you're less likely to see these well-defined patterns in kids. Mixed states by and large do not do as well, but that's not to say that a number of these kids don't do just fine. We've seen kids with mixed episodes who've done very well.

In our experience, many teenagers go into very long and stable periods of remission. These kids can look horrible, be dysfunctional, need hospitalization, but then they can go into remission. Yes, it's a lifelong illness, but people can have periods of time where they don't cycle. You can't really predict.

So, with this hope about the teenager's future firmly in mind, let us discuss some of the truly dark moments that a parent and a bipolar adolescent are bound to experience during the teenage years. There will probably be disagreements over medication compliance, acting out at home, and situations where the teen's judgment is simply bad or nonexistent. Such issues as the choice of friends, behavior in school and in the community, sexual promiscuity, and alcohol and drug abuse may pit parents and children against each other.

The task of adolescents is to separate from their parents and step out into the world as people with ideas and goals that need to be accomplished. Adolescents are typically in a state of expectation, excitement, and vulnerability. They are searching for their place in the world and are extraordinarily concerned with the opposite sex and what their peer group thinks of them.

They become desperate to fit in. Because adolescents know that social acceptance depends on how good they look and how cool they are, no flaws can be tolerated.

It's a wonder how anyone survives adolescence unscathed (and maybe nobody does). But now take a teenager who has bipolar disorder. He or she may enter adolescence with a reputation in shambles, a deteriorated relationship with exhausted and wary family members, a scholastic record hobbled by bad grades and time lost from school, and few champions among the school's administration or faculty. A teenager who takes medication may enter adolescence with even more acne than his or her nonbipolar peers and almost always with more weight than is acceptable in the perfect, perfect world most teenagers long to belong to. (For an individual with a penchant for perfectionism, as is the case with many bipolar kids, adolescence throws up a mirror that reflects every painful flaw imaginable.)

If a typical teen has to deal with a life now infused with sexual feelings and longings, a bipolar teen may have to deal with a much more intense hypersexuality. If a typical teen has to deal with the task of separation, the bipolar teen has to deal with severe separation anxiety, which makes it extremely difficult to negotiate the primary developmental task posed by adolescence. If the nonbipolar adolescent can experiment with alcohol and marijuana, the bipolar adolescent is more prone to addiction, and he or she may see the course of the illness worsen as the moods fluctuate with the use of alcohol and drugs.

Bipolar teenagers arrive at young adulthood with so much baggage, with such low self-esteem, that they can feel very isolated and defective.

Meantime, this is all unfolding as parents are entering middle age and worrying about their own increasingly elderly and infirm parents. At the same time, the parents may be going through their own identity and marital crisis. How are their own careers going? How is their marriage? Is their retirement income going to be sufficient? In addition, their child's college or post–high school years are fast approaching, and the future has to be reckoned with. Where will their child go to college—especially if his or her grades are not good or the child has learning disabilities or a history of suspension and poor attendance? How will this young person who has always been so dependent move away from home and into the hustle and bustle of college life or vocational school? Many difficult decisions await this already stressed family.

In the pages that follow we discuss these issues and some ways of smoothing the transition into these years.

If the teenager had early-onset bipolar disorder or had early symptoms but the full force of the disorder is only beginning to manifest itself, then nothing good can happen until there is stability. Medication compliance is going to be one of the major negotiating tasks of the teenage years.

MEDICATION COMPLIANCE

Teenagers are extraordinarily concerned with their body image. They are going through a period where everything is changing, and they are growing at a rate not experienced since the first year of life.

As a young person's hormonal levels shift, teenage acne sprouts on the face and body, and an adolescent can become obsessed with every pimple and blackhead. After a lot of hyperfocusing on the face and its deficiencies, this intense and very unforgiving gaze moves down to the body. Every curve is examined, breasts are found to be too small or too large; dieting becomes a major activity. Boys have their own concerns: Their chests are too concave, their voices are not low enough or crack embarrassingly.

Now imagine asking a teen to take a medication that causes acne and weight gain. Medication compliance is going to be a major problem.

"I always sympathize with my young patients," says child psychiatrist Rosalie Greenberg. "I never minimize what the side effects of medications mean to adolescents, and I send them to a dermatologist to get the acne under control (with the caveat that Accutane is not to be prescribed—it can cause depression). I also send these youngsters to a nutritionist so that we can better control the weight gain and so that they can feel that they are proactively fighting it. I promise them that I will try to switch the medications to minimize the weight gain if it becomes necessary."

But Dr. Greenberg first reminds now-stable teenagers how bad they used to feel and how much better they're getting along with their families and friends now that they *are* stable. She also reminds them that problems of weight gain and other side effects may not be lifelong as new drugs are always in the pipeline.

The support and sympathy of a confiding relationship with a therapist is invaluable in trying to help teenagers cope with the upsets of an illness like this and the side effects that arise from its treatment.

Medications also can become a power struggle between the parents and the adolescent. The parents who've lived through instability and episodes can become desperate for the teenager to stay compliant with the medication regimen, and a clash of wills may ensue as the adults pressure, hover, question, and cajole.

Adolescence is such a vulnerable time: A young person is struggling to move out of the orbit of parental supervision and to achieve independence. The idea of taking any medicine, and especially a psychotropic drug, can activate highly charged psychological issues. The medicine becomes a reminder that something within is not working as it should. This deficit makes the teenager more vulnerable in relationship to his or her peers and has the potential for decreasing the teenager's sense of self-worth. There may be a strong motivation to deny the illness and stop taking the medications entirely.

Parents will have to learn to play a different part around the medication treatment once a child becomes an adolescent. Where once they were the sole dispensers, now their involvement can become a problem for the teenager and a source of conflict. Teens may find the taking of medications an ideal subject to fight about and exhibit their own sense of control over the illness and the parents' wishes.

If parents can recognize the changes taking place in the child and back off a bit, and let the teen discuss all of this with the therapist, the young person probably will make the right decision. In most cases the terrible feelings the adolescent had before the medications worked are usually not worth reexperiencing for the sake of some weight loss. Many teenagers reach this conclusion if it doesn't become the issue to fight over.

Parents should encourage their teenager to fill the prescriptions at the pharmacy and to set up a schedule for remembering to take the medicines. Also, the teen should be encouraged to keep a diary of side effects and how well he or she thinks the medications are working, and discuss everything with the psychiatrist. These children need to learn to own their illnesses. A support group of teenagers with bipolar disorder would be ideal, and parents could talk to the guidance counselor at school or a psychiatrist in the area to help organize one.

The leader of a NAMI Child and Adolescent group told us that one of the most often asked questions by parents at the monthly meetings she chairs is how to get an adolescent to be compliant with the medications. Her answer? "The dangle of car keys. Teenagers will do anything for the privilege of the car. Sometimes that's your only ace in the hole." Parents who live in a city will have to find an equally regarded privilege.

ALCOHOL AND DRUGS

Parents who believe that drugs and alcohol are not easily accessible to any teenager are burying their heads in the sand. Thirteen-year-olds from "nice" suburban families are smoking pot and getting drunk—and on a regular basis. A leftover hippie from the 1960s has a harder time finding drugs than a teenager in America today.

Bipolar teenagers have an inordinately high risk of becoming addicted. It was commonly thought that people with mood disorders who abuse substances were self-medicating—they were either prolonging the highs of hypomania with stimulants or calming the anxiety and the irritability of depression with alcohol.

But recently researchers have begun examining the pairing of substance abuse and bipolar disorder more closely. They are asking the following questions about this "comorbidity": Is the association actually due to attempts at self-medication? Is the tendency to crave drugs and alcohol something heritable that travels in the company of the gene or genes that predispose one to mania or depression? Or do abused substances induce cycling? Or, as we mentioned in Chapter 6, is alcoholism a different manifestation of bipolar disorder?

Whatever the answers, the comorbidity of substance abuse and mood disorders has been vastly underestimated. In a random sample of five hundred members of the National Depressive and Manic-Depressive Association, almost half of the members reported that they abused alcohol and drugs prior to the correct diagnosis and treatment of the mood disorder, compared to 13 percent among patients properly diagnosed and treated.

The Epidemiologic Catchment Area data compiled early in the 1990s pinpointed an even higher statistic. It revealed that 61 percent of bipolar patients had a history of substance abuse. Of that number, 15 percent used drugs alone, 20 percent used alcohol alone, and 26 percent used both substances.

Dr. Kathleen T. Brady, the clinical director of the Center for Drug and Alcohol Programs at the Medical University of South Carolina, and Dr. Susan C. Sonne found that patients with substance abuse disorder and bipolar disorder have a much earlier age of onset—some seven years earlier. Other studies have found that substance-abusing bipolar patients are more likely to have irritable and paranoid episodes of mania rather than the elated kind. They are also more likely to relapse and have 50 percent more hospitalizations.

All this means that it is vital for parents to talk with their children and warn them that they will more likely become addicted to alcohol or drugs and suffer a worse course of illness. For the bipolar teen, drugs and alcohol are not "recreational" and something "everyone experiments with." They are mood-altering substances that impact powerfully on a very easily disturbed central nervous system. In this case, it's important for the teenager to view him- or herself as different, likely to have a far more serious reaction to the drugs than a hangover, and to remove him- or herself from the scene. Too much is at stake here, and the teenager needs to know that the consequences are not worth the short-term activity.

When All Your Efforts Fail

Despite all the family discussions, parents may come to learn that their son or daughter is abusing drugs or alcohol and spending time with a crowd of like-minded teenagers. It is natural to think that "all kids experiment, hopefully this is just a passing phase." But if it becomes apparent that the adolescent is spiraling downward and the teenager is becoming more unstable and his or her future is becoming closed off (or there is trouble with the law), parents will have to have a plan and be ready to enact it.

There are some teenagers who recognize they need help, and know deep inside that they need to be separated from their peer group. If the family has economic means, a therapeutic boarding school that has a dual-diagnosis program may be what's truly needed. However, the child may not be allowed to come home for months or even a year, and the costs are prohibitive (some can cost $5,000 a month and the adolescent typically attends such a school for a year or eighteen months).

Twelve-step programs that are in or nearby almost every community in this country may be helpful, but a person experienced with teenagers and recovery must be guiding the adolescent and family members. (Parents should understand that the twelve-step program was originally designed for adult men and that the needs of an adolescent are different.)

These programs seem to work best when the family attends Alanon meetings while the teenager attends his or her meeting. The family must work as a unit on recovery. People who have had experience with these programs advise attending a particular meeting at least three or four times before trying another group in the area.

When the best answer is to remove the adolescent from the negative peer environment, parents can investigate one of the so-called wilderness programs. These are typically eight-week programs that take place in states out West, such as Utah, Colorado, and Montana, although there are also programs in the Carolinas.

One program, Wilderness Quest in Utah, is highly esteemed for its work with recovering teenagers and they are quite adept at dealing with bipolar teens on medications who need special watching.

In a wilderness program such as this the teenagers learn to not just "talk the talk" but also to "walk the walk." They are out in the desert learning to love and respect the environment, themselves, and each other. This program involves the family initially, and one day is spent where the adolescent can only listen to the family members' point of view and say nothing; the next day, the family has to listen to the teenager and say nothing. After three days, the family leaves and the teen lives in a small group, learns to make fire, cook (think *Survivor),* takes night hikes, and learns to trust him- or herself and others. This program incorporates a drug rehab program with the wilderness program. (A program such as Wilderness Quest also has an adult program for people age eighteen to twenty-eight.)

Getting the adolescent to such a program may be so difficult that a parent has to resort to an escort service. This is a situation where two people come to the house and escort the teenager to the airport, onto the plane, and then into the program. This is harrowing for parents, but, expertly handled, it often goes more smoothly than expected. Most kids, once they find themselves in a no-exit situation, make the best of it and eventually see that the parents were trying to save their lives.

A book called *Shouting at the Sky* by Gary Ferguson profiles the Aspen Achievement Academy, and gives an accurate picture of the essence of these kind of programs, why they work, and how the teens, the staff, and the parents feel during the experience.

An eight-week experience like this costs in the neighborhood of $16,000, and may be the beginning of the road back. "I have found the wilderness programs to be the most effective way to get teenagers to internalize the need for profound change," says Thomas J. Croke, educational consultant and president of Thomas Croke and Associates in Latrobe, Pennsylvania. "For recovery to last, however, it must become as much a part of the teenager's lifestyle as drug-related activity has been." In other words, the adolescent may still need a more structured environment than home can reasonably provide following that wilderness experience.

If a family can afford it, a therapeutic boarding school may offer the teenager the best chance to consolidate recovery and self-esteem. If it is decided that the teenager should stay closer to home, many communities have intensive outpatient facilities—typically associated with a psychiatric hospital—that offer special programming for adolescents (they often attend after school). If you look at the Yellow Pages of the phone book under "Drug Abuse and Addiction Information and Treatment," you will find programs offered in your community.

To investigate wilderness programs, log on to http://www. bridgetounderstanding.com and check the listings. There are also educational consultants throughout the country who can help match your teenager or young adult to special schools or programs that deal with the bipolar disorder and the substance abuse problems. To locate someone who serves your area, contact the Independent Educational Consultant Association at http://www.iecaonline.com or by calling 703-591-4860. Their members have to have experience, credentials, and ethics, and must have visited over one hundred programs prior to membership so that they can truly match a teenager to a program.

SEXUALITY

It is estimated that about 50 percent of American high school students are having sex. The question becomes not should they have sex but how should a parent prepare a teenager about sex in the likelihood that he or she starts "dating" someone and the opportunities keep presenting themselves? Teens must be counseled to protect themselves both from pregnancy and a life-threatening disease.

If parents of typical teenagers are in a quandary about the entire subject of sex, consider the even more complicated situation a parent of a bipolar teen may be dealing with. Their teenager—if not medicated properly—can have periods of hypersexuality where the drive is *imperative.*

So many parents have described watching with horror as their daughters get "dressed" in the skimpiest of outfits and attempt to go out flaunting their bodies to cadres of boys in the neighborhood and school. One girl we know was so hypersexual that she and her boyfriend were practicing heavy petting in the school library for all to see.

The first thing the parents of such a teenager should do is call the treating psychiatrist and get the teen's blood levels checked. The hypersexuality may be a sign that the levels have dropped or the teen is being noncompliant. (In an adolescent with no history of the disorder, the hypersexuality may be a symptom of the impending illness, not an indication that the teen is amoral.)

Perhaps the adolescent should be kept home from school for a few days while the meds are adjusted and to keep her or him out of trouble. If there is a party that Saturday night, common sense dictates that this adolescent should not be allowed to attend. Sending a hypersexual teen to a party is an incendiary situation—one that can bring grave consequences to a teenager and the family.

The provocative dress and behavior may not only be a sign of hypersexuality; but it may be very tied to the psychology of the teen. Having a mood disorder can leave an adolescent feeling so defective and with such low self-esteem that the arena of sex may be a place where a girl finally feels attractive, valued, and in control. The girl may need to be so desired and loved that the cravings may be just as psychological as physical.

Parents will be desperate to avoid a pregnancy and the trauma of abortion or adoption. They will be so afraid of their daughter's impulsiveness and lack of forethought that the idea of a shot of Depo-Provera—a hormone that suppresses ovulation for about ninety days—seems to cover a lot of bases. But Depo-Provera contains medroxyprogesterone acetate, and progesterone is known to cause depression or exacerbate a mood disorder. And if it does so, it is present in the bloodstream for at least ninety days. Therefore, it's not a good option for a girl with bipolar disorder.

The mini pill—oral progesterone—may be a better option because it can be stopped if it becomes apparent that the progesterone in it is adversely affecting the mood disorder. But parents and teenagers should be aware that the mood stabilizers carbamazepine (Tegretol) and oxcarbazepine (Trileptal) can interfere with the contraceptive ability of birth control pills. They accelerate their normal breakdown and make them less reliable. (Depakote and lithium do not cause this.) Tegretol also diminishes the accuracy of pregnancy tests.

In the best of all possible worlds, a sexually active teenager would use a combination of a condom and a diaphragm with the spermicide and HIV-killing nonoxynol-9 gel with every sexual act. But teenage sex doesn't often afford such privacy and planning, and, paradoxically, many teenagers feel that if it just "happens" they won't be embarrassed by seeming aggressive and calculating. It lends a more innocent and romantic quality to the "unexpected" turn of events.

Probably the only thing parents can do is ensure that their children are well informed and understand the risks of pregnancy and sexually transmitted disease so that their fear overcomes any embarrassment and they take care of themselves. They need to know the benefits of monogamy and of knowing who their partner is. There are no easy answers here.

RECKLESS DRIVING

Even more of a nightmare than a sexually active teenager is an impulsive and reckless teenager behind the wheel of a car. If parents think the first few months of an infant's life left them sleep-deprived, wait until they have a daughter or son out with the car at night.

Unfortunately, research indicates that adolescents with ADHD are three to four times more likely to have an accident than teens who don't have ADHD. They are more likely to be involved in one or more accidents in which they are the cause; they are more likely to receive multiple speeding tickets and have their licenses suspended. Inattention, impulsiveness, and an attraction to daredevil antics can be a lethal combination behind the wheel of a car.

So if this is the case for adolescents with ADHD, and it is estimated that 94 percent of bipolar adolescents also exhibit ADHD symptoms, these terrifying statistics also apply to bipolar teens.

How can parents better protect the safety of their children and everyone else on the highways? In some states, teenagers have to undergo driver education training or a defensive driving course before they can get their license, but parents should think about investing in a special safety course no matter what the state requires. Personnel at the high school's driver education department or in the police department can no doubt advise parents as to what's available in the community.

A contract between the parents and teenager that spells out that he or she must take any prescribed medications diligently, wear seat belts, always drive the speed limit, never drink and drive, and meet all curfews in exchange for the use of the car may help curb some irresponsible tendencies on the part of the teenager.

Also written into the contract should be a clause about the teenager's not being a passenger in a car driven by a friend who's been drinking or taking drugs. The teenager will be loath to call his or her parents and ask to be picked up because he or she will be questioned and put in a position of getting that friend in trouble. Therefore, the contract should stipulate that no questions will be asked; you just want the teen to take no risks and arrive home safely.

LYING

In our survey, some 50 percent of the parents responding checked the phrase "Frequently lies" about their children. In many in-person and over-the-telephone interviews as well, parents discussed their children's lies. These parents were confused and upset because, even when confronted with evidence of the lie, the children and teenagers continued to deny their guilt. Audacious as it may sound, the teenagers—knowing full well they were lying—got angry at the parents for even *suggesting* they were not telling the truth.

But is lying a symptom of bipolar illness? Studies show that almost all teenagers lie. They do so to avoid getting into trouble, to maintain a certain zone of privacy, and to avoid confrontation. They often do it to manipulate a situation or to get what they want. They may lie at home and not so much in the outside world. As author Anthony E. Wolf writes in *Get Out of My Life But First Could You Drive Me and Cheryl to the Mall?*:

> Lying as a teenager is not an especially reliable indicator of whether or not that teenager is, or will become, an honest person. A good part of teenage lying is a function of the strange amorality of the at-home self. We should always confront them with their deceit when they are caught, and we must communicate our outrage. But a disaster, a tragedy, such deceit is not. Their sliminess may be deplorable, it is also normal, as it was when we were adolescents.

Dr. Wolf's wise discussion helps take the fear and steam out of the issue and place everything in perspective. But we need to explore this issue a bit further in the case of bipolar children.

There may be additional reasons why these kids lie. Some lies help establish the child's power. The child knows he or she is lying, and the parent knows it as well but is helpless to prove it. By lying, the child can test and challenge authority, and this may be an especially attractive form of power to a bipolar child who cannot accept parental authority without feeling a loss of self. In Chapter 1 we described a young boy who in response to his mother's exasperated question: "Why can you never listen to me and do as I say?" responded: "Oh, I couldn't. That would mean you had power over me. I am the master of my universe."

Lying would certainly be a provocative and teasing way to keep that power challenge going in the right direction for that child. There may be some other specific reasons for lying also. A twenty-one-year-old girl filled out our questionnaire and frankly checked off "Lies frequently" on the symptom checklist all through her childhood and adolescence. Since she was being so forthright about it, we homed in on this and asked: "How often do you lie, and why do you think you do it?"

She described what she felt was the underlying basis for her lying:

I lie all the time. It's a compulsion. It's easier to lie than to tell the truth. It's more comforting. It removes me from the constant feeling that I am incompetent and always failing.

For instance, this morning I was a half an hour late for work because I was sitting and daydreaming and time just passed. I don't know what happened to it, it just passed, and I couldn't pull everything together. So I told my boss that there was a three-car accident on the road and a slew of helicopters and all the news media blocking the way and I couldn't get through. The drama appealed to me. I don't know why I do this. I know they know it's not true. I don't know what they must think of me.

School Avoidance

According to Dr. Russell Barkley, the director of the Child and Adult Attention-Deficit Disorder Clinics at the University of Massachusetts and a leading authority on attention-deficit disorder, approximately 21 percent of teenagers with ADHD skip school. They are also at risk for dropping out (35 percent) or of being suspended (45 percent). Adolescents with ADHD and mood disorders may find school such a place of failure because they are so distractible and can't concentrate, and feel themselves slipping further and further behind.

While no statistics exist for bipolar teenagers, those just quoted don't bode well for this population.

Many teenagers with bipolar disorder experience school phobia, and tell their parents they have stomachaches, headaches, and impending flus in order not to have to attend. When parents detect signs of school refusal, they have to act quickly and locate the source of the problem.

If the adolescent has never been tested for learning disabilities, or never had special accommodations put in place to compensate for symptoms of bipolar illness, this is an avenue that should be explored immediately (see Chapters 10 and 11). It could be that the teenager is falling behind and feeling a lot of stress at school and trying to avoid that stress. While parents get to the bottom of things academically, they must make it very clear that unless the teenager has a fever, he or she is going to school. Parents should not cover for their child.

Certain mood stabilizers, in conjunction with medications such as Risperdal, can be very sedating and can make it difficult for someone taking them to get up in the morning. This possibility should be assessed by the treating physician who can perhaps advise that the meds be taken earlier in the evening or who can make some changes in the medication regimen.

At the same time, parents should be noting what time the teenager is getting to sleep at night. If he or she is having difficulty getting to sleep, it may be a sign that the condition is beginning to influence the sleep cycle—hypomania may be beginning to develop. Again, the doctor should be consulted, and he or she can assess the situation.

Parents should make it crystal clear to the teenager that if he or she is truant from school (some of them check into homeroom and then don't attend the rest of the day), the car and the car keys are going to be taken away for an extended period of time.

CURFEWS

Most teenagers, in their effort to establish independent relationships and a social identity apart from their parents and family, need to be with their peers constantly. They tend to congregate or "hang" into the late hours of the night.

Unfortunately, for a person with bipolar disorder, a disturbance in the sleep/wake cycle can become a window through which hypomania or mania can occur. A regular bedtime is essential to the teenager's health.

Parents should explain that they understand how important their teenager's social life is but that an irregular sleep/wake cycle can trigger episodes of illness. This needs to be addressed with the treating psychiatrist, and a reasonable curfew should be imposed, perhaps with some latitude on one weekend evening. If the teen is going to sleep at a friend's house, it must be made clear to the parents of that friend that "all-nighters" are dangerous for their son or daughter; their help must be enlisted to make sure the teens get to sleep at a decent time.

COLLEGE BOUND

Before a parent turns around, his or her world becomes filled with the subject of SATs and grade-point averages, and the coffee table overflows with brochure packets and videotapes from colleges and universities across the nation. Spring and summer vacations turn into car trips to campuses near and far. It's a heady and frightening time. This child is about to be launched.

Many, many questions and considerations are going to arise for bipolar adolescents. How far should they go away from home? Who will treat their disorder in a different community? Can they deal with the academic and social demands of campus life? What kind of school should they look for? At what point do you address the medical diagnosis and academic disabilities that may accompany the disorder?

Today, thanks to the Americans with Disabilities Act and the Individuals with Disabilities Act, an IEP can be put in place through the age of twenty-one, and many colleges have developed learning centers where students who have a disability can get help, tutoring, and have programs designed for them that take their disability into consideration (see Chapter 10 for a complete description of the IEP process). An educational consultant would be a good person to turn to for advice on suitable programs.

Jayme Stewart, the director of College Guidance at the Yorke Preparatory School in New York City, advises a bipolar student to look for a small, nurturing school (with about 1,500 to 2,000 students), one with an active learning center. She told us that the admissions office receives the IEP packet and information about past academic difficulties from the high school, but that they will not be involved with that student once the admissions process is complete, and it is extremely important that the dean of freshman students be contacted and put on notice that the student needs special accommodations. The parents need to let the dean know that they are expecting him or her to keep an eye out for that student. She gives all the parents of her learning-disabled graduates the following letter for them to make that contact. This letter should be sent return receipt requested:

Dean of Freshman Students   Date
College
Address

Dear Dean of Freshman Students:

Our (son/daughter) is about to enter (college name) as a freshman in the class of 20____. We are writing to you now at the suggestion of (his/her) high school guidance counselor. We would like to have an understanding with (college) that (child's name) is a documented LD student (see enclosed reports). Should it become necessary, we request that (name) will be allowed to take untimed exams in college, have a note taker for certain courses, have a lighter-than-usual course load, and be able to use "books on tape" if available. (He/She) will, of course, fulfill the required work during summers or as part of a fifth year.

In addition, we will arrange with the Academic Support Center to set up a tutoring schedule in order to give (name) whatever help (he/she) needs outside of class. Please feel free to contact me if you need any further information.

We, and (name), are very happy about (his/her) enrollment at (college) and we look forward to (his/her) becoming a productive and successful member of your student body.

Sincerely

Your Name

Enclosure

Jayme Stewart also advises parents to arrange—and pay for—the services of a mentor—a junior or senior with good grades who can tutor the new student and assist him or her socially. She said: "A student mentor is more natural than an adult tutor, and has the added advantage of taking the new student to parties and helping him or her assimilate into campus life. Knowing a mentor is in place means knowing that someone is checking in on the young adult and making sure everything is going smoothly."

Also, if an IEP is in place, the parents can ask for a note taker for every class. This is something done all the time for students with learning disabilities.

Ms. Stewart definitely recommends that a bipolar student look into something called a "quiet dorm." This is something new on college campuses; these dormitories have rules that forbid loud music or parties so that students can study without distraction and get enough rest. However, she does not think a bipolar student should ever have a single room. "This student could disappear from the scene and no one would know it. A roommate is company and can get help for the student if a period of instability arises," she explained.

It will be important for parents to contact and stay in touch with the senior resident assistant of the dorm. Because the school must view its students as adults and not intrude on them, the senior RA may be the only person who can keep an eye out for the young person who may become noncompliant with medications or begin to founder.

Ms. Stewart had several other recommendations to help ease the way into an entirely new life. She said: "I think bipolar students should schedule classes later in the day, as I know getting up in the morning can be difficult. I also think there is nothing wrong with taking five or even six years to complete a degree (this is becoming common even among non–learning-disabled students). If the pressures and stresses are kept to a minimum, the student has a better chance of experiencing success and really blossoming as a student and as a young adult."

This still leaves the question as to when parents alert the school about the bipolar diagnosis. Because stigma is not a thing of the past, it is probably best to reveal this information after the acceptance letter arrives and the student's place has been secured.

If the adolescent is not stable and is still acting out, it may be a better idea for him or her to attend school locally with the full support of the home environment and the treating psychiatrist and therapist. There may be excellent schools within driving distance of the home, and as the young person matures and stabilizes, he or she probably can attend another college full time, but then with a more secure academic and social base.

TO EVERYTHING THERE IS A SEASON

It is interesting to note that adolescence in Western society was something reserved only for the upper social classes until the early twentieth century. The poor never experienced adolescence because they were expected to proceed dutifully from an obedient childhood into an obedient adulthood without benefit of the period of transition from childhood to adulthood.

So, thanks to the emancipation of the working classes and the advent of the youth movements of the early 1900s, adolescence is something all parents get to "enjoy." As Dr. Louise J. Kaplan writes in her book *Adolescence,* "Now that adolescence is accessible to the multitude and not restricted to gentleman and lords, many adults are taking alarm at what seems to be a barbaric horde of scruffy girls and boys out to dismantle the structures of society. It is hard to see any virtue at all. What the grown-ups see in its stead is considerable evidence of pride, covetousness, anger, gluttony, envy, sloth, and a great deal of lust."

We hope this chapter has provided some perspective for the dicey years the parents of a bipolar teen will have to endure. Adolescence is a difficult phase—for any family.

But that's what it is, a phase, and one that passes. In the majority of cases, a more reasonable, more centered adult rises from the ashes of adolescence. It's never easy, but parents should remember that much of what they say, teach and advise eventually does get through, despite all evidence to the contrary.

Surprisingly, the parents of a bipolar adolescent may have a unique advantage over other parents: They have become particularly attuned to this child and his or her emotional state, and they may be in a better position to troubleshoot and stave off potential problems. They have had to confront uncomfortable truths early on. These parents have been tempered by the fires of a bipolar childhood and may be more flexible, more realistic, and better able to withstand the shock of adolescence without losing their footing. In fact, these parents—*and* their teenagers—may be surprised at their ability to handle adolescence and all its accompanying tumult.

When a Child Is
Hospitalized

Parents who've brought a newborn home from the hospital nursery usually have an indelible memory of the experience. It's impossible to pass through the hospital's corridors on that first journey home and not encounter people smiling broadly and voicing good wishes for the fledgling family. There is such excitement and hope about the special days and months ahead. And as the new young mother and father head out toward a brand-new future, all of their love, thoughts, efforts, and intentions are focused on helping this infant thrive and get off to the best possible start in life.

Never, *ever,* do parents dream that—not so many years later—they may be forced back into another kind of hospital because that child has a psychiatric condition that now makes him or her "a danger to self or others." Parents who make the agonizing decision to hospitalize a child will never forget either the events that led up to its necessity or those first disorienting days on a child psychiatric unit.

It is not uncommon for a child or adolescent to require hospitalization, and families should almost expect that a crisis might occur at some point in the child's life. Therefore, we want to outline the procedures and introduce the professionals that a child and his or her family encounter throughout the period of a hospitalization. We also want to include the wise advice and counsel of other parents who have had a child in crisis and

who, in hindsight, assessed the hospitalization as a positive experience—
for their child as well as for the family as a whole.

WHEN SHOULD A CHILD BE HOSPITALIZED?
WHAT CAN IT ACCOMPLISH?

It's time to think about a hospitalization when a child is so out of control
that he or she may be hurting him- or herself, threatening to harm a family member, unable to stop raging, experiencing delusions or hallucinations, or talking about or planning suicide.

*No two human beings, no matter how dedicated, have the stamina to see a child
through the intensity of such a crisis alone.* The right and appropriate course
of action is to have a professional staff take over at this time.

A psychiatric unit is a protected environment where a team of professionals can keep the child safe, observe the child's full range of behaviors
and reactions, meet with and talk to the family on a regular basis, participate in the diagnosis (or rediagnosis) of an illness, order and administer
medication trials, and note any untoward effects.

Years ago a psychiatric hospitalization often lasted a month or two. Today, with the cost-containing practices of managed care, a child is typically preauthorized for four days on a psychiatric unit, and all future days
must be reauthorized as the insurer's utilization review board monitors
the progress of the child's condition. Doctors often have to fight to make
a case for additional hospital days, but the average length of stay ranges
from six to fourteen days. A Band-Aid, yes, but often a necessary Band-
Aid.

We asked one father to tell us about his twelve-year-old daughter's
hospitalization in the adolescent psychiatric unit of a Chicago teaching
hospital. While he talked about the trauma of making the decision, he
said that ultimately there was no choice. She became more and more agitated and began acting in a threatening manner. He picked her up, put
her in a taxi, and headed toward the emergency room of the hospital.
Looking back, he felt that it was absolutely the right thing to have done,
and he ticked off the benefits:

- It offered respite and safety for her.
- It offered respite and safety for us.
- We got to "fast-track" a medication regimen.

- It supplied a concrete recognition of her illness and the crisis we were in.
- We got eight more confirmations of her diagnosis as the staff got to talk with her and observe her behavior. When people asked, "Did you get a second opinion?" we were able to answer: "Yes. We got eight of them."
- She got to meet other teenagers struggling with bipolar disorder and she didn't feel so alone or alien. They liked her and helped prove to her that she was okay, despite her problems.
- The other kids told her never to go off her medications. (They had, and that is why they were repeating the hospital experience.) They also told her that she should "never mess with alcohol and drugs" because it would make everything worse. (No one but another teenager could have made that all-important message stick.)

Other parents we interviewed had experiences that, on the whole, paralleled this family's, where the hospitalization—although traumatic for everyone at first—made perfect sense in view of the crisis situation and ultimately proved beneficial in many other ways.

But make no mistake, psychiatric hospitalization always raises the issues of stigma. No matter how enlightened, most people feel a sense of shame and disgrace that the private life of their family is now no longer private. The absence of the child from home must be explained, the seriousness of his or her illness must be acknowledged, and all of this must be thought through at a time when the family is exhausted and grief-stricken.

One mother who felt protective of her son's reputation (Would other parents let their children play with him when he got home? Would people gossip? Would they blame her and her husband?) admitted: "I found myself saying 'he has a neurological illness.' I felt ashamed telling people that I had put him in a psychiatric unit. When I had a choice between two hospitals, and one was Children's Hospital and the other began with 'The Psychiatric Institute of . . .' I opted for the name that revealed the least, or didn't make my heart skip a beat every time I was forced to mouth it."

Sadly, stigma adds to the already overwhelming burden these families feel. However, this mother has since rallied and was very eager to tell other parents how to avoid falling into the trap that had made her situation all the more difficult.

She said:

Your tendency is to contract and isolate yourself. But it's so important that the parents push themselves to reach out and break down the barricades of their isolation. I advise them to go home, and get on the phone with a NAMI or NDMDA chapter and ask someone at the chapter to put you in touch with another family who's had to hospitalize their child. I finally did this, and when a family member called me, it was such a lifeline. Here were people who were so empathic, who had been through the experience and who had survived it, and who could walk us through the days ahead and offer counsel and comfort.

This mother also had great praise for her son's psychiatrist during this crisis period:

She expressed such compassion. She acknowledged our struggle and offered us hope that this crisis would pass and we would have our little boy back. She also encouraged me to call her as often as I wanted and cry my heart out. Often I didn't need to speak to her, I just left messages on her machine. I needed to keep connected, keep her informed and vent a little.

IF YOU HAVE A CHOICE, WHICH HOSPITAL SHOULD YOU CHOOSE?

Since over 85 percent of the people who are insured in this country are enrolled in some type of managed care insurance program, today parents have limited choices when it comes to a psychiatric hospitalization. As we discuss in Chapter 14, most managed care plans have contracted with a few hospitals in your area for behavioral health treatment, and you will have to hospitalize your child in one of these facilities.

Most hospitalizations must be preauthorized and planned forty-eight hours in advance. (If it's an emergency and you cannot get preauthorization from the insurer, you have no choice but to go to the emergency room of a hospital and wait for a bed there.)

If a hospitalization seems imminent, it's best to call your insurer and get it on record that matters are deteriorating and find out your choices (if any). The child's psychiatrist arranges the preauthorization, but one mother whose two children had been hospitalized advises parents to do a lot of checking and even to tour the units and get a gut feeling about the facilities. Hospitals vary, and she wrote:

My oldest son was just hospitalized two months ago. I took him to University Hospital in San Diego. They got him a bed right away. The staff was great, I feel that it did help him. He says he wasn't scared and that they were good to him. He liked the classes and I liked his new child psychiatrist. So, it was a positive experience for us.

However, my youngest son is ten years old and is bipolar also. We had to put him in the hospital when he was nine years old because he tried to kill himself. We took him to a different hospital required by our insurance company. It was awful. He was there for seven days. He was only allowed to call home once a day and cried, told me how scared he was, and that the people were mean. I could hear the staff shouting in the background at him to get off the phone. He was scared of the dark and I had told them that, but they continued to close his door at night. They would only allow me to visit him for one hour each night. My son begged me to take him home every day. After four days I tried to and they told me it was against the doctors' advice and that basically Special Services would take him away from me if I did. I felt completely guilty for taking him there. I was a nervous wreck and cried all the time. I felt like an awful parent.

When he came home he was scared to leave my sight. He followed me everywhere, including the bathroom. He slept with my husband and me for a few weeks. We had to constantly reassure him that he was safe and he would never go back to that hospital again. He still is scared to tell things to his therapist because he says the therapist will send him back to the hospital. So, his therapist wrote a promise note telling my son that he promised he would never send him back to *that* hospital. He is just now, one year later, feeling okay to talk to his therapist about everything.

The only positive thing about my younger son being in that hospital—and this is not insignificant—was that his doctor there did properly diagnose him.

I would tell other parents—and I do tell them at groups I attend—to check out the hospital yourself first.

We asked Dr. Victor Fornari, the assistant chairman for training and clinical services at Schneider Children's Hospital in New Hyde Park, New York, if it is typical for a parent to tour the hospital. "If you have some choice," he said, "by all means make an appointment and come in to see the facility, meet some of the staff and become familiar with the point of view of people who might be working with your child. You may not be taken up to the children's unit, but you'll get a feel for the facility and the people in charge of its program."

We then asked him: "If you had to hospitalize one of your children on a psychiatric unit, what would you look for and what would you tell other parents to assess?"

He advised a parent to:

- Learn about the leadership of the unit. Who runs it and what is his or her philosophical orientation? What is the staff-to-patient ratio?
- Make sure you see more registered nurses than psych technicians (often called milieu therapists) and aides. One registered nurse is not enough. Naturally, the units with small children should have a greater ratio of staff to children than an adolescent unit.
- Research the policies and procedures governing seclusion and re-straints and involuntary administration of medication. While each state has regulations governing seclusion and restraint, there's a philosophy that guides how liberally either seclusion or restraints are used, and you want to know that it's for the safety of the child, used infrequently and as a last resort, and never applied punitively.
- If the child is very young and the separation from the parent is go-ing to be a big problem, ask if the hospital will let you "shadow" the child—sleep in the parents' lounge and participate in some of the day activities. If the staff doesn't advise that, listen carefully to their reasons and determine for yourself if they seem reasonable.
- Take a look at the programs for parents. Is there an attempt to ed-ucate parents and help them work through the trauma? Is there a siblings group? And how much thought seems to go into dis-charge planning? There are alternate levels of aftercare that in-clude more than discharge to home and therapist.

Parents should also keep in mind that private rooms and fancy facili-ties are not assurances of quality treatment. One family from Florida ad-mitted their son to a psychiatric hospital with tennis courts and swimming pools, and for three weeks the staff did nothing to benefit the boy positively. When their insurance ran out, he was transferred to the county hospital. There he was looked after by a doctor who diagnosed him correctly and prescribed a combination of medications that worked.

This child has been stable for a year. He had formerly suffered school phobia, and the school year was a nightmare for him and his family. His mother told us with such joy in her voice that he recently returned to school and he came home one week and announced: "You know, I'm really loving school and I think my teacher is great and I'm going to work hard this year and move ahead."

The diagnostic abilities and treatment philosophy of the psychiatrist running the unit are far more important than the interior design and the gym equipment.

COSTS OF A HOSPITALIZATION

Parents are going to need to read all the fine print on their insurance policies and probably log a bit of time on the phone with their plan's administrators, so that they understand completely what they will be responsible for when the bill for a psychiatric hospitalization is finally tallied.

Some of the questions that need to be asked are:

- How many days in a psychiatric hospital are covered?
- Do you have a choice in the hospital, or must it be in one of the plan's participating hospitals?
- If a child is hospitalized through the emergency room of a hospital not in the plan, how much of the bill will be covered?
- Is there a ceiling to the dollar amount reimbursed?
- What is the deductible?
- Are partial hospitalizations (for instance, day hospital programs) and other alternatives to inpatient care covered? For how many days or weeks?
- If you have several policies, when does one pick up from the other?

We discuss all of this in Chapter 14, and we understand how difficult it is to read fine print and legalese in the middle of a crisis, but the more information you have going in, the less likely you'll be to fantasize financial ruin over a hospitalization, and the more secure you'll feel when the issues of money and insurance are raised.

If your coverage is inadequate, the hospital's business office may be able to initiate a Medicaid application, help arrange a bank loan, or negotiate another payment method.

Families should also be aware that there is a form of hospital "Catastrophic Medicaid" that covers patients who are not currently receiving Medicaid and whose inpatient hospital care exceeds 25 percent of their annual income. This coverage is valid for only six months from the date of application and covers only inpatient care.

What would twelve days of a psychiatric hospitalization of a child or adolescent cost? The charges are variable, and a city, county, or state hospital will naturally cost less, but a child admitted to a private hospital would incur bills that would range from $10,000 to $17,000 just for the hospital bed rate. (These range from approximately $700 to $1,400 a day.) In addition, the parents of the child will be billed for selected services and specific treatments that would approximate these:

Electrocardiogram (ECG)	$175
MRI brain scan	850
ECT (10 treatments)	5,000
Therapy fees, including daily M.D. visits	1,600
Consultation fees	600
Psychological testing	400
Medications	300

Fees approximating $20,000 or more should motivate every parent to examine his or her insurance situation with a magnifying glass. If a person does not have coverage and lacks financial resources, a public hospital will take care of the treatment and initiate a Medicaid application.

PREPARING FOR ADMISSION

What to Take to the Admissions Office

A telephone call to the admissions office of the child psychiatry unit will fill you in on what's required for the admitting procedure. In all probability you need to take the following:

- Completed questionnaires and paperwork sent to you by the hospital prior to admission; similarly, any questionnaires completed by your child's teacher
- Your child's immunization record
- Any previous psychiatric, psychological, or medical reports

- A complete listing of all medication trials and the responses your child had to them
- Your child's insurance card
- The Social Security card or phone number of the person who will bear the responsibility of the bill
- Name, address, and phone number of the person to be notified in case of an emergency
- A checkbook or credit card (some hospitals require a deposit)

What Clothing Should You Pack for Your Child?

While each unit is different and will advise you about clothing and personal articles, many units ask that you supply enough clothing for one week and recommend that you iron in name labels or identify all clothing. Typically, a child needs:

Underwear 7 sets
Socks 7 pairs
Pajamas 3 sets
Bathrobe 1
T-shirts 7
Tops 7
Sweater 1
Pants/jeans 4
Slippers 1 pair
Shoes 1 pair
Sneakers 1 pair
Shampoo (in a plastic container)
Comb/brush (plastic)
Toothbrush/toothpaste
Soap
Coins for phone calls
A favorite stuffed animal, but no other toys, cords, or strings, which
    may be dangerous for a child in crisis

For the safety of the child and others on the child unit, do *not* pack or take the following: scissors, glass objects, tobacco products, matches, clippers, cameras, medications, Walkmans, radios, hair dryers or other electrical items, glue, paste, tape recorders, or soda cans.

After Admission

After the parents sign authorization-for-treatment papers, the family is escorted to the unit. In many hospitals, the nursing staff handles the orientation and intake procedure. Most hospitals hand you brochures with a Patient's Bill of Rights and a statement of the unit's philosophy of treatment as well as all kinds of information about life in this therapeutic community. The parents and the child will be told all about the therapy programs, the rules of the unit, visiting hours, the daily schedule, and so on.

Next the nurse takes a medical and psychiatric history from the parents. The nurse's intake not only helps orient the child and family to the new surroundings, but gives the people who are working most closely with the child a chance to get to know him or her and you.

Once the intake is complete, the psychiatrist responsible for the child begins a medical and psychiatric workup. In some cases, the private psychiatrist who admitted the child to the hospital will be his or her private attending physician and will thus be familiar with the child's history; in units that assign their own staff to each new patient, typically there will be an extensive workup of the child's developmental, medical, and psychiatric history. The family history should be explored and all medication trials and responses will be noted.

Physical Examination

All children admitted to a unit are given a physical exam and routine screening tests such as blood tests and a urinalysis. The results of these tests may point to a physical cause of the psychiatric problem or may unearth a coexisting medical problem. They also will guide the psychiatrist in the choice of psychotropic medication. For example, a child with a history of seizures would need psychotropic medications that would have less of a potential for lowering the seizure threshold. (Many neuroleptics lower it to some degree, as does the antidepressant Wellbutrin.) Depending on the clinical picture, the psychiatrist may call for a medical consultation with a neurologist, an endocrinologist, a cardiologist, or a specialist in psychopharmacology.

After all of these exams are completed, the treatment team and plan are put into action. Under the psychiatrist's direction, a team of psychologists, social workers, the nursing staff, occupation and activities therapists, and an education specialist continuously review, discuss, and treat the child.

Hospital Team

The child will be evaluated and treated by different staff professionals throughout the hospital stay, and it is important for parents to know who they are, how they can help, and what kind of training they have. The following brief descriptions should answer these questions:

- The *child psychiatrist* is a medical doctor who specializes in the diagnosis and comprehensive treatment of psychiatric disorders. After completing four years of medical school, he or she completes three years of an adult psychiatric residency and two additional years of a child psychiatry fellowship. The education encompasses medical treatment approaches as well as psychotherapeutic approaches. The child psychiatrist, as a medical doctor, is the only mental health professional (in most states) who can prescribe medications and perform electroconvulsive therapy. The child psychiatrist supervises and coordinates the entire treatment team and plan.

- The *clinical psychologist* is also called "doctor," but here the title refers to a Ph.D. degree or its equivalent in clinical psychology. The psychologist completes three years of course work as well as an internship in a psychiatric hospital or mental health clinic. In addition, most Ph.D. programs require a dissertation on a research topic. While a psychologist cannot prescribe medication, he or she is trained to do psychological testing, psychotherapy, and research.

- *Psychiatric nurses* are registered nurses who have been specifically trained to work with children who have psychiatric disorders. These are the professionals who spend the most time with the children on a psychiatric unit, and their manner can set the tone of the whole unit and do much to make a child and his or her family feel safe and at home. Not only do the nurses dispense the medications ordered by the child psychiatrist, but they closely monitor the side effects. The nurses' daily report gives the rest of the treatment team valuable information about the child's medical and mental status. Some nurses have master's degrees, and some are nurse practitioners trained to do psychotherapy and run groups, and even prescribe medications in some states.

- The *psychiatric social worker* can be invaluable to the family as well as to the child. After four years of college, the psychiatric social worker completes a two-year course with an internship in a psychiatric setting and is awarded the degree of master of social work (M.S.W.). If the initials A.C.S.W. appear after the social worker's name, it means that he or she has met the requirements of and is certified by the Academy of Certified Social Workers. L.C.S.W. means that the social worker is a licensed clinical social worker. Not only can this professional conduct group and individual therapy sessions, but he or she assesses and coordinates the needs of the child and family members during and after the hospitalization. The social worker helps with the discharge treatment plan and may initiate Medicaid applications where they are appropriate.

• The *rehabilitation therapist* on some children's units coordinates each child's daily schedule, which includes school, therapeutic activities, group therapy, and other milieu groups. He or she plans and leads a variety of action-oriented groups that address the child's problems and assets and focuses on skill development.

• Many units also have *activities therapists* who specialize in art therapy, dance or music therapy, or recreational therapy. They are graduates of accredited bachelor's or master's programs that emphasize the therapeutic application of art or physical education. The activities programs are designed to encourage self-awareness and the exploration of feelings as well as to provide the children with an opportunity to engage in structured leisure activities that promote socialization and the improvement of interpersonal skills. (These activities could include sports, hobbies, woodworking, crafts, cooking, and the like.) The activities therapist understands the treatment goals for each child and attempts to reinforce them through the projects undertaken.

• Most child and adolescent units have a *teacher* who conducts a school program for two to three hours a day. He or she keeps in close contact with each child's home teacher and receives the assignments and curriculum so they may be completed during school hours on the unit. This way the child can keep from falling far behind classmates during the hospitalization.

In addition to the professionals just mentioned, the child comes into close contact with other hospital personnel: the physician's assistant, who may do physical exams, psych technicians, and nursing aides. In a good hospital, these people not only do their jobs but offer children reassurance and encouragement.

Daily and Weekly Schedule on a Children's Unit

Treatment for children suffering with psychiatric disorders begins with an integrated plan to diagnose, ameliorate the symptoms of the illness, help the child reestablish a sense of self-esteem, educate the child and the family as to the nature of the illness, and develop a practical outpatient treatment that will serve to prevent rehospitalization. The many meetings, medical rounds, and social and therapeutic interactions throughout the hospital stay are aimed at accomplishing these agendas.

Typically each morning the staff assembles for "rounds." This is the nurses' report on the medical and behavioral status of each child on the unit. If there are psychiatric residents and child fellows on the unit (as there would be in a teaching hospital), the residents may report at this time also. Any questions about changes in the treatment plans, or concerns about a response to a medication or a family visit, are brought up at this time.

Many psychiatric units divide the patient responsibilities into two teams. Detailed discussions of each child are conducted in team meetings several times a week. If a child is experiencing any neurological or medical problems, consultants are called in and supplemental medical rounds are conducted.

Individual, group, and family meetings are scheduled throughout the week. Naturally, there are hours set aside for school, meals, showers, quiet times, and visiting hours.

Behavioral Programs on an Inpatient Unit

Every unit runs differently, but most have a system or set of rules designed to encourage behavior that will help a child reach his or her therapeutic goals as well as limit behaviors that result in distress or that are dangerous or disruptive. Some units run on a point system with a token economy. The more often the child maintains control and achieves certain goals set for him or her, the greater the number of points he or she receives, and these points can be converted to "behavior dollars" at the unit's store or result in special treats or privileges (such as time at the Nintendo game).

Behavioral programs should be explained thoroughly to the parents and the child during the intake process.

Safety Measures and Discipline

Some children are so aggressive, suicidal, or out of control that it is decided they need more contact with the nursing staff. Part of the treatment plan, then, is a period of time where the child has "one-on-one," or constant observation. This means that a nurse or milieu therapist is assigned to stay close to that child at all times and make frequent or verbal contact with the child.

If a child cannot control his or her behavior, there are a number of disciplinary procedures designed to keep the child safe, help him or her regain control, and also keep the other children as well as the staff on the unit safe.

One of these procedures (familiar to all parents) is "time-out." When there is a problem behavior, the child is asked to sit in a chair, away from social stimulation. If a parent visits during a time-out, the parent is usually asked to wait for the completion of the time-out before the visit can begin.

At the conclusion of the time-out, the staff discusses with the child what happened and how he or she might have dealt with the situation more appropriately.

Ideally, the child goes to a "time-out chair" cooperatively; if, however, he or she does not respond to the request to take a time-out, the child is typically helped to the chair by a staff member who holds the child's hand or arm. The child is given three chances to sit down. If he or she does not or cannot, the child is informed that he or she has the alternative of the quiet room.

If no cooperation is forthcoming, the child is gently escorted to the quiet room. The door is locked only if it is necessary to provide safety, and a doctor must order this and assign a staff person for constant observation for the time the child is in seclusion. Children should never be alone.

The Quiet Room, Seclusion, and Physical Restraints

Strict state regulations govern any use of a quiet room or seclusion. The following discussion may sound awful to people who've never dealt with a raging, aggressive, and abusive child, or a child who is hallucinating and feeling panicked or paranoid, but parents who've tried to deal with such a child by themselves have told us that they *wished* they had a seclusion room at home to protect their child, their other children, themselves, and all of their possessions when their child is totally out of control and kicking in the walls of their home. (At least four parents wrote and said they *had* jerry-rigged their own versions of a seclusion room at home. They felt it was necessary to keep the entire family safe.)

In a hospital setting, a seclusion room is a room stripped of any sharp or heavy objects that could be used by a patient to hurt him- or herself or the staff. Often the walls are covered with padding, and there is a mattress on the floor for the patient to rest and sleep on. (A bed frame has too many sharp angles.)

The seclusion room is a measure of last resort. It can be used only to prevent a child from hurting himself or others, and only when other treatments are ineffective. The psychiatrist must write the orders for seclusion, the child's behavior must be observed and documented frequently (there is a window in every seclusion room), vital signs (blood pressure, pulse, respiration rate, and temperature) must be taken periodically, and if the child is not sleeping, he or she must be released and taken to the bathroom every two hours.

There may be times—for instance, if the child is banging his or her head against the wall or trying to do damage to him- or herself in some way—that physical restraints are deemed appropriate. Again, each state has laws determining what kind of restraints can be used. (A rubber blanket that limits kicking and punching may be placed over a very agitated child or a restraining sheet with special padding may be used.) Again, this may look medieval to someone who has never dealt with this kind of extreme rage or aggression, but many parents have spent hours in their own homes holding a raging child down or wrapping a child in blankets. The authorized hospital restraints limit the potential damage to self or others that a child may cause. They may lessen the stimulation and feelings of overarousal a child is experiencing; they also may frighten a child terribly, and parents need to make sure that the policy of the unit is to have an empathic adult with that child at all times and to inform the family when restraints or seclusion are being used.

Having strangers make a decision to seclude or restrain your child is bound to bring up a lot of feelings of uneasiness and guilt for family members. But one young woman who was secluded in a quiet room for a time recalled how she felt about it on the "inside":

I had been running around trying to do a thousand things and my mind was going a million miles a minute. I was exhausted, and the room seemed a quiet and simple place for me. The pressure was off. I didn't have to accomplish anything. I could just slow down and rest. I'm sure a seclusion room must enrage or frighten some people—it's all so individual—but for me, the time in a seclusion room was a retreat. It seemed an appropriate place for me to be at that time.

Whom Can You Call to Check on Your Child and Whom Do You Turn to If You Have a Complaint?

It's always a good idea to ask who will have the most contact with your child and whom you can call to check in and see how he or she is doing. Typically, one nurse on each shift is assigned to each child, and that professional is in the best position to answer your questions. When you have the nurse's name, ask him or her when would be the best time to call.

If there is anything that concerns you about the treatment of your child, do not hesitate to talk to the unit chief or the head nurse. If you are still not satisfied, make an appointment to speak to the doctor in charge of your child or to the director of clinical services. He or she should be able to resolve any problem, but if not, consult the admissions brochure you were given at the start of your child's hospitalization and look for the name of the patient representative. This person is a direct link to the hospital's administration and should be able to help find a solution.

Should Siblings Visit?

Parents have a tendency to try to shield their children from situations that seem unpleasant, but when we asked Dr. Victor Fornari whether siblings should visit, he said:

> By all means. Everyone is affected by the hospitalization, and siblings need to understand what is happening and see their brother or sister. In addition, the hospitalized child needs to be kept involved in their family's life. I do think, however, that the visit should take place not on the unit, but in a waiting room or some other room off the unit.
>
> At Schneider Children's Hospital, we have a sibling group that meets once a week where the brothers and sisters can talk about their many feelings about the patient and his or her hospitalization and

the problems that led up to it. They begin to see that they are not alone with all their feelings.

Parents should not underestimate their other children's extreme sensitivity and capacity to imagine things far more terrible than reality. Watching their sibling removed from the home may have filled them with fear or triumph or any of a number of complicated feelings. There has been a supreme rupture in family life. Seeing their brother or sister at the hospital would do much to help these children replace uncomfortable fantasies with firm and guilt-free facts. Also, during a visit they get to witness the parents' deep involvement and concern for their ill child; this will allay any anxiety that the parent sent the ill child away because he or she was "bad" and "too much trouble." They may fear that this will also happen to them if they misbehave.

While Your Child Is in the Hospital

Parents need to remember to take very good care of themselves during this time of crisis. They are grieving. Experiencing your child grabbing on to you crying and begging "Don't leave me, Mommy, please don't leave me here alone" is not something easily forgotten. The guilt parents feel and the uncertainty about the drastic measures they've been forced to take are very unbalancing at first. A mother from Texas whose young son had several hospitalizations devised a way to deal with some of the sadness for everyone in the family:

When Billy is in the hospital we do "Billy" projects—something that sort of "commemorates" him. During one hospitalization, I made a quilt. Every stitch I took in was filled with my thoughts and love for him. It was very therapeutic for me because it was a way of keeping him close. It gave me a way to deal with the fact that someone else was taking care of him. It also gave me something to tell him about on visits and phone calls. He would get all excited and want to know how far I'd gotten each time. He sleeps with that quilt now, and it's his prized possession.

We also do projects to give the same "therapy" to his sister, Jamie. For example, we each have scrapbooks for Billy that we work on during hospitalizations. We incorporate photos, drawings, thoughts, and all kinds of things. She gets very sad when we see something or go somewhere and Billy's not there. So I encourage her to take pictures for the scrapbook—anything that she wants to share with him. He loves feeling like she's his "eyes" on the outside. He gets a sense that he's with us always and that we've not forgotten about him.

Parents are often confused as to what to tell neighbors, friends, and schoolmates. Several parents mentioned how kind neighbors were and how meals appeared at their doorsteps nightly. But one mother said, "No one can help you if you keep it all secret. You just feel more isolated."

Not all parents will want the child's classmates to know what has happened, but classmates can't send cards and stuffed animals unless they know your child is in the hospital. It's very sad that stigma keeps such natural inclinations at bay, so a parent has to think long and hard how his or her child is going to take a lack of contact and warm wishes from friends while in the hospital, as well as the possible future teasing that could result from some children frightened about the thought of a psychiatric hospitalization. Much depends on you, your child, the teacher, and the community you live in. A mother whose daughter was hospitalized told us that her daughter's classmates sent a big poster on which all of them had signed their names and written little notes. "She put it up on the wall in her room and she was so proud," said the mother. "The nurses told me that this was the first time a child on the unit had received anything from his or her classmates."

Coming Home

A three-week hospitalization gives a medical staff time to titrate medications and stabilize a child. Unfortunately, today insurance companies want a child out of a hospital as soon as the child is nonpsychotic and seems less "a danger to self or others." Thus a family may have a child who is not stable coming home in six or twelve days.

Before the child comes home, however, the staff meets to determine a discharge plan. It is hoped that the staff has given this a lot of thought, and each child is not discharged simply to "home and therapist." Alternate levels of care should be explored with the parents: Would a partial hospitalization, a day school, intensive outpatient care, a residential placement, or a private school be more appropriate aftercare? Much will be determined by the parents' insurance or ability to fight for funding, but all alternatives should be explored and some kind of plan be detailed.

When the child does return home, it's best if the parents don't expect too much, or press their other children to turn the homecoming into a joyous celebration unless the sisters and brothers want to mark the return of their sibling that way. The family needs some time to get used to each other again and to let the harshness of the preceding crisis fade a bit.

PARTIAL HOSPITALIZATION

After a hospital stay, a partial hospitalization or day program is often the best step-down level of care for a child who has been in crisis. Also, if a child is not dangerous to "self or others," is not psychotic, does not need twenty-four-hour medication monitoring, and has a stable living environment, then a partial hospitalization is not an unreasonable option to pursue in lieu of a complete hospitalization.

Partial hospitalization is usually a day program where a child spends from four to six hours a day, three to five times a week, and receives some of the support and therapeutic benefits of a full hospitalization without being separated from his or her family.

Typically a child attends a partial hospitalization program for several weeks, or again, as long as the insurer authorizes the treatment option. Sometimes school districts pay for a day program if they do not have an appropriate placement available (see Chapter 10).

Each morning the child is seen for a medical evaluation; there also are group meetings, therapy, school, classes in coping skills, and recreational activities. The parents are usually involved in a weekly meeting with the child and the psychiatrist, and there is a communications log where the therapists report to the parents each afternoon and the parents write back about the events of the evening.

A mother of a young boy wrote about day hospitalization:

I had to put Robby in this kind of program when he was twelve. It was a "kinder, gentler" place. He was there Monday through Friday from 7:45 to 3:15. In addition to therapy, he had regular seventh-grade classes so the psychiatrist, the social worker, and the special ed teacher could all observe him in a real environment. I really had to fight my insurance company over this, but now they are believers.

Another level of care is an *intensive outpatient program* (IOP), sometimes referred to as a "partial-partial." This is a program that lasts two to three hours a day and often takes place after school. The child attends his or her own school most of the day, and then goes to the hospital to receive clinical services.

Parents should also investigate a new type of program known as a *subacute program.* This is overnight care that may provide respite for the child and the family and a very structured environment at a time when the child may still be fragile.

It has to be said: The insurers are going to want to see a reduction in services as quickly as possible, and the psychiatrist involved in the child's care will have to be very smart and persistent to make sure the child's interests are best served. A solid alliance between the parents and the psychiatrist is invaluable at all times, but especially during and after a crisis situation.

COMMITMENT LAWS FOR OLDER ADOLESCENTS OR "EMANCIPATED MINORS"

A parent of a young child or adolescent can simply sign commitment papers requesting psychiatric hospitalization. But at a certain age, and in certain circumstances, a young person is no longer considered a minor, and the commitment process becomes much more complicated. In most states, once a "child" reaches the age of eighteen or twenty-one, he or she is viewed by the law as having reached adult status; or if an adolescent has been living away from home for a certain period of time, he or she is regarded as an "emancipated minor." A fifteen-year-old girl who has given birth may be by definition a mother *and* an emancipated minor. And if that young adult or emancipated minor does not see the need for a psychiatric hospitalization, and the parents do, then the only recourse the parents have is to pursue an involuntary commitment.

And now we enter the very complicated world of commitment law and all its attendant guilt and furor.

The purpose of commitment law is to enable persons who are mentally ill to be hospitalized for treatment before they harm themselves or others, even if they do not believe they need treatment. Each state enacts its own legislation governing commitment, and the laws of each state are constantly changing.

Commitment laws actually rest on two legal foundations: (1) *parens patriae,* the right of the state to act as a parent and protect the well-being of a citizen who cannot care for him- or herself (this concept evolved from English common law, which held that the king was "father" of all his subjects); and (2) the right of the state to protect its citizens from a person who is dangerous. This means that if a person is so disabled that he or she cannot recognize the need for treatment, cannot provide for his or her own basic needs, or may otherwise be dangerous to him- or herself or to others, that person may be committed to a psychiatric treatment hospital for a specified period of time.

In the 1960s, however, civil libertarians focused on issues of freedom for individuals and pushed for tighter and tighter restrictions governing involuntary commitment. In 1975 a U.S. Supreme Court ruling dictated that a state cannot confine a patient who refuses voluntary hospitalization and who can manage outside a hospital alone, or with the help of family or friends. Thus states began to demand proof that a person is mentally disturbed and a danger to self or others.

Some states are a little more flexible and do not rely strictly on "dangerousness" criteria. (The *parens patriae* rationale still plays a part.) For example, the state of South Carolina says that a person can be committed if "he is mentally ill, and needs treatment because he (1) lacks sufficient insight or capacity to make responsible decisions with respect to his treatment, or (2) there is a likelihood of serious harm to himself or others." The chances of getting a commitment in a state such as this are greater than in New Hampshire, whose law has no such latitude and states that a "person must exhibit dangerousness to self or others."

But what proof demonstrates that a person is dangerous to self or to other people? The least stringent level of proof is "clear and convincing evidence," while the "beyond a reasonable doubt" level of proof demanded by states such as California, Kentucky, Massachusetts, New Hampshire, and Oregon makes commitment more difficult.

State law also dictates the procedure for initiating commitment. The following paragraphs describe the process in the state of New York, but the reader can check the procedure in his or her state by calling the admissions office or emergency room of the nearest hospital, by calling the police, or by contacting the county mental health association or the state's local NAMI chapter (see Resources on page 420).

In the state of New York, if a family member or responsible adult sees that a person is exhibiting conduct that is dangerous to self or others, he or she can try to get the person into a hospital either by calling the police or by going to the State Supreme Court and filing a petition for commitment. (The patient must have made a suicide attempt or have acted in a menacing fashion, such as punching people or harboring a weapon such as a knife; or the patient must be dazed or confused and seem unable to take care of him- or herself.) If the responsible adult calls the police and they fail to check out the situation (they more often do respond—and quickly), the responsible adult must go to the Supreme Court and file a petition (an affidavit), setting forth the reasons why this person needs to be hospitalized and why the person is a danger to self or others.

If the judge who hears the argument is convinced of its validity, a warrant is issued, and the police can then find the person and take him or her to the emergency room of a hospital for an evaluation. In order for the patient to be admitted, the evaluating psychiatrist must decide that the person is a danger to self or others. Within seventy-two hours, a second doctor must confirm that opinion or the patient is released. However, if the second doctor does confirm the need for hospitalization, the patient can be held under an emergency commitment status for a period not to exceed fifteen days. The patient is released at the end of this time unless the director of the hospital or the family petitions the court for a longer period of commitment.

If the person is still delusional or dangerous at the end of the fifteen days, his or her status can be converted to a longer-lasting commitment only when two psychiatrists sign a certificate and a family member or responsible adult living with the patient signs a petition requesting a longer commitment and outlines the reasons for doing so.

At any time, the patient has the right to go to court and contest the commitment. A mental health information lawyer represents him or her at a hearing held before a judge. (Usually a judge's chambers is located in the hospital.) The patient, family members, and examining psychiatrist testify at the hearing, and normal judicial rules of evidence and due process apply.

Today the national trend is toward making it easier to commit involuntary patients with psychiatric illnesses. Addressing the issue, the American Psychiatric Association has devised a model commitment law that would allow commitments not only when patients are dangerous to self and others but also when they are suffering and would likely deteriorate without treatment; in the presence of a major psychiatric illness that could be treated, provided the treatment is available; and when patients are incapable of deciding for themselves.

In the past few years Arizona, Delaware, Hawaii, Iowa, Oklahoma, New York, and South Carolina amended their laws and made it easier to commit a psychiatrically ill patient to a hospital.

It takes an enormous amount of stamina and courage to press for an involuntary commitment, but the relative who decides to do so needs to understand that he or she is probably the only person who stands between the patient and the dangers that exist during an acute phase of the illness. We have had patients write to us and tell us that once they became stable, they were grateful to the relative who took such a stand. One person who had been in a delusional state said: "If a family member won't take care of me when I'm in this condition, who will?"

We wish we could say that, with excellent treatment, a child will never need hospitalization. But the very nature of being a child—a growing person whose height and body weight and metabolic processes change daily—makes treatment a tricky proposition. In puberty, the cascade of estrogens, progesterone, luteinizing hormone, and gonadotropins can induce or inhibit genes that affect neurotransmission and neuropeptide systems and potentially make the adolescent more vulnerable to breakthrough episodes (episodes that occur despite treatment), or relapse. And most adolescents decide to stop taking their meds at least once, either because they are uncomfortable with the idea of being different or uncomfortable with the side effects, or they feel well and are convinced that they don't have a problem anymore. Hospitalizations may be needed to finetune the medications, to calm extreme agitation, or to prevent self-injurious behavior.

This is why we so strongly suggest that parents check their insurance policies and visit the hospitals in the networks of managed care companies. Then, if anything happens, the family is more comfortable with their decision. Naturally, the ideal would be complete stabilization at home, but hospitalization is not a sign of failure. Remember, the goal is not to avoid hospitalization so much as it is to keep the child alive and well.

The Insurance
Maze

We doubt that there's a person on the planet who, when asked the proverbial question "What do you want to be when you grow up?" answers enthusiastically: "I want to accumulate an absolutely enormous amount of knowledge about neurological brain disorders; I want to know as much about Section 504 of the law as any educational attorney; and I want the vocabulary of managed care to come so trippingly off my tongue as to astonish all those around me."

And yet the parents of a child with bipolar disorder must assimilate and master all this and much, much more.

These parents have an enormous burden: Life inside the home can be a virtual war zone; life outside the home seems fair game to the intrusion of strangers. September is a nightmare because the stresses of the school year begin; June is a nightmare because just as the stresses of the school year end, the unstructured, endless days of summer begin. . . . Nothing is simple; nothing can be taken for granted, and parents are always scrambling for new strategies and better solutions.

So to add financial strain, serious debt, and, in some cases, near financial ruin in order to pay for diagnostic consultations, weekly visits to psychopharmacologists and psychologists, neuropsychological testing, multiple medication trials of long-term and often costly prescriptions, and individual, couples, and family therapies seems downright unfair.

While there is much we can't change, we hope that this chapter serves to allay some of the anxiety and clear up the confusion about paying for this enormously expensive illness. After we discuss the sea change in the delivery of mental health care that arrived with managed care, we'll move into the world of public insurance. These discussions should help children get the services they need—even when it looks as if all avenues are closed. Built into the system are options and appeals and "unadvertised" financial support programs. In the following pages, we explore some of them as well as the economic realities of the mental health marketplace.

PRIVATE INSURANCE FOR MENTAL HEALTH CARE

Private medical insurance and all the plans that, for a premium, seek to cover doctor's fees and hospitalization fees are called *fee-for-service* plans. The insurance company underwrites some of the patient's health care, but it is the patient's responsibility to locate the doctor to supply it and then file the claims for reimbursement. The doctor determines the medical treatment, and the insurance company asks few questions. Once a person meets a *deductible,* the service is reimbursed; typically the insurance company covers 80 percent of the incurred medical fees; the patient, the remaining 20 percent.

But the provisions for mental illness in such plans has always been more restrictive than for "medical" illness. Insurance companies typically limit their risk by capping the dollar amounts of annual and lifetime mental health benefits; requiring preadmission certification for hospitalization; limiting services covered, often with incentives for outpatient care; charging higher copayment and deductible amounts; and excluding coverage for certain disorders. These practices are discriminatory, and people with serious psychiatric illnesses are often denied sufficient coverage and have few choices but to try to obtain treatment from public mental health services or even to go without treatment entirely.

Group policies that cover employees through their place of business, union, or professional organization are much less expensive and usually more generous than individual policies, but not always when it comes to psychiatric coverage. Often an employer can choose just how broad or limiting the psychiatric coverage might be, but the standard policy typically pays for twenty to thirty days per year of inpatient care and for perhaps $1,000 for outpatient consultation or counseling. Employees are used to paying for most of their own therapy bills themselves. (Due to stigma, many people never avail themselves of the little coverage offered because they refuse to process claims for mental health services through the company.)

And then there are preexisting illness clauses written into most policies. Questions such as "Have you or any named dependent within the past five years had any mental or physical disorder?" may eliminate benefits for a certain period of time or deny them completely.

So, it's good to keep in mind that psychiatric coverage never really had a "Golden Age." In almost all cases it was inadequate, but especially for someone with a chronic psychiatric disorder.

MANAGED CARE: A RADICAL CHANGE IN THE DELIVERY OF HEALTH CARE

Today some 85 percent of America's employees are enrolled in some kind of managed care program. It is a system of organizing, financing, delivering, and evaluating services that deliberately seeks to control costs while promising to deliver high-quality health care.

The original idea behind the health maintenance organization (HMO) concept was to have health insurance and health services integrated by the same organization, under the same roof. This system provides a follow-through on patient care and an emphasis on preventive care. HMO members pay a fixed monthly or quarterly premium and receive health care from a team of physicians, nurses, technicians, and other health professionals. This model for the delivery of health care eliminates deductibles, reimbursement forms, charges minimal copayments, and provides plenty of patients for doctors.

Today's managed care organizations are simply networks of independent physicians who are called *providers* and who sign on to panels and agree to direct a patient's treatment according to guidelines set by the managed care companies. The doctors are reimbursed according to a fee structure also set by the managed care company.

Why on earth would doctors agree to this system? Well, as employers thrilled to the idea that there might be a brake on skyrocketing costs of health care and signed contracts with managed care companies to provide health care for their employees, physicians not associated with these managed care networks lost the possibility of treating many of these patients. Most doctors simply decided to ride the horse in the direction it was going.

Moreover, managed care companies instituted a system known as *capitation*. They give doctors a fixed amount of money every month and guarantee them a certain income if the doctors agree to provide a range of services to a specified group of patients. If the patient never shows up, or if the doctor can provide the services for less than the capitation received, the doctor can keep the difference. If, however, the doctor provides more extensive services than the capitation covered, the doctor underwrites the difference.

But built into this system is an incentive to limit the range of services or watch profit margins slip to razor-thin proportions.

The balance of power has shifted from the physician to insurers. Insurers decide which tests financially (not medically) can be conducted, what kind of treatments may be offered, and how often those treatments can occur by limiting what they will pay for. And because many of today's managed care companies are "for-profit" organizations, insurers are looking to the bottom line and are answering to shareholders, not necessarily to the patient's needs or the doctor's medical opinion of these needs.

Some organizations forced doctors to sign (the now-infamous) "gag rules": Doctors were told not to inform patients of alternative treatment strategies or medication options if they were viewed as more expensive. Fortunately these restrictive practices are being regulated out of existence.

Not only are doctors chafing under this new system of care, but patients are extremely anxious about physician choice. If their doctor is not on the panel of the company that provides their benefits, then they must leave their physician in order to receive maximum reimbursement. Most managed care plans do have a *dual-option plan* that allows a patient to seek care outside the network, but the patient must pay deductibles and co-payments and claims are reimbursed at a far lower rate. And the specialist must be referred to by the *primary care physician* (the PCP) whom the patient accepts when he or she signs on for the insurance.

A PCP is typically a family practitioner or an internist who acts as a "gatekeeper" to a network of specialists. Managed care philosophy is that a patient should first see a generalist who can explore whether a patient really needs the attention of a more expensive specialist or further testing.

For example, under the old fee-for-service plans, a patient who was troubled by headaches could make an appointment with a neurologist of his or her choice. The neurologist, in turn, would probably order a brain scan and other expensive tests, and the patient would then submit the bills to the insurer for reimbursement.

The managed care company argues that the patient should see a generalist first—a doctor who knows and understands the patient—and who may determine that the headaches are caused by stress, by allergies, by the wrong eyeglass prescription, or by masked depression, and attempt to solve the problem with commonsense, low-tech, and certainly less costly solutions. If none of these possible causes is at the root of the problem, then the patient may be referred to a specialist.

This sounds good and reasonable until you learn that managed care companies are not fond of doctors who make too many referrals to specialists and spoil their profit picture. Since the doctor's referral rate is keenly watched by the managed care company, there is a subtle pressure to be very conservative with referrals to specialists. Access to care is a grave concern.

Another thorn in the health care professional's side is that he or she must answer to an employee of the managed care company—the *case manager*—who has nowhere near the physician's level of training and expertise and who questions the physician about his or her treatment plans based on formulas and company policies driven by economic considerations. Add to these intrusions the lack of confidentiality between doctor and patient that this system insists upon, endless paperwork, and often slow-paying methods of the managed care companies, as well as the fact that the reimbursement fees are far below doctors' customary fees (moreover an established authority in his or her specialty is reimbursed with the same fee as a doctor straight out of a residency-training program), and you have a group of disgruntled, demoralized people providing you with health care.

Oddly, the managed care companies have taken a combative stance with the very people who are the bedrock of their existence—doctors and patients. Many doctors are disenrolling from panels; some are leaving medicine entirely.

Patients are beginning to fear that while preventive care is handled nicely by managed care, a truly serious illness would find them fighting for their lives as well as their pocketbooks. A poll taken by *Time* magazine and CNN in July 1998 found that fewer than half of the people questioned were confident that their current managed care health plan would pay for treatment if things turned serious and expensive.

In the film *As Good As It Gets,* the mother played by Helen Hunt begins to rant about her asthmatic son's treatment under managed care. So many movie audiences cheered and burst into spontaneous applause that the professional association for managed care companies filmed a rebuttal ad in which they claimed that Helen Hunt's (fictional) son would have fared better in an HMO than a fee-for-service plan. Few multiplexes opted to screen the ad, however.

Something else is being lost in this bottom-line mentality. America's academic training and research center hospitals are in great jeopardy. Because these institutions are traditionally more expensive than nonacademic ones—due to their taking on the most severely ill patients and the costs of education—managed care companies tend to contract with the nonacademic hospitals for the sake of cost efficiency. Thus important centers of research and postgraduate training, which typically develop and offer more innovative treatments, are suffering financially, and parents with bipolar children often don't have the option of having their child hospitalized in such centers.

These days no one can afford to blink when observing the managed care revolution. As quickly as employers embraced the HMO models, this form of restricted care is being superseded in recent enrollments by the *preferred provider organization* (PPO) model. Members can go to doctors and hospitals outside of the network, but it costs them more. At least they don't have to be funneled through gatekeepers to specialists who may not be of their choosing.

There may be some good news in the mental health arena of managed care, referred to as "behavioral health care." Some of its benefits and philosophies (at least on paper) may be more advantageous than those offered in the fee-for-service policies.

For example, one recent Aetna-U.S. Healthcare policy we looked at allowed sixty days of hospitalization in a psychiatric unit (there was a choice of three hospitals in the area), and there was no lifetime cap on psychiatric inpatient days. Many families with fee-for-service policies have lifetime caps of $25,000 for mental health. Since children develop bipolar disorder early in life and may undergo several hospitalizations, the lifetime cap can be reached after one or two hospitalizations.

The lifetime cap on psychiatric benefits is something every family with a child with bipolar disorder needs to investigate. Thanks to the passing of the 1996 Mental Health Parity Act, all group health plans with fifty or more workers must equalize the annual and lifetime limits imposed on mental and physical health care. This means that if there is a $1 million lifetime cap on medical illness, then the theoretical lifetime cap on psychiatric hospitalization must be the same. But we hear stories of health plans limiting access in subtle ways. (This also means that companies with under fifty employees are exempt from this law, and companies that have opted to choose policies that have medical caps can legally have caps on mental health benefits also.)

While many policies offer about twenty outpatient office visits to a psychiatrist a year, a senior staff psychiatrist at Kaiser Permanente told us that medication visits (office visits where prescriptions are reviewed, renewed, or written) are unlimited. This is a vital benefit for families of children with early-onset bipolar disorder who will need medication and monitoring for such a long time.

Employees of U.S. Healthcare told us that their company offers a *conversion of benefits* provision. A policyholder can choose to convert inpatient days for outpatient psychotherapy visits as well as aggregate visits for family therapy. For example, if a family decides that family therapy is the most appropriate use of outpatient visits, they can utilize twenty visits of one family member, and then the twenty visits of the next, and so forth. Medical directors are aware that the people closest to the patient—the family—can suffer from stress-related medical illnesses, and they view family therapy as a preventive type of medicine.

This all sounds good, and the prescription coverage of most policies is a boon that cannot be underestimated, but the doctor who understands how to treat bipolar disorder in children is the cornerstone on which any quality of life for the child and the family rests. If possible, it is best to check which child psychiatrists are on the panel before signing on. Not only is it terribly difficult to find a child psychiatrist who understands this illness, but it's not clear how many of those who participate in a panel that reimburses them far below their customary fee do have such knowledge and skill.

How Does Your Policy Read?

Look carefully at the wording of any policy before or even after enrolling. (Even if you have no choice, it's important to imagine a future in which there might be a crisis or a need for extensive psychiatric care.) If a benefits package uses phrasing such as "adequate mental health care" or "care where medically necessary," find out what this means in the insurer's lexicon. Find out the answers to the following questions:

• Which child psychiatrists, pediatric neurologists, and psychologists are on the panel of this insurer? In other words, which doctors are "in-network"? What if none of these physicians has experience treating early-onset bipolar disorder? How will I be reimbursed if my child continues to see his or her out-of-network psychiatrist?

• Will the psychologist's bills be covered if there is no psychiatrist practicing in the same office?

• How many outpatient visits are allowed each year? If the visits are for medication monitoring, are they unlimited? At what point does the psychiatrist have to ask approval for additional sessions?

• For hospital care, what is the maximum amount of days and the dollar cap per year allowed by the policy? What is the lifetime cap, assuming that the company has less than fifty employees and is exempt from the Mental Health Parity Act?

• Should my child need psychiatric hospitalization, which hospitals in my area are in-network? If I go to the emergency room of an out-of-network hospital, will it be covered? How much of it will be covered? What if the hospitals are unsatisfactory to me?

• What is the prescription plan? Is there a limit on the number or total costs of medications each year? What is the charge if I choose brand-name medications over generic ones? (See discussion of the differences in Chapter 4.) Are expensive, nongeneric medications such as Risperdal, Zyprexa, and Clozaril on the list of approved prescription medicines (the formulary) that the health plan agrees to pay for? Is the child psychiatrist allowed to prescribe these expensive brand-name drugs, or must he or she get authorization from the managed care company beforehand? Will this approval be difficult to get and be frowned upon, adding to the doctor's discomfort and reluctance to prescribe?

• Does the plan offer alternative service options such as day treatment (partial hospitalization), residential care, or intensive outpatient care in time of crisis? How many days are usually covered?

• How do I appeal decisions and file a grievance if I am not satisfied with the decisions being made about the psychiatric care of my child or my child's access to care?

If you feel you're being denied access to care, each managed care company has a phone number to call and a procedure for initiating an appeal process. Consumers and physicians sit on the grievance committee. (And new legislation may provide the right to appeal a managed care decision by going to an outsider.) It's not unlikely that an appropriate request will be granted in the appeals process. Managed care companies are very concerned about consumer satisfaction because if valued employees are not happy, then the employer paying for the coverage is going to consider switching managed care companies when the contract comes up for review.

One mother (who said she was willing to go to any lengths to avoid confrontation) described her mother lioness behavior when it became important to face off with the managed care company in order to ensure the proper treatment for her twelve-year-old son. She said:

> We are in an HMO insurance plan and we live out of the network area. For our mental health benefits we were referred to a gatekeeper. The gatekeeper psychiatrist met with us for fifteen minutes and then referred us to a psychiatrist in their network. She was good with Daniel but was clueless as to what his problems were. She diagnosed him ADD and maybe depressed and put him on Ritalin and Adderall. BIG MISTAKE! He was soon out of control big time, and she said that she had done all she could and he needed a "higher level of care."
>
> At this point the insurance company wanted to send him to a psychiatric hospital in our area, but one that cared mostly for kids with drug problems.
>
> I threw the biggest fit and told them I was not putting a twelve-year-old on a unit with drug addicts. I refused to back down and kept going up their higher chain of command. I literally had to browbeat the insurance company into placing him in a child and adolescent psych center that I approved of. It wasn't an easy or pleasant thing to go through, but now the insurance company listens to me. Anytime Daniel needs something they won't provide, I start going up their chain of command again and they back off.
>
> I would advise people not to let an insurance company make them use a psychiatrist they are not comfortable with. (After all, it was the psychiatrist's incorrect diagnosis and prescription of Ritalin and Adderall that precipitated the mania and resulted in the need for hospitalization.) Never back off—it's our right and we are the ones paying for the insurance.

PUBLIC INSURANCE

People who work full time for a company that employs more than fifty people on its payroll usually receive health benefits through that company. But employees whose place of work has fewer than fifty people may have to purchase medical coverage for their families by themselves, at huge costs.

Self-employed workers also have to purchase their own policies. If they belong to a professional organization that offers a group health plan, most likely they can purchase coverage through that association, but the premiums to cover a family typically cost more than $650 a month. (Buying a single-family policy without benefit of a group is prohibitive for most families, in the range of $1,200 a month.)

What happens to people who don't work full time or who are out of work? How do these parents obtain medical insurance for their families? What if they had a child suffering with bipolar illness—how would they cover the phenomenal medical expenses?

Fortunately, the federal government—acting through state programs—provides money for public health insurance and disability insurance to those who can't afford private medical coverage and who qualify for these programs.

"Qualify" is the operative word here. There are strict guidelines governing the granting of the entitlement programs. First we'll discuss Medicaid and Medicaid waiver programs mandated by certain states that offer financial aid to children who have special needs. Then we'll explore the new children's insurance program that was passed by Congress in 1998. It is called the State Children's Insurance Program (SCHIP), and it expands health insurance to a great many uninsured children. Finally we'll discuss Supplemental Security Income (SSI), which is available for some children who are disabled by a psychiatric problem.

Medicaid

Medicaid is a federally mandated national program of medical assistance for people and families who have limited incomes. The program is financed by federal, state, and local taxes and administered by local public assistance programs. (Look in the telephone book under City Government Departments and scan down the sublistings until you find Social Services; or sometimes it's listed under Government and Community Services under the heading "Medicaid.")

The Medicaid program provides children with mental illnesses with a comprehensive benefits package. It covers diagnostic screening and assessment, psychological testing, psychotherapy, prescription drugs, lab tests, and hospitalizations (inpatient and partial as well as day treatment), and the family is not responsible for deductibles or copayments. The disadvantage of Medicaid is that it reimburses professionals and hospitals with very low fees. Consequently, many doctors and hospitals do not accept Medicaid patients, and most often a child will be hospitalized in a city, county, or state facility. (But as we mentioned in Chapter 13, that is not necessarily a bad thing.)

How does a family qualify for Medicaid? It's complicated. Children under the age of six whose family income is up to 133 percent of the national poverty level—and children born after September 30, 1983, whose family income is up to 100 percent of the poverty level now qualify for Medicaid in every state.

If the national poverty level for a family of four is $16,450, multiply that figure by 100 or 133 percent and you will arrive at the allowable family income that qualifies a family for Medicaid.

Certain income, assets, and possessions are excluded when determining the family's income: the home the family lives in and the land it's built on are not counted; the family car usually does not count either.

Once the family meets the poverty guidelines, the child has to be suffering with a disability that is on the Supplemental Security Income (SSI) medical listing.

Generally, the definition of "disability" for children requires that:

- A child have a physical or mental condition or conditions that can be medically proven and results in marked and severe functional limitations
- The medically proven physical or mental condition or conditions must last or be expected to last at least twelve months
- The child cannot be working at a job that is considered substantial work

So a child with a documented history of bipolar disorder should be able to obtain a Medicaid card if the family income and the clinical history meet the disability criteria requirements.

Every three years a child has a disability review, and, at the age of eighteen, the eligibility of the child is redetermined.

Medicaid's Home and Community Waivers and the Katie Beckett Story

Medicaid's limitations on income levels are quite rigid, but in some states there are exceptions to the rules. These exceptions are referred to as *waivers,* and they come into existence when a state applies for (and is granted) exemptions from the standard Medicaid regulations. In other words, waivers allow the state to provide services that are not available under the state Medicaid Plan.

These waivers are often referred to as Home and Community Waivers. In Maine, Wisconsin, Iowa, New Hampshire, and the District of Columbia they are called Katie Beckett Waivers.

According to Medicaid regulations, if a child is hospitalized or institutionalized for thirty consecutive days in a given month, the government begins to pick up the costs after that thirty-day period, no matter what the parents' income. But if a child goes home to be cared for by the family, all payments from the government cease if the parents' income exceeds the SSI eligibility guidelines.

In the early 1980s Katie Beckett, a young child in Iowa, was hospitalized on a respirator after contracting viral encephalitis. She was in the hospital for two and a half years when the doctors considered her stable enough to go home on the respirator, with her parents trained to care for her. But the Becketts were told that if Katie came home, their income would count against her for SSI and she would no longer be covered by Medicaid.

Her mother, Julie, sat down, did the math, and realized that it was costing over $200,000 a year to keep Katie in the hospital. With the proper medical equipment, however, Katie could come home, be surrounded by those who loved her, for about one-sixteenth of the costs accruing in the hospital. Julie Beckett also figured that if the Medicaid benefits stopped, they couldn't afford to care for their daughter.

This kind of bureaucratic idiocy made Julie Beckett very angry, and she decided to do something about it. She enlisted the help of her congressman, Tom Tauk, who took Katie's case to then–vice president George Bush, who was head of the Regulatory Reform commission. He spoke with President Reagan, who involved Surgeon General C. Everett Koop. In time, Medicaid waivers were created so that Katie and children like her can be at home with their families and their medical costs still be covered.

Thus one impassioned mother was able to change Medicaid law.

Taking their lead from this groundbreaking legislation, other states began to apply for Medicaid waivers. Some are named after Katie Beckett, for other children, or are simply called Home and Community Waivers. Some of the waivers address the needs of children with mental illness, but each state decides which ill population it wishes to serve. For instance, the state of Connecticut has a small Katie Beckett Waiver and has earmarked funds for elderly persons who might otherwise have to live in nursing homes.

You can call your local Medicaid office and ask if you qualify for such a waiver. These waivers are not advertised. Just ask: "What waivers do you have, and what populations do they serve?" You're looking for one that serves children with severe psychiatric disorders.

All families should know about a wonderful grassroots organization called Family Voices in Albuquerque, New Mexico. Family Voices is a network of families and friends speaking on behalf of children with special health care needs. The people at this organization can give you all the information about each state's waiver programs. They will tell you if you qualify, refer you to your state coordinator, and match you with a family that has applied for the Katie Beckett or Home and Community Waiver and who can guide you through the process. Contact Family Voices at 1-888-835-5669 or at www.familyvoices.org.

A mother from Maine applied for a Katie Beckett Waiver and faxed us a note about its benefits. She said:

We have private insurance and that is used first for Keith (my nine-year-old son). Katie Beckett picks up whatever our insurance doesn't cover. It pays for prescriptions. We get a monthly Medicaid card in the mail, and all I did was present his Medicaid card and number to the pharmacy one time and we were all set. I don't see any bills. I believe the pharmacy must bill Medicaid.

Katie Beckett will pay for services within your state. Our doctor is out of state, but we were able to get authorization from our local doctor stating that her expertise was not sufficient for the refractory nature of his disorder and that we needed to go to a research center specializing in the treatment of bipolar children. They allowed a six-month grace period and then asked that we find services in-state.

This waiver pays for all "services needed." It covers lab work and is currently paying for the treatment component of Keith's residential program.

You are supposed to bring your Medicaid card with you to the doctor, the hospital, and the pharmacy before receiving services. I just fill out our private insurance information, and there is always a slot for Medicaid and other insurance. Katie Beckett also paid for part of Keith's hospitalization last year; $2,000 wasn't covered by our private insurance and the waiver picked up the balance.

It was a lengthy financial application to apply for the waiver, and it took about six months to process the application, but it's definitely worth it, and I advise all parents to look into their state's waiver programs.

State Children's Insurance Program (SCHIP)

On August 5, 1997, Congress signed the Balanced Budget Law, which, among other things, created a new children's health program that purchases health insurance for uninsured children. The legislation became effective on October 1, 1997.

Each state has the opportunity to create its own children's health program or to expand its current Medicaid program. If the state does choose to create a new children's health program, it has enormous flexibility in defining the benefits covered, selecting health plans, using managed care, and setting payment rates, but each state's proposed plan must meet the requirements outlined in the law and be approved by the secretary of Health and Human Services.

While the basic benefit package must include inpatient and outpatient hospital services, physicians' surgical and medical services, lab and X-ray services, and well-baby and well-child care, it is not guaranteed that all states will profile plans that include mental illness benefits. Out of the thirty-eight state plans currently submitted, however, only the state of New York declined to pay for inpatient psychiatric services, although its mental health benefits covers twenty outpatient visits a year, prescription drugs, and emergency medical services.

SCHIP is a program designed for the working poor—for people whose incomes are somewhere between 150 and 300 percent of the poverty level. Again, if the national poverty level for a family of four is $16,450, then a family in the state of South Carolina (a 150 percent state) must make less than $24,675 to qualify; while a family in the state of Missouri (a 300 percent state) must make less than $49,350 to qualify. (We have heard repeatedly that some people with children suffering with bipolar disorder look carefully at a state's SCHIP before taking a job in that state. For a family without private insurance, and with one or two children with bipolar disorder, this decision is not something to treat lightly.)

To check on your state's plan and get eligible children enrolled in SCHIP, call toll-free at 1-877-KIDSNOW (543-7669), or go online www.insurekidsnow.gov/.

Supplemental Security Income (SSI)

Supplemental Security Income (SSI) is a federal program that provides financial and medical assistance to children under the age of eighteen who are blind or who have a severe disability or chronic illness and who are financially needy. In 2002 children who were eligible received close to $545 a month (and more in the states that supplement this federal benefit; for instance, the state of Massachusetts will contribute an additional $100 per month). A child qualifies solely because of need, and naturally the more money the family makes, the smaller the check will be. But once a child receives even one dollar a month from SSI, he or she always receives free health care through Medicaid.

And it's the Medicaid benefits that are so important to the parents of a bipolar child. In thirty-two states as well as the District of Columbia, a child eligible for any amount of SSI is enrolled in Medicaid. In Alaska, Idaho, Kansas, Nebraska, Nevada, New Mexico, Oregon, and Utah, children who qualify for SSI are automatically enrolled in the Medicaid program, but the parents must fill out a separate application to apply for the benefits.

The other eleven states—Connecticut, Hawaii, Illinois, Indiana, Minnesota, Missouri, New Hampshire, North Dakota, Ohio, Oklahoma, and Virginia—do not automatically enroll children in Medicaid, but once the children qualify for SSI, they typically go on to qualify for Medicaid.

Once a child has been diagnosed as having bipolar disorder, it is not hard to document that the child is disabled and "has marked and severe functional limitations" from a mental condition, and that the condition is expected to last at least twelve months. Social Security has a "Listing of Impairments" that are laid out in its book *Disability Evaluation Under Social Security*. On pages 179 through 181, they list the criteria for mood disorders in children with a requirement that a number of symptoms be present to meet the impairment. A child with bipolar disorder would meet every one of the criteria listed, so the impairments of early-onset bipolar disorder will not be in dispute (especially if all records of hospitalization, time lost from school, and documentation from doctors are included with the application), but it's the financial piece of the picture that is very complicated and takes a bit of explaining.

Financial Eligibility
If a child with bipolar disorder lives with parents or stepparents who do not receive SSI themselves, Social Security counts the parents' income and resources, then subtracts certain types of resources and income. The resources that are not counted are:

- The family home and the land it sits on
- Personal belongings, furniture, and other household goods worth up to $2,000
- A car
- Life insurance policies that, combined, have a cash surrender value of less than $1,500; a pension fund or Individual Retirement Account; and property needed for work, such as farmland and equipment

Not counted as income are:

- Benefits received by other family members, such as welfare payments, SSI, and veteran's pensions
- Food stamps and housing or home energy assistance
- Foster care payments
- One-third of child support payments received
- Grants or loans for education

So what does count as income? Any wages, salary, or tips paid to family members through employment by others or for themselves (earned income) and any monies that don't come from employment. This includes a portion of child support, veteran's benefits, interest, unemployment, or workers' compensation, and most public benefits.

The chart that follows should give an idea of the maximum amount of monthly earned and unearned income parents can have to be eligible for SSI benefits for their child. Two parents with two children—one with bipolar disorder and one without—can earn about $37,500 a year before their child would become ineligible, and more than that amount in states that provide supplements.

Income Eligibility

Parents' maximum monthly income for a child with a disability to be eligible for at least $1 of SSI. (The dollars are for 2002. They change each year to reflect inflation.) **The maximum levels are higher in states that supplement SSI.**

COUNTABLE *EARNED* MONTHLY INCOME

Number of Other Children with No Disability in the Household	When Eligibility Ceases	
	One-Parent Household	Two-Parent Household
0	$2,305	$2,849
1	$2,577	$3,121
2	$2,849	$3,393
3	$3,121	$3,665

COUNTABLE *UNEARNED* MONTHLY INCOME

Number of Other Children with No Disability in the Household	When Eligibility Ceases	
	One-Parent Household	Two-Parent Household
0	$1,130	$1,402
1	$1,402	$1,674
2	$1,674	$1,946
3	$1,946	$2,218

Note: The monthly limit for either type of income increases by $272 for each additional child with no disability in the household.

What Kind of Financial Proof Does Social Security Require?

If it looks as if the child will qualify for SSI, the parent should go to the local Social Security office or call Social Security at 1-800-772-1213 between 7:00 A.M. and 7:00 P.M. on weekdays. Try to avoid Mondays and the first week of every month, because they are very busy.

A parent needs to bring the following items and documentation when filling out the forms and talking with the Social Security worker:

- Child's Social Security number.
- Child's birth certificate or proof of age.

- Information about the family's income and resources: payroll slips, income tax return of the year before, bank books, insurance policies, and car registration.
- Medical records and documents from doctors' offices and hospitals that detail the child's condition and limitations.
- Reports from any provider who has worked with the child in the past year: psychiatrists, psychologists, therapists, social workers, teachers, etc. (Ask providers to submit short written reports with their formal records. In these reports they should list specific examples of the child's medical, mental, and functional limitations.)
- Any charting of the illness the parent has recorded (see Chapter 5).

All of this information will be sent to an examiner at the state Disability Determination Service. This examiner may call or write for more information, and it should be supplied as quickly as possible. It is not unusual for a psychological exam to be scheduled also.

Typically it takes six months for a determination of disability to be made. If the child qualifies, a letter will come in the mail and the SSI payments will be paid retroactively back to the first day of the month after the parent filed the application.

Appeals

If the child is not considered eligible, a parent has sixty days to appeal to the next level of decision making. There is a form that requests reconsideration, and it should be filed immediately. Any new reports about the child's condition should be submitted with the reconsideration request.

If the answer is still "no," the parent should not give up. The next step is a hearing before a Social Security Administrative Law Judge (ALJ). This is the only chance to meet with the person who will reconsider the decision made about the disability. Parents should know that ALJs reverse more than half of all denials. It is advisable to bring a trained advocate or lawyer to this informal hearing. The local legal aid or bar association or the state Protection and Advocacy agency can usually supply a lawyer. (Call 202-408-9514 to find the state P&A agency; or check its website at www.protectionandadvocacy.org.) Witnesses such as doctors, teachers, social workers, therapists, and friends can testify and discuss the child's functional limitations at this hearing.

If the child is found not eligible at this level of appeal, a parent has sixty days to request a review by the Social Security Appeals Council, and from there the matter can go to a federal court.

Once a child is found eligible, his or her case is reviewed and reevaluated every three years.

As we were writing this chapter, we often needed to call government agencies (or to find out which government agencies we should call). We spent whole days listening to recorded messages prompting us to select any of a number of options, only to feel that we'd simply gone around in circles. When we did link up finally with a helpful person, all the "Title-this" and "Title-that" programs and the unfamiliar phrasing of the laws and regulations were hard to grasp. And no sooner had we nailed down one piece of information than we were told that each state had its own regulations or that legislation was pending that would amend that rule or limit that program or, in the case of SCHIP, expand that program. One young woman in charge of a Connecticut Entitlement Program finally said: "You want 'one-stop shopping' and it just doesn't exist in the world of insurance."

But it does, sort of, we came to find. There *are* grassroots organizations that are willing and able to guide the consumer through the maze of insurance and to help parents get their children the medical care they need. The day we stumbled across Family Voices on the Internet and called their number in New Mexico, we felt as if we'd come in from the cold. Finally we'd found an organization that knew every state Medicaid waiver and was set up to help a family apply for those as well as for SSI benefits if they qualified. And it's comforting to think that an organization like NAMI can also offer guidance and direction.

You are really not alone; but you will need patience and a lot of persistence. New and dense and difficult subjects take getting used to. After some exposure a few things make sense, and in a while more things make sense, and one day soon you'll be speaking the lingo so well you'll be able to explain it knowledgeably to someone else. Best of all, armed with a newfound understanding of the system and your rights, you'll be able to advocate for your children and get them the treatment they need and are entitled to have.

PART IV

Life Goes On

Agenda
for the Future

The year we spent on the BPParents listserv not only gave us a rare view of the day-to-day lives of hundreds of families with bipolar children but allowed us to watch the arc of emotional growth that these parents were experiencing. When these mothers and fathers first introduced themselves to the group, you could sense how tentative they were—how hard it was for them to step out and tell their stories. Many wrote how relieved they felt to find out that they weren't the only parents whose children were having these problems. (For years they'd thought they were all alone.) They felt blamed by others for their child's illness, intimidated by mental health professionals, and totally confused about the medications and their side effects. Most were angry at managed care companies and all the "ifs, ands, or buts" of the policies surrounding psychiatric care. All were mystified by the laws that governed accommodations in schools.

Months later, however, these parents were reaching out to welcome other newcomers to the listserv, eager to share the information they'd gained from sitting down every day and reading 175 posts; purchasing and reading the recommended books; and searching for—and absorbing—article after article in the professional literature. We were watching these parents turn into fledgling advocates.

What impressed us time and time again was that these people were on the front lines of a war inside their own homes, getting little support from the outside world, yet wanting to turn a nightmare into something shining and good by helping others in the same situation.

These parents want to channel their anger and energy in a direction that will create a better future for their children and others like them. Currently their "voices" exist only on screens in cyberspace (and now in the pages of this book), but they are beginning to be heard in their own communities. Soon they will make inroads beyond. As one woman put it, "I am now so knowledgeable about early-onset bipolar disorder that I've gone from shaking my head to nodding my head; and now I'm going to find a place to direct all this anger and knowledge and sorrow."

When Tomie Burke invited us to become members of the listserv, we opted not to post directly to the group because we did not want to intrude on this special community. As we read through the seasons of their year, however, we were able to hear time and time again what these parents need and want and are beginning to advocate for. A national agenda could be discerned among the blizzard of pages we downloaded from their daily postings over a twelve-month period, an agenda that requires the talents and energies of physicians, mental health professionals, policy makers, educators, and all family members to highlight areas of neglect and develop models of treatment, research, services, information, and advocacy. Such a national agenda would help ensure a better future for all children suffering with bipolar disorder.

Parents Want a Quicker Diagnosis and Less of a "Wait-and-See" Attitude

Parents want mental health professionals to leave the *DSM-IV* on the bookshelf and make the diagnosis based on current understanding of how early this illness can onset and how different it appears from the adult form of the disorder. They want doctors to take a long, hard look at the family history and at the subtle signs of a developing mood disorder—to recognize that this illness has myriad symptoms that can look like other childhood psychiatric disorders—and to intervene quickly and knowledgeably with medications that *will not worsen the course of the illness*. They want the residency training programs and the continuing medical education programs to begin to teach what is already published in the psychiatric literature and is becoming increasingly obvious in the psychiatric research community. In short, they want doctors to practice medicine based on today's findings, not yesterday's myths.

Parents Want the DSM-IV *Updated to Reflect the Realities
of Early-Onset Bipolar Disorder*
Until the editors of *DSM-IV* form some kind of emergency committee
and amend the criteria for mood disorders in children, diagnosis, research,
and clinical treatment is going to founder on the shoals of outdated and
skewed information. When diagnosing early-onset bipolar disorder, doctors should look to Dr. Barbara Geller's modified KIDDIE-SADS developed at and available from Washington University in St. Louis, or at the
K-SADS-PL, developed at the University of Pittsburgh and available via
the Internet at www.wpic.pitt.edu.

*Parents Want the Mental Health Professionals to Regard Them
as Collaborators on the Treatment Team for Their Children*
They do not want to be blamed or told that they are "overinvolved." They
want doctors to anticipate their questions and needs, and recognize that
the parents are the on-site experts who are responsible for administering
all the medications, watching carefully for side effects, and dealing with
the child on a twenty-four-hour basis.

They do not want to hear: "I'll call you if there's a problem with the
lithium level; you don't need to know it." *These parents need to know it.*
They are charting their sons' and daughters' course of illness, and they
will likely need to make corrections in the treatment plan with that doctor or another. Would a doctor tell a parent of a child with cancer "You
don't need to understand the treatment"? We think not.

*Parents Want All Doctors—Whether Psychiatrists, Neurologists,
or Pediatricians—to Know About New Treatment Trials*
Some children will not respond—or will respond only partially—to commonly prescribed medications. Their parents need to know what other
options exist in the psychiatric research community. They need doctors to
look for and learn about any new protocols that may help their children.

*Parents Want Managed Care Companies to Stop Placing Limitations
on Access to Care*
They want managed care companies to understand that when their children are at risk for suicide, they need immediate hospitalization. They do
not want to be told: "She's only slightly suicidal, so we can't admit her."
(One mother read that story on the listserv and shot back, "Oh, and if she
kills herself, will she be only slightly dead?")

They want the parity laws spoken about in Chapter 14 to be adhered to so that families do not "max out" on their insurance benefits. They want the government to take a closer look at the subtle ways mental illness discrimination is being practiced all over the land and access to care is being denied.

Managed care companies, parents, and doctors who treat these children know that it takes weeks to stabilize a child, not four "preauthorized" days. Doctors are not being allowed to use their best judgment; often they are forced to plead for authorization for a few more days of hospitalization. That is an untenable situation for a physician to be in. More often then not, all efforts fail, and these children are sent home sick and unstable, only to return to the hospital several days or weeks later. In between, the parents are playing ER at home with a child in crisis, at a soul-crushing cost to the family.

Parents Want More Research Focused on This Devastating Illness of Early Childhood

In 1997 the total NIMH budget was $700 million. Of that, $32.5 million went to research on bipolar disorder and a paltry $8.8 million went to child and adolescent bipolar disorder research. This is an appallingly small amount of money to fight an illness that is destroying children and entire families. In 2001, this research budget was increased to $18.1 million. Hardly sufficient.

Stepping into the breach are two foundations: the Stanley Medical Research Institute (SMRI) and the National Alliance for Research on Schizophrenia and Depression (NARSAD).

The Stanley Medical Research Institute funds research directly related to the causes and treatment of bipolar disorder. Today the foundation supports eleven research programs. One is a multisite Bipolar Disorder Treatment Outcome Network; the other is a program called the Early Intervention Initiative, which is collecting data from families all over the country and attempting to determine early intervention protocols for the treatment of bipolar children. SMRI publishes the *Bipolar Network News,* a free quarterly newsletter detailing its research findings. (See Resources for information on how to get the newsletter.)

In its first fifteen years of grant making, NARSAD has awarded $120 million to scientists on the faculty or staff of 175 universities and medical research institutions around the world. NARSAD is dedicated to the idea that all funds solicited go exclusively for research grants. In other words, a dollar donated is a dollar spent on scientific research. (See Resources for NARSAD's address and phone number.)

The recently launched Juvenile Bipolar Research Foundation is solely dedicated to funding research that will advance our knowledge about childhood-onset bipolar disorder. Current areas of study include diagnosis and phenomenology, neuroimaging, neuropsychology, molecular genetics studies, chronobiology, and neuroendocrine studies (see Resources for JBRF's address and website).

Parents Want More Outreach to, and Education for, Families Struggling with This Disorder

Several national organizations are addressing these issues; all addresses and phone numbers are in the Resources section.

In 1999, just as we were readying the manuscript of the first edition for publication, a group of parents and one physician who met on Tomie Burke's BPParents listserv founded the Child and Adolescent Bipolar Foundation. True to its mission, the foundation offers a great deal of information, support, and advocacy for families with children suffering with early-onset bipolar disorder.

In the winter of 2002, the National Alliance for the Mentally Ill created the Child and Adolescent Action Center to focus attention on systems of care reform and to help young families in need. The Center intends to drive the debate on child and adolescent psychiatric illness system reform, ensure improved treatment outcomes for children and adolescents by advancing evidence-based practices, and provide outreach to underserved populations, among other agendas. A free quarterly newsletter called *Because Kids Grow Up,* offers up-to-date information on legislation, research, and treatments, as well as model programs that help families cope.

The National Mental Health Association has 340 affiliates around the country. The NMHA advocates on the state and federal level with the juvenile justice system and for juvenile justice legislation, and is responsible for several initiatives that focus on children's mental health. Three years ago it launched Mental Health Awareness Week, which occurs the first week in May.

The National Depressive and Manic-Depressive Association, which has over eight hundred affiliates in the United States, is an organization of individuals who have been diagnosed with depression or manic-depression and their family members. Many of the affiliates are beginning to start groups for the parents of bipolar children and adolescents. NDMDA publishes a newsletter, runs a national bookstore, and is a good source of information and referral.

Parents Want Schools to Educate Teachers and Other Staff About This Disorder

Because so many students are suffering from mood disorders, there should be annual educational seminars for teachers, psychologists, guidance counselors, and administrators to raise awareness about these disorders. Model IEPs—taking into consideration periods of depression and activation—should be developed and implemented. Bipolar students should have a place to go to pull themselves together and a person on staff who understands what they are going through. Social skills programs should be offered.

Parents Desperately Need a Greater Choice of Smaller, Therapeutic Schools That Would Be Appropriate for Children with Bipolar Disorder

There are far too few specialized schools and programs, often long bus rides away, and far too many waiting lists. Bipolar children do not belong in classes with children whose IQs are far below theirs; nor do they belong in classes with juvenile delinquents. New programs are going to have to be instituted.

Parents Want Drug Prevention Programs in Schools Tailored to Their Children

Students in middle school should be taught about the risks of addiction. Parents want the programs to incorporate the findings that people with bipolar disorder are vulnerable to becoming addicted to substances like alcohol or drugs.

Parents Want Twice-Yearly Screening for Suicide Beginning in the Fourth Grade

Trudy Carlson, author of *The Life of a Bipolar Child,* is lecturing all over the country, proposing that there be biannual screenings for depression and bipolar disorder to identify children at risk. Her well-taken point is that schools routinely screen for vision, hearing, and scoliosis problems. Yet with millions of children suffering from undiagnosed mood disorders, and an estimated five thousand teen and preteen suicides annually in the

United States, there is no screening to identify these at-risk children and adolescents.

Ms. Carlson feels that a simple paper-and-pencil test would bring the problems into high relief for educators and the students themselves, and that programs could be set up to help these students get treatment. She recommends the Birleson Screening Instrument for fourth to sixth graders (it is in the public domain and is easily scored) and the Burns Depression Checklist for middle school and high school students.

Parents Do Not Want the Juvenile Justice System to Become the Hospitals of the Future

Because many states have slashed budgets for adolescent psychiatric hospitals and managed care makes it so difficult to hospitalize an adolescent, and because adolescents with bipolar disorder and conduct disorder act out so many of their problems, there's a good chance that the only place they can be "parked" is in jail. Adolescents do *not* belong in juvenile detention centers. Communities and policy makers must make major efforts to create more child and adolescent psychiatric units in general hospitals. Parents are going to have to survey their communities, identify the services lacking, and start fighting to get them in place. The Federation of Families is working to create wrap-around services that bring together families, personnel from child welfare, juvenile justice, and the school system, who, as a team, help devise an integrated plan that fits the needs of the child and the family and keeps the child in the community. Federation of Families has a program that trains people to deliver these integrated systems of care.

It is a huge agenda, and one that has been jump-started by parents and family members. Organizations like NAMI, the National Mental Health Association, and the National Depressive and Manic-Depressive Association have been advocating on behalf of the mentally ill for years, but only recently with a focus on children with psychiatric disorders. The ranks of such organizations need to be swelled by these families so that legislators listen even more carefully to their concerns.

Closing Thoughts

We wish our readers could see the hundreds of emails and letters that parents from all over the country sent helping us to better understand the problems that bipolar children and their families face. We have been inspired by their dedication to their children and their heroic efforts to find solutions. We are in awe of these children who get up each morning and struggle through each day, knowing—and also never really knowing—how a day can unfold. We have felt privileged to have been a part of this community.

A few months ago a new member of the BPParents listserv composed the following song in tribute to parents struggling with bipolar children. She prefaced it by saying: "I have always found that by writing I can get through almost anything. The only thing I could not write about was my relationship to my son due to this illness. Joining this group has changed that and I want to say thanks to all of you. I wrote this song for us. Each and every one of us. I hope that at some point, maybe, it will help someone get through a rough time."

With the permission of the composer Dianne MacKenzie, we reprint a section of it here.

Keepers of the Storm

We have watched the seasons change, within a single day,
We've seen their searing heat succumb—to lonely skies of winter's
    gray.
We have seen their silver lining fade before our eyes.
Clouds with scorched and blackened edges scattered in the skies.

Lightning out of nowhere, storms that rage within.
Dreamscapes filled with terror, nightmares never end.
Heaven lies before them, submerged in fiery flames.
Calling through the silence, we hear them speak our names.

For we are the watchers,
The keepers of the storm.
We have tamed the lightning,
Protecting them from harm.
Ever standing sentry,
Holding back the rains,

Sheltering their wearied souls,
From thunder's harsh refrain.
Dams that won't be broken,
We detain the flooding tides.
A vigil left unspoken,
Until the front subsides.

We hope the day comes soon when these children can run and play and swing on swings that have *nothing* to do with shifts in moods. When parents can rejoice in the great creativity this illness can confer but can watch a child grow with stability, reaching toward a future that is bright, filled more with sunlight than threatening clouds.

This will happen only if we *all*—researchers, doctors, parents, educators, drug companies, journalists, and policy makers—get involved and make these children's future a national public health priority. We need to reach, so they can reach. We need to reach, so they can soar.

The Bipolar Child
Questionnaire

This questionnaire was displayed on the website Parents of Bipolar Children, and copies were distributed by the leaders of NAMI Child and Adolescent Support Groups and through mental health professionals in our network. The symptom checklist, provided in Chapter 3 of this book, was attached.

Age _____

Date of birth _____

Current grade level _____

Are you the child's mother, father, or other? _____

Child's current psychiatric diagnosis _____

State of residence _____

Age and sex of siblings _____

1. How old was your child when you first noticed any behavioral symptoms (for example, temper tantrums, night terrors, excessive clinginess, separation anxiety, hyperactivity, rapid speech, periods of sadness, periods of irritability or elation, obsessive thoughts)? Please describe what you observed.
2. What did you think these symptoms represented? What did your family, friends, or even strangers tell you they represented?

3. Did any school professionals suggest that your child receive a psychological or psychiatric evaluation? Which school professional made the recommendation? What did he or she think the diagnosis might be? How old was your child at the time?

4. At what age did your child first see a mental health professional? Did you see a social worker, psychologist, psychiatrist, pediatric neurologist, or other? What were the conclusions reached at that evaluation? Were medications prescribed? If yes, which ones? Did the mental health professional inquire about a possible family history of psychiatric illness or alcohol and/or substance abuse?

5. Is there a history of alcohol or substance abuse in the family? If yes, who has the problem?

6. Do you or your spouse suffer with any of the following psychiatric disorders?
Mother: depression, manic-depression (bipolar disorder), phobias, OCD, panic disorder
Father: depression, manic-depression (bipolar disorder), phobias, OCD, panic disorder

7. Do you or your spouse take psychotropic medications? If so, who is taking them, and which ones have been effective?

8. Have you or your spouse ever been hospitalized for depression, mania, or a mixed state?

9. Does anyone on either side of the family have recurrent depression or manic-depression? If yes, who has the illness (e.g., maternal or paternal grandmother or a maternal or paternal uncle, sibling, etc.).

10. Have there been any suicides in the family? Please specify.

11. Were you aware that manic-depression (bipolar disorder) can be manifested in childhood?

12. Did you or your spouse experience symptoms of a mood disorder or any other psychiatric condition in childhood? Please specify.

13. Were you or your spouse ever afraid to have children because of a personal or family history of mood disorders? If yes, please explain.

14. Did you worry about and/or watch your children uneasily?

15. Before your child received any medications, how would you describe your child's behavior in the classroom? Did the child have attentional problems? Did the child fidget and not sit still? Did the child skip school or disregard authority? Did he or she at-

tempt to be the class clown? Was it hard for your child to make and sustain peer relationships?

16. Please describe what problems your child may have had with peer relationships.

17. Does your child have any learning disabilities? If yes, please specify.

18. Was your child ever put on Ritalin or another stimulant? Who prescribed the medication? How did your child respond to the medication?

Attention:	Improved	No change	Became more distractible
Mood swings:	Improved	No change	Mood swings increased
Hyperactivity:	Decreased	No change	Increased

If the behavior of the child worsened after treatment with Ritalin or another stimulant, please describe what you observed.

19. If your child was initially diagnosed as depressed, was antidepressant medication prescribed?

Which one(s)?

If yes, how did he or she respond?

| Mood improved | No change in mood | Mood swings increased |
| Became more aggressive | Had trouble sleeping | Other (please specify) |

If the behavior of the child worsened after treatment with an antidepressant, please describe what changes in behavior you observed.

20. If your child was diagnosed with bipolar disorder, was he or she placed on a mood stabilizer such as lithium or Depakote or some other medication(s) in combination or alone? If yes, please detail the type of medications, the maximum daily dose, the length of the trial, and the response.

21. Once your child was diagnosed with bipolar disorder, how did you and your spouse initially react to the diagnosis? Did you seek a second opinion? How did you feel about putting your child on medication?

22. What was the original episode of illness? Depression or hypomania or mania? What was the duration of the first episode? What is the episode frequency pattern now? Full episode within a 24- to 48-hour period? Full episode within a week? One episode per month? Four or more full episodes per year? One episode per year?

23. How would you describe your child's daily activity level? (For example, difficult to arouse in the morning and increasingly active at night?) Is there a discernible pattern? If so, please describe.

24. Were the child's educators supportive? What did they say or do?

25. How did you explain the illness to your child? How did you explain the illness to his or her siblings?

26. How has the illness changed the relationship between the child and his or her siblings? How has the illness affected the family as a whole?

27. How did you and your family attempt to deal with your child's difficult behaviors? Were any measures particularly effective?

28. Were there any stressors (such as a job loss, a move to another community, marital difficulties, or a death in the family) that affected your family in the year prior to the emergence of symptoms in your child? If so, please describe.

29. Has any form of talking therapy been recommended for your child? If yes, what kind (individual, family, group, other)? How has it been helpful?

30. What in your opinion constitutes a good doctor? What would you advise someone to look for?

31. Would a support group for parents of children with bipolar disorder be helpful? Why? If you belong to a support group, how does it help?

32. Is there anything you would especially like to say to us, or any issues you hope will be covered in this book?

33. About early-onset bipolar disorder: What do you know now that you wish you had known when the illness first manifested itself in your child?

Resources

ORGANIZATIONS
The Juvenile Bipolar Research Foundation
49 S. Quaker Hill Road, Pawling, NY 12564
email: info@bpchildresearch.org
http://www.bpchildresearch.org

Child and Adolescent Bipolar Foundation (CABF)
1187 Wilmette Avenue, # PMB 331, Wilmette, IL 60091
847-256-8525
http://www.bpkids.org

NDMDA (National Depressive and Manic-Depressive Association)
730 N. Franklin Street, Suite 501, Chicago, IL 60610
1-800-82-NDMDA
http://www.ndmda.org

NAMI (The National Alliance for the Mentally Ill)
200 N. Glebe Road, Suite 1015, Arlington, VA 22203-3754
703-524-7600/FAX: 703-524-9094
1-800-950-NAMI
http://www.nami.org.
For newsletter *Because Kids Grow Up,* contact Monique Lewis: monique@nami.org

The Stanley Foundation Bipolar Network
5430 Grosvenor Lane, Suite 200, Bethesda, MD 20814
1-800-518-7326
http://www.bipolarnetwork.org

NARSAD (National Alliance for Research on Schizophrenia and Depression)
60 Cutter Mill Road, Suite 404, Great Neck, NY 11021
516-829-0091
http://www.narsad.org

The National Mental Health Association
2001 N. Beauregard Street, Alexandria, VA 22311
1-800-969-NMHA
http://www.nmha.org

Federation of Families
1021 Prince Street, Alexandria, VA 22314
703-684-7710
http://www.ffcmh.org

Family Voices
3411 Candelaria NE, Suite M, Albuquerque, NM 87107
1-888-835-5669
email: kidshealth@familyvoices.org
http://www.familyvoices.org

Lithium Information Center
c/o Madison Institute of Medicine
P.O. Box 628365, Middleton, WI 53562-8365
608-827-2470/FAX: 608-827-2479

INTERNET RESOURCES
The Bipolar Child (website of Demitri Papolos, M.D., and Janice Papolos)
http://www.bipolarchild.com
In-depth information about the disorder, noteworthy email newsletter, model IEP, bookstore, the Bipolar Child Questionnaire, and authors' contact page and lecture schedule.

Juvenile Bipolar Research Foundation (JBRF)
http://www.bpchildresearch.org
Information about juvenile bipolar disorder, descriptions of foundation-sponsored research, screening questionnaires, professional listservs for physicians and therapists treating the children, Grand Rounds Program (bimonthly online clinical case conferences with parental questions addressed by international experts), discussion forums for parents and educators.

Child and Adolescent Bipolar Foundation (CABF)
http://www.bpkids.org
Important interactive website offers online support groups (including Tomie Burke's BP-Parents), chat rooms, message boards, learning center, database of professional members and local support groups, resource page with information on Social Security, drug database, and international resources.

BPSO
http://www.BPSO.org (click on Children and Adolescent icon)
Internet support group for people in relationships with someone who has a bipolar disorder (children, parents, siblings, spouses, etc.).

Pendulum Resources
http://www.pendulum.org

McMan's Depression and Bipolar Web
http://www.mcmanweb.com
This site contains nearly two hundred highly readable articles, including articles on early-onset bipolar disorder. Online weekly newsletter presents the latest research to new therapies to social and legal issues to book and movie reviews. Available on a subscription basis, but go to website for free samples.

Dr. Ivan Goldberg's Site
http://www.psycom.net/depression.central.html

National Library of Medicine
http://www.nlm.nih.gov/medlineplus
Free access to Medline, where over four thousand biomedical journals are archived. Click on "Other Resources" and then on "MEDLINE" to conduct a search of articles dating back to the 1960s. Some full-text articles are available; others are abstracts. Refine your search by using Boolean operator "and." For instance, if you search "lithium" and "neuroprotection" and limit the search from 1996 to 2002, ten references appear.

Teaching LD.Org
http://www.teachingLD.org
The new website for the Division of Learning Disabilities for the Council of Teaching Exceptional Children, this should be a great resource for teachers who are working with children with bipolar disorder. Not only are there general discussion bulletin boards, but the site features information on research-based teaching strategies and approaches and interviews with experts in all aspects of learning disabilities. Particularly helpful to teachers with questions about the best way to work with bipolar children is the "Find a Colleague" section in which a teacher can build a profile and search a database in order to find other teachers and mentors who are dealing with a child of the same age with the disorder and then share knowledge and strategies of what has been effective.

OTHER WEBSITES AND HELPFUL PRODUCTS
The Mood Tree
Helps parents and therapists chart the child's moods, feelings, and actions at a particular point in time. This tangible communication tool is rather like a board game with Colorform-like apples. These apples can be chosen by the child and placed on the tree to illustrate what he or she is feeling. High-energy states as well as low ones and mixed states can be captured by the placement of the apples. The Mood Tree is available in a child or adolescent version for $39.95.
Order online at www.moodtree.com or call 850-386-3455

Sensory Comfort Catalog
Provides a selection of products that help children with sensory integration difficulties and attentional problems, such as seamless socks, junior ear muffs that reduce noise levels, blankets that don't itch, soothing tapes that calm or aid attention, and an Easy Focus Center (portable study carrel) that reduces visual stimulation and aids in concentration. 1-888-436-2622; or www.sensorycomfort.com

The Courage to Change Catalog
This catalog for life challenges is a resource for children and their parents, teachers, and therapists. Features products such as games and books that help children deal with anger and low self-esteem, as well as improve social and decision-making skills. Catalog also includes the popular *Magic Island* audio tapes: guided imagery that helps to quiet the mind, sooth the emotions, and expand the imagination. 1-800-440-4003.

Bibliography

CHAPTER 1

Duke, Patty, and Kenneth Turan. *Call Me Anna.* New York: Bantam Books, 1987.

Geller, Barbara, Marlene Williams, et al. "Prepubertal and Early Adolescent Bipolarity Differentiate from ADHD by Manic Symptoms; Grandiose Delusions; Ultrarapid or Ultradian Cycling." *Journal of Affective Disorders* 51 (1998): 81–91.

Gershon, Elliot, et al. "Birth-cohort Changes in Manic and Depressive Disorders in Relatives of Bipolar and Schizoaffective Patients." *Archives of General Psychiatry* 44 (1987): 314–319.

Hershman, D. Jablow, and Julien Lieb. *Manic Depression and Creativity.* Amherst, N.Y.: Prometheus Books, 1998.

Hunt, Swanee. "I Couldn't Help My Daughter." *Good Housekeeping* (November 1996).

Klerman, Gerald, L. Lavori, et al. "Birth Cohort Trends in Rates of Major Depressive Disorder Among Relatives of Patients with Affective Disorder." *Archives of General Psychiatry* 42 (1985): 689–693.

Kramlinger, K. G., and Robert Post. "Ultrarapid and Ultradian Cycling in Bipolar Affective Illness." *British Journal of Psychiatry* 168 (1996): 314–323.

Kranowitz, Carol Stock. *The Out-of-Sync Child.* New York: Penguin Putnam, 1998.

Lewinsohn, Peter M., Daniel N. Klein, and John R. Seeley. "Bipolar Disorders in a Community Sample of Older Adolescents: Prevalence, Phenomenology, Comorbidity, and Course." *Journal of the American Academy of Child and Adolescent Psychiatry* 34 (1995): 454–463.

McInnis, Melvin G., Francis J. McMahon, et al. "Anticipation in Bipolar Affective Disorder." *American Journal of Human Genetics* 53 (1993): 385–390.

Papolos, Demitri, and Janice Papolos. *Overcoming Depression,* 3rd ed. New York: HarperCollins, 1997.

Popper, Charles. "Looking at Anger." *American Academy of Child and Adolescent Psychiatry Newsletter* (Fall 1990).

Popper, Charles. "On Diagnostic Gore in Child's Nightmares." *American Academy of Child and Adolescent Psychiatry Newsletter* (Spring 1990).

Steel, Danielle. *His Bright Light.* New York: Delacorte Press, 1998.

Torrey, E. Fuller. *Surviving Schizophrenia,* 3rd ed., New York: HarperCollins, 1995.

CHAPTER 2

Adams, F. *The Extant Words of Aretaeus, the Cappadocian.* London: The Sydenham Society, 1856, 301–302.

Akiskal, Hagop S. "The Prevalent Clinical Spectrum of Bipolar Disorders Beyond DSM-IV." *Journal of Clinical Psychopharmacology* 16, Supplement 1 (1996).

Akiskal, Hagop S. "Subaffective Disorders: Dysthymic, Cyclothymic, and Bipolar II Disorders in the 'Borderline' Realm." *Psychiatric Clinics of North America* (April 1981): 25–46.

Akiskal, Hagop S., Walker Parks, et al. "Bipolar Outcome in the Course of Depressive Illness: Phenomenologic, Familial, and Pharmacologic Predictors." *Journal of Affective Disorders* 5 (1983): 115–128.

American Psychiatric Association. *Diagnostic and Statistical Manual of Mental Disorders,* 3rd ed. Washington, D.C.: American Psychiatric Association, 1980.

American Psychiatric Association. *Diagnostic and Statistical Manual of Mental Disorders,* 4th ed. Washington, D.C.: American Psychiatric Association, 1994.

Anthony, E. James, and Peter Scott. "Manic-Depressive Psychosis in Childhood." *Journal of Child Psychology and Psychiatry* 1 (1960): 53–72.

Ballenger, James C., Victor I. Reus, and Robert M. Post. "The Atypical Clinical Picture of Adolescent Mania." *American Journal of Psychiatry* 139 (May 1982): 602–606.

Biederman, Joseph, Steven V. Faraone, et al. "Attention-Deficit Hyperactivity Disorder and Juvenile Mania: An Overlooked Comorbidity?" *Journal of the Academy of Child and Adolescent Psychiatry* 35 (August 1996): 997–1008.

Biederman, Joseph. "Is Childhood Oppositional Defiant Disorder a Precursor to Adolescent Conduct Disorder?: Findings from a Four-Year Follow-up Study of Children with ADHD." *Journal of the American Academy of Child and Adolescent Psychiatry* 35 (September 1996): 1193–1204.

Bleuler, Eugen. *Dementia Praecox or the Group of Schizophrenias.* New York: International Universities Press, 1950.

Bolton, P. F., A. Pickles, et al. "Autism, Affective and Other Psychiatric Disorders: Patterns of Familial Aggregation." *Psychological Medicine* 28 (1998): 177–183.

Bowring, Margaret Ann, and Maria Kovacs. "Difficulties in Diagnosing Manic Disorders Among Children and Adolescents." *Journal of the American Academy of Child and Adolescent Psychiatry* 31 (July 1992): 611–614.

Carlson, Gabrielle A., Shmuel Fennig, and Evelyn J. Bromet. "The Confusion Between Bipolar Disorder and Schizophrenia in Youth: Where Does It Stand in the 1990s?" *Journal of the American Academy of Child and Adolescent Psychiatry* 33 (May 1994): 453–459.

Carlson, Gabrielle A., and Frederick K. Goodwin. "The Stages of Mania." *Archives of General Psychiatry* 28 (February 1973): 221–228.

Davis, Richard E. "Manic-Depressive Variant Syndrome of Childhood: A Preliminary Report." *American Journal of Psychiatry* 136 (May 1979): 702–705.

Delong, George Robert. "Children with Autistic Spectrum Disorder and a Family History of Affective Disorder." *Developmental Medicine and Child Neurology* 36 (1994): 659–660.

Delong, George Robert, and J. Dwyer. "Correlation of Family History with Specific Autistic Subgroups: Asperger Syndrome and Bipolar Affective Disease." *Journal of Autism and Developmental Disorders* 18 (1988): 593–600.

Faedda, Gianni L., Ross J. Baldessarini, Trisha Suppes, et al. "Pediatric-Onset Bipolar Disorder: A Neglected Clinical and Public Health Problem." *Harvard Review of Psychiatry* 3 (1995): 171–195.

Faraone, Stephen V., Joseph Biederman, et al. "Bipolar and Antisocial Disorders Among Relatives of ADHD Children: Parsing Familial Subtypes of Illness." *American Journal of Medical Genetics (Neuropsychiatric Genetics)* 81 (1998): 108–116.

Faraone, Stephen V., Joseph Biederman, Janet Wozniak, et al. "Is Comorbidity with ADHD a Marker for Juvenile-Onset Mania?" *Journal of the American Academy of Child and Adolescent Psychiatry* 36 (August 1997): 1046–1055.

Feighner, John P., Eli Robbins, Samuel Guze, et al. "Diagnostic Criteria for Use in Psychiatric Research." *Archives of General Psychiatry* 26 (January 1972): 57–63.

Filipek, P. A., P. J. Accardo, G. T. Baranek, E. H. Cook, Jr., et al. "The Screening and Diagnosis of Autistic Spectrum Disorders." *Journal of Autism and Developmental Disorders* 29 (1999): 439–484.

Filipek, P. A., P. J. Accardo, S. Ashwal, G. T. Baranek, E. H. Cook, Jr., G. Dawson, et al. "Practice Parameter: Screening and Diagnosis of Autism: Report of the Quality Standards Subcommittee of the American Academy of Neurology and the Child Neurology Society." *Neurology* 55 (2000): 468–479.

Frazier, Jean A., Robert Doyle, et al. "Treating a Child with Asperger's Disorder and Co-morbid Bipolar Disorder." *American Journal of Psychiatry* 159 (2002): 13–21.

Geller, Barbara, Louis W. Fox, and Karen Clark. "Rate and Predictors of Prepubertal Bipolarity During Follow-up of 6–12-Year-Old Depressed Children." *Journal of the American Academy of Child and Adolescent Psychiatry* 33 (May 1994): 461–468.

Geller, Barbara, Louis W. Fox, and Miriam Fletcher. "Effect of Tricyclic Antidepressants on Switching to Mania and on the Onset of Bipolarity in Depressed 6–12-Year-Olds." *Journal of the American Academy of Child and Adolescent Psychiatry* 32 (January 1993): 43–50.

Geller, Barbara, and Joan Luby. "Child and Adolescent Bipolar Disorder: A Review of the Past Ten Years." *Journal of the American Academy of Child and Adolescent Psychiatry* 36 (September 1997): 1168–1176.

Geller, Barbara, Kai Sun, et al. "Complex and Rapid-Cycling in Bipolar Children and Adolescents: A Preliminary Study." *Journal of Affective Disorders* 34 (1995): 259–268.

Geller, Barbara, Kristine Bolhofner, et al. "Psychosocial Functioning in a Prepubertal and Early Adolescent Bipolar Disorder Phenotype." *Journal of the American Academy of Child and Adolescent Psychiatry* 39 (December 2000): 1543–1548.

Geller, Barbara, Betsey Zimmerman, et al. "Bipolar Disorder at Prospective Follow-up of Adults Who Had Prepubertal Major Depressive Disorder." *American Journal of Psychiatry* 158 (January 2001): 125–127.

Geller, Daniel A., Joseph Biederman, et al. "Obsessive-Compulsive Disorder in Children and Adolescents: A Review." *Harvard Review of Psychiatry* 5 (1998): 260–273.

Goodwin, Frederick K., and Kay Redfield Jamison. *Manic-Depressive Illness.* New York: Oxford University Press, 1990.

Kestenbaum, Clarice J. "Children at Risk for Manic-Depressive Illness: Possible Predictors." *American Journal of Psychiatry* 136 (September 1979): 1206–1208.

Kovacs, Maria. "Presentation and Course of Major Depressive Disorder During Childhood and Later Years of the Life Span." *Journal of the American Academy of Child and Adolescent Psychiatry* 35 (June 1996): 705–715.

Kovacs, Maria, and Myrna Pollock. "Bipolar Disorder and Co-morbid Conduct Disorder in Childhood and Adolescence." *Journal of the American Academy of Child and Adolescence* 34 (June 1995): 715–723.

Kraeplin, Emil. *Manic-Depressive Insanity and Paranoia.* Edinburg: E. & S. Livingstone, 1921.

Lisch, Jennifer D., Susan Dime-Meenan, et al. "The National Depressive and Manic-depressive Association (DMDA) Survey of Bipolar Members." *Journal of Affective Disorders* 31 (1994): 281–294.

Maj, Mario. "Evolution of the American Concept of Schizoaffective Psychosis." *Neuropsychobiology* 11 (1984): 7–13.

Mellior, C. S. "First Rank Symptoms of Schizophrenia." *British Journal of Psychiatry* 117 (1970): 15–23.

Papolos, Demitri F., and Janice Papolos. *Overcoming Depression,* 3rd ed. New York: HarperCollins, 1997.

Piven, Joseph, Jeanne Gayle, et al. "A Family History Study of Neuropsychiatric Disorders in the Adult Siblings of Autistic Individuals." *Journal of the American Academy of Child and Adolescent Psychiatry* 29 (1990): 177–183.

Piven, Joseph, Gary A. Chase, et al. "Psychiatric Disorders in the Parents of Autistic Individuals." *Journal of the American Academy of Child and Adolescent Psychiatry* 30 (1991): 471–478.

Pope, Harrison G. "Distinguishing Bipolar Disorder from Schizophrenia in Clinical Practice: Guidelines and Case Reports." *Hospital and Community Psychiatry* 34 (April 1983): 322–328.

Pope, Harrison G., and Joseph F. Lipinski, Jr. "Diagnosis in Schizophrenia and Manic-Depressive Illness: A Reassessment of the Specificity of 'Schizophrenic' Symptoms in Light of Current Research." *Archives of General Psychiatry* 35 (1978): 811–822.

Pope, Harrison G., Joseph F. Lipinski, Jr., et al. "Schizoaffective Disorder: An Invalid Diagnosis? A Comparison of Schizoaffective Disorder, Schizophrenia, and Affective Disorder." *American Journal of Psychiatry* 137 (August 1980): 921–927.

Popper, Charles. "Diagnosing Bipolar vs. ADHD: A Pharmacological Point of View." *The Link* 13 (1996).

Puig-Antich, Joaquim, et al. *Schedule for Affective Disorders and Schizophrenia for School-age Children (Kiddie-SADS).* Pittsburgh: Western Psychiatric Institute and Clinic, 1986.

Schneck, Jerome M. *A History of Psychiatry.* Springfield, Ill.: Charles C. Thomas, 1960.

Strober, Michael, Carolyn Lampert, et al. "The Course of Major Depressive Disorder in Adolescents: Recovery and Risk of Manic Switching in a Follow-up of Psychotic and Nonpsychotic Subtypes." *Journal of the American Academy of Child and Adolescent Psychiatry* 32 (January 1993): 34–42.

Taylor, Michael A., and Richard Abrams. "The Phenomenology of Mania." *Archives of General Psychiatry* 29 (October 1973): 520–522.

Torrey, E. Fuller. *Surviving Schizophrenia,* 3rd ed. New York: HarperCollins, 1995.

Weller, Elizabeth, Ronald Weller, and Mary Fristad. "Bipolar Disorders in Children: Misdiagnosis, Underdiagnosis, and Future Directions." *Journal of the American Academy of Child and Adolescent Psychiatry* 34 (June 1995): 709–714.

Weller, Ronald, Elizabeth Weller, and Mary Fristad. "Mania in Prepubertal Children: Has It Been Underdiagnosed?" *Journal of Affective Disorders* 11 (1986): 151–154.

Whybrow, Peter C., Hagop S. Akiskal, and William T. McKinney, Jr. *Mood Disorders: Toward a New Psychobiology.* New York: Plenum Press, 1984.

Wozniak, Janet, and Joseph Biederman. "A Pharmacological Approach to the Quagmire of Comorbidity in Juvenile Mania." *Journal of the American Academy of Child and Adolescent Psychiatry* 35 (June 1996): 826–828.

Wozniak, Janet, Joseph Biederman, et al. "A Pilot Family Study of Childhood-Onset Mania." *Journal of the American Academy of Child and Adolescent Psychiatry* 34 (December 1995): 1577–1583.

CHAPTER 4

Allison D. B., J. L. Mentore, M. Heo, L. P. Chandler, et al. "Antipsychotic-induced Weight Gain: A Comprehensive Research Synthesis." *American Journal of Psychiatry* 156 (1999): 1686–1696.

American Academy of Child and Adolescent Psychiatry. "Practice Parameters for the Assessment and Treatment of Children and Adolescents with Bipolar Disorder." 36, Supplement 176 (October 1997): 157.

American Psychiatric Association. "Tardive Dyskinesia: Summary of a Task Force Report of the American Psychiatric Association." *American Journal of Psychiatry* 137 (October 1980): 1163–1172.

Balaban, M. T. "Affective Influences on Startle in Five-month-old Infants: Reactions to Facial Expressions of Emotions." *Child Development* 66 (1995): 28–36.

Baldessarini, Ross J. *Chemotherapy in Psychiatry,* 2nd ed. Cambridge, Mass.: Harvard University Press, 1985.

Baldessarini, Ross J. "Fluoxetine and Side Effects." *Archives of General Psychiatry* 47 (1990): 191–192.

Baldessarini, Ross J. Personal written correspondence, September 12 and 25, 2000.

Baldessarini, Ross J., and Leonardo Tondo. "Antisuicidal Effect of Lithium Treatment in Major Mood Disorders." *Harvard Medical School Guide to Suicide Assessment and Intervention.* Douglas Jacobs, ed. San Francisco: Jossey-Bass Publishers, 1998.

Baldessarini, Ross J., and Leonardo Tondo. "Does Lithium Treatment Still Work?" *Archives of General Psychiatry* 57 (2000): 187–190.

Baldessarini, Ross J., Leonardo Tondo, Gianni Faedda, et al. "Effects of the Rate of Discontinuing Lithium Maintenance Treatment in Bipolar Disorders." *Journal of Clinical Psychiatry* 57 (October 1996): 441–448.

Baldessarini, Ross J., and Martin H. Teicher. "Dosing of Antipsychotic Agents in Pediatric Populations." *Journal of Child and Adolescent Psychopharmacology* 59 (1995): 1–4.

Bertogali, Mark W., and Carrie M. Borcharch. "A Review of ECT for Children and Adolescents." *Journal of the American Academy of Child and Adolescent Psychiatry* 29 (1990): 302–307.

Biederman, Joseph. Personal correspondence, September 21, 2000.

Biederman, Joseph. "Olanzapine in the Treatment of Bipolar Disorder in Juveniles." An abstract presented at the American Psychiatric Association, 2000 Annual Meeting; Chicago, Illinois.

Botteron, Kelly N., and Barbara Geller. "Pharmacologic Treatment of Childhood and Adolescent Mania." *Child and Adolescent Psychiatric Clinics of North America* 4 (April 1995): 283–304.

Brunet, G., et al. "Open Trial of a Calcium Agonist, Nimodipine, in Acute Mania." *Clinical Neuropharmacology* 13 (1990): 224–228.

Burgess, John R., Laura Stevens, et al. "Long-chain Polyunsaturated Fatty Acids in Children with Attention-Deficit Hyperactivity Disorder." *American Journal of Clinical Nutrition,* 71 (2000 supplement): 327–329.

Cade, John F. "Lithium Salts in the Treatment of Psychotic Excitement." *Medical Journal of Australia* 195 (September 1949): 349–352.

Calabrese, Joseph R., Tricia Suppes, et al. "A Double-blind, Placebo-controlled Prophylaxis Study of Lamotrigine in Rapid-cycling Bipolar Disorder." *Journal of Clinical Psychiatry* 61 (2000): 841–860.

Calabrese, Joseph R., Charles L. Bowden, et al. "A Double-Blind Placebo-Controlled Study of Lamotrigine Monotherapy in Outpatients with Bipolar I Depression." *Journal of Clinical Psychiatry* 60 (1999): 79–88.

Chen, Guang, Wei-Zhang Zeng, et al. "The Mood-Stabilizing Agents Lithium and Valproate Robustly Increase the Levels of the Neuroprotective Protein bcl-2 in the CNS." *Journal of Neurochemistry* 72 (1999): 879–882.

DelBello, Melissa P., et al. "Prior Stimulant Treatment in Adolescents with Bipolar Disorder: Association with Age at Onset." *Bipolar Disorders* 3 (2001): 53–57.

Delong, G. Robert. "Lithium Carbonate Treatment of Select Behavior Disorders in Children Suggesting Manic-Depressive Illness." *Journal of Pediatrics* 93 (1978): 689–694.

Denicoff, Kirk D., Earlian E. Smith-Jackson, et al. "Comparative Prophylactic Efficacy of Lithium, Carbamazepine, and the Combination in Bipolar Disorder." *Journal of Clinical Psychiatry* 58 (November 1997): 470–478.

Dose, M., et al. "Use of Calcium Agonists in Mania." *Psychoneuroendocrinology* 11 (1986): 241–243.

Dubovsky, Steven L., and Randall D. Buzan. "Novel Alternatives and Supplements to Lithium and Anticonvulsants for Bipolar Affective Disorder." *Journal of Clinical Psychiatry* 58 (May 1997): 224–242.

Dubovsky, Steven L., and Ronald D. Franks. "Intracellular Calcium Ions in Affective Disorders: A Review and Hypothesis." *Biological Psychiatry* 18 (1983): 781–797.

Dunn, Robert T., Mark S. Frye, et al. "The Efficacy and Use of Anticonvulsants in Mood Disorders." *Clinical Neuropharmacology* 21, no. 4: 215–235.

Earl, N., Ascher J., et al. "New Information Confirming the Importance of Dosing and Rash with Lamotrigine." Presented at the 41st annual meeting of the New Clinical Drug Evaluation Unit; Phoenix, Arizona, May 2001.

Emrich, H. M., M. Dose, and D. von Zerssen. "The Use of Sodium Valproate, Carbamazepine, and Oxcarbazepine in Patients with Affective Disorders." *Journal of Affective Disorders* 8 (1985): 243–250.

Emrich, H. M., T. Okuma, and A. A. Muller, eds. *Anticonvulsants in Affective Disorders.* Amsterdam: Elsevier Science Publishers, 1984.

Faedda, Gianni L., Ross J. Baldessarini, et al. "Pediatric-Onset Bipolar Disorder: A Neglected Clinical and Public Health Problem." *Harvard Review of Psychiatry* (1995): 171–195.

Faedda, Gianni, Leonardo Tondo, Tricia Suppes, Mauricio Tohen, and Ross J. Baldessarini. "Outcome After Rapid vs. Gradual Discontinuation of Lithium Treatment in Bipolar Disorders." Paper presented at the Fifth Meeting of Biological Psychiatry, Florence, Italy, June 1991.

Fatemi, S. H., D. J. Rapport, et al. "Lamotrigine in Rapid-cycling Bipolar Disorder." *Journal of Clinical Psychiatry* 58 (1997): 522–527.

Fine, Max. "ECT Update—1997." *Psychiatric Times* (April 1997).

Frazier J. A., M. C. Meyer, et al. "Risperidone Treatment for Juvenile Bipolar Disorder: A Retrospective Chart Review." *Journal of the American Academy of Child and Adolescent Psychiatry* 38 (1999): 960–965.

Geller, Barbara, L. W. Fox, and M. Fletcher. "Effect of Tricyclic Antidepressants on Switching to Mania and on the Onset of Bipolarity in Depressed 6–12-Year-Olds." *Journal of the American Academy of Adolescent Psychiatry* 32 (January 1993): 43–50.

Gershon, Elliot, et al. "Birth-cohort Changes in Manic and Depressive Disorders in Relatives of Bipolar and Schizoaffective Patients." *Archives of General Psychiatry* 44 (1987): 314–319.

Goodnick, Paul J. "Treatment of Mania: Relationship Between Response to Verapamil and Changes in Plasma Calcium and Magnesium Levels." *Southern Medical Journal* 89 (February 1996): 225–226.

Gorman, Jack M. *The Essential Guide to Psychiatric Drugs,* 3rd ed. New York: St. Martin's Press, 1997.

Green, Wayne Hugo. *Child and Adolescent Clinical Psychopharmacology,* 2nd ed. Baltimore: Williams & Wilkins, 1995.

Hibbeln, Joseph. "Fish Consumption and Major Depression." *The Lancet* 351 (1998): 1213.

Horrobin, David. "Depression and Bipolar Disorder: Relationships to Impaired Fatty Acid and Phospholipid Metabolism and to Diabetes, Cardiovascular Disease, Immunological Abnormalities, Cancer, Aging and Osteoporosis: Possible Candidate Genes." *Prostaglandins, Leukotrienes and Essential Fatty Acids* 60 (1999): 217–234.

Horrobin, David. Personal correspondence, April 20, 2001.

Hughes, Jennifer, B. Barraclough, and W. Reeve. "Are Patients Shocked by ECT?" *Journal of the Royal College of Medicine* 74 (April 1981): 283–285.

Isovari, Jouko I. T., et al. "Polycyctic Ovaries and Hyperandrogenism in Women Taking Valproate for Epilepsy." *New England Journal of Medicine* 329 (1993): 1383–1388.

Kafanteris, Vivian, Daniel J. Coletti, et al. "Adjunctive Antipsychotic Treatment of Adolescents with Bipolar Psychosis." *Journal of the American Academy of Child and Adolescent Psychiatry* 40 (2001): 1448–1456.

Kafantaris, Vivian, Magda Campbell, et al. "Carbamazepine in Hospitalized Aggressive Conduct Disorder Children: An Open Pilot Study." *Psychopharmacology Bulletin* 28 (1992): 193–199.

Katz, Abraham. "Magnetic Depression: Scientists May Zap the Blues Away." *New Haven Register,* September 4, 1997.

Klerman, Gerald L., et al. "Birth Cohort Trends in Rates of Major Depressive Disorder Among Relatives of Patients with Affective Disorder. *Archives of General Psychiatry* 42 (1985): 689–693.

Knoll, James, Kristine Stegman, and Trisha Suppes. "Clinical Experience Using Gabapentin

Adjunctively in Patients with a History of Mania or Hypomania." *Journal of Affective Disorders* 49 (1998): 229–233.

Kusumaker, Vivek, and Lakshami N. Yatham. "An Open Study of Lamotrigine in Refractory Bipolar Depression." *Psychiatry Research* 72 (1997): 145–148.

Kutcher, Stan. *Child and Adolescent Psychopharmacology.* Philadelphia: W. B. Saunders Company, 1997.

Loppman, Steven. "A Comparison of Three Types of Lithium Release Preparations." *Hospital and Community Psychiatry* 34 (February 1983): 113–114.

McClellan, Jon, and John S. Werry. "Practice Parameters for the Assessment and Treatment of Children and Adolescents with Bipolar Disorder." *Journal of the American Academy of Child and Adolescent Psychiatry* 36, Supplement (October 1997): 157–176.

Meesters, Ybe. "Case Study: Dawn Simulation as Maintenance Treatment in a Nine-Year-Old Patient with Seasonal Affective Disorder." *Journal of the American Academy of Child and Adolescent Psychiatry* 37 (September 1998): 986–988.

Moise, Frantz N., and George Petrides. "Case Study: Electroconvulsive Therapy in Adolescents." *Journal of the American Academy of Child and Adolescent Psychiatry* 35 (March 1996): 312–318.

Morrow, David J. "Lusting After Prozac." *New York Times,* October 11, 1998.

Papolos, Demitri F., and Janice Papolos. *Overcoming Depression,* 3rd ed. New York: HarperCollins, 1997.

Pazzaglia, Peggy J., Robert M. Post, et al. "Preliminary Controlled Trial of Nimodepine in Ultra-Rapid Cycling Affective Dysregulation." *Psychiatry Research* 49 (1993): 257–272.

Reinstein, Michael J., John G. Sonnenberg, et al. "Comparative Efficacy and Tolerability of Oxcarbazepine versus Divalproex Sodium in the Treatment of Mania." A poster presented at the American Psychiatric Association Conference, New Orleans, 2001.

Rosenthal, Norman E. *Winter Blues,* rev. ed. New York: Guilford Press, 1998.

Rosenthal, Norman E., Alytia A. Levendosky, et al. "Effects of Light Treatment on Core Body Temperature in Seasonal Affective Disorder." *Biological Psychiatry* 27 (1990): 39–50.

"Safeguards Needed for Carbamazapine." *FDA Drug Bulletin* 20 (1990).

Sandrolini, Mark: Telephone conversation with Janice Papolos, September 20, 2000.

Schou, Mogens. *Lithium Treatment of Manic-Depressive Illness,* 2nd ed. Basel: Karger, 1983.

Schou, Mogens. "Lithium Perspectives." *Neuropsychobiology* 10 (1983): 7–12.

Segal J., M. Berk, and S. Brook. "Risperidone Compared with Both Lithium and Haloperidol in Mania: A Double-blind Randomized, Controlled Trial." *Clinical Neuropharmacology* 21 (1998): 176–180.

Simoupoulos, Artemis P. *The Omega Diet.* New York: HarperCollins, 1999.

Spencer, Thomas, Timothy Wilens, and Joseph Biederman. "Psychotropic Medication for Children and Adolescents." *Pediatric Psychopharmacology* 4 (January 1995): 97–121.

Stevens, L. J., S. S. Zentall, et al. "Omega-3 Fatty Acids in Boys with Behavior, Learning, and Health Problems." *Physiological Behavior,* April–May 1996, 915–920.

Stoll, Andrew. *The Omega Connection.* New York: The Free Press, 2001.

Stoll, Andrew L., Emanuel Severus, Marlene P. Freeman, et al. "Omega-3 Fatty Acids in Bipolar Disorder: A Preliminary Double-Blind, Placebo-Controlled Trial." *Archives of General Psychiatry* 56 (1999): 407–412.

Tohen, Maurizio. Telephone conversation with Janice Papolos, September 22, 2000.

Tohen M., T. G. Jacobs, et al. "Efficacy of Olanzapine in Acute Bipolar Mania: A Double-blind, Placebo-controlled Study." *Archives of General Psychiatry* 57 (2000): 841–849.

Tohen, M., T. M. Sanger, et al. "Olanzapine vs. Placebo in the Treatment of Acute Mania." *American Journal of Psychiatry* 156 (1999): 702–709.

Tohen, M., Zarate C. A., Jr., "Antipsychotic Agents and Bipolar Disorder." *Journal of Clinical Psychiatry* 59 Suppl. 1 (1998): 38–48.

Tondo, Leonardo, and Ross J. Baldessarini. "Reduced Suicide Risk During Lithium Maintenance Treatment." *Journal of Clinical Psychiatry* 61 [Suppl. 9] (2000): 97–104.

Tondo, Leonardo, Ross J. Baldessarini, et al. "Lithium Treatment and Risk of Suicidal Be-
    havior in Bipolar Disorder Patients." *Journal of Clinical Psychiatry* 59 (1998): 405–414.
Valenstein, Elliot S. *Blaming the Brain: The Truth About Drugs and Mental Health.* New York:
    The Free Press, 1998.
Wehr, Thomas A., and Frederick K. Goodwin. "Can Antidepressants Cause Mania and
    Worsen the Course of Affective Illness?" *American Journal of Psychiatry* 144 (November
    1987): 1403–1411.
Willins, Timothy E. *Straight Talk About Psychiatric Medications for Kids.* New York: The Guil-
    ford Press, 1999.
Wong, Ian, George E. Mawer, and Josemir W. Sander. "Factors Influencing the Incidence of
    Lamotrigine-Related Skin Rash." *Annals of Pharmacotherapy* 33 (1999): 1037–1042.
(The FDA approval of fish oil at dosages up to three grams per day as safe in all age groups
    can be found in the Federal Register Vol. 62, No. 108, June 5, 1997.)

CHAPTER 6
Egeland, Janice A. "Amish Study, III: The Impact of Cultural Factors on Diagnosis of Bipo-
    lar Illness." *American Journal of Psychiatry* 140 (January 1983): 67–71.
Fibiger, H. C. "Neurobiology of Depression: Focus on Dopamine." *Neurobiology to Treatment.*
    New York: Raven Press, 1995.
Ginns, Edward I., Pamela St. Jean, et al. "A Genome-Wide Search for Chromosomal Loci
    Linked to Mental Health Wellness in Relatives at High Risk for Bipolar Affective Disor-
    der Among the Old Order Amish." Proceedings of the National Academy of Science 95
    (December 1998): 15531–15536.
Iarovici, Doris. "New Hints About Genetic Factors in Psychological Traits." *Journal of NIH
    Research* 7 (November 1995).
Lachman, Herbert M., Bernice Morrow, et al. "Association of Codon 108/158 Catechol-O-
    methyltransferase Gene Polymorphism with the Psychiatric Manifestations of Velo-cardio-
    facial Syndrome." *American Journal of Medical Genetics* 67 (1996): 468–472.
Lachman, Herbert M., Demitri F. Papolos, et al. "Human Catechol-O-methyltransferase
    Pharmacogenetics: Description of a Functional Polymorphism and Its Potential Applica-
    tion to Neuropsychiatric Disorders." *Pharmacogenetics* 6 (1996): 243–250.
Lubs, H. A., et al. "Genetic Bases of Developmental Dyslexia: Molecular Studies." *Neuropsy-
    chological Foundations of Learning Disabilities.* San Diego: Academic Press, 1994.
McGuffin, Peter, Michael J. Owen, et al. *Seminars in Psychiatric Genetics.* London: Gaskell
    Press, 1994.
Papolos, Demitri F., and Herbert M. Lachman, eds. *Genetic Studies in Affective Disorders.* New
    York: John Wiley & Sons, Inc., 1994.
Papolos, Demitri F., Sabine Veit, Gianni Faedda, et al. "Ultra-ultra-rapid Cycling Bipolar
    Disorder Is Associated with the Low Activity Catecholamine-O-methyltransferase Allele."
    Molecular Psychiatry 3 (1998): 346–349.
Papolos, Demitri, Sabine Veit, and Robert Shprintzen. "Chromosomal Abnormalities and
    Bipolar Affective Disorder: Velo-Cardio-Facial Syndrome." *Medscape Psychiatry Journal* 2
    (August 1997): 1–13.
Plomin, Robert. "The Role of Inheritance in Behavior." *Science* 248 (April 1990): 183–188.
Tiihonen, Jari, Tero Hallikainen, Herbert Lachman, et al. "Association Between the Func-
    tional Variant of the Catechol-O-methyltransferase (COMT) Gene and Type I Alco-
    holism." *Molecular Psychiatry* (in press).
Todd, Richard D. "The Link Between Parental Alcoholism and Childhood Mood Disorders:
    A Family/Genetic Perspective." *Medscape Mental Health* 2, no. 4 (1997).

CHAPTER 7
Anch, A. M., and C. P. Browman, et al. *Sleep: A Scientific Perspective.* Englewood Cliffs, New
    Jersey: Prentice-Hall, Inc., 1988.

Arkin, A. M., et al. *The Mind in Sleep: Psychology and Parapsychology.* New Jersey: Lawrence Earlbaum Associates, 1978.

Borbely, Alexander. *Secrets of Sleep.* New York: Basic Books, 1986.

Borzel, Nicolas L. "Nightmares and Night Terrors: The Horror Movies of the Mind." http://sawka.com/spiritwatch/borzel.htm.

Bowlby, John. *Separation.* New York: Basic Books, 1973.

Bowlby, John. *Attachment,* 2nd ed. New York: Basic Books, 1982.

Brazelton, T. Berry, and Bertrand G. Cramer. *The Earliest Relationship.* New York: Addison-Wesley, 1991.

Dubovsky, Steven L., and Ronald D. Franks. "Intracellular Calcium Ions in Affective Disorders: A Review and an Hypothesis." *Biological Psychiatry* 18 (1983): 781–797.

Hershman, D. Jablow, and Julian Lieb. *Manic Depression and Creativity.* New York: Prometheus Books, 1998.

Hofer, Myron. "Early Social Relationships: A Psychobiologist's View." *Child Development* 58 (1987): 633–647.

Joels, Marian, and E. Ronald De Kloet. "Effects of Glucocorticoids and Norepinephrine on the Excitability in the Hippocampus." *Science* 245 (September 1989): 1502–1505.

Kagan, Jerome, Richard B. Kearsley, and Philip R. Zelazo. *Infancy: Its Place in Human Development.* Cambridge, Mass.: Harvard University Press, 1980.

Kramer, Mark S., Neal Cutler, John Feighner, et al. "Distinct Mechanism for Antidepressant Activity by Blockade of Central Substance P Receptors." *Science* 11 (September 1998): 1640–1645.

Mahler, Margaret S. *The Selected Papers of Margaret S. Mahler: Volume 2.* New York: Jason Aronson, 1979.

Mahowald, Mark W., and Carlos H. Schenck. "Diagnosis and Management of Parasomnias." *Clinical Cornerstones (Sleep Disorders)* 2, no. 5.

Ohayon M. M., P. L. Morselli, et al. "Prevalence of Nightmares and Their Relationship to Psychopathology and Daytime Functioning in Insomnia Subjects." *Sleep* 20, no. 5: 340–348.

Ohayon, M. M., et al. "Night Terrors, Sleep Walking, and Confusional Arousals in the General Population: Their Frequency and Relationship to Other Sleep and Mental Disorders." *Journal of Clinical Psychiatry* 60 (April 1999): 268–276.

Papolos, Demitri F., and Janice Papolos. *Overcoming Depression,* 3rd ed. New York: HarperCollins, 1997.

Pine, Fred. *Developmental Theory and Clinical Process.* New Haven, Conn.: Yale University Press, 1985.

Popper, Charles. "On Diagnostic Gore in Child's Nightmares." *American Academy of Adolescent Psychiatry Newsletter* (Spring 1990).

Reich, Annie. "Pathologic Forms of Self-esteem Regulation." *Psychoanalytic Study of the Child,* vol. 15. New York: International Universities Press, 1960.

Salzman, Leon. *Treatment of the Obsessive Personality.* New York: Jason Aronson, 1980.

Winnicott, D. W. *The Maturational Processes and the Facilitating Environment.* Madison, Conn.: International Universities Press, 1965.

Winson, Jonathan. *Brain and Psyche: The Biology of the Unconscious.* Garden City, N.Y.: Anchor Press, 1985.

CHAPTER 8

Aston-Jones, G., and Floyd E. Bloom. "Activity of Norepinephrine-containing Locus Coeruleus Neurons in Behaving Rats Anticipates Fluctuations in the Sleep-waking Cycle." *Journal of Neuroscience* 8 (August 1981): 876–886.

Berger, Ralph J., and Nathan H. Phillips. "Regulation of Body Temperature During Sleep." *Comparative Physiology of Sleep, Thermoregulation, and Metabolism From the Perspective of Energy Conservation.* New York City: Wiley-Liss, 1990.

Blakeslee, Sandra. "Biologists Close in on the 'Tick-Tock' Genes." *New York Times,* December 15, 1998.

Bradley, M. M., P. J. Lang, and B. N. Cuthbert. "Emotion, Novelty, and the Startle Reflex: Habituation in Humans." *Behavioral Neuroscience* 107 (December 1993): 970–980.

Cahill, L., et al. "Amygdala Activity at Encoding Correlated with Long-term, Free Recall of Emotional Information." *Proceedings of the National Academy of Sciences* 15 (July 1996): 8016–8021.

Changeux, Jean-Pierre. *Neuronal Man.* New York: Pantheon, 1985.

Charney, Dennis S., et al. "A Functional Neuroanatomy of Anxiety and Fear: Implications for the Pathophysiology and Treatment of Anxiety Disorders." *Critical Review of Neurobiology* 10 (1996): 419–446.

Chorpita, B. F., and D. H. Barlow. "The Development of Anxiety: The Role of Control in the Early Environment." *Psychology Bulletin* 124 (July 1998): 3–21.

Conlan, Roberta, ed. *States of Mind: New Discoveries about How Our Brains Make Us Who We Are.* New York: John Wiley & Sons, 1999.

Coscina, Donald V., et al. "Induction of Rage in Rats by Central Injection of 6-Hydroxydopamine." *Pharmacology Biochemistry and Behavior* 1 (1973): 1–6.

Ehlers, C. L., et al. "CRF/NPY Interactions: A Potential Role in Sleep Dysregulation in Depression and Anxiety." *Depression Anxiety* 6 (1997): 1–9.

Evans, B. "Cyclical Activity in Non-rapid Eye Movement Sleep: A Proposed Arousal Inhibitory Mechanism." *Electroencephalography and Clinical Neurophysiology* 86 (February 1993): 123–131.

Farrant, Mark, and Stuart Cull-Candy. "Gaba Receptors, Grabule Cells, and Genes." *Nature,* January 28, 1993, 302–303.

Fibiger, H. C. "Neurobiology of Depression: Focus on Dopamine." *Depression and Mania: From Neurobiology to Treatment.* New York: Raven Press, 1995.

Glavin, Gary B. "Stress and Brain Noradrenaline: A Review." *Neuroscience and Biobehavioral Reviews* 9 (1985): 233–243.

Goleman, Daniel. *Emotional Intelligence.* New York: Bantam Books, 1997.

Halaris, Angelos, ed. *Chronobiology and Psychiatric Disorders.* New York: Elsevier, 1987.

Inui, A., M. Okita, et al. "Anxiety-like Behavior in Transgenic Mice with Brain Expression of Neuropeptide Y." *Proceedings of the Association of American Physicians* 110 (May 1998): 171–182.

Jacobson, Lauren, and Robert Sapolsky. "The Role of the Hippocampus in Feedback Regulation of the Hypothalamic-Pituitary-Adrenocortical Axis." *Endocrine Reviews* 12 (1991): 118–134.

Joels, Marian, and Ronald De Kloet. "Effects of Glucocorticoids and Norepinephrine on the Excitability in the Hippocampus." *Science* 245 (September 1989): 1502–1505.

Kramer, Mark S., Neal Cutler, et al. "Distinct Mechanism for Antidepressant Activity by Blockade of Central Substance P Receptors." *Science* (September 1998): 1640–1645.

Kranowitz, Carol Stock. *The Out-of-Sync Child.* New York: Penguin Putnam, 1998.

Lachman, Herbert M., and Demitri F. Papolos. "Abnormal Signal Transduction: A Hypothetical Model for Bipolar Affective Disorder." *Life Sciences* 45 (1989): 1412–1426.

Landsberg, Lewis, and James B. Young. "Fasting, Feeding, and Regulation of the Sympathetic Nervous System." *Seminars in Medicine of the Beth Israel Hospital, Boston* 298 (June 1978): 1295–1300.

LeDoux, Joseph, and William Hirst. *Mind and Brain.* Cambridge: Cambridge University Press, 1986.

Lee, Gregory P., David W. Loring, Kimford J. Meader, and Betty B. Brooks. "Hemispheric Specialization for Emotional Expression: A Reexamination of Results from Intracarotid Administration of Sodium Amobarbital." *Brain and Cognition* 12 (1990): 267–280.

Leeman, Susan E., James E. Krause, and Fred Lembeck, eds. *Substance P and Related Peptides.* New York: New York Academy of Sciences, 1991.

Logothetis, Nikos K., David A. Leopold, and David L. Sheinberg. "What Is Rivalry During Binocular Rivalry?" *Nature,* April 18, 1996, 621–624.

Lombroso, Paul J., and Robert Sapolsky. "Development of the Cerebral Cortex: Stress and Brain Development." *Journal of the American Academy of Child and Adolescent Psychiatry* 37 (December 1998): 1337–1339.

Lumer, Erik D., Karl J. Friston, and Geraint Rees. "Neural Correlates of Perceptual Rivalry in the Human Brain." *Science* 280 (June 1998): 1930–1934.

Malkoff-Schwartz, Susan, Ellen Frank, et al. "Stressful Life Events and Social Rhythm Disruption in the Onset of Manic and Depressive Bipolar Episodes." *Archives of General Psychiatry* 55 (August 1998): 702–707.

Mandell, Arnold J., and Suzanne Knapp. "Asymmetry and Mood, Emergent Properties of Serotonin Regulation: A Proposed Mechanism of Action of Lithium." *Archives of General Psychiatry* 36 (July 1979): 909–916.

Manji, Husseini K., Gregory J. Moore, and Guang Chen. "Bipolar Disorder: Leads from the Molecular and Cellular Mechanisms of Action of Mood Stabilizers." *British Journal of Psychiatry* Suppl 41 (2001): s107–s119.

Manji, Husseini K., Gregory J. Moore, et al. "Neuroplasticity and Cellular Resilience in Mood Disorders." *Molecular Psychiatry* 5 (2000): 578–593.

Marder, Eve. "From Biophysics to Models of Network Function." *Annual Review of Neurosciences* 21 (1998): 25–45.

McGeer, Patrick L., Sir John C. Eccles, and Edith G. McGeer. *Molecular Neurobiology of the Mammalian Brain.* New York: Plenum Press, 1978.

Migliorelli, Ricardo, Sergio E. Starkstein, et al. "SPECT Findings in Patients with Primary Mania." *Journal of Neuropsychiatry and Clinical Neurosciences* 5 (1993): 379–383.

Mirabile, Charles S., and Bernard C. Glueck. "Separation of Affective Disorder into Seasonal and Nonseasonal Types Using Motion Sickness Susceptibility as a Marker." *Journal of Neuropsychiatry* 5 (Summer 1993): 330–334.

Monk, Timothy H. "Research Methods of Chronobiology." Chapter 2 in *Biological Rhythms, Sleep, and Performance,* Wilse B. Webb, ed. New York: John Wiley & Sons, 1982.

Moore, Gregory J., Joseph M. Bebchuk, et al. "Lithium-induced Increase in Human Brain Grey Matter." *Lancet* 356 (2000): 1241–1242.

Murphy D., B. Costall, and J. W. Smythe. "Regulation of Hippocampal Theta Activity by Corticosterone: Opposing Functions of Mineralocorticoid and Glucocorticoid Receptors." *Brain Research Bulletin* 45 (April 1998): 631–635.

Ostrow, David, Angelos Halaris, et al. "State Dependence of Noradrenergic Activity in a Rapidly Cycling Bipolar Patient." *Journal of Clinical Psychiatry* 45 (1984): 306–309.

Papez, James W. "A Proposed Mechanism of Emotion. 1937." *Journal of Neuropsychiatry Clinical Neuroscience* (Winter 1995): 103–112.

Pettigrew, John D., and Steven M. Miller. "A 'Sticky' Interhemispheric Switch in Bipolar Disorder?" *Proceedings of the Royal Society of London* 265 (1998): 2141–2148.

Papolos, Demitri F., and Janice Papolos. *Overcoming Depression,* 3rd ed. New York: HarperCollins, 1997.

Restack, Richard. *The Brain.* New York: Bantam Books, 1984.

Schulkin, Joseph, P. W. Gold, and Bruce S. McEwen. "Induction of Corticotropin-releasing Hormone Gene Expression by Glucocorticoids: Implication for Understanding the States of Fear and Anxiety and Allostatic Load." *Psychoneuroendocrinology* 23 (April 1998): 219–243.

Tache, Yvette, and Catherine Rivier, eds. *Corticotropin-Releasing Factor and Cytokines: Role in the Stress Response.* New York: New York Academy of Sciences, 1993.

Teicher, Martin H., Carol Glod, et al. "Circadian Rest-Activity Disturbances in Seasonal Affective Disorder." *Archives of General Psychiatry* 54 (February 1997): 124–130.

Tornatzky, Walter, and Klaus A. Miczek. "Long-term Impairment of Autonomic Circadian Rhythms After Brief Intermittent Social Stress." *Physiology and Behavior* 53 (1993): 983–993.

Trimble, Michael R., and E. Zarifian, eds. *Psychopharmacology of the Limbic System.* Oxford: Oxford University Press, 1985.

Warren, Wade S., Thomas H. Champney, and Vincent M. Cassone. "The Suprachiasmatic Nucleus Controls the Circadian Rhythm of Heart Rate Via the Sympathetic Nervous System." *Physiology and Behavior* 55 (1994): 1091–1099.

Webb, Wilse B., ed. *Biological Rhythms, Sleep, and Performance.* New York: John Wiley & Sons, 1982.

Wehr, Thomas A. "A Brain-warming Function for REM Sleep." *Neuroscience Biobehavioral Review* 16 (Fall 1992): 379–397.

Whybrow, Peter C., Hagop S. Akiskal, and William T. McKinney, Jr. *Mood Disorders: Toward a New Psychobiology.* New York: Plenum Press, 1984.

Winson, Jonathan. *Brain and Psyche: The Biology of the Unconscious.* Garden City, N.Y.: Anchor Press, 1985.

CHAPTER 9

Featherstone, Helen. *A Difference in the Family.* New York: Penguin Books, 1981.

Greene, Ross J. *The Explosive Child.* New York: HarperCollins, 1998.

Papolos, Demitri, and Janice Papolos. *Overcoming Depression,* 3rd ed. New York: HarperCollins, 1997.

Popper, Charles W. "A Haven from Rage." *American Academy of Child and Adolescent Newsletter* (Spring 1991).

Popper, Charles W. "Looking at Anger." *American Academy of Child and Adolescent Newsletter* (Fall 1990).

Secunda, Victoria. *When Madness Comes Home.* New York: Hyperion, 1997.

CHAPTER 10

Anderson, Winifred, Stephen Chitwood, and Deidre Hayden. *Negotiating the Special Education Maze: A Guide for Parents and Teachers.* Bethesda, Md.: Woodbine House, 1997.

Cutler, Barbara Coyne. *You, Your Child, and "Special" Education: A Guide to Making the System Work.,* 3rd ed. Baltimore: Paul H. Brookes Publishing Co., 1997.

Davidson, Howard. *Just Ask!: A Handbook for Instructors of Students Being Treated for Mental Disorders.* Calgary: Detselig Enterprises Ltd., 1993.

Dornbush, Marilyn P., and Sheryl K. Pruett. *Teaching the Tiger.* Duarte, Calif.: Hope Press, 1995.

Haerle, Tracy. *Children with Tourette Syndrome: A Parents' Guide.* Bethesda, Md.: Woodbine House, 1992.

Latham, Peter, and Patricia H. Latham. *Attention Deficit Disorder and the Law.* Washington, D.C.: JKL Communications, 1997.

Lynn, George T. *Survival Strategies for Parenting Your ADD Child.* Grass Valley, Calif.: Underwood Books, 1996.

Quackenbush, Doug, Stan Kutcher, et al. "Premorbid and Postmorbid School Functioning in Bipolar Adolescents: Description and Suggested Academic Interventions." *Canadian Journal of Psychiatry* 41 (February 1996): 16–22.

CHAPTER 11

Bearden C. E., K. M. Hoffman, and T. D. Cannon. "The Neuropsychology and Neuroanatomy of Bipolar Affective Disorder: A Critical Review." *Bipolar Disorders* 3 (2001): 106–150.

Cohen, Jonathan D., et al. "Temporal Dynamics of Brain Activation During a Working Memory Task." *Nature* 386 (1997): 604–608.

Comings, David. *Tourette Syndrome and Human Behavior.* Duarte, Calif.: Hope Press, 1990.

Courtney, S. M., et al. "Transient and Sustained Activity in a Distributed Neural System for Human Working Memory." *Nature* 386 (1997): 608–611.

Dornbush, Marilyn P., and Sheryl Pruitt. *Teaching the Tiger.* Duarte, Calif.: Hope Press, 1995.

El-Badri, S. M., C. H. Ashton, et al. "Electrophysiological and Cognitive Function in Young Euthymic Patients with Bipolar Affective Disorder." *Bipolar Disorders* 2 (2001): 79–87.

Goldberg, Elkhonon. *The Executive Brain: Frontal Lobes and the Civilized Mind.* New York: Oxford University Press, 2001.

Harwell, Joan M. *Complete Learning Disabilities Handbook,* 2nd ed. Paramus, N.J.: The Center for Applied Research in Education, 2001.

Kay, Kiesa, ed. *Uniquely Gifted: Identifying and Meeting the Needs of the Twice-Exceptional Student.* Gilsum, N.H.: Avocus Publishing, Inc., 2000.

Ratey, John J. *A User's Guide to the Brain.* New York: Pantheon Books, 2001.

Roberts, A. C., T. W. Robins, and L. Weiskrantz. *The Prefrontal Cortex.* New York: Oxford University Press, 1998.

CHAPTER 12

Alexander-Roberts, Colleen. *ADHD and Teens: A Parent's Guide to Making It Through the Tough Years.* Dallas: Taylor Publishing Company, 1995.

Bauman, Lawrence, and Robert Riche. *Ten Most Troublesome Teen-age Problems: And How to Solve Them.* Secaucus, N.J.: Citadel Press, 1998.

Cassell, Carol. *Straight from the Heart: How to Talk to Your Teenagers About Love and Sex.* New York: Simon and Schuster, 1987.

Dendy, Chris, and A. Ziegler. *Teenagers with ADD: A Parents' Guide.* Bethesda, Md.: Woodbine House, 1995.

Ekman, Paul. *Why Kids Lie.* New York: Charles Scribner's Sons, 1989.

Kaplan, Louise J. *Adolescence: The Farewell to Childhood.* New York: Simon and Schuster, 1984.

McGlashan, Thomas. "Adolescent Versus Adult Onset of Mania." *American Journal of Psychiatry* 145 (1988): 221–223.

Pogany, Susan Browning. *SexSmart: 501 Reasons to Hold Off on Sex.* Minneapolis: Fairview Press, 1998.

Wexler, David B. *The Adolescent Self.* New York: W. W. Norton & Company, 1991.

Wolf, Anthony E. *Get Out of My Life, But First Could You Drive Me and Cheryl to the Mall?* New York: Farrar, Straus, Giroux, 1991.

CHAPTER 13

Levy, Robert M., and Leonard S. Rubenstein. *The Rights of People with Mental Disabilities.* Carbondale, Ill.: ACLU Southern Illinois University Press, 1996.

Papolos, Demitri F., and Janice Papolos. *Overcoming Depression,* 3rd ed. New York: HarperCollins, 1997.

Roth, Loren H. "A Commitment Law for Patients, Doctors, and Lawyers." *American Journal of Psychiatry* 136 (September 1979): 1121–1126.

Schneider Children's Hospital Child Psychiatry Inpatient Unit Parents' Guide. New Hyde Park, N.Y.

Torrey, E. Fuller. *Surviving Schizophrenia,* 3rd ed. New York: HarperCollins, 1983.

CHAPTER 14

Academy of Child and Adolescent Psychiatry. "New Children's Health Program Becomes Effective October 1, 1997." Legislative Alert Issued by the Department of Government Affairs of the Academy, September 8, 1997.

Ammer, Christine, with Nathan T. Sidley. *The Common Sense Guide to Mental Health Care.* Brattleboro, Vt.: The Lewis Publishing Company, 1982.

Bazelon Center for Mental Health Law. *SSI: Help for Children with Disabilities.* Washington, D.C.: Bazelon Center Publications, 1997.

Bazelon Center for Mental Health Law. *Your Family and Managed Care.* Washington, D.C.: Bazelon Center Publications, 1996.

Beckett, Julie. Telephone conversation with Janice Papolos, February 12, 1999.

Center for Health Policy Studies. *Mandated Mental Health Benefits under Private Insurance: A*

Review of State Laws. Prepared for the National Institute of Mental Health, December 1983.

Freudenheim, Milt. "H.M.O.'s Cope with a Backlash on Cost Cutting." *New York Times,* May 19, 1996.

Freudenheim, Milt. "Insurers Tighten Rules and Reduce Fees for Doctors." *New York Times,* June 28, 1998.

Freudenheim, Milt. "(Loosely) Managed Care Is in Demand." *New York Times,* September 29, 1998.

Gorman, Christine. "Playing the HMO Game." *Time,* July 13, 1998.

Greenley, Dianne. "Insurance and Other Third-Party Coverage for Persons Who Are Mentally Ill: Issues and Possibilities." Report written for the National Alliance for the Mentally Ill, February 1986.

Hall, Laura Lee, Elizabeth Edgar, and Laurie Flynn. *Stand and Deliver: Action Call to a Failing Industry.* Arlington, Va.: National Alliance for the Mentally Ill, September 1997.

Malloy, Michael. *Mental Illness and Managed Care: A Primer for Families and Consumers.* Arlington, Va.: National Alliance for the Mentally Ill, 1995.

National Committee for Quality Assurance. "Draft Accreditation Standards for Managed Care Behavioral Healthcare Organizations," April 1996.

Nerney, John. "Fire." *AMI-NYS News,* November 1995.

Papolos, Demitri F., and Janice Papolos. *Overcoming Depression,* 3rd ed. New York: Harper-Collins, 1997.

Torrey, Fuller E. *Surviving Schizophrenia,* 3rd ed. New York: HarperCollins, 1995.

U.S. Department of Health and Human Services. *Disability Evaluation Under Social Security.* SSA Publication No. 64–039, January 1998.

U.S. Department of Health and Human Services. *Social Security Handbook.* SSA Publication No. 05–10135, July 1984.

CHAPTER 15

Butterfield, Fox. "Prisons Replace Hospitals for the Nation's Mentally Ill." *New York Times,* March 5, 1998.

Pear, Robert. "Insurance Plans Skirt Requirement on Mental Health." *New York Times,* December 26, 1998.

Index